people that knew him on a real level.

The untold stories behind his gre̶   ̶ ̶ng
bring to light just how remarkable h   ̶e,
accurately framing the scope of his ta̶

The perspectives added by his close confidants lend an insight into Brian's mindset and attitude that opens up Pandora's box, allowing a deeper analysis of not only Pillman, but of the industry he found most enthralling.

In the true spirit of Brian, however, it feels pertinent for me to point out the duality held within. What was designed to be a feel-good, upbeat reflection filled with fond memories and funny stories, brings with it tales of woe that are every bit as much a part of his life, impossible to ignore when approaching with honesty. The thrills of his awe-inspiring grit and overachievement are simultaneously tempered with the distressing realities that came with living a lifestyle that frequently played with fire.

As you'll soon learn, it's perfectly in keeping with Brian's outlook, perhaps deserving to be his true legacy. A college-educated athlete that was as complex as he was primitive. An outlandish eccentric, a hilarious guy that could be as intelligent, caring and calculating as he could be impulsive, whimsical and aggressive.

Some stories in the book may be a little X-rated. Rather than mindlessly adding them for the sake of shock or humor, I'd learn from his friends that such situations were a good portion of who he was. He had a partiality for the preposterous, but with it, a psychology to use his antics to impact people's perception of him.

One of the major takeaways for me after completing this book is that, 20 years later, there are a litany of valuable lessons to be learned from Brian's life still relevant today. For wrestlers to take chances rather than settle for a spot, to study beyond their understanding and evolve. For the people behind the characters to ground themselves in reality, difficult as it may be in a fantasy world. And for promoters, one in particular, to take a long hard look in the mirror at the environment they choose to foster and the permanent ramifications it can have on the people within it.

I have always held Brian Pillman as a figure of reverence and still do. I'm a lifelong fan of pro wrestling and always will be. But neither is or was perfect, and there are times within this book where it'll be explored.

Saying that, constructing this book has been one of the most satisfying and rewarding experiences of my life, chasing the answer to the question of what it was about Brian Pillman that I found so compelling on that first impression years ago. As I'd come to learn, it would quite literally take a book to describe. From one fan of his to another, I sincerely hope you enjoy it.

∞

I want to take this opportunity to extend my gratitude to everybody I spoke to about Brian Pillman for this project, those named within and those not, or assisted in any way with the production of the book. I'd especially like to thank Linda Pillman, Brian Pillman Jr., Brittany Pillman, Kim Wood, Dave Meltzer, Alex Marvez, Bruce Hart, Bob Johnson, John Pollock, Chris Hughes, Shane Douglas, Jim Cornette, Mark Coleman, Raven, Mark Madden, Les Thatcher, Mike Johnson, Jeremiah Evans, Billy Paige, Rip Rogers, Colin Bowman, Dale Gay, Matt Holt, Craig Atkinson, Sheri Benjamin Naud, Paul O'Brien, Tim Hornbaker, John Haddock and Matt Doran. Your input was and is deeply appreciated.

I also want to give a nod to the various written sources credited throughout this book, for their reporting served as a tremendous reference point throughout the process.

A special thanks to my brother Kieran for planting this idea in my head two years ago and being an invaluable sounding board the entire time.

And most of all, to my beautiful soulmate Stacey for supporting me every step of the way and being a constant inspiration in my life. I love you more than I could ever do justice with the written word.

CRAZY LIKE A FOX

THE DEFINITIVE CHRONICLE OF

BRIAN PILLMAN

20 YEARS LATER

LIAM O'ROURKE

Editor and Formatting: Liam O'Rourke (@LiamORourke86)
Cover and Text Design: John C. Haddock (@RebelCityProps)
Cover Photo: George Tahinos
Back Cover Photos: George Tahinos, Scott Grant and the Pillman family.

This book is set in Garamond.

This book was printed and bound in the United States.

ISBN-13: 978-1976541247
ISBN-10: 1976541247

CONTENTS

INTRODUCTION

When the idea was first conceived to write a book about Brian Pillman, I saw it turning out much differently to the book you are about to read. The plan was to compile notes from various sources on a man that led a well-chronicled life, adding in some little-known facts and putting Brian in the type of context I felt had been previously missing. With his name first appearing in print in 1979 as a star football player in Norwood, Pillman was in the spotlight for most of his time on earth. Certainly, a broad knowledge of his general story exists among wrestling fans, in itself creating an almost cult icon status that has sustained for two decades.

But I kept going back to my earliest impression of him. As a kid, there was something compelling about Pillman that almost came through the television screen, something others didn't have. There was just an inate quality about Brian that drew me in and made me want to know more from the first time I saw him. You could almost sense he was different from the rest. As I began seriously considering this project, I understood quickly that the original concept would have been an absolute disservice.

When WWE did their DVD on Brian Pillman in 2006, the common sentiment was that it was one of their better efforts. That may be the case, but as time passed, it bothered me tremendously to think that a new generation of wrestling fans could watch it and think that was all there was to one of the most captivating men to ever grace professional wrestling. So much of the real story, almost all of it in fact, was missing. Perhaps that's a symptom of trying to capture 35 years in just 90 minutes. Possibly, they weren't privy enough to the situation to depict Brian accurately. Or maybe it's because the elements that make him such a fascinating subject delves into themes and areas they didn't want to address, fearful of speaking to the true nature of the profession.

Through hours and hours of research and phone calls, looking to pick up every anecdote and detail I could, it became clear that this crazy story was going to be an incredible challenge to tell. Thankfully, it was an utter joy to compile, the tale itself naturally enriched with every wrinkle provided by the

"It's not the size of the dog in the fight, it's the size of the fight in the dog."

-   Originally by Mark Twain, one of
    Brian Pillman's favorite real-life sayings.

1 - THE EARLY LIFE OF BRIAN

What turned out to be anything but a normal life appeared to begin in an archetypal manner. Brian William Pillman was born on May 22nd, 1962 at the Jewish Hospital in Cincinnati, the last of five children. His father, Howard, served in the U.S. military and happened to be stationed in Cardiff, where he first met a young lady named Mary Perkins. The two hit it off and had their first child, Susan, in Wales. The budding family later moved to Howard's home country, where they eventually welcomed Angie, Philip, Linda and finally Brian into the world. For a very short time, they were a picture-perfect family.

Raised in Norwood, Ohio, a working-class enclave of Cincinnati that was economically dependent on the local General Motors and Fisher Body auto assembly plants, Brian's lifelong struggle with challenging circumstances began only a couple of months into his existence. His father Howard passed away suddenly of a heart attack in August 1962 at the age of 50, stepping off the bus to the post office annex where he worked.

His mother Mary, who worked as a waitress at the Dockside VI restaurant, had the unenviable task of playing the role of both parents to five kids simultaneously. "This was in 1962", recalls Linda Pillman, "So I'm not sure how much she would have gotten in help from Social Security for us kids, because we were all under eighteen." Luckily, Mary wasn't alone, and was able to rely on family to assist. "My grandmother and aunt lived on the second floor of our house", says Linda, "So they were able to watch us in the evening while my mother worked."

The pressures of such a family dynamic were only amplified when polyps began growing on the two-year-old Brian's vocal cords. In a case like Brian, contracting the problem so young, this posed a bigger issue than usual. The vocal cords sit at the top of the windpipe, comprised of two folds of tissue stretched across the larynx. As the polyps grew in tremendous volume inside such a small area, they consequently closed off Brian's windpipe, making it exceedingly difficult to breathe. The problem led to a number of trips to hospital with a very legitimate fear for his life. In one such instance, Brian's heart refused to function correctly, stopping three times in one day as the battle for survival continued. Dr. Sidney Peerless eventually saved his life by performing a tracheotomy, allowing Brian to take in a steady flow of oxygen.

With breathing being such a challenge, the decision was made by the Cincinnati Children's Hospital to put Brian in an oxygen tent to assist him. Confined to his own world, the restless Brian had little to do. Seemingly out of boredom, he began poking holes in the oxygen tent with his crayons one day. At the time, the Children's Hospital had nuns working at the facility, and their response was to literally strap him to his bed to prevent him from doing further damage. "My Mom went in to the hospital one day, and he was laying bound in his bed - his arms were tied down. She had a fit", remembers Linda. "She said, 'I'm paying for those oxygen tents, he can destroy as many as he wants! I'm paying for these, just bill me for them!' Of course, she didn't have the money to pay the bill, but she was going to get billed regardless, so she didn't care how many she had to pay for." Mary untied Brian herself, called in the doctor and transferred her son that afternoon to the Jewish Hospital across the road.

In the aftermath, Pillman underwent a litany of surgeries in an effort to scrape the polyps off his vocal cords. The polyps grew back as soon as they were removed, and would do so until they were dealt with at the root. One such surgery almost ended in disaster when Brian was four years old. In the recovery period, an obstruction in his trachea caused him to stop breathing. His face turned an ominous shade of blue. It was a pediatric roommate that identified the problem and bellowed to a nearby nurse that help was needed. Brian would never find out who he was, but indeed, the mystery savior extended a life that seemed almost destined to be tragically short.

With his issues, Brian spent a lot of his early childhood in hospital in his ongoing fight for existence. He once spent almost nine straight months at the Jewish Hospital where he quickly became a fixture, leaving only once – for Christmas. But with Mary's nature, the health problems only caused the bond between her and her youngest son to grow stronger. "Brian and my Mom were very close", says sister Linda. "When he was young and in the hospital, she'd get up in the morning and go and sit in the hospital until four in the afternoon. Then she would come home and visit with us, then get ready and go to work at the restaurant until about midnight or 1am. She'd go to bed and do the same thing all over again the next day."

Eventually the doctors were able to get to the roots of Brian's polyps, but the amount of work that had to be done severely damaged his vocal cords. He was barely able to talk at all. This began the second wave of operations, procedures designed to restore his voice to functional levels. As new technologies were trial-and-errored on Brian, prolonged periods of non-speaking after surgery were required and the normalities of a regular happy childhood were forcibly abandoned. For a period of time, Brian had to communicate with others by writing on a notepad. Brian's mother once told Cincinnati Magazine of her son's ordeal that, "It was very frustrating for him. You couldn't hear him crying, but you'd see the tears rolling down his face." It did, however, introduce Brian to the characteristics that would become hallmarks of his – determination, courage, resilience and discipline. Even if said introduction was a baptism by fire that no parent would wish on their child, or anyone else's.

His voice returned slowly as he began spending more time at home, which was a far more positive environment for him. "We were all real close growing up", says Linda. "Very much protective of him. But times were different back then, everyone looked out for each other. Even the neighborhood kids, my neighbor's mother was just like my mother. If she told me to do something, I did it. Everybody looked out for everybody back then."

Given his difficulties, doctors urged the Pillman family to send Brian to a public school so as not to separate him from his built-in circle of friends, which they did. "Back then, you went to school with everybody that lived on your street and you all walked together, so everybody knew him and knew his history", says Linda. Unfortunately, it led to him being mocked for his ongoing troubles by those who didn't know him. He was given the nickname "Squeaky" by classmates due to the high pitch of his voice, and they weren't the only ones to take issue with it.

The grade school began its singing program, and a young Brian was disappointed when his teacher told him that he wouldn't be allowed to participate, declaring that he couldn't sing. Brian was noticeably upset when he returned home and told his inquiring mother the story, raising her ire. "My Mom went right to them and had it out with them", states Linda, "Brian ended up singing. He wasn't going to be treated any differently because he had a croaky voice. He was allowed to sing…after Mom went to school."

Still, the throat was a recurring problem in his early stages of education. It was decided that Brian would have to constantly wear a tracheotomy in his throat to help him breathe, which he did for two full years.

There was one area where Brian excelled, in which participation brought him a great deal of happiness and allowed him to ignore his traumatic beginnings - athletics. His introduction to the world of football came mostly in a neighborhood kids game on Grove Avenue, which Brian relished with a zeal that would further blossom with time. Rudimentary as it was, the local kids practiced throwing the ball high in the air, with the one who caught it running for his life until he was ultimately tackled to the concrete. Then they'd get up and do it again. Along with the scrapes, bruises and bloody noses that resulted, Brian found himself inspired by the feeling that came with the game, his pent-up aggression finally able to come out. He soon developed an affinity for the physical contact and rush of adrenaline that came as part of the package. "For being as sickly as he was, he was a little bugger", remembers Linda. "He was tough. It didn't stop him from doing anything. I mean, he was out playing baseball and everything with the tracheotomy in his throat."

His love of playing sports helped make the Pillman house a local favorite for the kids, and it was common for all the children to congregate in the backyard where a baseball diamond was carved into the grass. In time, it became a checkpoint for the parents. If they didn't know where their son or daughter was, they'd almost always be at the Pillman's. It was the place where everybody buried their pets, or spent hours working together to dig a giant hole to make a pond. As for Mary? She didn't care what happened to the backyard – this way at least she knew were everybody was.

The sense of community would come in handy whenever Brian would get annoyed with his tracheotomy. There were two tubes that were inserted in his windpipe, an outer tube and a smaller inner one that would have to be cleaned out several times a day, causing him to gag and cough repeatedly. It was miserable. Worse for Brian, when he would run around playing sports the two tubes rattled together, which he hated with a passion. Seeking a respite, the crafty youngster would remove the inner tube from his throat and hide it. That way, he could run around uninhibited. It was a semi-regular event for Mary to call the local kids together and offer a dollar for the one who found Brian's tube. "It was like an Easter Egg hunt every other week", laughs Linda. "Except you were looking for the tracheotomy tube."

Loving the ability to be active after being cooped up in hospital for so long, Brian played everything he could, falling in love with ice hockey in elementary school. Right as it became clear that Brian had a natural talent for the game, a local hockey team came into Cincinnati and was being heavily promoted. As luck would have it, the restaurant where Mary worked was next to the hotel where the players stayed when they first came to town. As she got to know them and told them of Brian's skills, he was able to get involved, soon becoming part of the traveling team himself.

Not limiting himself to one sport, Pillman tried out for his junior high football team in the seventh grade. Of course, this while being undersized by the standards of the other players, going in at under 125 pounds. Unfazed, he got on the team, starting every week as a defensive back.

It's interesting to note how the two sports that Brian gravitated to the most, football and hockey, both involve a great deal of physical danger. After going through so much trauma at an early age, Brian seemed to play fearlessly, using his body as a weapon against kids much bigger and older than him. This undaunted attitude had become part of his DNA. Going forward, Pillman seemed to live every aspect of his life, athletically and socially, without many of the reservations most tend to have.

Hockey was his true passion, and he went to extreme measures to work on his skills. The Pillman home had a detached two car garage at the back of the property, which, like most homes, housed clutter rather than vehicles, which were instead parked outside. Seeking an opportunity to practice, the mischievous Brian went to work. "One winter, Mom went down to use the wash machine in the basement", begins Linda. "The washing machine wouldn't work because the thing was frozen." As Mary looked around, she saw that the back door was left wide open, with the garden hose running up the steps and hooked up inside the basement. "Brian had the garden hose out to the garage and flooded it to make an ice rink. He had pulled everything out and put it all up in the attic, and he had a goal out there. His friends who didn't play hockey and didn't have skates were just sliding around out there in their shoes. But he had a good three-inch base out there. Turns out he'd done it over two days."

Brian wholeheartedly attacked every sport he could when he got to Norwood High School, playing basketball, track, shotput, as well as hockey and football, excelling in all of them. As a 15-year-old freshman hockey player, he was such a standout that he was playing on another traveling men's hockey team despite being underage.

Regardless of his obvious athletic overachieving given his smaller frame, Brian still faced problems. As the youngest on the team, he was again often mocked for his voice by both opponents and his own hockey roommates. But this time, it was a mistake. As if the nature of football and hockey weren't enough to channel his frustrations, Pillman stood up for himself, getting into a couple of fistfights and coming out on the better side of it. Even in situations with grown men, a ferocious tenacity and refusal to back down further crafted the toughness that carried him through his initial years in hospital. Size be damned, he didn't have to be the kid with the tube in his throat quietly crying any longer.

Sadly, his talent made him a target as well. When somebody on another team questioned Mary about her son, the proud mother fired off, "He's only fifteen, he's going to be sixteen in May!" The information was then relayed to the officials in order to get Brian Pillman kicked out of the league. While disappointed, he continued to play all through high school, eventually playing on the all-city and all-state teams.

In football, Pillman switched to playing safety in his freshman year and ended up playing every game on the reserve team as a sophomore, even though he'd earned a spot as a starter with the varsity team. It was in his sophomore year that a huge shift would occur in Brian Pillman's football life, when Don Rahe became Norwood's head coach.

Don Rahe had won 7 letters at Moeller High in football, track and wrestling, played middle guard at the University of Cincinnati and worked as an assistant coach under Bob Lewis for some 9 years at Wyoming High prior to coming to Norwood. At the team's first workout under the new coach, Rahe, who was unfamiliar with the entire roster, called a random name, "Brian Pillman", to the front of the group to lead calisthenics drills. When the 5-foot 7-inch, 145-pound Pillman stepped to the head of the team and began instructing the squad in his squeaky voice, Coach Rahe had absolutely no idea what to think, even going so far as to ask his assistants if it was a practical joke. It was with this in mind that Rahe began to watch Brian practice, only to be blown away by what he saw. "He was the smallest player on the field, but he was the best hitter on the entire team", Rahe would later recount to the Cincinnati Enquirer.

Rahe and Brian developed a strong friendship, starting a pattern that would continue throughout Pillman's life of gravitating to older, wiser figures in the absence of a father.

In Brian's junior year he was tried out at another position, this time filling a team void at linebacker in addition to his role as a halfback on offense. While that position entailed going nose-to-nose with guys much bigger than Brian, the Norwood squad wasn't very good (even playing Pillman at linebacker, Norwood failed to win a single game in Brian's sophomore or junior years), so they decided to experiment with the position to see if it stuck. Against the odds, it somehow seemed to click for him personally and he immediately became the team standout.

His aberrant pre-game preparations became notorious, as Brian would suit up, don his helmet and begin headbutting lockers, throwing hard elbows at them and screaming obscenities at himself in a blind fury as his teammates watched on with an anxious unease. Just when the aggression would hit its peak, he would inevitably vomit in the toilets or trash can. Without skipping a beat, he'd fasten the chinstrap and be ready to go.

Though the team failed to accomplish much as a collective unit, Brian's performances stuck out like a sore thumb. One such effort was against Colerain, who were not only undefeated up to that point in the season, they hadn't even been scored on. On offense, Pillman ran a dive and got hit squarely at the line of scrimmage and blew straight though two huge tackles. At that point Mark Taylor, a defensive back who not only was all-city that year but ended up playing alongside Brian at Miami of Ohio later on, came over to take on Pillman one-on-one. Brian steamrolled him and ran 55 yards for a touchdown.

With Brian considered easily the best player on the squad, Don Rahe nominated him to be on the league's all-star team. What happened as a result ended up having long term implications on Brian's life, as Rahe's nomination was entertained up until the point he read out Pillman's height and weight. Another coach in the room laughed out loud, wildly entertained by the notion of somebody with those statistics playing at that high a level. Consequently, Brian didn't get one vote for the all-star team. Rahe, who had already grown close to Brian and sympathized with his plight, went to Pillman honestly and told him the situation. Brian nodded, silently taking in the message, no doubt disgusted by what he'd heard. "OK Coach", Brian mustered, heading straight for the weight room.

That aside, his reputation as a player grew. Pillman became known for his incredible instincts for the game, being able to read plays like few else could and getting into the right position quickly. In addition, his grit and unshakeable will was raising eyebrows, as he'd maintain the same intensity throughout the game regardless of what was on the scoreboard for his team. But convinced by the overbearing laughter of that coach that it would never mean quite enough to get him where he wanted, Brian befriended the school's power-weightlifting team and gained thirty pounds over the summer before his senior year.

On a personal level, Brian's confidence was boosted when, after another throat operation (he had a total of thirty-one throat surgeries by the time he was 21), combined with his body maturing, his voice noticeably changed. Pillman's enthusiasm was such that he returned to school proudly proclaiming to everybody that would listen, "I can talk!"

Whether it was the added size or the confidence, Brian Pillman, already the best player on the team, exploded in his senior year. Not only was he a little bit taller and a lot heavier and stronger, but his speed also saw major gains. In his junior year, Brian was running a 5.2 second 40-yard dash. As a senior, he ran 4.7's and 4.6's. He began focusing even more on the defensive side of the game and evolved into one of the best football players in all of Cincinnati, leading the city in tackles and quarterback sacks. As his senior year came to a close, he was named to the 1979 all-city team and eagerly began looking around, anticipating college scholarship offers that were surely heading his way.

Brian had continued playing hockey throughout high school, which was truly his biggest interest. "He was an excellent hockey player", confirms Linda. "He was a better hockey player than he was a football player." However, it was becoming clear as Brian's senior year came to an end that a difficult decision was forthcoming. His two passions would both require singular focus in order to progress. "Coach Rahe would be calling the house looking for Brian because he wasn't in school that day", says Linda Pillman. "I answered the phone one day and said, 'He's not here'. He was on the road at a hockey game with the traveling hockey league, and he was missing school. Coach

Rahe was upset because some scout from a college was there to take a look at him and interview him, and he was out playing hockey."

Rahe saw great things in Pillman and encouraged him to focus on football. To illustrate how impressive Brian had become, Norwood would go on to retire his high school football jersey, No. 41. More impressive yet, it was the first football number ever to be retired by Norwood High. On a personal level, Pillman had made such an impression with his superiors that one of the Norwood coaches named their own son Brian in his honor.

Pillman had a tough decision to make, having to choose between his new passion and his first love. Seeing that football offered far more scholarship opportunities, he decided to ride that wave as far as it would take him.

2 - WALKING ON

As it turned out, Pillman didn't get a single scholarship offer. Not one. The records and the videotapes were impressive, but coaches still weren't buying that Brian was big enough. He was clocking in at under 200 pounds, but while his weight was acceptable at a high school level, the size deficit was only going to be more pronounced against the cream of the crop in college. There, he could easily get run over on defense, and taller quarterbacks would throw at a trajectory that the now 5-foot 9-inch Pillman couldn't reach. Don Rahe reacted with disbelief, sending videotapes to Eastern Kentucky, Ohio University and the University of Cincinnati to encourage them to pick up Pillman, but the responses were eerily similar. Eastern Kentucky even wrote back raving about him, saying he was doing things in the videos that they'd never seen before. But still, he was too small to consider, and the general belief was that his 40-yard dash numbers were being exaggerated. Only the Air Force Falcons didn't pass judgement on his size. People told a discouraged Pillman to try Division III football, but settling for less wasn't part of the plan.

One school did express a modicum of interest, that being Miami of Ohio. The Miami Redskins (now RedHawks) defensive coordinator Tim Rose came to talk to Brian and expressed the common concerns amongst colleges: they didn't believe in his size or speed, and nobody wanted to risk a scholarship on a 5'9" linebacker. Pillman's previous success aside, they told Brian to come to Miami of Ohio as a walk-on (a player without a scholarship who takes to the field and attempts to out-do scholarship athletes) as a middle guard. He even told Brian that if he worked really hard, he might make the traveling squad by his senior year. Almost tone deaf to just how low the bar of expectation was set for him, Brian responded with, "What are my chances to start?" Don Rahe advised Brian against the offer, but undeterred, he went ahead and walked on, listed originally as the eighth-string middle guard for the Redskins.

On the first day of practice, history repeated itself. Just like the day Don Rahe watched the kid with the squeaky voice dominate the field, Miami's head coach Tom Reed had no idea who Brian was. The first port of call was conditioning drills, designed to push their cardio to the limit and see who, of the handpicked athletes recruited, would excel. Of the 150 players being worked until they were gasping for air and their faces were purple, Brian Pillman, the walk-on, came in third, only behind two starters. When they took to the line of scrimmage Pillman was all over the place, refusing to be ignored, fighting tooth and nail to prove he warranted a better spot. By the end of the first practice, Reed, who would later compare this first day performance with the Tasmanian Devil, was looking for answers from his assistants, "Who is that guy? Brian Pillman, who is he?"

Brian smashed the original projection by making the traveling squad three weeks in. Halfway through the 1980 season, Brian earned the chance to start as the team's middle guard and got a scholarship. His walk-on gamble had paid off due to the exceptional heart and desire to succeed, to the point that Tom Reed would later say that, "Brian Pillman, as a freshman, was a better middle guard than the senior we started."

So determined was Brian that he first took to the field to start with both ankles badly sprained at the time. Facing injury as Miami of Ohio went against Western Michigan, Pillman blocked a punt from Alton Laupp that resulted in a tie-breaking touchdown, eventually leading to a Miami victory.

Brian ended up being a part of NFL history before his junior year when his mother managed to land tickets to the AFC Championship game in 1981. As they prepared to watch the Cincinnati Bengals take on the San Diego Chargers, the temperature dropped to the coldest (in terms of wind chill) in NFL history in a game that became known as the Freezer Bowl. "Mom said she was sitting down and had six inches of snow in her lap", laughs Linda Pillman. "I drove them down and during the game they had all the snow. They were just going to walk to one of the downtown hotels because there were no buses running or anything, the roads were terrible. The hotels were all booked, they didn't have anywhere to stay. So, me and my aunt drove downtown to get them, and on a good day it's a ten-minute drive, but it took us almost two hours. And it was so cold that the heater in the car, the defroster, couldn't keep up, and my aunt was sitting in the backseat with an ice scraper, scraping the *inside* of the windows that were icing up." Even in the worst of conditions, Brian was enthralled by the game, and couldn't help but fantasize about playing in Riverfront Stadium as he watched the Bengals capture the championship.

As much progress as Brian had made in his first two years at Miami of Ohio, he didn't settle, constantly looking for the next hurdle to overcome and the next way to gain an edge in the fiercely competitive environment. Knowing how important size was and having nudged his weight up to 195 pounds by 1981, Brian looked to further enhance his physique. He turned to his high school friend, Don Gay. Gay was a 112-pound amateur wrestler at Norwood High, who over time had transformed his physique to the point of being a bodybuilder, winning Mr. Cincinnati in 1980, Mr. Ohio in 1981, and would go on to place first at the 1982 National Physique Committee USA Championships in the Light Heavyweight division. Pillman, Gay and hockey player Kevin Warner spent the summer in the gym, as Brian altered his regimen, eating six times a day and ingesting over 5,000 calories, dedicating his entire existence to growth.

Eat. Work out for two hours on a body part. Eat again. Work out on another body part for two more hours. Brian's family even chipped in, assisting his laser focus by buying him steaks and protein drinks, as the amount of time being dedicated by Brian didn't allow him to get a job of his own to subsidize the initiative. "My Mom would go to these yard sales or big consignment shops and would buy these big meat platters, and that's what they would eat off", remembers Linda Pillman.

Though he was serious in his approach, Brian's emerging, distinctive sense of humor was blossoming throughout the entire process. On one occasion, Brian went out to eat with Don and his father, Paul. After ordering a huge meal and feasting like a pig, Pillman saw the opportunity to joke at his friend's expense. Excusing himself to use the restroom, Brian disappeared. Several minutes passed without his return. Eventually, Don figured out that Pillman bailed from the restaurant, leaving Paul to pay the entire bill by himself.

When Brian first dabbled with anabolic steroids is unknown. He'd had significant weight gains after his association with both the powerlifters in high school and now the bodybuilding crowd, as Pillman successfully shot his weight up to 225 pounds by the end of the summer. Local newspapers wrote about his ever-improving statistics in 1982, bench pressing 425 pounds, squatting 600 pounds, running a 4.5 40-yard dash, with the ability to slam dunk a softball through a basketball hoop (he couldn't palm a basketball). Brian even won some college weightlifting competitions, scoring the highest deadlift total at Miami of Ohio.

Mark Coleman, who would go on to become the first UFC Heavyweight Champion and won the 2000 Pride Open Weight Grand Prix, still remembers his first encounter with Pillman at this time. "I'm a little scared freshman, you know what I mean?", he begins. "My training partner and I are in the weight room, and there's fucking Brian Pillman. He was a monster, and he was so freakin' strong. He had so much weight on the bar it was sick. And I'm just sitting there like, 'Oh my God!' I'm spotting him on preacher curls. He's got like 225 pounds on the preacher curl. He does his reps and gets to eight. He's starting to fail and I'm supposed to be spotting him. All of a sudden he puts the weight down and says in that voice, "WHAT THE FUCK!?" He just screams at me. I must admit, I was a little bit intimidated. More than intimidated. I was embarrassed that he was yelling at me, but that was his intensity. He was one of the most intense guys I've ever met in my life."

On campus, people referred to Brian as "the Incredible Hulk" during this period of evolution, and it wouldn't be an outrageous assumption to make that if steroids weren't a part of his high school life, there certainly were by this point. The external pressures to fit a certain criteria, combined with an abnormally heightened internal pressue to succeed, led to Brian rationalizing the dangerous leap. The coaching staff were as shocked as the team by the transformation, but in awe of what Brian, the walk-on, was now capable of.

Some of the fondest memories Brian's sister Linda has are of this period, seeing her brother finding his groove at nose tackle. "He liked hitting people, he loved playing defense", she says. "He'd come out and bang his head on the goal posts before the game. He threw up before every football game. If he didn't throw up, something was wrong. He did it all through his college career too. I guess it was just intensity. He was very, very intense."

As good as Pillman was before, he truly came into his own in the 1982 season. During a September game opposite Northwestern University, Miami were up 20-13. After having trouble rushing against the Miami defense, NU made an incredible push with five minutes left to play, bombarding Miami with short passes. Getting from their own 26 yard line to Miami's 37, NU were at fourth down with two yards to go. The defensive signal from the bench was to prepare for a jet pass, since Northwestern's rushing game hadn't worked previously and their method of success was obvious. Brian's gut told him different, and he flagrantly ignored the coach's call, positioning himself for the run. Sure enough, running back Ricky Edwards took the ball, but was met head on by the seemingly omnipresent Pillman. Brian made such contact that he had to be assisted from the field himself, but he didn't give up a single inch in what was the biggest play of a game Miami went on to win.

The Redskins went undefeated for the first half of the season. The NFL at the time were in the middle of a players' strike, and thus a number of college games were used to fill time on television. One such game was Miami of Ohio against Bowling Green State, and Pillman took the opportunity to steal the show. Brian was all over the field, bombarding the offensive unit with crushing tackles and leading his team to victory. The CBS announcers, amazed at what they were witnessing, declared that Brian was the defensive player of the game.

The awareness of Brian's talent was spreading and teams began to build their offensive plays around dealing with him, often giving him double coverage to offset his tenacity. Teams that Miami would defeat often had many of the same remarks to newspapers in the aftermath. Kent State head coach Ed Chlebek, after seeing his team go down 20-0, said, "I was especially impressed by the nose (Pillman), he's one of the better ones in the league."

Brian saved his best efforts, however, for the two teams that had burned him when seeking out a scholarship, Ohio University and the University of Cincinnati. Against Ohio U, Pillman was sensational, racking up almost twenty key tackles. When the game was over, Brian brashly walked over to the same coach who had told his mother, Mary, that Brian just wasn't big enough in 1980. The coach sheepishly acknowledged his misgivings, complimenting Pillman on a great game. Against UC, Brian was such a force that he ended up being triple teamed on every play to shut him down as a priority.

By the end of November, as the team looked at a 7-4 record, Brian was one of the ten finalists for the Mid-American Conference Football Player of the Year honors, and unanimously voted to the MAC all-star team. He set an all-time Miami of Ohio record for season tackles for a loss at 25, for a total of 119 yards. When it came time to decide the Miami of Ohio defensive MVP for 1982, Pillman took the award with ease.

Additionally, Brian was becoming as big a hit off the field on campus as he was on it. "This guy ruled Miami of Ohio", says Mark Coleman, who became friends with Pillman after their introduction. "Everybody at the school feared this man. When he was walking, people stepped out of his way. The only people that would fuck with him would be people that didn't know him. If he ever got into a fight at Miami of Ohio, he always won."

Explaining the context of Pillman in the environment, Mark continues. "I hated the place. It was a beautiful campus, but it was a bunch of rich, stuck up, preppy snobs. At the same time, Brian was just basically mean and tough. A badass. He got the chicks and he whooped some ass. He was a mean, hungry, tough ass kicker on the football field and on the campus."

Being the star player and a good-looking guy with a bodybuilder physique got him a lot of female attention, and his taste for the wild life flourished in the environment. "A lot of it I think was that, being a kid and shut in a hospital", begins Linda, "He had so much energy pent up inside him. I think he was making up for lost time."

Brian made up for it with a vengeance, frequently being the life of the party, doing things that would be the talk of the town. Stories of his female conquests ranged from the ridiculous to the sublime. Rumors flooded the halls of Brian taking on an entire cheerleading squad by himself, topped only by the most absurd of all, an incident where he hung a girl wearing nothing but gravity boots to a pull up bar, performed a handstand and had sex with her upside down.

He and his roommate John Harbaugh (current head coach of the NFL's Baltimore Ravens) were almost roguish in their shared appreciation for practical jokes. Together the two were renowned for being pranksters off the field, stealing the tires off people's cars and going to ridiculous lengths to mess with fellow students.

This isn't to imply that Pillman was a simple-minded jock, as the truth is quite the contrary. Up to that point, Brian was doing well in his studies as a sociology major with a minor in criminology, and was considered one of the sharpest students on the course. Classmates would sit in frustration as Brian seamlessly breezed through the tougher aspects of learning. "He was such an intelligent guy", recalls Les Thatcher, who would go on to meet Pillman much later in life. "A couple of the kids he played football with at Miami of Ohio had said to me that they would sit and beat themselves to death trying to study for a test, and Brian would just run through it once and get it."

As he engaged himself academically, he told people around him that he enjoyed his minor far more and ultimately wanted to become a private investigator. After the 1982 season, the impulsive Pillman changed his major to political science for his senior year, eyeing up a potential run in law school after Miami of Ohio. Juxtaposing his brash reputation even further, he distracted himself by being an avid coin and old money collector, picking up pieces of historical significance. But football was his true love and as the 1983 season approached, Brian, having been named team captain, spent as much time studying the game as he did anything else.

When things got underway for the Miami Redskins in '83 they faced a number of challenges, between first-year head coach Tim Rose and a new quarterback struggling with bad luck. Getting off to a rough start, the team lost their first four games straight. Highlighting Brian's individual performance, he was still awarded the game ball after a loss to Bowling Green State. His incredible efforts against offenses that were now regularly assigning two or three men to him on every play earned him plaudits, with Jack Harbaugh (John's father and head coach of Western Michigan at the time) stating that, "Brian Pillman is the best defensive player in the Mid-American Conference, and from that standpoint controls a game like no other player I've seen since Tim Davis played at Michigan in the 60's."

After Ohio University bested Miami, coach Brian Burke stated to the Cincinnati Enquirer, "If you don't double team him, he's in your backfield. He's a great football player. Our protection sometimes was breaking down because of the things we were trying to do against Pillman."

The team struggled their way to a 4-7 record by the end of the season, victims of a young offense unravelling. The losses were no reflection on Brian, who had an incredible year. Blitzing his own record from the year before, Brian executed 40 tackles for a loss, totaling 142 yards, despite increased coverage.

His efforts earned him the Mid-American Conference Defensive Player of the Year award, as well as picking up his second Miami of Ohio defensive MVP honor. Even more impressive, Pillman was voted to the Associated Press All-American second team in the middle guard position. The man voted to the first team was the 300-pound William "Refrigerator" Perry of Clemson, who would go on to be a part of the Super Bowl winning Chicago Bears team of 1986. "He was a two-time All-American at Miami of Ohio", says Linda Pillman. "That just goes to show how much respect he had, because it was the coaches that voted on them. Miami wasn't a top tier college, not like your Michigan or Ohio State colleges, it was a level below that. So for him to get second team All-American behind a first-tier college, that was something right there."

So remarkable was Pillman that in the book *Schoolboy Legends: A Hundred Years of Cincinnati's Most Storied Football Players* by John Baskin and Lonnie Wheeler, Brian was listed on the Cincinnati All-Time College Team at linebacker. In 1999, the Cincinnati Enquirer voted on a Miami of Ohio all-century team. Pillman was listed at middle guard.

Some of Brian's records still stand at Miami of Ohio to this day, holding the benchmark for career tackles for a loss (77), season tackles for loss for his 1983 efforts (40), as well as the total tackles for lost yards record at 346.

Brian maintained a 2.8 grade average throughout most of 1983, but in spending so much time focusing on his final year on the Redskins, he fell behind in his studies and never completed his degree. He vowed to return and finish it one day, but life took him in a different direction.

As he wrapped up his run at Miami of Ohio, Brian told the Enquirer, "I'll be awfully sad when the whistle sounds for the last time. These four years have been a continuous thrill. I'll miss college football dearly."

Brian had come a long way since being given the worst uniforms to wear as a high school freshman, treated as the undeserving runt of the litter that was lucky to even be on the field. But as he began to talk to pro scouts, the same concerns about his size painfully seared into his ears, and he had to face the fact that there may be no place for him to continue his career. Not sure if his run in football was over, he tentatively considered staying at the college as a coach. However, his desire to play was too strong. After being such a star at Miami of Ohio, the prospect of entering a regular field of work or doing anything else was simply unappealing. He'd loved the game so much and there was only one mountain left to climb. With nothing to lose, Brian made the decision. He was going to make the National Football League.

3 - MAKING THE BENGALS

As he prepared for pro football, Brian spent hours every day in the Miami of Ohio gym, running five miles a night around campus to keep in peak cardio condition. At that time, most NFL middle guards were closer to 280 pounds, and the consensus was that if Brian was to make the pros, he'd fit in better at linebacker, his old high school position. Readily aware that life as a linebacker would be much different at the pro level after four years at nose tackle, Pillman knew he needed some time to work at it, and found himself at an impasse.

Despite his status as the star player in college, his record setting ability and the fact that he was a two-time All-American, Brian's name didn't get called in the NFL Draft. With the same size concerns as always going through the minds of the key coaches, Pillman was forced to endure the same disappointment he'd faced at the end of his high school days.

After going unsigned, he eagerly anticipated the United States Football League draft. But it took until the tenth round for the Denver Gold to pick Brian, making him the last All-American selected. Disheartened and feeling slighted, Pillman didn't even accept the offer, turning down a small bonus and a $35,000 per year contract (dependent on making the team). He expected more for himself.

He began looking at the Canadian Football League as an alternative and opened up talks with the Montreal Concordes, who quickly offered him a free agent trial. Pillman did feel encouraged when the then-Green Bay Packers defensive co-ordinator Hank Bullough (who had coached with the Cincinnati Bengals previously under head coach Forrest Gregg) told him he felt he was big enough to play inside linebacker in the NFL. Seemingly taking an interest in Brian, Bullough gave him a workout and agility program to prepare for a free agent tryout, which the Packers had also decided to offer him.

Before long, the home team came calling, as the Cincinnati Bengals offered a free agent trial deal as well. Interestingly, there was a strong Bengals connection to Miami of Ohio, dating back to franchise founder Paul Brown attending in 1941. Brian's origin as a Norwood street kid would make a spot on the team a local success story in the media, who were already fond of Pillman. That, combined with the Bengals losing two linebackers to the USFL in the off-season, opened the door for Brian to be offered a chance that many in his position perhaps wouldn't get. Seeing the window of opportunity as more open in Cincinnati given the recent departures, Brian Pillman officially agreed to a free agent contract with the Bengals on May 3rd, 1984. "We had a champagne celebration", remembers his sister, Linda.

"I'm ten feet off the ground right now", Pillman told Peter King of the Cincinnati Enquirer. "It's always been my dream to play for the Bengals. This is like a dream come true."

Enthusiasm aside, it was always going to be tough for Brian to earn a spot on the active roster, fighting tooth and nail with draft picks and free agents for a place on the team, all the while learning linebacker at the pro level. The previous year, the Bengals had 13 free agents attend the training camp in Wilmington, and none of them were signed. For the 1984 season, Pillman was among 16 free agents looking to beat the odds.

Wasting no time, he got in his rusty 1974 Monte Carlo, a car that could generously be called a heap of shit, complete with a speedometer that stopped working 10,000 miles prior, and headed to the Bengals. With the training camp starting in mid-July, Brian had two months to prepare and work on his new position. With size on his mind (as always), he headed to the gym. It was here that he first met Kim Wood.

Wood, a former running back for Wisconsin himself, was the strength and conditioning coach for the Bengals dating back to 1975, a post he would keep for almost three decades. Years before, Wood had fallen in with Arthur Jones, the inventor of infimetric and akinetic exercise equipment and founder of Nautilus. Wood set up many top college and pro weight programs and worked closely with Jones as the company grew. Later, Kim became good friends with Pete Brown, the son of Bengals' founder Paul, and the two went into business together selling Nautilus machines in the Midwest. Through the connection, Wood got the job with the Bengals, becoming one of the first (if not the first) full time strength coaches in professional sports. Later, he would become one of the founders of Hammer Strength, another hugely successful weight machine company.

Kim would go on to play a pivotal role in Brian's life, but in the summer of 1984 the intention was different. "The first time I actually met him was when the Bengals had signed him, and he just showed up at our training facility", recalls Wood. "They called me and they said, 'We just signed this kid, do whatever you want to him. Whatever you want to do with this guy, do it, see what he's got'." With the free agents, the directive was to throw as much work as possible at them to test their meddle and, in many ways, run off the pretenders.

"I'm not saying I tried to kill him…but damn close", says Wood, who shares further insight on the Pillman experiment from the Bengals' perspective. "It was a nice gesture to sign him. There was no way he was going to make the team. To get where he had to go would have been virtually impossible. If you're undersized, or if there's something about you that's different, football doesn't want anything to do with you even if you can do it. Even if you could actually play, because they don't want other people laughing at them because winning is so hard to do. You can't lose in a unique fashion."

But Pillman wasn't to be denied, and threw his heart and soul into handling whatever was thrown in his direction at mini-camp, agonizing as it may be. During one session, Wood instructed Brian to perform 50 squats on the Nautilus squat machine with each individual leg, an experience that Pillman later joked went beyond the point of pain, since he felt dead at the 15-rep mark. In the Cincinnati Enquirer, two days before the training camp was to start, Kim Wood spoke of Brian's progress. "Talk about a strong son of a gun", Wood told the paper, "He's an intense, determined guy who's made so much progress in five weeks that he's got guys coming up to him asking what he's doing."

With a mountain of a task ahead of him, Brian Pillman at least felt prepared as he checked into Pickett Hall, the player's dorm, on July 15th. With steroids, he'd managed to push his weight all the way up to 240 pounds. Eating like a king at the Bengals cafeteria that night, he mentally prepared for the next morning. The chance to play in the NFL, as well as prove his doubters wrong once again, was in touching distance in his mind.

On his first day of practice, Brian was faced with the reality of just how high the mountain was. While his aggression always did him well, being back at linebacker after years away, and this time as a pro, was a wake-up call. He struggled to mentally click in the position and his usual ferocity suffered. Brian was tentative and slower off the mark than usual. He returned to his room that night vowing to return to the field a better player.

The next day, Pillman put on a performance reminiscent of the one that earned him the "Tasmanian Devil" tag back at Miami of Ohio. Pillman read a screen play and steamrolled the 270-pound Bruce Kozerski, a rookie center, at full speed. Later that day, Pillman dislocated the left shoulder of starting halfback Stanley Wilson, an injury that would keep him out for over three weeks. Pillman had already taken out Mike Martin right before the training camp began, giving him a bruised arch, and the coaches started to take notice of the common denominator. Wilson went on to tell the papers, "If he keeps going like he is, they're going to have to find a spot for him." Pillman left the field sore, but redeemed.

He took to the field the next day looking to carry that momentum on. It started out with more of the same, as Pillman tackled running back Robert Williams, giving him a deep thigh bruise that kept him out of practice for a few days. Pillman was a wrecking machine, throwing every fiber of his being into every play. He was feeling right and playing well, when he was suddenly faced with the worst-case scenario. On a play designed for Pillman to follow the running back in motion and suddenly shift directions, he planted his left foot into the ground and sprung out with his right leg. Upon landing, he felt a pop in his right hamstring. When the play ended, he limped off the field, denying the severity of the injury to the trainer, who quickly saw through the façade and instructed Pillman to the training room. As Coach Sam Wyche entered and told him to rest, Brian couldn't help but feel absolutely crestfallen. His odds were slim enough to begin with, but an injury on the third day of practice put him behind the eight ball even more.

Icing and stretching his torn hamstring regularly, Pillman was forced to watch from the sidelines, studying the role of linebacker diligently as others competed for the job he wanted so badly. Unable to participate, Brian's spirits were crushed as the days went by, one after the other, hoping each morning would be the one where nature cooperated with him. Brian had never missed a game at Norwood High or Miami of Ohio, regardless of injury. Seven years without absence and now, with an NFL spot on the line, his body had failed him.

After eight days of inactivity, Pillman was able to slowly jog without pain and his spirits immediately lifted. Holding Brian Pillman off the field at a time like this was the very definition of holding a tiger by the tail. His teammates grew more familiar with his over the top personality, as he would brazenly set the electronic muscle stimulator treatment on his hamstring to maximum voltage, taping pads to his forearms and driving them into the wall full bore, much to the players' disbelief.

Twelve days after suffering the injury, Pillman was back on the field, practicing with his teammates. The following day, he fell to the ground once more, having strained the hamstring further. He'd be out a few more days. To say Brian was maddened would be a vast understatement.

Unable to make an impression on the field, Brian refused to be forgotten off it. A couple of days after his latest setback, the Bengals held their family picnic, attended by General Manager Paul Brown, as well as all the coaches and players who brought their loved ones along. Brian Pillman decided to take the opposite approach, showing up with a black prostitute, dressed for action, much to the amusement of the team. Brown himself took notice, taking the time to set Brian at ease about his injury, advising him not to rush back.

Brian was determined to be an attribute to the team while unable to practice, and would routinely fire off encouraging words of wisdom to his colleagues. His sarcasm-laden tirades would usually be enjoyable, if not effective. One of the more humorous examples would backfire when Pillman used his unique brand of inspirational speaking to try and fire up Anthony Munoz. Munoz, a legendary offensive lineman who would end up being elected into the Pro Football Hall of Fame in his first time on the ballot, was known for being a true gentleman. Indeed, his charitable exploits off the field were highly regarded and his demeanor was such that he won the Cincinnati Bengals Man of the Year award five consecutive times. Munoz, not one to approve of outbursts of profanity, sat in disbelief as Brian Pillman, a free agent rookie, stood before him ranting almost maniacally, violently detailing what he needed to do to the opposition in his first pre-season game. Using every vulgar curse word under the sun, Brian's speech fell on completely deaf ears, a fact he chose to ignore as his colorful tirade went on. If nothing else, the other players were entertained watching, though Munoz himself glared at

Brian as if he belonged in a mental institution.

Another memorable incident off the field came when Brian bit back against Reggie Williams. Williams, a fellow linebacker who started with the Bengals in 1976, had taken it upon himself to taunt the rookie Pillman unmercifully throughout his tenure as part of the typical hazing initiation. Part of training camp tradition was to hold a "rookie show", where the newbies were given carte blanche to ridicule the veterans in retaliation. Brian did so in grand fashion on the African-American Williams, painting his own face black and donning a three-piece suit to resemble him, before parodying his elder in hilarious fashion. His impersonation highlighted the night and earned him a standing ovation.

Brian waited a week before he started jogging with his teammates again, testing the waters and trying desperately not to exacerbate his injury. Having missed so much time, Pillman's chances to make the cut were undoubtedly hurt, but his determination showed through. He was almost religious in treating his injury, constantly icing and stretching it, never missing a session with the trainers and studying the plays and practices meticulously to come back as ready as possible. Coach Wyche couldn't ignore how hard Brian was working to return.

Three weeks after the initial injury, he was finally ready. Stepping onto the field, he knew he had to make up for missed reps and went full speed ahead. The Bengals were preparing for a preseason game against the Tampa Bay Buccaneers and with Brian on the shelf so long, he didn't expect to be figured in. Much to his surprise, he was told he'd be playing his first NFL game. Even with the Bengals losing 21-13, Pillman was stood on the sidelines the entire time, itching to get the call to run on the field and make a difference. With his hamstring injury fresh on everybody's mind, the call never came.

But seeing his unbreakable drive was inspiring, and the coaches began flirting with the idea of putting Pillman on special teams. Indeed, with his characteristics, a spot on the suicide squad seemed apropos. "As a football player Brian showed that he was totally fearless", says Kim Wood, "Which in that world is valuable currency. He wasn't gonna' last too long in pro football, but people loved him as a little guy who tried his ass off." Bruce Coslet, a coach at the Bengals, would add to that sentiment telling *Schoolboy Legends* that, "He would hit anything that moved. Even if it was his own guy, he didn't care."

Seeing this as a way to get some game time, Pillman was elated to find his name on the lineup for the upcoming battle against the Chicago Bears, where defensive backfield coach Trent Walters had him positioned as a wedge-buster on the kickoff team. It was a spot custom made for somebody looking to get aggressive and do some serious damage, and Brian fit the bill.

As Saturday finally arrived, Pillman walked into Soldier Field with a purpose. Time to make an impression. The special teams unit got in position for Brian's first play in the NFL, a kickoff that sent the ball screaming past the end zone for a touchback. But Pillman neglected to notice, instead eyeing up Wilber Marshall, the Bears outside linebacker and first round draft pick, and careened into him with a body-block. The two exchanged hot-tempered profanities as they were separated. "I wasn't about to run 40 yards and not hit anybody", Pillman later told the Enquirer. They would collide again on the second kickoff, with Brian this time driving his forearm directly into Marshall's head, sending him to the turf and getting the figurative victory. As the game progressed, Pillman tackled Walter Payton to the ground, internally reveling at manhandling a legend.

Regardless of only getting four plays in the game, Pillman was satisfied as the Bengals took the victory. Things got more encouraging when Brian survived a round of cuts made two days later and was given his special teams spot in the last exhibition game of the preseason, where the Bengals were set to face the Detroit Lions at Riverfront Stadium in Cincinnati.

In very real terms, this was the last chance, as it was for every free agent signing, to make a definitive statement that they belonged on the team. A few days after this game the final round of cuts would take place, and Brian had a lot of ground to cover.

He walked onto the field in front of 41,715 of his townsfolk. Among those in attendance was Hank Bullough, who originally tried to recruit Pillman to Green Bay, but had since become coach of the USFL's Pittsburgh Maulers. He wanted to see how the man he saw major potential in fared, hoping there was still a chance he'd play under his tutelage if he didn't make the Bengals.

Like a man possessed, Pillman went on a tear. As if willing him to a great performance, the fans would rise and cheer every time Brian was in on a play, or his name announced on the public-address system. He paid off their enthusiasm tying the team lead in total tackles with six, forcing a fumble on special teams and getting in on some plays as inside linebacker to boot. But by far the biggest moment of the game for Brian came in the second quarter. On a kickoff, the ball was caught by Kenneth Jenkins of the Lions, who ran out to the 15 yard line where he was met by a sprinting Pillman, propelling himself like a heat-seeking missile. Pillman drove himself into Jenkins with reckless abandon, the resulting thud echoing around Riverfront Stadium. "It was as hard a hit as I ever saw in over 30 years of NFL coaching", says Kim Wood, "You could hear it throughout the stadium, which was unusual." The Enquirer simply referred to it as "an aggravated assault" in their coverage. The Cincinnati natives roared with approval as Brian rose to his feet, a reeling Jenkins wondering if he'd been hit by a truck.

As the game came to an end, Pillman beamed inside hearing receiver and sometimes roommate Cris Collinsworth telling him how well he'd done.

The performance, and particularly the tackle, got the attention of those who mattered. "He was on the bubble at the cut-down date", says Wood, "The hit made him a favorite with the Bengal coaches." The following day, Pillman's brutal tackle was the talk of the team, as Coach Sam Wyche reviewed and rewound the tape in front of the players, proudly spotlighting Pillman's proudest moment.

As the buzz of the game wore off and with the final round of cuts coming, the uncertain Pillman was riddled with anxiety, nervously awaiting the final verdict. He'd done all he could, but missing those three weeks had to be a killer for his chances.

Cut day came. This was it. Assistant Player Personnel Director Frank Smouse called Brian and invited him down to Spinney Field, the Bengals training ground. Surrounded by waste sites and factories, Spinney was a true reflection of the city's balancing act between major league aspirations and working-class roots. Wondering which side of the divide he was about to fall on, Pillman listened intently.

Smouse told Brian that the club needed to reduce their roster to 49 players, meaning they needed to cut nine names, and Pillman was amongst those being waived. Brian was initially crushed at the news, before Smouse told him not to consider it as being written off. To the contrary, Brian could still be recalled to the roster if the Bengals shifted a couple of names to the injured reserve list the following day. Leaving the office with mixed emotions, Pillman went straight to the field and practiced with the team, choosing to remain optimistic.

The decision to put Pillman on the waivers list was strategic. By being waived, there was the possibility of another NFL team swooping in and taking Brian, as others had until noon the following day to make a grab. Since he'd originally gone undrafted, it was a relatively safe decision to put Brian on waivers while they decided how many other players could go on injured reserve, opening up spots for free agents.

It wasn't as cut and dry in reality, however. The Philadelphia Eagles had started expressing interest in Brian as well, which was only amplified after watching him in action at Riverfront. And he still had his options in the USFL and CFL if things fell through.

As it turned out, there was nothing to fear. At 2pm the following day, Frank Smouse called back with the news that Brian Pillman was officially a Cincinnati Bengal for the 1984 season.

He'd done it. The little guy with the squeaky voice, that was too small to play in high school, had made it all the way to the National Football League. "He had a real underdog rep which helped him be seen as a totally fearless and almost magical player", says Kim Wood. "Once in a while guys like that come along. If you find somebody who is fierce and fearless, sometimes teams just like to have a guy like that around. He really was a special talent."

And on that day, Brian Pillman couldn't have been happier.

4 - LIFE IN THE NFL

With his official signing, Pillman was, at the time, one of only five men who actually went to high school in Cincinnati that made it to the Bengals, joining Neil Craig, Walter Johnson, Vic Koegel and Clem Turner on that list. Such was the local enthusiasm for his success that he was honored by the City of Norwood, who instituted the Brian Pillman 3D (Determination, Desire and Dedication) Scholarship Fund in a ceremony at Norwood Senior High School gym.

As Pillman prepared to don the stripes for the first game of the season against the Denver Broncos, he was surrounded by a confident team. The offense looked especially promising, with two strong options at quarterback. Ken Anderson, who signed with the Bengals in 1972, held the role as the Bengals' starting quarterback and had led them to eight winning seasons, four playoff appearances and one Super Bowl appearance. In 1984, Anderson was the Bengals all-time leading quarterback in most statistical categories. Anderson was aging in the role, but the appropriate replacement had been drafted in that year in Boomer Esiason. Esiason, a 6'5" behemoth with a rocket arm, would go on to be a four-time Pro Bowler and set a number of team and NFL records. 1984 and 1985 would be the transition period between the two, and at the start of the season it almost looked like it would be hard to fail.

It was with this mindset that defeat came as a bitter pill to swallow for the Bengals, as the Broncos took the win 20-17 in a game that Cincinnati, by all rights, should have won. As Broncos starting quarterback John Elway went down in the third quarter, the Bengals had the lead. They'd be stifled by two missed field goals, a fourth quarter touchdown pass from Gary Kubiak to Clarence Kay, and finally a fumble with two minutes remaining to throw the game away. While Pillman was personally enthused with his contribution, the team was disappointed.

It got worse. The following week the Bengals played the Kansas City Chiefs at Riverfront and gave up several opportunities to win. When a mad scramble for a fumble recovery led to a safety rather than a touchdown for the Bengals, it was clear it wasn't their day. They left the field defeated and dejected once again. To make matters worse for Brian, he ended up with a broken nose from a collision in the last kickoff of the game.

But Pillman, never one to let a single defeat keep him down, thrust himself into the Bengals lifestyle full throttle. The attention he was afforded fit perfectly into Brian's personality, and as a legendary carouser he'd been given the keys to the kingdom. Being able to play the NFL card in local bars went down well, and the stories he'd come back with seemed more outrageous by the week.

Brian began getting confidential fan mail from a woman in Detroit. She wrote to him for about six straight weeks, revealing that she was a single mother taken aback by what a great guy Brian was, and how he had such an outstanding character. In true Pillman fashion, he read all the letters aloud to the other players in the training room before practice, as they sat around getting their ankles taped. Eventually, the woman came down from Detroit to see Brian, who took her to a hotel in Norwood ten minutes from his house and proceeded to seal the deal. After the woman fell asleep, Brian quietly left the room and walked home. In the middle of the night, the woman was awoken suddenly by the sound of the housekeeper banging on the door, kicking her out. Brian, as it turned out, had only paid for the hotel room for four hours.

A long way from home and stranded, the woman headed back to Detroit and wrote an indignant letter to him for what he did. Wildly amused, Brian read it aloud to his teammates, who lapped up his latest adventure. "He would do these terrible things when he was with the Bengals", joked Kim Wood, "And he would be the center of attention, the guys couldn't believe it. They'd have their mouths open, going, 'This guy's a rookie!'"

Brian had learned a very vital lesson in preseason, one that stayed with him for the rest of his life. After going down to injury and being unable to beguile the coaches with his ability, he'd circumvented the problem by getting over with key people so strongly off the field. With his wild personality and outlandish antics, people wanted to be around him, affording him unlikely opportunities in the process.

Not all the attention Brian got was positive, however. "I think because of his reputation, people would try him and figure, 'Let's see how tough you are'", says Linda Pillman.

Brian would get into fights that typically ended in spectacular fashion, and word would travel fast. Back in college, he was sitting in the back seat of a car with his friends when another car full of guys pulled up next to them, looking to start trouble. The war of words between open windows quickly became something more when the doors of the other car started to open. Brian got out, grabbed the first person to approach him and swiftly broke his arm, right in front of his shocked friends. The injured man actually attempted to sue Brian as a result, but with multiple witnesses identifying him as the instigator, it was thrown out.

While Brian never actively sought a physical confrontation, he wasn't one to shy away from it either, and the stories of his confrontations had already made him an alehouse legend in Cincinnati. "I remember Brian used to say he would be out in a restaurant and somebody would think they were taller than him or bigger than he was, so they could take him on", elaborates Linda. On one occasion, Pillman had gone out to dinner and was approached by a larger man clearly looking to goad him into a fight. As the stranger began firing obscenities in his direction, Brian responded the same way he did at the line of scrimmage – by blowing kisses at him. Again and again. The unorthodox tactic seemed to work, as the man backed down.

Another time, things escalated a little further, resulting in Pillman being permanently banned from a popular bar in downtown Cincinnati. On the second floor of the club, which had a balcony overlooking the dance floor, Brian bumped into a girl he'd been out with before. Things had ended badly then, and she threw a drink in his face upon seeing him. Brian responded by firing off an insult in her direction, which raised the ire of the man the girl came the club with. He quickly came after Brian, but Pillman turned the tables, knocking him to the ground. The fight ended with Brian throwing the man over the balcony and holding him upside-down by the ankles over the dance floor. He wasn't welcome back.

Such was his standing as a street fighter at the time that when *Schoolboy Legends* did their write-up on Brian, they opened with the following passage: "He was the answer to the trivia question: 'Who do you want on the barstool next to you when the fight breaks out?' In any contest of Brian Pillman vs. a buzzsaw, the saw got the long odds."

Part of Brian's charm as a multifaceted, complex personality was that his calm, caring side was every bit as endearing as his intensity was intimidating. He was prone to random acts of kindness, and stories of his fondness for animals (especially cats) appear sporadically throughout his life. "He'd have these crazy spurts", recalls Linda Pillman, "But at the same time, he was down at the Bengals practice field one day. I'm a big animal lover, and he brought me a bird that he found down on the field. It had been injured but it was okay, it only needed a week of rehab. And here he is bringing me this bird home in a shoe box, and when it was better he took it back to the field in the same shoe box and released it where he found it."

Looking to get back in the saddle on the gridiron, the Bengals headed to New York to face the Jets. It was more doom and gloom in Cincinnati, as the Jets beat them decisively, 43-23. Moreover, Pillman reaggravated his right hamstring injury on a special teams kickoff coverage and was back out of practice. He managed to make it to the following games against the St. Louis Rams and Pittsburgh Steelers, but the nagging setback refused to go away. Morale only got worse as the Bengals ended up losing their first five games in a row, with questions and finger pointing in every direction as to what the team was doing wrong.

As they prepared to face the Houston Oilers in their sixth season game, changes were made at the head of the horse. The Bengals opted to start with Boomer Esiason instead of Ken Anderson at quarterback, and the results were immediate. Though the Oilers weren't as tough opponents as they'd faced previously, a win was much needed, and the Bengals got their first of the season, 13-3, right there at Riverfront. But for Brian Pillman, the victory was bittersweet. It was after this game that he had to face the fact that his hamstring just wasn't ready, and the coaches put Brian Pillman on injured reserve on October 13th. By doing this, Pillman would be ineligible to play for four weeks.

Forced to the sidelines again, Brian looked on as his team strived to fight up from the hole they were in. Despite teammate's objections, Brian was back in practice two weeks later.

In many ways, the method that got Pillman his roster spot was also his undoing. In the very same pre-season game against the Detroit Lions when Brian made his jaw-dropping tackle and earned his place, Bengals defensive back Bobby Kemp dislocated his right shoulder, forcing him to the injured reserve list. The timing was fortuitous to Brian, in that it was this injury that left the roster spot available for him to step into after being waived. But with Brian's hamstring limiting him he was forced onto IR himself, right as Bobby Kemp was ready to return to a spot on the active roster.

The weeks passed by, but Pillman remained on injured reserve. Even after the hamstring healed, the team didn't want to swap out any of the newly drafted or high dollar players for the free agent kamikaze.

Regardless, he practiced daily with the team, fighting to contribute in any way he could. But it was impossible to get past the depressing feeling that came having to take the road trip and watch the game, rather than be in it, every Sunday afternoon.

As the season approached its conclusion, it became apparent Brian wouldn't return to the active roster. The Bengals managed to rally back, winning three games in a row down the stretch and going into their final game of the season with a 7-8 record. Somehow, they only needed one more win, against the Buffalo Bills, to have a chance at the playoffs. At home, Cincinnati succeeded, convincingly beating the Bills 52-21 and finishing the season at 8-8. But the playoffs weren't locked in yet – they needed the Pittsburgh Steelers to lose to the LA Raiders in order to win the AFC Central division title that seemed so far out of reach earlier in the season. The Bengals were forced to scoreboard-watch, their hearts sinking as the Steelers won 13-7, dashing their 1984 playoff hopes for good.

In many ways, Brian Pillman's year mirrored the Bengals' season at large. A tale of fighting against the odds, somehow making an opportunity when it would have been far easier to write off success as a far away fantasy, but being denied when it counted the most.

But the intestinal fortitude, outright gutsy nature and over the top personality of Pillman didn't go unnoticed. Every year, active members of each NFL team vote for one player who, to them, "exemplifies commitment to the principles of sportsmanship and courage", for the prestigious Ed Bloch Courage Award. In 1984, the Cincinnati Bengals award was given to Brian Pillman.

As the season came to a close, Sam Wyche told the Cincinnati Enquirer of

Pillman, "As far as his future with the team goes, I'm sure he'll be back at training camp again next year, and then it'll start all over again for him."

But Brian didn't make it to the 1985 training camp. On May 16th, 1985, he was officially waived by the Cincinnati Bengals. With his release came a letter from Paul Brown, the Bengals owner, telling Brian that if he ever needed a job, he could come and work for him at any time.

∞

It goes without saying that Brian was disappointed in hearing the news about being waived, but his feelings towards football were dampened for reasons beyond that. Playing pro football had been a goal and an impossible dream for years. When fantasy became reality, however, life as an NFL football player wasn't exactly what Pillman envisaged.

"I don't think it was what he thought it was going to be", states Linda Pillman. "I think he realized it was more business than the game. They're going to keep the people they've invested the most money in, that kinda' thing."

Business first was a different approach to what Brian was used to. In his prior experience as the star player at Miami of Ohio, it was all about the rush of going on the field, the adrenaline of working as a team, battling another for superiority. It was pure, and it was all about the football. The mentality was different in the NFL. He saw it in the players, and he felt it with some of the coaches.

"With college football when you're in game mode, you're in game mode from the time you get on the bus to go to the next city", explains Linda. "I remember Brian saying to me that one of the coaches commented to Brian when he was getting on the bus, 'You've got your game face on already? It's not for two more days'. Brian was trying to carry his football from college into pro and it didn't make the transition. He was more serious about football than some of them. He just wanted to play football, he didn't care about the glam."

After his experience in the Bengals, Brian wound up being somewhat disillusioned with pro football. He still loved the game, however, and it wouldn't take long for Brian to find a new home. One month later, Pillman was picked up by the Buffalo Bills, who were now being coached by Hank Bullough after the Pittsburgh Maulers folded following the 1984 season.

When working for the Bengals, Bullough would catch the local media talking about how fierce Pillman was as a nose tackle at Miami of Ohio, and sought out footage to see for himself. When he did, he was suitably impressed. Bullough had always seen major potential in Brian, and his mind raced with the possibilities of what Brian was capable of if used correctly in the NFL. While Pillman was signed for the Bills as a linebacker, Bullough was strongly considering the idea of putting Brian in as a nose tackle, an unheard of idea for a guy his size in pro football. As previously mentioned, Pillman was fifty pounds lighter than the average NFL middle guard. The position typically required a large athlete with formidable strength and staying power to demand and then ward off double teams, turning the middle of the field into a pileup while the linebackers run free to the football. But Hank thought Brian's quickness and unique ability to foresee how plays would unfold in that position could revolutionize the entire game. The records at Miami of Ohio spoke for themselves in Bullough's eyes, and he believed it could translate to the NFL.

However, things had changed for Brian. With his time off, he began scrambling for the answer to hitting a wall in the NFL and was having trouble finding it. He decided that the safest bet would be to get bigger, gaining more weight. As he prepared for a shot at Buffalo, he bulked up to 250 pounds. The downside was that he wasn't in the same shape that made him an exceptional player in the first place. Even worse, he knew it.

Brian Pillman headed to Buffalo and practiced as a linebacker for the duration of training camp. He was impressive enough that he was considered on the team for the regular season, but when the final round of cuts were made, the last man told he was no longer a Buffalo Bill was Pillman.

There were a number of factors working against Brian. With his added size, he'd lost the speed that allowed him to maneuver in a way that other teams couldn't deal with. The Bills were wanting Brian to play on the outside and he just wasn't fast enough. In addition, he wasn't as mentally focused in camp after his past experiences and the awareness of his size was a problem. "He just said he went too far into trying to be big because everybody told him he was too small", says Linda Pillman. "He didn't have the mindset at the time, and he knew he wasn't in shape when he went up there." Certainly, the days of the impressive blowouts in training forcing the coaches hand had passed.

Furthermore, an assistant coach was alerted that the housekeeping lady who would go into the dorm rooms at training camp was fearful to go into Brian's room because it was so filthy. From a lifestyle perspective, the room was simply a place to land in the early hours for Brian, who had a reputation for leaving rooms looking like a tornado had hit them. It has also been reported that another assistant coach found a vial of anabolic steroids with Brian's name on them. While drug use in the NFL at that time has been documented as widely prevalent, it was a knock against Brian that he didn't need, with size being such a key concern surrounding him already. With the belief that he was small guy that didn't belong all juiced up and concerns that Pillman's carelessness could ultimately be trouble for the team, he was axed.

With no second year in the NFL, Brian was at a loose end and in need of a new direction. He'd kept in touch with several people at the Bengals that he'd personally liked, including strength coach Kim Wood. It was in talking with Wood that a new occupation was discussed.

Kim had followed professional wrestling for years, and was convinced that Brian Pillman was the inch perfect candidate to make a living inside the squared circle.

Pro wrestling almost seemed like a natural transition for former football players at the time, and the laundry list of individuals who made the leap reads a mile long, with varying levels of success. The combination of still being in the spotlight, the adrenaline rush, and being involved in a physical endeavor that, if you made it big, had the potential to pay significantly better than your average job brought with it a natural allure.

Interestingly, wrestling wasn't really something that crossed Brian's mind previously, as he had very little exposure to it. With the exception of his early years in the hospital where he'd watch cartoons all day, he never watched a lot of television – he was too busy playing sports. His grandmother, however, regularly watched Big Time Wrestling which played to Ohio, promoted by The Sheik. Doubling as the main attraction of the territory, Sheik was one of the most notorious heels in the history of the game, and his wild, bloody antics would be viewed regularly by Brian's elder relative. Though he wasn't really paying attention, the sight of the out-of-control mad man was vivid enough to become Brian's earliest wrestling memory.

Besides, background knowledge wasn't the reason it was a match made in heaven. From a personality perspective, it was ideal. "Pillman knew that, outside of sports or something like wrestling, he was going to have a tough time in life", elaborates Wood. "He wasn't going to be an insurance salesman, you know. And he knew that this was the perfect thing for him because he was a wild guy and a tough guy, and a legendary fighter in Cincinnati. The fascinating thing with pro wrestling is the stuff behind the scenes, and Pillman just loved it. Because that's the way he was in college and football." When asked if this assessment was accurate, Brian's sister Linda simply laughed, "Yeah, I couldn't see him sitting behind a desk."

"You didn't have to grow up in pro wrestling", begins Alex Marvez, who has covered the NFL for over 20 years and served as the president of the Pro Football Writers of America. "When Brian grows up as an athlete and he's a football player, he's a guy who was the big man on campus. Even though he wasn't the most physically gifted player on the football field because of genetics, he was the meanest. He was so darn tough, and you could stay 12 years old forever when you play in the NFL, at least as it was at the time. It's the same thing in pro wrestling - you can be even more immature quite honestly."

With his reputation as an eccentric personality, Brian started to see what Wood was talking about as Kim shared stories about how unique the business was. By its very nature, it was a prerequisite for a newcomer to have great resolve, be headstrong, in great shape, and to have a larger than life personality to get noticed and connect with the masses.

Along with that, it must be said that wrestling in the eighties was an odd beast, filled with a vast array of potential pitfalls. From being manipulated and taken advantage of by promoters to the inherent drug and steroid use, to the homosexual casting couch tendencies of several trainers and executives, it was a minefield. Wrestling had the curious dynamic of requiring its main attractions to portray boisterous personalities in front of the camera but to be docile behind the scenes, to be used and dictated to. The Wild West nature of the game strongly juxtaposed the fact that talent was viewed as disposable, a wrestler's spot gone and replaced with the stroke of a pencil.

On the flip side, the money, fame, camaraderie and other rewards that go to those who manage to navigate to success are often impossible to turn away from. Furthermore, the menagerie that comprised the rosters of the various troupes always turned up stories and antics that appealed to Brian's sense of humor. "Wrestling's not like the circus. It *is* the circus!", says Kim. "Pillman knew that he could live this fantasy life of fucking as many women as he possibly could, good looking ones. He could get in fights and he could live that way. He was this real alpha male with a bunch of guys who played the role of alpha males that really weren't very tough."

Wood was always eager to learn more about the business. His fascinations had previously led to him seeking out wrestling from all over the world and later becoming good friends with Dave Meltzer. Meltzer wrote the Wrestling Observer Newsletter, the foremost insider publication covering the business.

"Dave and I became good friends, in part, because I used to buy tapes from him over 30 years ago", says Kim Wood. "I would get tapes of the Japanese stuff and then initially the Pancrase stuff, but I would buy it from Dave. He claims that I helped put one of his ex-girlfriends through college."

Meltzer's newsletter started from humble beginnings, but before long wrestling promoters around the country were switched on to Dave's worldwide coverage and insight on the industry. Over time, the Observer grew as the readership and sources developed, with almost all of the important power brokers in the business subscribing to find out the inside word on their own line of work. With professional wrestling being a very closed off, insular industry, it wasn't always easy for the major players to keep tabs on what was really going on. But since Meltzer spoke to everybody and developed the ability to separate fact from fiction, the newsletter carried great weight. Promoters would pay close attention to Dave's analysis of business figures, or sense for what was or wasn't working with the public.

"When Vince (McMahon, WWF/WWE owner) would get the Observer, he would immediately have 25 or 30 copies Xeroxed to give to his main people to find out what was going on", explains Wood. "Of course, Dave was talking to all of Vince's people. They were ratting out Vince, but were desperately fearful Dave would rat them out. But he never did."

Dave's journalistic roots saw him earn a degree from San Jose State University, starting out as a sports writer for local papers alongside his work with the Wrestling Observer. Ultimately, he had to choose between a full-time career as a sports writer or dedicating his time to the newsletter. He put the Observer first, listening to the wrestling obsession that dated back to when he was 10 years old, watching Roy Shire's wrestling in California.

"He's an absurd guy", jokes Wood. "He's written significantly more pages than the Bible. A lot of the real legitimate sports writers really respect him. But he's a great guy. He is like the hidden mystery, even though everyone knows about him, focal point of wrestling. The person that really runs the thing, and kind of pulls the strings in an inadvertent way, is Meltzer."

The Wood-Meltzer connection was a massive benefit for Pillman's new career, and would go on to have tremendous implications throughout Brian's life. "One of the reasons I mention Dave, not that you're writing a book on

Meltzer", details Kim, "I was certainly, I feel, good friends with Dave before I ever met Brian, and definitely before he went into wrestling. But I made it a point for Brian to become good friends with Dave, which he did. It became a thing where Brian realized that his whole future involved having a strong relationship with Meltzer." One of Kim's first acts was to sign Pillman up with an Observer subscription to learn from an inside perspective as soon as possible. Through the years, Dave would be an invaluable sounding board for Pillman. "He genuinely liked Brian, and genuinely helped Brian", says Wood.

"Kim would tell me about this football player friend of his who had a good physique. He thought that he was tailor made for pro wrestling before Brian knew he even wanted to be a wrestler", says Meltzer. "I thought Kim was kind of a genius, personally. He was sort of like Brian's father figure, that was the impression I always kind of had anyway."

Brian was eager to pick Kim's brain for this new venture, and it was clear that the two had grown very close by this point. "Meltzer says I was like a father surrogate to Brian, I don't know about that", says Kim. "I actually lent Brian money at one point, and he was the only guy I ever lent money to that actually paid me back. I got close to a lot of the guys I coached…" Kim pauses for a second, reflecting on the friendship, before confirming, "But I guess I was a father figure to him."

Pillman was on board with the new direction. Kim shot a series of pictures of Brian, looking to ship them off to certain training schools. Originally, Kim was looking at sending Pillman to Minnesota to be trained by Brad Rheingans. Rheingans had represented the United States on the Greco-Roman wrestling team at the 1976 and 1980 Summer Olympics, and had two Pan American Games gold medals (1975 and 1979) to his name as well. Breaking into wrestling in Minnesota under American Wrestling Association promoter and perennial champion Verne Gagne (with a helping hand from Billy Robinson), Brad was now a staple in the AWA and helping train the next crop of talent. Minnesota had an excellent reputation at the time for turning out a lot of the current top-flight wrestlers such as Ric Flair, Ricky Steamboat, Curt Hennig, the Road Warriors and Rick Rude.

As it turned out, the entire plan was put on hold. Pillman had received a call from Calgary to play in the Canadian Football League for the Stampeders, again offering him a spot at linebacker. While the pro wrestling idea was intriguing to Brian, he felt this was his last opportunity to make it in football, or at least spend serious time playing the game he loved, and opted to accept the deal.

Moving to Calgary, Brian was in better shape than when he tried to earn a spot at the Buffalo Bills and was a regular starter for the season. The Stamps, led by new head coach Bob Vespaziani, played hard in their first month, losing their first two games but rallying back to win the following two. Brian got some publicity for scoring a pair of sacks against the Hamilton Tiger-Cats quarterback. But once again, just as he started to gather momentum, he suffered a left ankle injury and was considered expendable by mid-season.

Brian had a harsh reality to face. Like so many, his time in pro football was coming to a fork in the road. After being resigned to a different professional future once his tenure ended at the Bengals, he knew it was time for a change. He spoke to Kim Wood who told him that, since he was up in Canada any way, it would be worth calling the Hart Brothers' wrestling school, which was also located in Calgary and had its own reputation for success. While he could always give Paul Brown a call, Brian wanted something else to pursue and was already turned on to what that would be.

He picked up the telephone and began the next chapter of his life.

5 - NEW BEGINNINGS

Stu Hart was a fascinating character.

Stu began promoting Klondike Wrestling, running shows in Edmonton, Alberta, back in 1948. Running a successful operation, within three years Stu Hart began his odyssey of promoting in Calgary under the banner of Big Time Wrestling. To rejoice, Stu purchased what would become "Hart House", an extravagant mansion built on a hill, majestically overlooking the city of Calgary. Surrounded by acres of gorgeous land, the brick fortress was the ultimate victory for a man of Stu's humble beginnings. Having been born into a farming family, Stu was raised on a curriculum of pride, self-sufficiency and tireless work ethic in his formative years. It was at the local YMCA, however, that Stu found his true calling.

He discovered wrestling by observing it from a distance at first, his eyes and ears drawn to the screams of anguish and pleas for mercy. Youngsters were being twisted and tormented by knowledgeable grapplers with a variety of punishing holds, stretching their tendons and ligaments to the limits of nature's intentions. Eventually, Stu got involved and was treated exactly the same, the immense suffering taking his body to the brink of unconsciousness. But unlike so many others, who were happy never to relive the pure torture they went through, Stu ended the experience with an appreciation for the art form and was eager to learn. After a tough upbringing that included seeing his father bullied out of his land and later arrested to boot, he was keen to acquire the knowledge and skills that meant he never had to take a backseat to anybody. Ever.

Stu became a stud, winning city and provincial amateur wrestling championships, before falling into the professional ranks. Even after his success as a wrestler and promoter, the true guts of what made Stu what he was could be defined by one room. Inside a house adorned with chandeliers, accompanied outside by a growing fleet of Cadillacs, was the famed "Dungeon". It wasn't simply the family basement, it was a testament to and constant reminder of the life that brought Stu there. Beside a collection of free weights was a large canvas stretched across the floor, stained with the blood, sweat and tears of countless men learning the trade of professional wrestling. As Hart's promotion evolved to Wildcat Wrestling, then finally Stampede Wrestling, the natural churn of talent resulted in many a newcomer offering himself up for training at Stu's hands.

Athletes, local tough guys, even die-hard fans, all sauntered up to Hart House with a relaxed reserve about their own place in the world of toughness. As Stu got them to the ground, he would inevitably take control of the unassuming individual and begin his syllabus of suffering, teaching the same first lessons to hundreds of men that he himself had to learn. Stretching them to the point where it felt like major injury was a given and they'd be lucky to leave with their lives, Stu indoctrinated respect for wrestling in everyone that walked down his basement steps. Many would flee, never to return. But those that came back time after time, Stu would teach, and the list of Dungeon graduates by this point featured names such as Superstar Billy Graham, Joe Blanchard, Archie "The Stomper" Gouldie, Greg Valentine, Rick Martel, and of course, a number of his sons. Bret, Bruce, and later Owen were the more involved of Stu's twelve offspring, all of whom were drawn in to the family business in one form or another. Stampede Wrestling would bring in everybody from Andre The Giant, the iconic special attraction known the world over for popping territories and drawing their best houses of the year, to the diminutive Dynamite Kid, a relative unknown from Wigan that would revolutionize the in-ring style of the business. Stu endured the peaks and valleys of the industry, some years more prosperous than others.

The world had changed for Stampede Wrestling with the ascension of Vince McMahon and the World Wrestling Federation. After purchasing the company from his father in 1983, Vince McMahon went on a calculated nationwide surge that broke the territorial boundaries that the business was forged on for decades. While McMahon took American wrestling by storm with his ruthless approach, he extended his vision for dominance to all of

North America. In August 1984, Jim Barnett called Stu, proposing a deal on behalf of McMahon to purchase Stampede for $1 million. Vince would pay $100,000 to Stu annually for ten years, as well as give him a cut of all shows run in Edmonton and Calgary. Stu was sixty-nine years old, leading a struggling promotion with a myriad of issues and decided it was time to get out. As part of the deal, Stu insisted that the WWF pick up his son Bret, sons-in-law Davey Boy Smith and Jim Neidhart, and the remarkably talented Dynamite Kid. Vince agreed, and Stu's promotion became a thing of the past, a legend to be remembered as part of the fabric of prairie lore.

Funnily enough, the WWF struggled to do any business in Edmonton or Calgary. While Toronto was an instant hotspot for McMahon, the former Stampede stomping grounds weren't economically viable for Vince and he reneged on his agreement with Stu only one year in. Claiming he couldn't afford the $100,000 payment as promised, McMahon gave Stu the all-clear to return to promoting. Stu loved the business, and it was often said that his year out of the game never sat well with him. His undying passion led to Stampede Wrestling making its return in October 1985. With many of his best performers now working for McMahon, there was an outreach for new talent, as sons Keith and Bruce ran the training for anybody with the inclination to break in.

"There were some football players that were on the team up here that kind of knew us", says Bruce Hart who, as well as wrestling and training newcomers, was also the company booker at the time. "They called me up and said they had a guy who was playing for the Stampeders, but that he was hoping to get into wrestling and it was part of the reason he signed to play in Calgary." After flirting with the idea for months, Brian Pillman made the phone call. He dialed Keith Hart's number and asked what he needed to do to get trained by the Harts. With a simple invitation, Pillman was on his way to Hart House.

The Dungeon had seen many a football player in its time but, while there were exceptions, most men that had long, successful NFL runs stayed away. "Brian was actually one of the few football players, one of the few I can think of, who was on the team, pretty successful and well-regarded as a player", details Bruce. "Most of the others you hear about, they were at the end of their football career. They were, more or less, guys who never made it or got cut, then later on they pretended they were superstars." Certainly, taking a player straight from the Calgary team and into the ring had its benefits from a publicity standpoint as well.

Brian, once he began comprehending what pro wrestling was all about, took to the training like a duck to water. Although contradictory to his often-outrageous personality, he was extremely studious in his approach to wrestling right from the beginning. After training sessions were completed, Pillman would write down everything he was taught - every drill he went through, every bump he took, every move he learned, in a notebook. Recording his entire education helped him advance at a breakneck pace, as he would review his notes for hours and go through every step of the process in his mind, the pieces coming together the more he learned and reflected on past lessons.

"He was pretty good to train. I think he already had the work ethic and focus, and the understanding of applying yourself, before he came into wrestling", says Bruce Hart. "He had that same type of challenge, which he'd overcome and enabled him to be successful, in football. He and I hit it off pretty good."

Brian quickly became enamored with Stu, the respect for his toughness growing with every passing story he heard or picture he saw. He would regularly quiz the patriarch of the family, holding his answers in the highest regard, considering him the real deal. Similarly, Stu had an affinity for legitimate athletes and quickly became fond of the Norwood native. Despite the reputation of Calgary training evoking visions of Stu Hart viciously stretching trainees, Brian was able to sidestep that aspect, quite literally. "Pillman's the only guy that Stu never got", laughs Kim Wood. "Brian said he jumped on the kitchen table to get away from him, but he never got him."

It was apparent early on that Pillman was special, and his superior conditioning from football accelerated his progression. He stood above the rest athletically and before long was acting as the unofficial class president, motivating his fellow trainees and leading them through cardio drills. He'd serve as a pseudo-instructor on the Harts' endorsement and assist others in going over the basics he'd indoctrinated into his brain. He practiced constantly, immersing himself with every trick of the trade he could pick up.

With Stampede looking to capitalize on Brian's built in notoriety, he was very quickly rushed into the ring only a couple of months after his first lesson. Making his debut appearance on the October 24th, 1986 episode of Stampede Wrestling, Brian stood inside the squared circle surrounded by five other trainees. "Diamond" Jim Davies, the fedora-wearing cohort of Calgary institution Ed Whalen, held the microphone and quizzed Brian about the current class of students.

The interview was merely a prelude to justify Pillman's presence in the building for a later angle. John Fitzgerald, a journalist for the Calgary Sun, was also interviewed later in the episode by Ed Whalen to discuss his wrestling column. He was interrupted by Makhan Singh, a nefarious turncoat who was aligned with the top heel act in Stampede, the Karachi Vice. Makhan, the real-life Mike Shaw from Michigan, had previously declared himself a "born again Pakistani" to explain his affiliation, and objected to Fitzgerald's writing. After threatening to shove a copy of the Sun "where the Sun don't shine", Singh approached the writer, only for Brian Pillman to hit the ring and interject himself. With Singh looking on, Brian leaned into Whalen's microphone, saying, "He talks tougher and tougher week in and week out Ed. Now he's picking on a journalist. What's it going to be next week, a Sunday school teacher?" Before long, Pillman and his new nemesis were exchanging forearms, before Makhan's ally Gama Singh hit the ring to attack Brian from behind with a kendo stick. After the Karachi Vice threw Pillman through the ropes and slammed him on the concrete floor, a large, unknown individual began lurking around ringside. Soon enough, he was jumping in and making the save for Brian, running off the villainous duo. As it turned out, the mystery hero was new Australian import Outback Jack, who vowed to fight Makhan Singh in the future.

Seven days later in an interview with Ed Whalen, Pillman told of how the pain in his ribs had subsided and that he'd be wrestling his first match the following week, with his former teammates in the Calgary Stampeders attending at ringside (they had actually made the playoffs and had an off-week). As the Karachi Vice attacked Owen Hart after the main event, Pillman surged from the dressing room to clear the ring of the group, followed shortly afterward by Ben Bassarab. A six-man tag was announced for the following week, a strong introduction to get Brian in the swing of things.

Brian's debut match ended in chaos when the rest of the Karachi Vice attempted to hit the ring and the Calgary Stampeders held them off, leading to an all-out brawl. More importantly, Pillman showed promise in his limited involvement in the ring. Though very clearly green and inexperienced, the raw material was there, and the Harts were high enough on him to bring him right in at the top of the mix.

"I thought he was going to be good pretty early on", says Dave Meltzer. "You could tell in his first couple of matches in the sense that he had the athletic ability that was really good. At that point it was that he's a better athlete than most, he's got a good look, so he's on the right track."

While still associated with the CFL Stampeders team, it was shortly after this that Pillman's rights as a player were assigned to the Ottawa Rough Riders. It was clear Brian's interest was now elsewhere, and Ottawa opted not to sign him. "It was a good time for him to be hooking up with the promotion because we were in the rebuilding stage, and he was part of that", states Bruce Hart. "It was conducive to him getting a better opportunity than if the systems were firing on all cylinders."

Unfortunately for Brian, the opportunity wouldn't come immediately. After his debut, he continued to wrestle on the Stampede live shows, mostly teaming with either Owen or Keith Hart to help ease him into things, getting experience without overexposing the weaknesses he had as a novice. Regrettably, on a show on November 25th in Regina, Saskatchewan, disaster struck. While teaming with Owen against the Karachi Vice, Pillman was tossed to the floor by Makhan Singh, but lost his grip on the middle rope and crashed awkwardly on his shoulder on the concrete. He immediately knew he was hurt badly, but continued the match through to its conclusion.

Brian shrugged it off in the dressing room afterwards, denying the seriousness of the injury. He even tried to wrestle the next night in Victoire, Saskatchewan, but rode the ring apron in a tag match, doing very little. With the little he was able to do, his body was sending him a message. Upon heading to the hospital, he was diagnosed with a broken clavicle and torn ligaments. Doctors were initially fearful that Pillman's new career was over before it really began, such was the magnitude of the break. At minimum, he'd be sidelined for months.

Brian couldn't help but be deflated. It seemed as if injuries were cropping up any time he was able to gather any momentum, no matter what field he was plying his trade in. Not to be deterred, he vowed to return, rehabbing diligently and using his downtime to advance his understanding of the wrestling business.

With his early introduction to the territory and the business underway, Brian began collecting footage of Ric Flair and Dusty Rhodes promos, watching them again and again to try and understand what they did that made them so special. Brian began to understand and believe that they were, in their own way, geniuses in their ability to speak to the public in a way that drew money. He also saw that they were naturals, and only so much of what made them great could be reduced to words in his notepad. He started thinking about how to develop himself as a natural, but with a smart, educated approach. He hoped that with study, analysis and thinking, he could bridge the gap that separated the organic speaking skills of the Flair's and Dusty's from the rest of the pack.

He also contacted Dave Meltzer and began to build a rapport with him, just as Kim had suggested. "He was weary of me at first, he didn't really know me", begins Dave. "But Brian got pretty darn smart to wrestling, the big picture stuff. Brian was a really smart guy anyway, really funny and really smart, but Brian definitely picked up aspects of wrestling, and the people in wrestling, really quick. He could kind of see through people, kind of knew everyone for what they were. I remember with him it was one of those things where, you know the guys who were sort of dishonest? He could figure it out really quick and kind of knew how to approach different guys. I think he had a really good ability to read people."

Brian's homework included watching footage of the best matches he could get his hands on. In particular, the Tiger Mask Vs. Dynamite Kid series in New Japan Pro Wrestling caught his eye, matches that altered the way smaller wrestlers worked and were viewed by the public. The combination of Dynamite's vicious, picture-perfect attack that incited tremendous crowd heat and Tiger Mask's lightning fast kicks, dives and holds had made both of them stars. With the market-leader, the WWF, infatuated with size and many other companies doing the same in an effort to duplicate the success, the matches opened Brian's eyes to the possibilities of focusing on athletics.

"I would give Brian the tapes of Satoru Sayama (Tiger Mask)", says Kim Wood, "Because there was nobody in America that was doing anything like he was doing." Sure enough, upon his return to the ring, Pillman experimented with springboards, top rope moves, dives to the floor and leg lariats, finding what worked for him.

When asked about Brian focusing on a way to be outstanding so early, Bruce Hart elaborated on why he felt the timing of his debut was of particular note. "It was an interesting period when I was breaking Brian in", begins Bruce. "It was the exact same time Owen was breaking in, and Chris Benoit, and a non-descript Japanese guy called Keiichi Yamada. They had these people sneering at them like they were too small, that those guys would never make it because they didn't look like Hulk Hogan, Legion of Doom, Lex Luger and Ultimate Warrior. But it was one of the things that drove them.

That 'I'll show you assholes', mind over matter type thing. It was about wrestling not just being about veneer and bullshit. But that helped make all those guys as good as they were - they were all undersized with a chip on their shoulder, with an attitude and some swagger to them."

It wasn't just the WWF that saw an explosion in oversized meatheads coming through the doors. With the relaunch of Stampede, Calgary was seeing its fair share of muscle-bound lugs as well. Naturally, with the biggest promotion on the continent looking so superficially at the outside package, a barrage of individuals with little to no talent swarmed to the business, hoping for a shot at stardom. Many of those that gravitated to Calgary were individuals that Vince McMahon had his eye on, and Bret Hart had steered towards Bruce to get them experience.

"I was booking, but I was also in charge of training the talent", explains Bruce. "We were starting from scratch, and I had an overdose of these steroid freaks and slugs. Ted Arcidi, Bill Kazmaier, Tom Magee, that misfit from Australia that Vince sent us, who was a fucking abomination, named Outback Jack. I remember referring to them sarcastically with Owen as 'The Dinosaurs'. These ponderous, slow types, that reminded me of the early bad Godzilla Vs. King Kong Japanese movies. So I had this dichotomy of the big muscleheads and the smaller, faster, hungrier guys. Over time, it almost seemed like the dinosaurs became extinct. It was like a forerunner of what happened in the business years later."

This was the scene Pillman met upon his return to action. Since the shoulder took a while to heal, Brian first came back as a troubleshooting referee, the counter to Rod Hayter. Hayter was being used in the role of the nefarious heel official, prone to making decisions that benefitted the territory's top heels (a role Stampede used several times with different individuals), and the idea was to bring Pillman back in the mix to benefit from the heat Haytor had built up. In storyline, Haytor was a favorite of the Karachi Vice, and when Pillman began to offset him it was a natural segue for his return to the ring.

On the March 6th, 1987 episode of Stampede Wrestling, Pillman officiated a match where the Vice team of Makhan Singh and Ron Starr teamed up to face Johnny Smith and Ben Bassarab. The match saw Haytor get involved and bedlam ensue, leading to a challenge for the following week where Brian would join Smith and Bassarab in a six-man tag match against Singh, Starr and Haytor. In his comeback, Pillman was put over strong with his team getting the win. While still green, it was clear that his time off had not been wasted, as he seemed sharper and more confident between the ropes.

Stemming from the six-man tag victory, Pillman was booked against Makhan Singh for Stampede's North American Heavyweight Title. In spite of his rookie status, Brian was protected by Bruce's booking with the match going to a double disqualification. Though being in the ring with the underrated Makhan Singh helped, his improvement shined through once more. It appeared as though Brian was destined for big things as a singles player in Stampede, but a new idea was formulated shortly after that would set the course for the rest of his run in the promotion.

The Stampede International Tag Titles had been in turmoil for some time. The Viet Cong Express (Hiro Hase & Fumihiro Niikura) had vacated the titles at the end of 1986 when Niikura was sidelined, and a planned replacement in the team was injured during training. As a result, the belts had been dormant for a few months and there was a desire to resurrect them as a top priority. Pillman was already a close confidant of his trainer, Bruce Hart, and as Brian returned to the house show loop they began talking over the possibility of a tag team. "You'd spend a lot of time on the road, and that was where you hatched so many of the ideas", mentions Bruce. As the two began brainstorming, a concept was batted around that both men loved. The idea was to form a tandem that didn't fit the cookie-cutter model of 1980s tag teams, but one that had more of an attitude and would be borderline heelish while still cast as babyfaces.

"We wanted it to be sort of like those Clint Eastwood 'Dirty Harry' type movies. That idea of taking the law into your own hands, that the good guys are badder than the bad guys", explains Bruce. "So that was the whole point of the team - we were babyfaces, but mostly kick ass, which the people kind of liked. At that time it was pretty edgy stuff to have babyfaces be that cocky and brash. We're talking about an era where we had Hulk Hogan doing the 'Say your prayers and eat your vitamins' shtick. Most of the faces weren't that edgy, and that was sort of the design. Even the name was about dealing with the assholes of the world." The duo was christened Bad Company, named after the rock band out of London. "Brian and I were just kind of talking over the tag team, and I can't remember which song came on the radio, and he said, 'That's not a bad name, you know'", details Bruce.

Another major benefit to the team was that, given Brian's relative inexperience, it aided him to be paired with somebody who could guide him so early on. Certain elements of tag team wrestling help those who may not be the most complete, well-rounded workers, and being in a team would hide some of Brian's flaws as a rookie. In addition, it rejuvenated Bruce and spotlighted him in a more contemporary fashion, a win-win for both men.

"Bruce took him under his wing really fast", adds Dave Meltzer. "So that helped Brian a lot too because you have the booker who is your tag team partner, and I think Bruce liked the idea that with Brian he could get a second life. It's not like his career was over or anything, but with Brian it gave it a new start I thought."

"I enjoyed it because it was a refreshing departure for me", offers Bruce. "Up to that point I'd been more of a prototypical babyface that was doing everything within the rules, and all the Hart kids were like that. I had been a heel everywhere else I went, in Australia, New Zealand, Japan, Hawaii, but it was radical in that virtually everything we did was heel-type stuff. Punching and kicking and low blows, all in the name of doing justice to the bad guys. We were among the first teams to ever go that way. Brian's athleticism helped make it and gave it an extra layer."

The new team launched with a bang, winning a tournament held over two days to lift the vacant International Tag Team Championship, beating Ron Starr and Cuban Assassin in the finals on April 5th, 1987. It began to feel like Brian had found a true spot, and he and Bruce went all around the regular spot shows, perfecting their act and finding it to be a hit. Starting off without a distinct look and wearing trunks that didn't match, the duo quickly morphed into a proper unit. Between them, the two devised an image that was befitting of the name and attitude, adopting leather biker jackets, bandanas and wraparound shades as part of their look. Bruce was mindful of the big picture for the duo, while Brian loved working on the details. "He always had a lot of ideas, and he was real big on writing down any time he had a brain wave or a concept", remembers Bruce.

Brian was getting in the swing of things and began living the Stampede lifestyle. Calgary was renowned for being a crazy territory. From insanely long trips in the back of a jam-packed van with a vile odor permeating through the air, to the perks that came with being a local celebrity. Brian had never struggled to attract women and to the female fans of Stampede, Pillman was the pick of the litter. Before long, he had a gorgeous girl in every town on the loop. As always, Brian was never without a story to tell.

"He's up in Calgary", says Kim Wood. "He calls me in the middle of the night and he says, 'I gotta talk to you, there's this girl I've been going with.' I said, 'Yeah?' You know when somebody calls and complains about a girl, that's not new, but with Pillman you could expect anything. He says, 'Well the thing is, she's got these rape fantasies.' And I go, 'Well....okay!?' He says, 'I can't take anymore!' I said, "What are you talking about?" He says, 'We go to downtown Calgary outside and we go by the park down there, and she starts ripping her own clothes off and jumps over into the bushes and starts screaming.' And I said, 'What?' He says, 'Yeah, apparently that's the way she wants me to screw her, I guess. I don't know what to do.' I said, 'Yeah, I could imagine that'd be rough, you could get arrested.' And he says, 'Oh I'm not afraid of that. The thing that upsets me is - that's my thing.' I said, 'Your thing?' He says, 'Yeah! I like to rip their clothes off and throw them into the bushes and fuck 'em. It takes all the fun out of it when she does it.' And I just said, 'You're right Brian, there's a problem there, this isn't gonna' work out'."

Another of the Calgary hallmarks was the incessant ribs that would take place. With the road trips, temperature and living conditions straining the limits of mental toughness, the practical jokes ranged from harmlessly amusing to excessively dangerous, and occurred in great volume. Two of Stampede's greatest exports, the aforementioned Davey Boy Smith and Tom "Dynamite Kid" Billington, were notorious for what they'd subject their colleagues too. Their trademark was to initially befriend the victim and take them out for a drink. When the target in question would turn their head or run to the bathroom, Dynamite would spike their drink with a halcion, a drug medically used to cure insomnia. With the victim passed out, it would be open season.

Dynamite was the more rotten and sinister of the two, an incredible wrestler with a creative flair and mean streak to match. His Napoleon complex was legendary, amplified by a cocktail of steroids, uppers and downers that made him a walking powder keg, and he would regularly go to extreme lengths to impose his will on others. Davey wasn't as dark but was easily led, and together they were a deadly combination. Shortly after Outback Jack's arrival in Calgary, he was given the call to go to the WWF and ran afoul of the Bulldogs. After "helping" him pass out for the night, the Bulldogs took him up to his hotel room and stripped him naked. The Brits first tore his clothes to shreds and defecated on them. Then, with Jack completely at their mercy, they shaved his head bald, spray-painted his body pink, superglued his hands to his own face, then took him outside and dumped him in the snow in freezing temperatures. This is what qualified as a Calgary rib.

Alex Marvez talks about an incident involving two men he knew, a tag team called The Black Hearts, consisting of Tom Nash and Dave Heath (later Gangrel). "They were a good up-and-coming tag team", says Marvez. "But Nash ultimately left because the Bulldogs picked on them constantly. At one point they had Nash doing a handstand against the wall with his pants down and they were throwing syringes at his ass like a human dartboard. This is the type of shit that went on. It was depravity."

"Pillman understood right away - keep away from those guys", says Kim Wood. Luckily, he wouldn't have to cross paths with the Bulldogs much until later in his Stampede stay.

He did, however, have to deal with his running buddies, who were happy to take advantage of Brian's position as the junior member of the group to joke at his expense. "One of the ongoing ribs we'd do all the time", starts Bruce, "Bob Johnson used to line up all the talent, and we would set up these spot shows in the small towns. Owen and I had Bob Johnson get Brian to do these seemingly pointless things, and Pillman fucking hated them. We had Bob Johnson line up a 'Say No to Drugs' speech at a kindergarten in front of four-year-olds. Pillman had to get up at 7am after we were in Saskatchewan the night before, and Pillman was steaming about 'that fucking Johnson' lining up the speech. Owen and I did pretty good Stu impersonations, so we'd call Brian as Stu. 'Well eeeehhh, Brian…it's important that you eehhhhh…teach these kids.' Pillman would always be doing it because he didn't want to get on the wrong side of Stu, but he'd be saying to us, 'That fucking Johnson!'"

Another night in Kelowna, Brian was out around town with a female companion when Bruce and Pillman's roommate Owen Hart found a stray dog moping around the bushes outside the hotel. The mutt stank to high heaven and its hair was long and drenched. Thinking of the best way to utilize this unusual weapon, they took the dog into Pillman's hotel room and put it in Brian's bed dressed in Pillman's Bad Company gear, wrapping a bandana around its head, placing his sunglasses on its face, and leather jacket around its body. For good measure, Owen took the bulbs out of the room's lights and put a full bucket of water on top of the door. As Brian returned, he found himself bamboozled as to why the lights wouldn't work and why the room stank, before being drenched in water and chased from the scene by a rattled canine wearing his ring costume.

When Brian wasn't looking over his shoulder at the good-natured joking from Owen and Bruce, he was playing defense against some of the oddballs in the territory, and even one within the family. Smith Hart was almost considered the black sheep of the clan due to his propensity for erratic behavior that bordered on unexplainable (such as naming his daughter Satanic Ecstasy, or being banished from a German promotion for growing a small black moustache and goose-stepping around the ring). Brian got to witness some of this for himself. On one occasion, with Pillman at the house to hang out with Bruce, he caught Smith arbitrarily putting rat poison in his protein powder.

But this kind of insanity is what Brian thrived on, and he started getting with the program. "When he'd come home we'd think of the ribs we could play on Stu", jokes Kim Wood. "What we'd do is, I had this huge collection of wrestling stuff, so I'd get these old 8x10's and autograph them, 'To Stu, From Billy Goelz', or whoever it would be. Then Brian would go, 'Gee Stu, I ran into this guy and he wanted me to give you this and he sends his best', and Stu would say, 'Ehhh…Brian, that's great. The only problem is he died in 1956'."

One person who did successfully feel the sardonic wrath of Pillman was Bill Kazmaier. The 330-plus pound Kazmaier, best known for taking first place in three consecutive World's Strongest Man competitions from 1980 to 1982, turned his attention to pro wrestling in 1986. A remarkable physical specimen from the University of Wisconsin, Kazmaier once set the bench press world record with a 661.4-pound lift (sans bench shirt), and had all the physical dimensions to garner a prominent spot in the size-conscious wrestling world of the late eighties.

Upon his arrival in Stampede, he quickly earned the disfavor of the crew with his naiveté to the business, obnoxious statements, and simple-minded demeanor. Bill would frequently talk about how his size made it only a matter of time before he made it big in the wrestling business and left the small towns behind, all the while displaying no grasp of the industry whatsoever, in or out of the ring. After taking a loss, he'd sit deflated backstage, his hands on his knees and head hanging low. "What's the matter, Bill?", somebody would invariably ask, to which he'd respond dejectedly, "I lost, I let the fans down." Even when the realities of the business were explained to him (that he'd been *told* to lose), he'd repeat, "Yeah, but I let the crippled kids down."

A perfect illustration of Kazmaier's lack of fundamental understanding was when, on February 18th, 1987 in Estevan, Saskatchewan, Kazmaier had a match with North American Heavyweight Champion Makhan Singh. The storyline called for Bill to win the match and presumably the North American Title, only for the decision to be revealed as a disqualification. As a result, Singh would retain the title since the belt couldn't change hands in that manner. The scenario was repeated the next night in Medicine Hat, Alberta. After the second storyline miscarriage of justice, Kazmaier angrily called Stu Hart to complain, saying he didn't understand why he wasn't champion since the referee had now twice declared him the winner.

The dressing room was confounded by his thought process, and combined with a striking ineptitude as a worker, it made him an instant target. His outward disdain of recreational drugs earned him some sour feelings from certain members of the roster, and he had a sensitivity to offensive slurs that was all too easy to exploit. Of course, there was also the general resentment amongst the smaller workhorses that the business, as dictated by Vince McMahon's vision for the WWF, was currently all about guys of Kazmaier's ilk - muscle bound freaks with little appreciation for the skill required to excel. If there was a chance to weed him out, they'd take it. "He was an egocentic shithead", surmises Bruce Hart, "And he couldn't stand Pillman."

Brian's torment of Kazmaier was unrelenting, quickly nicknaming him 'Quagmire', a tag that would follow Bill around for the rest of his Stampede days. At a spot show in Edmonton, Pillman spotted a Japanese photographer in the hallway that was covering the progress of Keiichi Yamada, and saw Kazmaier walking around the corner. Pillman seized the opportunity and approached the photographer, who didn't even know who Brian was, and went into an animated diatribe about how he'd just broken the world bench press record. "I lifted 943 pounds on the bench", Pillman said loud enough for Bill to catch, "And I didn't just do it once, I did it five times for good measure!" Kazmaier, the gullible soul, immediately took the bait and began yelling repeatedly at the photographer, "He's a fucking liar! He hasn't broken it! He's a liar!" The photographer, who didn't speak a word of English, was terrified at the enormous, red-faced Kazmaier screaming at him with no idea as to why.

On one particular loop, Pillman looked to push Kazmaier to the breaking point. Bill decided he was going to sit in the front seat of the van, his seat reclined all the way back, taking his position as if he were a proud Emperor with an air of entitlement in his posture. Meanwhile, in the back, Owen, Benoit, Bruce, Pillman and several others were sat amongst a litany of bags, as Brian went into story mode.

"You know, I was running some sprints on the track in Cincinnati the other day, and this fucking nigger comes up to me and challenges me to race! I said, 'Why don't you put some money on it Sambo!'" Kazmaier's ears perked up at the deliberately offensive tirade. "I blew him away by ten yards. These reporters came running up to me and said, 'Do you know who that was? That was Carl Lewis!'" Playing the part, Owen, Bruce and Benoit sold Brian's story with awe. "Then this other time", Pillman continued, "I was shooting some hoops and this cracker geek comes up to me and challenges me to a game of H-O-R-S-E, and I beat his ass. Turns out it was Larry Bird." As the guys offered up more faux respect for this dubious accomplishment, Brian went on. "Then I was sparring at the gym one time, and this nigger with a gold tooth and a lisp comes up to me and offers to go a couple of rounds. I told him to put some money down and I knocked him out cold. The other fighters came up to me and said, 'Don't you know who that was? That was Mike Tyson!'" Bill shook his head in disbelief in the front seat, biting his tongue as the stories came one after another, having to not only hear the stories and the offensive language, but having to listen to everybody else believe the tall tales.

The long, drawn out spiel was approaching the one-hour mark, when Brian prepared for the punchline. "Then this one time when I was playing for the Bengals, we played against the Steelers. And I went up against this center and knocked him on his ass so many times he came up sobbing and begged me, 'Please don't tackle me any more, you're making me look bad'." On cue, Owen, with all the innocence of a young boy sitting on Santa's lap, asked, "And who was he, Brian?", to which Pillman burst out with, "MIKE FUCKING WEBSTER!" Not only was Webster such a legendary center to the point the Steelers to this very day have never reissued his jersey number, but he was Bill Kazmaier's ultimate hero having idolized him at the University of Wisconsin. "You're a fucking liar Pillman!", exploded Kazmaier. "This is all just fucking bullshit! All of it! You need to shut the fuck up Pillman!"

But Brian wasn't done. On the journey home, Kazmaier spotted a ring rat that he was fond of whose car happened to be broken down on the side of the road. Kazmaier asked for the driver to pull over, but Pillman urged them not to, causing Bill to pretty much yank the steering wheel off the driver and force them to pick her up. After they helped with the car, the crew offered her a ride. With Kazmaier up in the front seat, Brian worked his charm and before long, the groupie was providing Pillman with some oral gratification in the back of the van. With Owen, Benoit and Bruce offering a running commentary in graphic detail, Brian began selling the blowjob with exaggerated gusto, moaning loud enough to risk an avalanche. "I don't think Brian should be doing that with Bill in the van", the onlookers said aloud, "I thought that was Bill's girl." After so long, the passenger light came on - Kazmaier could take no more. "That's it!", vented Bill at the top of his lungs. "You're fucking dead, Pillman! When we get to Calgary I'm gonna kick your fucking ass!" But while Kazmaier was blowing a gasket, Brian didn't bat an eyelid.

For the rest of the journey, Owen, Bruce and Benoit spoke with a hushed voice, but obviously loud enough to be heard, about how tough Pillman is. "This isn't going to end well for Bill", and "Pillman even knocked out Tyson" echoed off the cold van walls for hours. Glimpses into the rear-view mirror exposed the growing doubt in Kazmaier's eyes as to how exactly things were going to turn out once the van got to Calgary. Stories of Pillman's toughness were legendary as it was before being heightened for comedic effect. As the van pulled up to its final destination, Kazmaier's fear exposed itself despite his 150-pound weight advantage and strongman plaudits. He bolted towards his car and sped off into the distance, an amused and fired up Pillman chasing after him, screaming, "Come on you gutless son of a bitch!" to the amusement of the crew.

"Pillman made his reputation as a tough guy up in Calgary by calling Kazmaier out, 'Let's fight you motherfucker!', over fifty times", says Kim Wood, "And he wouldn't fight because he'd never been in a fight in his life." Even with his immense size and strength, Kazmaier was known to be insecure, even sleeping with a gun under his pillow. Since it was clear that Kazmaier wasn't keen to fight, Pillman found another way to get under his skin.

"They were going from Yellow Knife to Medicine Hat in the van, and there was a black guy working with them named Gerry Morrow. So you've got fifteen white guys in the van and one black guy", Kim Wood explains, fondly remembering a story Brian told him. "And Morrow's in on it. They're all in on it except Kazmaier. So Pillman says, 'You're a fucking nigger', and goes on and on for five hours." As Pillman and Ben Bassarab went back and forth arguing with Morrow, it got increasingly uncomfortable and heated, the racial insults coming thick and fast. "So then they say 'That's it', and Pillman gets Bruce to pull the van over", said Wood. "They're literally in the fucking frozen tundra, and Pillman's got these guys all whipped up, 'I've had enough! I've had enough!' Poor Morrow hadn't done anything but argue and cry and everything. So they tie him to the bumper of the fucking bus, and the guy blades!"

In wrestling, blading refers to the practice of taking a cut-off piece of razor blade and slicing your own forehead to draw blood in the ring. The pouring crimson was key to eliciting crowd heat and drawing money, based on the heightened emotions the image conjures from the audience. To the outside world, the method seems barbaric. In the business, especially at that time, it was commonplace inside the squared circle. Going to this extreme measure for the sake of a rib in front of fifteen people, however, was something else entirely.

Having witnessed the racist rant, the victimization, and now the sight of Morrow bleeding from the forehead, Bill was terrified. "Morrow's screaming for his life and Kazmaier says, 'I'm outta' here!'", laughs Wood, "And he hitchhiked back to Calgary. By the time they got back, he'd packed his stuff and gone back down to Alabama." So ended the run of Quagmire in Stampede.

Years later, when Pillman was in Ted Turner's WCW, he was approached by Kazmaier, who was looking to get into the company. "Pillman called me from the road in Atlanta laughing his ass off", recalls Bruce Hart. "After the obligatory ass-kissing, Bill, after all the torment Brian put him through, tried making out that he was an old buddy from the Calgary circuit. After a while Bill asks him, 'Who was behind all those fucking ribs in Stampede?' Brian just looked at him right in the eye and told him, 'It was all Ross Hart'." Even today, Bruce laughs at the implausible accusation. "My brother Ross is very straight-laced, kind of the voice of reason. Kazmaier hears this and says to Pillman, 'The next time I see that motherfucker I'm going to fucking kill him!'"

This type of inimitable lunacy was part and parcel of what made wrestling attractive to Brian – it was a reflection of his own flair for the absurd, whether he was at the center of the story or analyzing it. After being given the lowdown before entering on the nature of wrestling and the people who thrived within it, he was happy to indulge himself in the theater of the bizarre. After all, unlike many others, he had the knowledge and self-confidence that he was tough and had success in a legitimate world. "You may have noticed, it was one of the things that made him as appealing and compelling as he was, it wasn't really that much of a work", says Bruce Hart. "With a lot of guys it's artificial contrived bullshit. Their personalities are nothing. Brian was quiet and didn't say too much at first, but I think the wrestling business was a good vehicle for him to manifest his personality a bit."

∞

Bad Company began feuding with the Karachi Vice, particularly the team of Cuban Assassin and the extremely underrated "Champagne" Gerry Morrow, clad in army fatigues as the Cuban Commandos. In a standout match on June 19th, 1987, Bruce and Brian went to a 45-minute draw with the Commandos, with a red-hot crowd in the Pavilion going crazy as Bad Company got closer and closer to victory without getting the elusive three count.

Around this time, it was becoming obvious that Brian's rate of progression was far superior to his contemporaries. While still rough in spots, he shined with his high dropkicks, electrifying top rope splashes and crossbody blocks. Not only that, he exuded a poise in the ring that belied his years, and the crowds were quickly taking to the double act with Bruce.

The constant interplay with the Vice kept the television show engaging. Whether Pillman was taking on Jude Rosenbloom, a bombastic yet cowardly manager, or fending off the seemingly indestructible Jason the Terrible, the eclectic cast of characters kept the story fresh. It also offered the glib Brian the opportunity to cut his teeth on promos regularly. In building a match opposite Mahkan and Morrow, Pillman ranted to announcer Jim Davies, "We're taking on the blimp and the pimp! And after we take the pimp and pierce the blimp, it'll make the Hindenburg disaster look like a camp fire!"

The matches with the combination of Gerry Morrow and Makhan Singh spanned several months in 1987 and were a tremendous boon to Pillman. The two teams traded the belts in November and the work ethic in the matches was undeniable. With Owen Hart, Chris Benoit, Hiroshi Hase, Biff Wellington and Keiichi Yamada all coming into their own and pushing the pace with the more established members of the crew, the spirit of friendly competition saw the territory undergo a minor resurgence as the year came to an end. The stir being made specifically by the Cincinnati local was enough to earn the attention of the industry's most studious fans. In the Wrestling Observer Newsletter's Year End Awards he was voted the 1987 Rookie of the Year, beating out Ron Simmons, Shane Douglas and Doug Furnas for the award.

With Bruce eager to keep the momentum going, he devised another new combination to work with, one that was as far removed from the cutthroat, diabolical Karachi Vice as possible. As were the Midnight Cowboys – Kerry Brown and Rip Rogers.

Brown had been a Stampede regular for a while and was a good worker, but had trouble breaking through the pack in his current incarnation. Rogers arrived in Stampede at the turn of 1988 coming from a run in Kansas City. Together, the two were given a fresh coat of paint as unambiguously gay heels. "It was right around the time of 'Adorable' Adrian Adonis, who was playing the obnoxious androgynous type in the WWF", mentions Bruce Hart. Seeing similarities in their physical attributes and bumping style, Bruce thought it might be just the thing to reinvent Kerry Brown. "We kind of patterned Kerry into being a little bit of a takeoff on that and it got over pretty good."

Rip Rogers had spent time in 1986 working with "The Exotic" Adrian Street in Continental Championship Wrestling, and was very familiar with the crowd-baiting tactics employed by one of wrestling's more flamboyant characters, appropriating some of them for himself. "The gimmick was a rib on Kerry", says Rogers. "He hated the pink stuff. He'd always been a tough rugged heel."

The team gelled immediately, and they were quickly put opposite Bad Company. As the rivalry began, the Midnight Cowboys were an easy foil, and Brian's promos went from being fairly glib and aggressive to showcasing his vicious wit.

"It really gave Pillman an opportunity to unleash his promo cutting", says Bruce. "They were good guys for Brian to incorporate his verbal assaults on, and at the time it was politically more acceptable to be making those kinds of anti-gay comments. Brian had a lot of fun putting them down and making double entendres or suggestive remarks about their sexual proclivities."

In one such instance, in hyping up an eight-man tag against the Cowboys, Makhan Singh and Johnny Smith, Brian stood beside Ed Whalen and went on a tirade in his raspy voice. "An eight-man tag? Correction Ed, four men, a blimp, a wimp, and two limp-wristed fellows. Last week, Toilet Bowl (Makhan Singh) said his team have a distinct advantage because he and his entourage grew up fighting on the docks. Technically, you could say the Midnight Cowboys did grow up on the docks because, to my understanding, they were 'reared' in the San Francisco Bay Area."

Brian's promos didn't need to rely on easy jokes to be effective, and his verbiage and ideas grew more and more creative. Referring to the squared circle as "The Badlands", he began experimenting with unique ways to convey the appropriate message. Pillman once brought a Cabbage Patch-esque doll of Makhan Singh to the ring, talking about how if you've had a bad day you could punch it in the face. Or, if you were depressed, you could look at it to know things could be worse in life. Or better yet, use it in the kitty litter box. Brian segued into the upcoming match, promptly offering the Karachi Vice "an eternity of tranquility in pine boxes".

The matches against the Midnight Cowboys and new Vice combinations were getting better and better, following the tried and tested Bad Company formula – Pillman would shine early before the diabolical heels isolated him, and he'd eventually make the hot tag to Bruce to clean house. "The veteran should save the rookie, not the other way around. First you learn to sell, then you learn to come back. But Brian was very good for his limited amount of experience", explains Rip Rogers. "Bruce knew the territory better than anybody, but he usually let us call the match. Brian got to learn to listen, execute, register, sell and fight back."

With more of the "dinosaurs" leaving the territory, it seemed that the inspired crew were pushing themselves harder with each passing show. Bruce had gotten into the habit of booking eight or ten-man tag matches on house shows and the wrestlers took pride in putting in serious time.

"He was working with good people because Calgary was a really strong place at that time", mentions Dave Meltzer. "It was a place where you're working five or six nights a week, that's a good place to improve. A lot of guys would come through for short periods of time that were really good."

On an untelevised event in Edmonton on February 27th, an eight-man Bunkhouse match pitting Makhan Singh, Steve DiSalvo, Akam Singh & Gerry Morrow against Wayne Hart, Owen Hart, Jason the Terrible & Brian Pillman went 47 minutes and received rave reviews. The long, hard-fought battles were done with such regularity that the wrestlers involved began dropping weight. When the April live events started incorporating a steel cage into the eight-man encounters, Brian was regularly soaring off the top of the structure, risking life and limb in front of a thousand people or less. The drive to make the territory succeed was making everybody better, and Pillman reveled in delivering hot matches at the top of the card that got people talking.

Unfortunately, Brian was about to get the attention of the wrong two people.

6 - A DINOSAUR TOO FAR

Brian's position brought with it its fair share of jealousy. As a rookie who was teaming with the booker and being treated so well, and clearly a family favorite, it is easy to see why it bred resentment. Within a unique industry that cherished tenure and had a sense of etiquette that novices were expected to adhere to (with some rules that may seem peculiar to the outside world), Pillman's natural personality was seen by some as unjustifiable cockiness given his situation.

Among the people that grew to dislike Brian were the British Bulldogs. Though Pillman was well aware that it was in his best interest to steer clear, Dynamite Kid and Davey Boy Smith often sought out trouble with a self-assured bravado. Though they still worked for the WWF at the time, the Bulldogs lived in Calgary, and with Davey Boy married to Diana Hart, the two were privy to all the goings-on throughout the Stampede circuit.

With their short-tempered, volatile nature, it would only take one incident to set them on their way, and one such situation developed that began the course for Pillman's tenure with Stampede to come to an end.

Living in Davey Boy's basement at the time was a regular of the Stampede circuit named Jeff Beltzner, who worked under the alias Brick Bronsky. Bronsky was a powerlifter out of Pennsylvania who qualified for the Mr. America bodybuilding competition before turning to pro wrestling. Predictably, Bronsky fit in the same category as the Ted Arcidis and Bill Kazmaiers before him, showing little aptitude for the business, hoping to cash in on the bodybuilder craze endorsed and encouraged by Vince McMahon.

Bronksy rode in a car with Bruce and Owen Hart, as well as Pillman, to head towards another spot show. Along the way, Bronsky was the subject of a harmless rib that had been played on newcomers for years. "There was this one town we used to drive through that was famous for unearthing a lot of dinosaur bones, called Drumheller", explains Bruce. "We'd get these rookies and talk about this massive statue of Stu that had been built in his honor. We'd be building it up for an hour before we drove through the town." As the car would finally arrive at Drumheller, with the rookie anticipating a breathtaking monument sculpted in the image of the iconic Hart, they would drive around the bend to see a 30-foot statue of a Tyrannasaurus Rex. At that precise moment, everybody in the car would break into their comical impersonation of Stu's distinctive voice, much to the amusement of the newbie.

Bronsky decided to relay the story to Diana and Davey once he returned home, who took that as all the ammunition they needed. Interpreting the practical joke as a mean-spirited insult to Stu, likening him to a dinosaur that was teetering on extinction, Diana and the Bulldogs were worked up. Naturally, with Bruce and Owen being family members, there was little that could be done. Pillman, on the other hand, was the outsider in the eyes of the Bulldogs, and he was fair game.

It should be said that Bruce, as company booker, was in a position that made him the subject of criticism on a regular basis anyway from the grumbling wrestlers, and Dynamite had longstanding issues with him. Bad News Allen, who took the bronze medal in judo at the 1976 Olympics and was a respected (and feared) man, had once advised Pillman to disassociate from Bruce, suggesting that any heat Bruce accumulated as the booker would rub off on Brian. Pillman heeded the warning but was loyal to his trainer. As it turned out Bad News was right, and to Dynamite, Pillman became an enemy by association.

After Drumheller, Davey and Diana had heard all they needed to back up Dynamite's viewpoint. Their answer was to fire up Bronsky, convincing him that he should beat up Pillman in retaliation under the guise of defending Stu. The Bulldogs implied to Bronsky that doing so would help his career, as a ringing endorsement from them and Stu to the WWF could get him where he wanted to be a lot quicker. And besides, Brian's a little guy and Brick was approaching 270 pounds of muscle. Before long, he was convinced.

As the crew arrived at the Victoria Pavillion in Calgary on May 27th, 1988,

Brian started to sense that things were different on this particular day. Unusually, all the Hart girls were in attendance, all dressed up in silent competition, as if encouraged to attend a special event. Brian and Bruce headed to get a coffee, walking past a lineup of individuals who were curiously stationed outside the dressing room area. Paying no extra thought to it, Pillman and Bruce entered. Brian had his gear bag over his shoulder and a styrofoam cup in the other hand, as he was approached by Brick Bronsky. Bronsky fired off a punch to the unassuming Pillman, catching him completely off-guard, knocking Brian on his ass into a bunch of lockers. Dynamite and Davey suddenly appeared on the scene with smug expressions plastered across their faces, as the setup became readily apparent. Bronsky stood firm, looking down and admiring his work, thinking his one sucker punch had accomplished the mission.

Sadly for Bronsky, Pillman picked himself right back up and charged him with the pace and aggression he was renowned for in football, tackling him into the lockers on the opposite side and sending them crashing to the ground. Brian immediately followed with a flurry of devastating punches. With Bronsky in major trouble, Brian continued the assault, kicking him repeatedly in the gut, then firing off kicks to the face which Bronsky couldn't defend, leaving his face a bloody mess. As Brick struggled to get up, Pillman stuck his thumb in the corner of his eye and hooked his eyeball out of the socket. The destruction was absolutely savage, and the Bulldogs quickly turned and left the dressing room. "I remember his cheekbone was protruding under his eye", recalls Bruce Hart, the disturbing memory still as clear as day. "It was just this stark white bone amongst the blood. Pillman pretty much beat the living shit out of him."

Brian left the scene the obvious winner, as the bigger, stronger Jeff Beltzner was laid to waste. As he left the locker room, the lengths the Bulldogs went to make this a production were revealed. The onlookers were still lined up outside, including the Hart girls, who were there to supposedly witness Pillman's ultimate humiliation, beaten and battered after 'disrespecting' Stu. Instead, Pillman walked out covered in Bronsky's blood. With everybody looking at him as if the wrong guy won the climactic gunfight in a cowboy movie, Pillman calmly said, "Yeah, there's a guy in there, he's pretty messed up, he's bleeding like a stuck pig, so you should probably take him to the hospital", and walked on his way.

In spite of how things looked on the outside, Brian didn't leave the fight unscathed. Pillman suffered a torn tricep muscle while charging Bronsky (which makes the subsequent ass-kicking all the more impressive), and was told he'd need to be out of action for two or three months. It was likely that Bad Company would have to vacate the International Tag Team Titles, but with the undeniable will of the gods, Brian didn't intend to take a step back. Pillman tried to rush himself into the ring in early July to help fill the cards, but reinjured his tricep in the process and became completely limited in what he could do. Regardless of his desire, this was another instance of having to accept his fate and take some real time off to heal properly. On July 22nd, Bad Company dropped the tag titles to the Cuban Commandos.

The fight and injury was a wake-up call to Brian. Even having come out on the better end of things, he had bigger aspirations than a personal feud with the Bulldogs. The muscle tear allowed him to see that he'd accomplished as much as he could in Stampede. Unlike his first ring injury when he'd barely gotten his feet wet, he'd now had a strong run and added to his reputation. But it was time for a change.

Conveniently enough, Pillman had been turning more heads than he realized, and word of the sensational flyer and red-hot rookie had traveled to the more studious players in the industry. Two of these players were Eddie Gilbert and Paul Heyman, who were working in the Continental Wrestling Federation in Alabama. "Hot Stuff" Eddie Gilbert was a sensational heel with a mind for the business that contradicted his youth, and also had the job as head booker. Heyman was a superb heel manager on-screen as Paul E. Dangerously, a hustler from Scarsdale, New York, and served as Eddie's booking assistant. Together, the two had turned around Continental, creating a product that won Eddie Gilbert the 1988 Booker of the Year award in the Wrestling Observer Newsletter. The two were always aware of wrestling's need to constantly create new stars to offset stagnation and scoured the landscape for talent. Heyman had watched a pirate tape of Stampede Wrestling and liked the look of Pillman immediately.

A call was made and Brian liked what he heard. Gilbert had designs on creating a stable of four hot heels in the guise of the Four Horsemen, the National Wrestling Alliance's legendary group led by Ric Flair, but with a youth movement overtone. Pillman, he figured, would be a natural for the role, and Eddie wanted to align him with Tracy Smothers, Scott Armstrong and Shane Douglas. Pillman agreed to make the move and subsequently gave Stampede his two-week notice.

Though the injury was preventing him from doing any of his trademark high flying, Brian was able to continue wrestling on it, being hidden in six-man tags until his final show on August 13th, where Bad Company and Jason The Terrible defeated Johnny Smith, Gama and Makhan Singh.

Pillman told Heyman and Gilbert about the damaged arm and everybody agreed that Brian should go home to Ohio, rest up properly, and start in Alabama on October 1st.

Brian said his goodbyes and headed home. Like his last absence from the ring, he used his downtime wisely. "I had recently gotten divorced and he came over to help with a few things", says Kim Wood, "One of the ways I paid him was I sent him to acting lessons." Pillman went to the University of Cincinnati to learn, as the area had a thriving acting community with ties to the Cincinnati Playhouse. As his arm slowly healed, he dedicated his time to working on every other element of his game via the classes. "He did very well with them", details Wood, "His mentality was that, 'I'm going to have to pick it up and I'm going to have to have an aptitude for it to be successful. But it does not hurt to have an academic approach, because ain't nobody else gonna' do that'."

As it turned out, Brian wasn't destined for Continental after all. After being announced on television as debuting the following week, Pillman's run in Alabama was scrapped due to circumstances beyond his control. Gilbert and Heyman left the territory after a blowup with the owner, David Woods, when Gilbert worked a shot in Kansas City while claiming he was injured in Alabama. Both men wound up instead working for the National Wrestling Alliance, the second biggest promotion in the country.

It left Brian at a loose end for the rest of the year. While Pillman was home and healing, Dynamite Kid played the bully one time too many in the WWF, this time to Jacques Rougeau. Rougeau waited for the opportune time and punched Dynamite in the face while clutching a roll of quarters. Dynamite was livid at being shown up and beaten, but was ordered not to retaliate by Vince McMahon. The typically proud Billington backed down submissively at the request of his boss. The Bulldogs abruptly gave their notice, leaving the WWF and going back to Calgary. Part of Stu getting both Bulldogs back in Stampede, however, was agreeing to Dynamite's demand that he replace Bruce as the booker. If Pillman did have designs on returning to Calgary, he was now given an extra incentive to seek work elsewhere.

While waiting for things to shake out, Brian stayed in Norwood and got the closest thing to a regular job he ever had, unloading semi-trucks at night. For six or seven of the coldest months of the year, Pillman was outside in coveralls during the early hours, loading and unloading vehicles, looking for his next opening in wrestling.

Looking to get his face seen, Brian went to a WWF show at the nearby Riverfront Coliseum in November. On his first impression of the biggest promotion in North America, Pillman got to witness how strange the political and psychological aspects of the company really were. Brian caught up with Owen Hart backstage, who had made the jump to the WWF and was in the middle of a run as The Blue Blazer. Attempting to market a high-flying hero, the WWF had repackaged Owen, who would now wear a mask and cape to the ring. As Owen and Pillman were talking in the basement of the facility, WWF road agent Jack Lanza walked by and spotted Hart without his mask on. Interjecting himself in the discussion, Lanza looked at Brian then turned to Owen, sternly insisting that he should have his mask on at all times if talking to non-WWF personnel. Owen and Brian were stupefied by the nonsensical edict, since they were standing in the bowels of the building in the dark, literally hundreds of yards away from anybody. Even after Owen explained their history as former roommates, Lanza was serious and stood in the doorway until Hart donned his hood. Weird dominance games like this were commonplace, it would seem, and Pillman shook his head in disbelief.

Contact was made with World Championship Wrestling by Kim Wood, who had gotten in touch with Jim Ross. Ross, a known avid football fan, was excited to hear from somebody within the field who spoke so fondly of the youngster's upside. Pictures and tapes were sent across along with a letter of recommendation from Wood, and Ross quickly saw the potential in Pillman, vouching for him to get a chance. Right at the tail end of 1988, NWA/World Championship Wrestling interim booker Jim Crockett came to an agreement with Pillman to bring him in, giving him a start date of February 12th, 1989 at the Omni.

Funnily enough, rumors of Brian's arrival started before Crockett's original offer. Legend has it that the plan was to bring Pillman in as a heel as part of a full-time tag team with Dennis Condrey. Condrey himself had only recently returned to the promotion as part of the Original Midnight Express tag team with Randy Rose, managed by Paul E. Dangerously. Crockett had a low opinion of Rose's look and work, and felt somebody with a more youthful image would better suit Condrey. The notion of Brian being the partner, however, isn't fully based in fact.

"That was Paul E's rumor", clarifies Jim Cornette, manager of the Midnight Express team of Stan Lane and Bobby Eaton. The Midnights were embroiled in a rivalry against the Original team of the same moniker. "I was in the conversation with Jimmy Crockett saying, 'I don't like Randy Rose's work, I'm going to find Dennis another partner, I don't know who.' But I guarantee you he couldn't pick Brian Pillman out of a police lineup at that point in time." Further explaining the origin of the myth, Cornette details, "Obviously Paul loved Brian, and plus he wanted a new hot talent. Paul E. started putting out the rumors that at least he was going to get somebody hot, or was trying to make a self-fulfilling rumor because then he could get Brian Pillman. So that's where that part came from, I believe."

Similar to the false start in Continental, a change in leadership seemed to thwart Brian's plans. WCW had recently been sold to Ted Turner's TBS, with Jack Petrik positioned as the new company President. Petrik was a longtime Turner bigwig with a reputation as somebody that you could give any project to and he'd find a way to make it profitable. In reality, the WCW appointment was a cushy position for Petrik who was on the home stretch of his career, and with little product knowledge he wasn't prone to the most educated decisions. He assigned Jim Herd, the husband of his wife's best friend, to be the new Executive Vice President, and hired George Scott to be the new permanent head booker.

George Scott had a sterling reputation as a creative mind, having had strong runs in the Mid-Atlantic area and for Vince McMahon's WWF leading up to and just beyond the first WrestleMania. But after his WWF departure in 1985, he'd gotten completely out of the business. It was revealed quickly that he hadn't kept tabs on upcoming talent, had no idea who Brian Pillman was, and therefore had no desire to use him. The planned start date was dropped.

With limited options immediately available but a keen desire to work, Pillman called Calgary and worked a handful of dates for Stampede, also lining up a quick tour of New Japan Pro Wrestling for April. To a student like Brian it was a personal thrill to land a gig in New Japan, even if it wasn't his preferred option. In the meantime, talk again started to circulate of a role for Pillman in WCW, this time in a heel tag team with Dr. Tom Pritchard, a polished worker from Continental. Eager to land a full-time spot with WCW, he kept his ear to the ground as he arrived in Japan. While he had less than ten matches on the tour, it was a lesson taught between shows that stuck with him.

Another American on the trip was "Mad Dog" Buzz Sawyer, a man noted for being a combination of an incredible talent in the ring and a notorious scumbag outside of it. Sawyer had been around the block and pulled Pillman aside as the tour began with some useful advice. "Whatever you do", said Sawyer, "It's really important that you're polite to all the Japanese people, especially the cab drivers." Pillman nodded, mentally taking note of the sagacious wisdom. He then got into a cab with Buzz Sawyer, who immediately went off on a profane, hot-tempered tirade at the Japanese driver that would make a sailor blush – "You motherfucker! You cocksucker! You MU-THA-FAK-KA!" After witnessing Sawyer's put-on, Brian was amazed. "Sawyer taught him something", says Kim Wood. "Brian picked up that you can work on just being crazy. Sawyer didn't really understand it, but he understood enough, and that is that you take the play to *them*." Pillman stored the lesson in mind. As it turned out, it would come in handy later in his career.

While Brian was in Japan, George Scott was fired as WCW head booker a mere three months into his run, replaced by an interim committee led by Jim Ross. Ross, who had championed to sign Pillman earlier in the year, got back in touch. As Brian returned from New Japan, the deal was put together. Pillman was signed to a contract for $104,000 per year. With less than three years in the business, he was about to ply his trade on a national level.

7 - FLYIN' SOUTH

When Brian signed his WCW deal in early 1989, the company was seemingly trying to find itself. It had been a rough couple of years for Jim Crockett Promotions prior to selling to Ted Turner, with Vince McMahon's World Wrestling Federation tightening its grip nationally and Crockett making the wrong moves at the wrong times. Still, being owned by Turner meant a greater, more stable platform than any wrestling promotion had ever had up to that point, and financial security as well. Everybody believed that if WCW could just get their ducks in a row, they could be viable and go toe-to-toe with McMahon.

The WCW booking committee had their eyes open for new, marketable talent, and the athleticism, appearance and attitude of Pillman fit the bill. He was introduced with a series of music videos, splicing footage of matches filmed at television tapings with Brian working out shirtless in the gym, or piloting a helicopter under his Flyin' Brian alias. Slow-motion shots of Brian launching dropkicks or soaring through the air with his top rope splash aired, accompanied by the sounds of Yellow's "Oh Yeah" or "Rocket" by Def Leppard, the latter of which would become Brian's handpicked entrance music.

To prepare for Pillman going on the road, Jim Ross approached Shane Douglas and Johnny Ace, at the time teaming together as the Dynamic Dudes, asking them to ride with Brian on his first loop. "Personally, we got along great", says Shane. "Brian could tell that I was a guy that cared about going to the gym, and he was fanatical about hitting the gym, fanatical about his diet.

He used to have this saying which was, 'White bread, white death'. Meaning he could eat no white pasta, no white bread, no white potatoes, nothing white. I mean, he was a lunatic on his diet and what he put into his body."

Looking to fit in, Brian would soon introduce his running buddies to his outlandish disposition. "He would always push the envelope with people", Douglas mentions. "Not with us, but with a waitress or a bartender or a bouncer in a club. We were always keeping an eye out for Brian. If a fight broke out and Brian started it, he would have major heat the next day and possibly get fired for it. WCW didn't want those kinds of stories. We were sort of babysitting him because it was in Brian's nature that, if we would go to some place and somebody was looking at some pretty chick on the dance floor, Brian would do something to get people looking at him."

While his vignettes ran on TV, Pillman began working on house shows on June 9th picking up a win over Bill Irwin in Albuquerque. He was lined up for a series of preliminary matches on the annual Great American Bash tour and racked up a series of losses, teaming with fellow newcomer Scott Hall against Mike Rotunda and Dan Spivey. The booking is indicative of WCW's view of Brian early on – they saw upside in him, but were in no rush to feature him as a star attraction.

This lack of focus was compounded by the fact that, whether due to nerves or just not clicking with Rotunda and Spivey (both of whom had styles that clashed with Brian's often-ambitious approach), Pillman's initial WCW offerings were not particularly impressive. Brian quickly got the stigma of being green; a work in progress that should be brought along slowly. "At the very beginning they didn't know what to do with him because he was inexperienced and everything", says Dave Meltzer. "They knew he was a good athlete, but it was like he had to prove something to them."

Brian's first high profile match for WCW saw him oppose Bill Irwin at the 1989 Great American Bash. The show is still considered among the best in company history, but Brian's contribution was minimal. After first appearing in the show-opening two-ring battle royal, Pillman pinned Irwin by leaping off the top turnbuckle of one ring into the other, connecting with a crossbody for the victory. The exciting finish and clean pin spotlighted Brian, who was positioned on commentary as one to watch for the future.

His doubters in the locker room were soon coming around on his work. In fact, Pillman was able to shake the 'new guy' label pretty quickly. "I remember this story, just because it shows how stupid a few of the guys were and how cool Brian was", begins Jim Cornette. "You know he had the fucking hair? He had the hairdryer, which a lot of guys carried, but he also had this big fucking diffuser thing that looked like Jimmy Hart's megaphone. When the guys saw him using that when he had first just come in and nobody really knew him, I remember some of the guys started giving him a raft of shit."

Having been well versed in the practice of ribbing for years, Brian knew exactly how to deal with being on the receiving end. "He didn't make a big deal out of it", says Cornette. "I think one night somebody went in and stepped on it and broke it or whatever. He didn't put it over, he didn't say anything. A little bit later on they would learn more of his background and found out that if he'd wanted to make an issue of it, he'd have probably ate their fucking eyeballs. So I think that got him over to a lot of the guys that, 'Okay, this guy's with it, he's not just a pretty boy, he can actually go and he's cool, and he just knows the women are fawning over him so he's gonna take care of his hair'."

WCW's next move was to put Pillman in his first program, working with his old Stampede nemesis Makhan Singh. Singh had since been repackaged in Jim Herd's vision of WCW as Norman the Lunatic, an escaped mental hospital patient under the guidance of Teddy Long. After Pillman pinned him on television in Baton Rouge, Norman attacked Brian, ramming him into the ringpost and giving him a splash from the second rope. To apparently multiply the damaging effects, Long placed a giant gold key on Brian's chest before Norman hit the splash. The key, of course, would be used by Long to keep Norman in line, the implied threat being that he would be shipped back to the mental asylum if he deviated from instruction.

Ideas like this were Herd's attempt to emulate Vince McMahon's WWF, who would often present childish or cartoonish gimmicks to try to appeal to the masses. For McMahon, some worked, some didn't. In WCW's case, though they were owned by a television company, their production was inferior in quality, which made over-the-top characters feel bush league and out of place. Even if that wasn't an issue, the NWA/WCW fanbase wanted something different from McMahon's wrestling and would reject such slapstick efforts. Things were struggling, and as the Bash tour wrapped up, top star and World Champion Ric Flair could take no more. Seeing a flurry of underwhelming houses on the traditionally hot circuit, Flair demanded he take the position of head booker to try and correct the course of the company.

For Brian, this was good news. He'd gone out of his way to get close to

Ric in the weeks prior and the two had hit it off. "Flair liked him a lot", says Jim Cornette, who joined Ric's committee shortly after Flair was given the book. "I think Flair saw guys like himself and Ricky Steamboat and all the young guys in the seventies in the Carolinas that came up, were athletic, worked hard, had the oomph and were pussy magnets. He saw that in Brian and he said, 'Well, here's a guy that needs to be a star'. I think that's what Flair saw. His work was wonderful, he can sell, he connects with the audience, girls love him, he's in great shape and he is a real legitimate athlete. You can tell with his personality he was with it. He was *with* the business. As a matter of fact, before long he'd get past it and was five years ahead."

Adding to that, their common fondness for girls and partying gave them an instant bond outside of the ring. Pillman was a huge fan of "The Nature Boy" dating back to studying Flair's promos in Stampede, and the two clicked off-screen with their similar gregarious personalities. Brian quickly became a drinking buddy for Flair, which, given Ric's real-life affinity for the sauce, ended up being a bit of an issue as the weeks went by.

"I got a midnight call from Brian", explains Kim Wood. "I said, 'What's the problem?' He said, 'Fuckin' Flair'. And I said, 'There's a problem? Well, fuck him, he's just another asshole.' I made a statement assuming something I shouldn't have assumed", clarifies Wood. "I said, 'Hey, some people don't like you, fuck it'. He says, 'Oh no, that's not the problem. He *really* likes me. He makes me go drinking with him every night. But two thirds of the drinks I pour into the potted plants. I'm only drinking one third of the liquor he is and I'm so fucked up I think I'm going to become an alcoholic! I can't live like Flair! But Flair loves me and I'm afraid if I say no to him he'll turn against me...and he runs the whole deal!'"

In the foray that caused the late phone call, Flair had paid extra money to keep the bar open late, a regular occurrence. As would also be a Flair signature, he had somebody run out to the parked limousine and bring in his ring robe. Before long, the Ric Flair show was in full effect. "He's got alligator shoes, long black socks, bleach blond hair like a woman and he's naked except for his ring robe and his belt", says Wood. "Then he's trying to fuck some stewardess on the dance floor. This is like four or five in the morning. Then he sleeps for a half hour and flies out at 8am the next day. And Brian's saying, 'I can't live like this!' I just laughed and said, 'Well, you wanted it!'"

With the new head booker seeing potential in the Norwood native and taking to him personally, Pillman's stock quickly started to rise. It helped that just about everybody on the new committee liked him as well. Kevin Sullivan and Jim Cornette were fans. Brian would schmooze Jim Barnett, and got especially close to Jim Ross. With their common interest in football, Brian would play it to the hilt with JR, asking him before big shows if he had his "game face" on. Additionally, Brian would get autographed pictures of Oklahoma football players and bring them to Ross, including one of former Bengals teammate Stanley Wilson. Over time, Ross became one of Pillman's closest confidants.

With the committee in his corner, Brian was given the victory over Norman at every town on the loop. Better yet, Flair himself started teasing an alliance on television with Pillman to try and shoot him up the ladder quicker than originally projected.

The build to Brian as Flair's protégé started abstractly enough, a throwaway comment from Ric during an interview on television, praising the relative newcomer. Later in the show, as Sting would be attacked by Gary Hart, Terry Funk, Great Muta and Dick Slater, Ric hit the ring looking for revenge, but was cut off by a spinning kick from Muta. With only the endorsement of Flair to justify his presence, Flyin' Brian hit the ring, flooring Slater with a springboard clothesline to attempt a save, before being outnumbered as well. Eventually, Ric made the comeback, the scene culminating with Flair, Sting and Pillman standing tall as the feature babyfaces in the company.

The emphasis on Brian was furthered at the September 12th Clash of the Champions VIII show on TBS. Pillman, accompanied to the ring by a flood of USC Gamecock cheerleaders, disposed of Norman in a hot match in three and a half minutes, later getting involved in the show's final angle. After Terry Funk pulled a plastic bag over Flair's head in an attempt to suffocate him, Pillman was the first on the scene, attending to him with medics as the broadcast left the air, trying to establish the new connection.

By sharing screen time with Flair, Brian's credibility was rising fast and the crowd reactions for his matches and appearances were suitably impressive. Which was just as well, as there would soon be a lot riding on him. One of the main attractions of the upcoming Halloween Havoc pay-per-view was to be Pillman's biggest match to date, challenging Lex Luger for the United States title. Brian had shot up so drastically that he was now in the ring with one of the top three stars in the promotion at a major event, and WCW continued their hard sell of Pillman to the public. On television, Brian was placed at number four in the "Top Ten" rankings, behind only the current champions and Sting.

Knowing that alone wouldn't be enough to create intrigue, a series of angles were shot to get Pillman perceived as a threat to Luger's title. It began with Lex issuing an open challenge that Brian accepted. When later pushed in a face-to-face confrontation to accept the title match for right there on television, Luger meekly offered that he would, but he was already booked against jobber Richard Sartain. Right as Lex's mismatch looked set to begin, Brian entered the ring to take Sartain's place. The unsanctioned encounter saw Pillman get the better of Luger at every turn, with Lex eventually running away from Brian two minutes in to the crowd's delight. To shine an added spotlight on Pillman's elevation, both Flair and Road Warrior Animal put Brian over in promos later in the show for outclassing Luger.

Lex appeared on the following week's show, repeatedly demanding that the footage never be aired on television again. Later in the hour, a Pillman squash match was interrupted by a bitter Luger, leading to a fight that ended up with both men rolling around on the concrete floor.

With Brian riding high at the prospect of his first huge WCW match and a genuinely strong push, he received some shocking news that brought him down to earth. As it turns out, he was about to be a father for the first time.

Earlier in the year, Pillman had a brief relationship with a woman named Jan, who broke the news to him that she was now pregnant with his baby. The two were not close (in fact Brian's family never met her when they were together), so the announcement was completely out of left field.

Oddly, after being told by Jan about the incoming addition to the world, Brian didn't hear back from her and the issue quickly became forgotten. Two full years went by without Brian knowing a thing, until one day he was contacted again. It was at that point that he was introduced to his daughter Danielle, who had been born on October 18th, 1989.

With the course of events being as odd as they were, Pillman doubted the validity of Jan's claim and asked for a DNA test to confirm whether or not he was the father. As it turned out, she was correct - Brian was a dad. Though the outcome caught him off-guard, it wasn't such a surprise to others.

"After I first saw Danielle I thought, why did you waste all that money on the DNA test?", jokes Linda Pillman. "Because she's dead-on Brian. She looks just like him, like he spit her out of his mouth! I don't know how he could deny that."

Jan raised Danielle and kept a degree of distance from Brian, but was happy to allow him to see his daughter when he wanted. Back in 1989, the initial news was a temporary distraction. While waiting for the situation to play out, he began focusing his energy on creating a match with Luger that would steal the show.

Pillman still had some doubters inside WCW. Having never been beaten on television, whispers about his size and true ability circulated among those in the locker room envious of his hasty push. On the contrary, Lex Luger was the company golden child. While he had his own skeptics, Lex's weaknesses were often overlooked in favor of the mountain of perceived potential. His Herculean physique, good looks and articulate nature had convinced many that he was the next Hulk Hogan. Fearing that Luger was WWF bound in 1987, Jim Crockett signed Luger to one the company's first contracts for $350,000 a year, with no track record of being able to back it up. For the three-year duration of the deal, efforts were repeatedly made to get Lex in the position to be a difference maker, but they never seemed to take. In his current run as a heel he'd had a tremendous series of matches with Ricky "The Dragon" Steamboat, carried by the veteran Steamboat. Being matched up with Pillman on the backside of it was seen as, of all things, a litmus test for Lex. After being carried by Flair in matches throughout '88, then by Steamboat in '89, the company saw Halloween Havoc as Luger's chance to finally do the carrying and prove he was at the level they wanted. Pillman, regardless of his obvious athletic skills, was yet to be considered a top-caliber worker.

Knowing that a great performance was imperative in such a high-profile situation, Brian visualized the match and took the lead in putting the entire thing together. Though Pillman was capable of spectacular things, arguably his greatest asset, even three years into the business, was his aptitude for mentally constructing major matches. Through the drama and excitement crafted by Brian, the battles would turn out even better than his level of fundamental ability.

That certainly was the case on October 28th at Halloween Havoc. Taking place on the heel-friendly turf of Philadelphia, the bigger star, Luger, was cheered over pretty-boy Pillman by the male-dominated audience. It didn't deter Brian at all, who put on a stellar effort in a match that massively overachieved. Luger looked like a seasoned pro, exuding as much poise as he maybe ever did, while Brian fought from underneath. The announcers spent most of the match putting over Lex, making it abundantly clear who the bigger star was, but the final flurry of near falls teasing the upset had the Philly fans on the edge of their seats. By the time it was over, every mission had been accomplished – Luger looked great in victory, Brian's standing rose in defeat and the two had the best match on the show. More to the point, the match was such an artistic success that WCW was convinced that Lex was finally where they wanted him to be. Time would tell that it simply wasn't the case.

"That kind of opened their eyes with the idea that they put him in a match, a match for him to lose", says Dave Meltzer. "But he looked really good and it was like, 'Wow, he's not just a pretty face.' Because they knew he was a good-looking guy, good physique and everything. A little on the small side which was fine. But there was that thing of, 'How good of a worker is he? He can do athletic moves but how good of a worker is he?' At the beginning, he was nervous in his first couple of TV matches and didn't impress them that much, but once he had the match with Luger they were like, 'Okay, yeah, he can work'."

Seeing value in prolonging the feud, a rematch was booked for the Clash of the Champions special in November. This time, Pillman was given a visionary pin over Luger after the referee was knocked down, a further sign of WCW's increasing faith in Brian. Luger picked up the victory, albeit after using a steel chair to crack Pillman's cranium.

The feud with Lex was phased down in the aftermath, with a couple of television matches and promos alongside Flair and Sting to transition Luger over to the two top stars for Starrcade, the final pay-per-view of the year. With plans for the key players to be involved with each other for the next few months, Brian was almost completely phased out of the main event mix.

Instead, the next battle plan formulated for Brian was for him to be put in a tag team. His partner was to be "The Z-Man" Tom Zenk, who himself was brought into WCW that year.

A former bodybuilder, Zenk won the titles of Mr. Minnesota, Mr. Twin Cities and Mr. North Country before entering the world of pro wrestling, training with Ed Sharkey. Zenk had a six-month stint in the World Wrestling Federation teaming with Rick Martel as The Can-Am Connection, before a discrepancy in pay created a rift that led to Zenk leaving the promotion. From there, Zenk plied his trade in Verne Gagne's American Wrestling Association and Shohei Baba's All Japan Pro Wrestling for a couple of years, before Jim Barnett began negotiating to bring him to WCW at the request of Ric Flair. With his strong position in All Japan being sacrificed to wrestle stateside full time, Jim Herd offered Zenk $156,000 per year and talked of making him a major babyface player to lure him to join. But since his arrival in September Zenk had been treading water, waiting for something substantial to sink his teeth into.

The team with Pillman and Zenk was one the committee believed could work. A pair of good looking guys to attract female viewers and fill a void that was present in the tag ranks. At the time of the team's inception, The Rock and Roll Express (Ricky Morton and Robert Gibson) had also been brought back for much the same reason. But as good as the team were in their day, time had changed the once teeny-bopper looks of Morton and Gibson, and their appearance didn't compare to the younger, fresher, more contemporary team of Pillman and Zenk.

The new pairing was always designed as a vehicle for Brian. With the big names working with each other at the start of the year, there was nobody free that could elevate Pillman as a singles player. This way, he'd still get to be the star of the show in his segments.

The team was introduced in an angle where, after Pillman beat Jimmy Jam Garvin, Garvin and partner Michael P.S. Hayes, collectively known as The Fabulous Freebirds, attacked Brian 2-on-1. The Z-Man ran in to make the save. The scenario led to a house show series with Pillman and Zenk being put over at every turn and looking very impressive in the process.

One of the more memorable moments from this early run opposite the Freebirds came on January 12th, 1990, when WCW ran a house show in Cincinnati Gardens. With it being Brian's first match in front of his hometown crowd, the show got a lot of local publicity with the returning former Bengal front and center.

Pillman loved the attention and status as a local celebrity, earning a reputation for being very accomodating with his fans. "Before WCW, being little kids with no filter, we used to just call his house all the time", remembers Jeremiah Evans, a fan that grew up in Cincinnati. "It sounds awful now as an adult but to Brian's credit, every once in a while we'd get him when he was at home. He never was a jerk, he would talk to us for ten minutes and then say, 'I gotta' go to the gym', or whatever. I once drew a picture of him and mailed it to his house, and I still have the postcard he sent me back, saying he hoped to wrestle in Cincinnati soon."

When the day came, over 4,500 fans turned out to see Flyin' Brian take on Michael Hayes. In a nice coup, Pillman was able to get Cris Collinsworth, a fellow former Bengal and future renowned NFL broadcaster, to be in his corner for the match. Collinsworth, who was from Florida, grew up a fan of Eddie Graham's territory and was in particular a big fan of Professor Boris Malenko. As a longtime enthusiast he felt he knew his role, and en route to Brian picking up the victory, Collinsworth began pounding the mat to whip up the crowd. Hayes responded by leaning over to Cris, unhappy with him dictating the rhythm of the audience and gave him the cue to stop with the helpful words, "Cut it out, prick!"

Surrounded by family and ex-Bengals after the show at Sorrento's sports bar, it was hard for Brian not to enjoy the atmosphere. The bar had sections dedicated to memorabilia of local sports stars, and it's worth noting that Pillman's section was similar in size to that of Pete Rose, such was his goodwill in the area.

"Traditionally, Ohio was always a hotbed for pro wrestling and Brian Pillman was always something that they claimed as their own", states Alex Marvez, who later moved to Cincinnati to cover the Bengals. Marvez, who would also be mentored by Kim Wood, got to see the scope of Brian's fame firsthand. "He was someone that, if you just said Brian Pillman, people's faces lit up. That's what he was around all the time when he was there. People knew him. He loved the adulation, he loved being in the spotlight, he loved being *Brian Pillman*. He loved everything that it brought him. With the local celebrity too, you have to understand the culture in Cincinnati. I covered the Bengals and I would go out to the supermarket and I get this - 'Ain't you the guy that writes the wrasslin' column?' I got that almost everywhere I went and on top of that, nobody asked me a question about the Bengals. Nobody. I wrote once a week on pro wrestling, I wrote five or six days a week about the Bengals, and nobody cared about the Bengals, but everyone cared about pro wrestling. It's crazy, but that's how it was, that was the environment at the time."

Pillman and Zenk were quickly entered into an eight-team tournament to crown the new United States Tag Team Champions. Rather than a demotion, the belts were intended to spotlight Zenk and Pillman as legitimate players. The sincerity from the committee, Flair in particular, was exemplified when Flair booked himself in feature matches against Zenk and Pillman at the beginning of 1990. The design behind the matches was twofold - they would bring attention to two of the more promising new babyfaces on the roster, and also serve a narrative function in Flair's own story. Flair, still WCW World Champion at the time, was in the process of turning heel and felt it would be a great way to demonstrate the shift in personality to victimize a couple of young, hungry lions.

Flair's match with Zenk, for the title, took place in Greenville on January 23rd. Both men started the bout playing babyface, with the crowd rallying behind Zenk and rooting for a title change as Flair played subtle heel throughout. Finally, with Zenk turning up the heat and coming close to pulling off the upset, Flair hooked the tights for the pin.

Two weeks later on February 6th, Flair went full-blown heel at Clash of the Champions X: Texas Shootout, as the Four Horsemen kicked Sting out of the group. Sting would return at the end of the night, storming the squared circle during the main event. With the Horsemen taking on The Great Muta, Buzz Sawyer and The Dragon Master in a steel cage, Sting attempted to climb the structure to exact revenge for the earlier attack, only to legitimately tear his patella tendon in the process. The injury would keep Sting on the sidelines at the worst possible time, and his planned World Title match with Flair was held back for months.

Elsewhere on the Clash, Pillman and Zenk defeated the MOD Squad in a match purely designed to showcase them as they prepared for the finals of the U.S. Tag Title Tournament, which would end up taking place on Worldwide on February 12th. It was there that the team came full circle, as they defeated The Fabulous Freebirds to become U.S. Tag Champions.

The team was clicking. The people were responding and they got along well personally. In an interview on Wrestling Observer Live in 2000, Zenk said of the partnership that, "My favorite tag team partner, in and out of the ring, was Brian Pillman, far and away. We had a lot of fun, that's when he was single, I was single, running around having a good time." Girls would flock to the duo at the bars, with a dark-haired choice in Zenk and the blond option of Pillman. "We had the line, 'Where can we go to have a good time, we're from out of town', and Brian would look at them with that choir boy smile and innocent looking face", said Zenk. As always, there were plenty of outrageous moments with Brian when it came to women.

"We're at the Waldorf Astoria, the best zip code in the country", says Zenk. "We're up there for the doll convention, the Galoob doll convention. We're both out rolling around Manhattan. He gets a friend...this chick, beautiful blonde, and we go back to the hotel. I had met some girl that was at the doll show that day. So I'm in my room, we split up, and usually our deal was to leave the doors open. You know, in case we needed a toothbrush or dental floss or something, you could just walk in. Anyway, I'm in there with this girl, one thing leads to another. All of a sudden, 30 minutes or an hour later, Pillman slides in...and we're there naked! He says, 'Tom, come here!' We'd been out and had a couple of beers, so I said, 'What is it?' He says, 'I'll leave the light on in the bathroom. I want you to slide in down low at the end of the bed and hold my feet, I need to get some traction!'"

Having a blast off-screen, things were looking better yet when Ric Flair worked one of his first matches as a full-blown heel, as planned, against Pillman - a non-title match for the February 17th WCW Saturday Night. It was a huge chance for Brian, the biggest opportunity yet to make an impression in a key position.

With Brian and Ric having become fast friends, Flair had every intention of doing what he could for Pillman. Ric even pitched that Brian beat him clean in the middle (since it was a non-title match), which would have made Pillman an instant superstar and elevated him to the top level in WCW. That proposed idea, however, faced some opposition.

Since Sting was injured, the company had been forced to turn Lex Luger babyface out of nowhere to work with Flair in the interim. Due to the hotshot nature of the Luger turn, the belief was that the first match with Flair Vs. Luger at WrestleWar, one week following the Pillman match, needed to be treated as the top priority in order not to fail. Kevin Sullivan talked Flair out of losing to Brian, arguing that the loss would switch the audience's focus from Luger to Pillman at an inconvenient time. Flair saw the logic and agreed.

The match itself was Pillman's finest hour to date. The crowd was hot from the outset, as Ric Flair walked to the ring sporting a stunning pink robe flanked by Woman, the real-life Nancy Sullivan who had recently become Flair's manager. With the crowd solidly behind him, Pillman put in a tremendous performance, firing chops back and forth with Flair throughout. The action spilled to the floor where a thumb in Brian's eye allowed Ric to build heat on the plucky youngster. Fans screamed as Flair applied his figure four leglock, urging Brian to turn to his stomach and reverse the pressure. When it came time for Brian's comeback, the crowd erupted with every backdrop, dropkick and suplex dished out. After Woman's involvement foiled a Pillman pin attempt, Flair took the advantage back, tossing Brian over the ropes. Ric gathered his wits, until Brian executed a springboard to the top rope, soaring off with his "Air Pillman" clothesline. As the referee dropped to count, the entire crowd was convinced it was over. Flair just about got the shoulder up at the last millisecond, half the crowd exploding with cheers thinking it was over, the other half booing at the kick out. Conveying the urgency of the moment, Brian went straight to the top rope for a crossbody, but Flair rolled through, grabbed a handful of tights and got the win. The Nature Boy rolled to the outside, looking as if he'd been in the fight of his life and barely survived, while Brian sold the agony of defeat.

The experiment was an unmitigated success. The show did a 4.0 rating with a 7.8 share, the best rating for WCW Saturday Night in three years. It was viewed in 2,130,000 homes, which was an all-time record for the show. The record, it should be mentioned, was never broken. It couldn't have gone better, and everybody on the booking committee was suitably impressed. In his big opportunity, Brian proved he could draw as a singles player.

Coming off their initial success as a team and showings against Flair, both Zenk and Pillman became the top candidates to take the empty fourth spot in the Horsemen, with Flair himself advocating Pillman for the role. After such a great effort against the WCW World Champion and head booker, things were looking good for Flyin' Brian. Lamentably, only five days after the Saturday Night match, Ric Flair resigned from the booking committee.

Flair and Herd had butted heads regularly, with Jim seemingly going out of his way to make life difficult for Ric. In addition to Herd's constant complaining and meddling throughout Flair's booking run, he was also a proponent of scaling Ric down on-screen. Herd felt Flair was simply too old be the feature attraction of the promotion as he inched towards his 41st birthday. Flair was in the ultimate hot seat, finding it difficult to juggle so many things at once. He was the booker and the top guy, which came with a great deal of responsibility and finger-pointing. With an overworked Flair getting pressure from all sides, stepping down seemed like the right thing. For him, it may have been. For WCW, he was undoubtedly wrong in that assessment.

Looking to unwind with the burden of the booking position off his shoulders, Flair hosted a party for his 41st birthday on February 25th in Greensboro. With most of the roster and some of his Flair's friends in attendance, it led to an incident with Brian and the 51-year-old Wahoo McDaniel. Wahoo, himself a former NFL star who had great success with the New York Jets and Miami Dolphins, was legendary for being a tough individual in his own right.

"Brian always had some little smart-ass comment, he was always just poking people, you know?", laughs Shane Douglas. "Either verbal jabs or physical. And Wahoo didn't take to that kind of thing. He kept telling Brian, 'Settle your ass down or I'll settle you down', and of course that just turned Brian on." With Pillman pushing Wahoo further, things quickly escalated.

"I remember Brian and Wahoo ended up wrestling on the ground", says Dave Meltzer. "I was right there watching it. I don't even know what happened, they were just rolling on the ground!"

"There's a ton of people at the party and I just remember seeing those two being pushed apart", mentions Shane Douglas. "Even though that was Brian's nature, there was method to his madness. I think Brian would have looked at that as, 'Hey, if I'm man enough to step up to Wahoo, the other guys will respect me'. Because Wahoo was one of those guys that was known for being a tough son of a bitch. In hindsight, it was almost like spraying his territory. He's going to come in there and get the attention put on him, not to get heat, but to get respect."

That aside, Brian was looking forward to his next angle, which had a great deal of promise. Pillman and Zenk had wrestled The Midnight Express in the semi-final of the U.S. Tag Title Tournament, and the chemistry was such that Brian was chomping at the bit to work with them more, specifically requesting to do so. Indeed, "Beautiful" Bobby Eaton and "Sweet" Stan Lane, managed by the wildly entertaining motormouth Jim Cornette, were the best and most complete team in the entire promotion. The Midnights had been downplayed significantly in the prior months, but Cornette had devised a scenario that promised to propel them back to the forefront and set up a run of hot, fresh matches.

"Flair thought the WCW Saturday Night match in February would be a good way to kind of start elevating Brian", says Jim Cornette. "That's when I said, 'Hey, Ric, if you like him and you're the booker who happens to be the world champion and my boss, have me and my tag team help get him over'."

At the TV tapings in Altoona, Pennsylvania, Pillman and Zenk defended the titles against The Midnight Express. The crowd was rabid as the action went back and forth, with Pillman firing down punches in the corner on Eaton as Zenk applied his finishing sleeper hold on Lane. With victory in Zenk's grasp, Cornette ran into the ring armed with his trusty tennis racket and blasted Zenk in the back, giving the babyfaces the win by disqualification. After dispatching the Z-Man to the floor, the Express turned their attention to Pillman. "Sweet" Stan hoisted Pillman into position, preparing for Bobby

Eaton to come flying off the top rope with the move they dubbed "The Veg-O-Matic". As "Beautiful" Bobby was about to leap, Cornette lowered the tennis racket directly over Pillman's throat. Eaton delivered the legdrop, and the female shrieks in the audience turned to gasps on impact. Lower card wrestlers hit the ring to attempt to stop the post-match attack, but were laid out one at a time by Lane and Eaton. Meanwhile, Cornette repeatedly drove the butt of the racket into Brian's throat, the crowd growing more vociferous each time as Jim Ross on commentary pleaded, "Somebody needs to come help Pillman!" Only when the Rock and Roll Express hit the ring did the assault come to an end, but not before Cornette stole the U.S. Tag Title belts at ringside, handing them off to his men to a chorus of thunderous boos.

It was a superb, heavy angle, done with the idea of bringing up Brian's throat surgeries as a child. The claim that Lane, Eaton and Cornette had undone all the restorative treatment Pillman had undergone on his voice as a kid would garner even more sympathy for the eternal underdog. Interviews were taped to tell the story, with Zenk and a barely audible Pillman promising retaliation on the dastardly Midnight Express.

The strategy was to build toward an eventual match with Pillman and Zenk against the Express, with Brian getting five minutes alone with Cornette if they won. Before the match, the Midnights would ambush Zenk and take him out of the picture, preventing the match and Brian's quest for revenge. Pillman, however, would insist on the match going ahead, take on Stan and Bobby by his lonesome and still come out victorious. Brian would then get his hands on Cornette, ending the rivalry by triumphing over all three. From there, Brian could move onto Flair.

It wasn't to be. At the booking meeting following the airing of the angle, Cornette was told that the throat aspect, the entire emotional crux of the feud, was to be dropped. It was argued that playing up internal damage may be too strong for TBS, and they didn't want it to seem exploitative to Pillman's situation. Doing the angle further harm was Jim Barnett, who convinced Herd that the whole scenario would somehow devalue Brian. "I'm reading this conversation that I wasn't in on", begins Cornette, "But Herd was there grumbling, 'What are they doing here with the Midnight Express', and Barnett, knowing Herd was fishing for any reason to knock us, said, 'Well it makes Brian look weak'. And that's where all that shit came from."

Barnett argued that such a heavy angle should be saved for when Brian was opposite a main event star. It should be noted that Barnett was a supporter of Pillman's and genuinely believed he had top guy potential, but ultimately helped ixnay the direction, and the interviews vowing revenge never aired.

With the throat injury dropped, the rest of the heat was built on the Midnight Express stealing the title belts. Inexplicably, two weeks after the first angle, Pillman and Zenk stole the belts back. What started as a red-hot rivalry was reduced to a sterile mid-card tag team feud, just with a far better quality of match.

The real reason for the dropped angles had more to do with the Midnight Express than Brian Pillman. Cornette had lost considerable clout on the booking committee ever since Flair resigned, and the long-term prognosis for the team wasn't good. Cornette approached Herd to discuss the Midnight Express' contracts which were coming due in May. Despite an excellent body of work as a unit, Herd wanted Cornette to quit managing to become a full-time color-commentator, and wanted to split up Bobby and Stan for good. With plans to offer Eaton a one year deal as a singles babyface and Lane a verbal 90 day agreement as a heel, the writing was on the wall.

In an act of self-preservation, Cornette proposed that he would only become a commentator and leave Eaton and Lane on the premise that Cornette would "sell their contracts" to Woman in storyline, and thus they'd become members of the Four Horsemen alongside Flair and Arn Anderson. The committee approved the idea, but when Jim Cornette returned from vacation one week later, he was told that Herd had shot down the plan in his absence. As a result, Cornette quit the booking committee on the spot.

In the fallout of that, Pillman and Zenk beat the Midnight Express all over the country on house shows. With an angle that had all the punch taken out of it and opponents that appeared to be on their way out, it was a testament to all four that it didn't show in the matches. To the contrary, the bouts were frequently the highlight of the card. Pillman and Zenk were mastering the art of gaining sympathy as they desperately fought to tag the fresh man in, and with the Midnights' polished act to riff off, it brought the best out in them. Pillman joked that working with Lane and Eaton was like working with air traffic control, in that if you just go where they tell you to, you won't get hurt. "When he first started working with us in the WCW run", states Cornette, "We had a bunch of code words that we would shout out or signals we'd give to draw the referee or whatever. He said one night, 'I look around me and all three of you are running in different directions. Just when I think you've all left, all three of you hit me at the same time'."

As April ended, Brian was given another opportunity to work with Ric Flair, this time in a very unusual situation. The AWA were hosting a show called Twin Wars on May 5th and as a political favor, one of the main advertised matches was Ric Flair defending his NWA World Title against Brian Pillman. The AWA had fallen on lean years and, even with a great TV slot on ESPN, was having trouble drawing in its own backyard in St. Paul, Minnesota. At the start of April they'd had trouble getting 2,000 people into the Civic Center for SuperClash IV, a stark contrast to the strength of the company in years gone by. The idea to use WCW stars did create some local interest, as the mention of Pillman's name as appearing at the upcoming Twin Wars show got a surprisingly loud response from the St. Paul crowd.

The match came and 4,000 people turned out to watch Flair and Pillman throw hard chops for over twenty minutes, with "The Nature Boy" bleeding heavily from the forehead. Attendees stated that the crowd reaction indicated it was the match people came to see, and the fans rallied behind Pillman the longer the match went. Brian himself told people afterwards that he felt it was the best match of his career up to that point, though no tape of the encounter would ever see the light of day. As it turned out, Pillman and Flair were the main attraction on the last show the AWA ever ran at the St. Paul Civic Center.

Ric and Brian were still partying frequently, with Pillman trying to figure out the mystery of Flair's drinking capabilities. With the aid of his traveling partners, Brian unlocked the secret. "Me, Brian, Zenk and Johnny Ace drove together", begins Shane Douglas. "We all pitched in some money to rib Flair, and the deal was we'd have to out-tip him. What Flair would typically do is, he'd go in a bar and tip the bartender $100 to start and more as the night went on. Every so often he'd drink a real one, but the majority of them would be virgins."

Looking to drink Flair under the table for once, they formulated their plan of attack. "I sat down with the bartender and lied to him", continues Shane. "I said, 'It's Flair's birthday tonight, he knows the guys are going to get him drunk, so he's going to try to get you to make him virgins. Whatever he tips you, I'll top. And Brian, Flair really trusted him. He wouldn't hardly talk to me, Johnny or Zenk, but Brian was his boy. So Brian's pushing him, 'C'mon Naitch, are you gonna party tonight or are you gonna pussy out?' He would just keep poking Flair. Soon enough, Ric comes over to the bar with the bartender I've already spoken to and I see him put the bill on the table. The bartender looks at me, and the cue was if I tap my hat, that means I'll top it. So Flair gets this great big tray of melon balls, which is what Flair would always drink. And Pillman's there going, 'C'mon Naitch, give us a toast!' All that type of shit. Flair does the big toast, gives a big "Whoo!" and everybody does their shot. And as Ric drinks his, he stops halfway and oversells it. It's a double. This went on all night long."

As the proceedings came to a close, Ric was blasted. But keeping up with Flair step-for-step came with a price. "We get in the car to drive back to our hotel", Douglas adds. "Zenk and Pillman are in the back, Johnny and I up front. By the time we get to the hotel, Pillman and Zenk had filled the floorboards of this Lincoln town car completely even with puke. It was like two swimming pools of vomit."

It was around this time that Brian received some more major news in his personal life - his on-again, off-again girlfriend Rochelle was pregnant.

The soon-to-be-mother, born Shawn Rochelle Law, was originally from Northern Kentucky. "I was close to her", reveals Linda Pillman. "She was like a sister to me. She had a big heart, she really did."

After meeting Brian in Cincinnati in the late eighties, the two began dating, with Rochelle even moving up to Calgary with him for a brief time after Brian tore his tricep. Rochelle worked and helped bring in the money for the two while Pillman was hurt and looking for a new place to land in wrestling. "They were together for some years", remembers Linda. "We always thought they'd get married. That didn't come to be."

Rochelle had her own difficult background and had to deal with confidence issues throughout the course of her life. "She was a beautiful gal", recalls Kim Wood, "As beautiful a gal as any." However, Wood explains that Rochelle had her own eccentricities. "She used to hang around my office over here and she'd be dressed up in like a bedsheet. And it's like...Oh, *okayyy*. She was originally some kind of stripper too, I think."

At the time Rochelle gave Brian the news of her pregnancy, the pair had recently split. With their unique personalities they could have their bust ups, but always gravitated back to each other. The infant on the way served as a catalyst to bring them together again. Rochelle later gave birth to a healthy baby girl, named Brittany, on October 26th, 1990.

Back in the NWA, the matches with Pillman and Zenk against the Midnights were getting better, with the two teams gearing up for their planned meeting at Capital Combat on May 19th. In an attempt to neutralize Jim Cornette, it was announced he'd be locked in a cage suspended high above the ring.

Given the political state of play, the pay-per-view outcome seemed like a foregone conclusion, but a pair of major political moves changed everything. A couple of weeks before the show, Jim Cornette and the Midnight Express had their existing deals renewed for a year when the booking committee went to bat for them without their knowledge, protesting Herd's warped vision for the team. The other, far bigger move was when Ole Anderson was given the job as head booker on May 9th.

8 - IT AIN'T 1934

The decision to go with Ole proved to be a controversial one. While generally regarded as a miserable bastard and disliked by the vast majority of those he encountered at this point, Ole Anderson had over 20 years as a top wrestler and booker to his name. Certainly, one could understand him being considered, but his idea for what World Championship Wrestling should be was a giant leap in the wrong direction.

In the issue of the Wrestling Observer Newsletter announcing Ole's new position, Dave Meltzer casually mentioned, "Expect Tom Zenk to be putting guys over with Anderson as booker." Unfortunately, this would be astonishingly accurate. Anderson's perception of Zenk was anything but positive, seeing him as a pretty-boy with a guaranteed contract and a tendency to quit when things didn't go his way. With cutting costs being one of his major priorities he wanted Zenk out the door, a reality that didn't bode well for him or Brian Pillman.

Sure enough, 10 days after Ole landed the job as booker, Zenk and Pillman lost the U.S. Tag Titles to the Midnight Express at Capital Combat. "By that time, they'd fucked the program up so bad", says Cornette. "Now it's gone, in three months, through three booking regimes - Flair, the committee and Ole. So instead of that being the program that started to get Brian Pillman over as a singles top babyface by beating all of us in the end, they'd beat us from the start. Then in the match where I was in the cage, the one the Midnight should have lost because the odds were even, then the Midnight Express win and win the fucking belts." In disbelief at the mishandling of what looked in the beginning like a certain success, Cornette laughs, "That was the perfect way to end that fucking program."

The result was indicative of a bigger issue. Under Ole's watch, a certain breed of wrestler was being targeted. Feeling that guaranteed money bred complacency and took too much power out of the promoter's hands, Ole sought to downplay the likes of Pillman and Zenk. Rather than make a long-term investment in the creation of talent and stars, which gave the wrestlers a semblance of control as valuable commodities, Ole took a different tact.

Instead, he aimed to bring in a steady stream of older and cheaper talent under less secure conditions of employment, ones he'd have the power to manipulate at will. Typically, they were guys that Ole had used in years prior, who could be relied on to be loyal and flexible due to their past associations and unstable deals respectively. Among Ole's crew brought in under this initiative were Paul Orndorff, Buddy Landell, Bob Orton and The Junkyard Dog. Tommy Rich, who had struggled to get over to any real level in 1989, was given a strong push as a feature babyface based solely on the fact he was red-hot back when Ole Anderson booked Georgia Championship Wrestling in the early eighties, and he was cheap. The Iron Sheik was brought back to television and looked awful. Fans began referring to the company as "The Seniors Tour", even joking that NWA now stood for the "Nostalgia Wrestling Alliance".

Ole's dated vision extended beyond bringing in his cronies from years past and bled into the angles he put on television. In an attempt to rekindle the magic Junkyard Dog had in the early eighties, particularly in Mid-South Wrestling under Bill Watts, Anderson decided the best way to attract the black audience was with a race-baiting angle. On one show, Ric Flair was told of an impending surprise for The Horsemen. With Rocky King, an African-American, in the middle of the ring, Flair approached Jim Ross at the announce position asking who the surprise was. Flair dismissively said, "I don't even talk to people like Rocky King." Flair and Anderson entered the ring asking Rocky who the surprise was, with Flair repeatedly calling King "boy", telling him, "You can't moonwalk with a broken leg." This prompted the Junkyard Dog to enter the scene and fight off Flair and Ole, before cutting a promo claiming, "This ain't 1939, this is 1990!" Sadly, the irony of the comment was lost on Ole Anderson.

The direction was clear – WCW was going back in time and actively seeking to eliminate the future in the process. Ole saw no sense in having

Brian Pillman and Tom Zenk as a top tag team when he could use the Rock and Roll Express in the same position for half price at $75,000 per year each. Consequently, the team of Pillman and Zenk was quietly demoted, and both men suddenly found themselves very low in the pecking order. Brian Pillman went from being Ric Flair's personal protégé and potential top star to working with The Iron Sheik, his promising future compromised as quickly as it developed.

Morale quickly plummeted, with almost everyone on the roster uncertain about what their spot would be going forward. Everything about the company was moving toward Anderson's antiquated ideologies, with no upside to the movement in sight.

Brian would look to make the best of a bad situation, cutting down Ole's booking in the locker room with his smart-ass, satiric wit. Trying not to let the shaky landscape destroy his spirits completely, Pillman decided to amuse the locker room. He'd been working a series of matches on house shows with Dutch Mantell, with Brian getting the win every night. One of the trademark attributes of Mantell was the sheer amount of body hair he had. One night, as Mantell fell asleep in the locker room, Pillman superglued a bath mat to Dutch's back hair. The result is best left to the imagination.

Since he was looking to get into high spirits, Pillman headed back to Cincinnati for the bachelor party of his old Bengals teammate Brian Blados at Jeff Ruby's Waterfront Restaurant. As would be expected, the liquor was flowing freely, and Blados especially was putting away beer like it was going out of style. Blados had a reputation for being able to drink a lot, but had consumed enough by the end of the night to be virtually paralytic. A group of boisterous punks decided to screw with Blados, pushing around the 320-pounder who was too drunk to defend himself. Never one to shy away from a fight, Pillman's response was almost legendary. "He beat 25 guys up", says Kim Wood, "Granted, they were all little guys, but he threw them in a pile!" The players jokingly referred to it as one of the greatest off-the-field moments in Cincinnati Bengals history, with Pillman tossing people around like a man possessed to protect Blados. "Brian was always involved in things that had a flair from the Old West", laughs Wood.

But it wasn't all fun and games, as Brian arrived at Clash of the Champions XI where he was booked to lose to Mean Mark Callous. Callous, who would become the WWF's Undertaker by the end of the year, was a fairly green and uncharismatic heel at this point. He was getting a push as Paul E.

Dangerously's new client and being groomed for a United States Title match with Lex Luger. Sacrificing Pillman killed two birds with one stone. Dismayed as he may have been with the relegation, Pillman worked hard to have a good match, true to the principles of David Vs. Goliath. Uncharacteristically, Brian blew a spot near the finish when he was supposed to be sent into the corner and come off the second rope, get caught by Callous and dropped throat-first on the top rope. Instead, Pillman had a momentary mental lapse, took the turnbuckle with his back and charged out full speed, before they repeated the sequence successfully. Pillman received a great deal of criticism from Callous and Ole after the match for the miscue.

Rather than be dejected by their complaints, Brian looked for the first opportunity to prove a point. It didn't take long, as Pillman went one-on-one against Arn Anderson for the TV Title in a match taped for the July 8th episode of WCW Main Event. While it was put together as a throwaway for Arn to win, the two men tore the house down in one of the better television matches of the year. The Pillman de-push was obviously unwarranted, but suggesting he was anything but a top-notch performer was a personal insult to Brian.

Regardless, one look at the Great American Bash on July 7th would make one think that Pillman thought himself lucky. Though downplayed, Flyin' Brian was still given a win in the opener against Buddy Landell. Comparing that with the treatment of his partner Tom Zenk was a wake-up call. Zenk was booked to lose to the debuting Big Van Vader in only five minutes. Since Zenk refusing a finish would be grounds for termination, he nodded his head compliantly. Only two minutes in, Ole Anderson gave them the cue to take it home early. It was an utter burial.

With concern brewing professionally, Pillman and Zenk opted to look at the positive side of things. "We just figured, hey, if they're not going to use us right, we're gonna' have fun after hours", said Zenk on Observer Live. "So we turned up the heat going out and had a great time." The attention Zenk and Pillman got from the fairer sex had its drawbacks, however. "We put heat on ourselves", Zenk detailed, "Because the top guys, their favorite saying was 'Don't you know who I am?' We could be losers (on TV) and the guys would look at me like I was some kind of a jerk, but we'd pull out girls in the bar and they didn't know, they could care less."

The resentment from married wrestlers at the top of the card towards young, single guys, who aren't treated as anything special on television but were main eventers in the female sweepstakes, was obvious. "I remember one time emphatically. We were out with Flair", said Zenk. "We were talking and girls were around, and Flair said that both Brian and I were married. This girl came up and stooged it off. So we went back to Flair and went, 'What are you doing? What are you talking about, we're not married!' He goes, 'I didn't say that'. I said, 'Flair, this girl told us!' So we brought the girl over, she says, 'Yeah, you told us they were married'. He goes. 'Well….I'm Ric Flair. I'm Ric Flair', and does his little jig, that little dance he does." Pillman was keen to have fun – it helped distract from the ongoing strife of being on the wrong side of the booker.

While Zenk and Pillman got along well at this point, it apparently wasn't always that way. "He got into a fight once in WCW with Tom Zenk", states Kim Wood. "Zenk crossed him, somehow. And he takes him (Zenk) out in the parking lot, and takes his head and puts it in the gravel, and scrapes it on the gravel for about a hundred feet. Then he starts kicking him in the face like a football and he made the guy cry. Meanwhile there's a crowd of like 200 people, wrestling fans, watching because these guys are supposed to be pals…and he made the guy beg for his life. If you talk to Zenk, he probably won't tell you about that one."

The house show numbers were falling hard, but Ole didn't get the message and continued down the same path. He brought in more guys on low, per-night deals such as Hector Guerrero, the Nasty Boys, Bob Armstrong, Buddy Roberts and an ancient-looking Ivan Koloff. The lineup for the September 5th, 1990 Clash of the Champions was especially indicative of the times. Cheap, outdated or green wrestlers filled the card while Brian Pillman was left off.

Somehow, while they were victimized since Ole's first day in, Pillman and Zenk were chosen to represent WCW on a famous episode of Family Feud, alongside WCW Champion Sting, Jim Ross, and Brad Armstrong under the ringname "The Candy Man". The WCW team beat the opposing GLOW (Gorgeous Ladies of Wrestling) team, but the choice to put Brian in the spot was truly puzzling given Ole's philosophy. He was looking to lower Pillman's profile in order to either hurt his negotiating leverage when his deal expired (and hopefully put him on a cheaper verbal deal), or to make his exit from the company a negligible loss. Halloween Havoc and Starrcade were booked without Brian Pillman scheduled to appear at all, and he continued to tread water for the rest of 1990.

Anderson began feeling the pressure from Jim Herd regarding the decreasing numbers and general discontent, and had very few supporters inside or outside WCW. The frustration finally defeated The Midnight Express, as Jim Cornette and Stan Lane quit the promotion. Cactus Jack had already abandoned ship. Non-contracted, pushed wrestlers Mean Mark and The Nasty Boys left and headed to the WWF.

Finally, in the first week of December, the axe fell - Ole Anderson was fired. After doing an awful job throughout the company and dooming newly-crowned WCW Champion Sting with an albatross of a storyline in 'The Black Scorpion' (supposedly a shadow from Sting's past returning to haunt him, but since none of the options were any good, they simply stuck Flair under the mask when it came time for the reveal), Jim Herd gave Ole his marching orders. It was reported that WCW lost $6.5 million in 1990, the majority of which was under the rule of Anderson, qualifying the period as an artistic and economic failure.

Brian was overjoyed at the decision. Surely, he thought, the company had hit its nadir under Ole's reign, and the only way from here was up. An interim committee was put in place consisting of Jim Ross, Ric Flair, Tony Schiavone and Kevin Sullivan, as Herd searched for a new full-time head booker.

The new committee seemed aware of a lot of the problems and took immediate action to get things back on track. Ole's recruits started dropping off the cards in short order and ideas were floated around on how to get the contract players back in the mix. Brian was lingering without an issue as Starrcade approached, but an intriguing idea was discussed for Pillman coming out of the show.

The theme of Starrcade 1990, beyond the painful final act of Sting and The Black Scorpion, was the Pat O'Connor Memorial International Cup. The idea was to have eight tag teams, each representing a different country, in a one-night single elimination tournament. Among those brought in for the show was Konnan, who teamed at the event with Rey Misterio (the uncle of the more famous WCW and WWE star Rey Mysterio). As a huge fan of lucha libre, Brian was eager to meet Konnan and the two became fast friends. Not only was the learned Pillman excited to talk lucha, but for the first time since his days in Calgary he had somebody who was used to practicing regularly before the show. Brian seized the opportunity, working out in the ring with Konnan and absorbing as much knowledge as he could.

The pre-show training in the ring did lead to one humorous moment that stuck with Pillman for years. As Brian and Konnan went through some lucha spots, Lex Luger came walking by them at ringside. With his face contorting, unable to comprehend what he was seeing, Luger said loud enough to hear in his whiny, almost effeminate tone, "Oh my God, do we have to start flying around now?"

Without pause, Pillman turned to Konnan, responding, "Don't listen to him, he's just a dick."

"He was super cool", revealed Konnan on MLW Radio, "He was wild and would say to a guy's face, 'That guy's a stooge, that guy's a stooge, you can't trust him, don't give him money, fuck him'." The two clicked so well personally that the idea being discussed was for Pillman and Konnan to become a regular tag team in 1991. The tandem was not to be, however. The WWF was pursuing Konnan at the same time with a more aggressive recruitment process and talked of creating a character that would be hugely marketed. The gimmick, which would become Max Moon, seemed like a serious investment from Vince McMahon. Konnan compared a full-blown push from the WWF side to a WCW offer coming from an interim committee, and felt the WWF was the safer bet.

With that plan out the window, Pillman awaited his next opportunity as the calendar turned to 1991. Changes were sweeping through the company, as Jim Herd accepted the reality that Sting's run as NWA Champion had failed to take the company to the Promised Land. While the lion's share of the blame has to fall on Ole Anderson's booking, it was generally felt that it was time to cut bait on Sting as the franchise, and Herd started looking for his next top guy. His eye immediately turned to Lex Luger who, like Sting, had been viewed as an heir apparent within the company for years. Whatever their plan was for the top babyface spot, they knew the best man to drop the belt to that new top babyface would be Ric Flair. As a result, Flair won the NWA World Championship once again on January 11th.

The interim committee began building up a War Games match for WrestleWar '91, originally scheduled as Sting, Luger, Pillman and the Steiners against the Four Horsemen and a mystery partner. With a Clash of the Champions show scheduled for the end of January on TBS (a perfect opportunity to promote WrestleWar the following month), it was announced that the main event would be Ric Flair defending his newly-won title against Brian Pillman. For Brian, it was the ideal way to erase six months of spinning his wheels and get back to working with top guys.

9 - LIVING 'THE DREAM'

"The American Dream" Dusty Rhodes was announced as the new WCW head booker at the start of January 1991, thus beginning the next period of adjustment. Rhodes had actually been hired for the job (a two-year deal for $300,000 per year) by WCW President Jack Petrik back in October, without the knowledge of Executive Vice President Jim Herd. Dusty was still finishing his dates in the World Wrestling Federation at the time. After receiving his WWF release on December 30th, Rhodes fulfilled his advertised appearance at the 1991 Royal Rumble, putting him in the bizarre position of wrestling on a WWF pay-per-view while officially occupying the position as WCW booker. The general feeling among the wrestlers was positive in that anything was deemed better than Ole, with a degree of trepidation from those with longer memories.

Rhodes had booked Jim Crockett Promotions during the promotion's peak in 1985-86, building the company around himself and Ric Flair to great success. As time passed the product grew stale, and Dusty's refusal to step aside as the top babyface became an albatross. A parade of overdone gutless finishes caused revenues to drop significantly. Combined with massive overspending (some of which was at Dusty's suggestion) and an inability to outmaneuver Vince McMahon in 1987, the company was left millions of dollars in debt as they entered 1988. Consequently, Jim Crockett Promotions had to be sold to Ted Turner to continue operations. Dusty remained as the booker during the shift in ownership, but had made many enemies with his decision making and was constantly battling politically with Ric Flair. As the man with the pencil, it was a war 'The Dream' felt he would win handily. With frustrations mounting, Rhodes booked Ric Flair to lose the NWA World Title at Starrcade 1988 to Rick Steiner in a few minutes, thinking he'd either damage Flair greatly or force him to quit.

Dusty's downfall was that in the sale to Turner, Ric Flair was the most valuable commodity the company had in Ted's eyes, not Rhodes. Herd knew Turner's viewpoint and overruled Dusty's Starrcade plan. Rhodes, not used to not having things his way, immediately shot an angle in which the Road Warriors stuck a spike in his eye, flagrantly breaking TBS' graphic violence and no blood policies. Dusty was fired and went to the WWF, where he'd stayed until January 1991.

But with the bar set so low, that wasn't as fresh in the mind. Concerns that Dusty's ego would lead to him making the product about himself were addressed early, as Rhodes' new position was given on the proviso that he stay out of the ring himself. There were early signs that the cronyism seen during Ole's reign remained, however. Dusty immediately surrounded himself with his crew, forming a booking team with friends and allies Barry Windham, Magnum TA, Mike Graham, Grizzly Smith, Kevin Sullivan, Ron West and Jody Hamilton. In addition, it was no secret his son, Dustin, would be on his way in as well.

One of Dusty's first decisions as booker was to rearrange the upcoming Clash, immediately switching Ric Flair's opponent in the main event from Brian Pillman to Scott Steiner. It was an unfortunate change for Pillman given what a great match with Flair on a big stage could have meant, and it was tough to hide his disappointment. Not only that, but the same week the switch was made, Pillman was booked to lose to Sid Vicious in four and a half minutes at the Meadowlands in New Jersey, the same major house show that saw Ric Flair take back the WCW World Title. Sid dominated the match, didn't sell much of Brian's offense, then beat him clean with the powerbomb.

Vicious was quickly becoming one of the most disliked individuals in the promotion. At 6'9" and 300 pounds, Sid had a physique that looked to be sculpted out of granite, outlined by a menacing face and a tremendously domineering presence. He embodied everything promoters wanted in the late eighties and looked like something straight out of a Vince McMahon wet dream. Unfortunately, he was as wooden as they came when the bell rang, with very little grasp on the mechanics of pro wrestling. Instead, he was treated as a destruction device, protected at all costs and rarely defeated.

WCW, swayed by his look and reactions of the live crowds, signed him for $250,000 per year guaranteed based on potential. Though they had high hopes and treated him like a star, Sid didn't produce at the box office when counted on. Halloween Havoc 1990, headlined by Sid Vs. Sting for the WCW Title, drew a lower buyrate than the two prior pay-per-views, and television ratings weren't noticeably different from anybody else when he was on the screen. Despite this, his sense of self-worth was ridiculously inflated, often saying and doing things that rubbed people the wrong way. Once, when directed to watch all-time greats Barry Windham and Arn Anderson to help improve his performances, Sid brazenly asked what they could possibly teach him, since he was already making more money than them. After suffering a punctured lung, Sid sat out long after he'd recovered claiming he was still on the mend, while actually indulging his true passion – playing on his local softball team. But his flaws were overlooked due to his perceived marketability, and Pillman found himself a casualty of WCW maintaining Sid's image.

That said, Brian was still penciled in for War Games in February, with the original plan changing to remove Luger and the mystery partner from the match. A precursor to the big pay-per-view showdown took place on the January 20th WCW Saturday Night, when the Horsemen team of Ric Flair, Arn Anderson, Barry Windham and Sid Vicious took on Sting, Pillman and the Steiners. What followed was a blistering encounter with a molten hot crowd. Pillman and Flair sought each other out as if to prove a point and had the fans on their feet. In keeping with Dusty's build to the Clash, it was Scott Steiner given the dramatic hot tag, leading to a wild brawl that caused the match to be thrown out. With the chaotic scene unfolding, Jim Ross provided the perfect soundtrack, stating, "This is an issue that only has one solution, the ultimate solution – the War Games!"

As the Clash of the Champions rolled around on January 30th, watching Scott Steiner have Flair beat for the World Title only to be denied by the time limit expiring was a bitter pill for Brian to swallow. The crowd didn't buy Steiner in the top role and Brian was convinced he would have been the better choice.

But Pillman liked Dusty, and the new booker was quick to defuse any skepticism Brian may have had about his future. Rhodes gave lip service to Brian about how he envisioned him getting over with the same blueprint used for Magnum TA. Magnum, when Dusty Rhodes booked him upon his arrival in Jim Crockett Promotions in 1984, was given a megapush out of the gate and beat opponents in short, convincing fashion, always with the belly-to-belly suplex. In many ways, Magnum wasn't ready for such a push, but he managed to prosper in it and got over tremendously. Pillman was encouraged by The Dream's big vision, and Dusty assigned Mike Graham to be Brian's mentor going forward. Graham became a constant point of reference for Brian behind the scenes, offering advice on how to survive as a smaller guy in a big man's business, and the two hit it off.

Only a couple of weeks later, Pillman was getting mixed messages about Dusty's long term ideas for him. With every sign pointing to being pushed as a singles star, talk began circulating about Brian being booked in a tag team with WCW's latest pick-up – Owen Hart. Having left the WWF in 1989, Owen had been working around the world doing tours of Mexico, Japan, and Europe. Hart had been courted by WCW back in 1990 to team with Brian (to replace Tom Zenk), but he had no interest in working for Ole Anderson. Dusty, however, had come to an agreement with the youngest of the Hart clan to start in March. With the prior Stampede connection, he too saw Pillman and Owen as a high-flying tag team, set to go by the name of "Wings". The impression was that the team would be the back-up plan if Brian's singles run didn't pan out, but one had to wonder how committed Rhodes was to Pillman's "Magnum push".

Still, with WrestleWar approaching, Brian was in a good position, rubbing shoulders with the most prominent players in the company and holding his own in matches and angles in every regard. After erroring in removing Pillman from the match with Flair at the Clash, Dusty's make-good was to create a story that would make War Games all about Brian. On the WCW Saturday Night taking place 24 hours before WrestleWar, with Sting and the Steiners already "in Pheonix" for the pay-per-view, the Horsemen ambushed Pillman, with Flair delivering a knee drop off the second rope to Brian's neck and shoulder. As the show wrapped up, Dusty (working on-air as an announcer) declared that he believed Brian would still be in War Games because his future in wrestling depended on it, but that he was risking his career by participating. It was a strong hook, executed well, and had the potential to be a star-maker had Brian been booked to overcome the odds at the big show.

As WrestleWar hit the air, Brian mentally prepared for his first pay-per-view main event. With his injury being the major story of the match going in, the spotlight naturally would gravitate to him and he was keen to make the most of it. War Games was an interesting concept, created by Dusty Rhodes years before, which saw two rings side-by-side, enveloped in a steel cage with a roof on top. Unlike WWE's later Hell in a Cell, however, this cage roof was only around eight feet from the canvas. It was a traditional blow-off match for the NWA/WCW, where blood was shed and victory was only attained by forcing the other side to "submit or surrender".

As the two sides lined up (with Larry Zybysko serving as a late replacement for an injured Arn Anderson), Barry Windham entered War Games first. Pillman, with his shoulder taped up to sell the previous night's attack, bolted past his partners against their wishes and started the match, laying a violent five-minute beating to Windham, whose face was covered in crimson early. The action was intense, as the bout continued picking up steam and firing up the crowd as the other members of both teams entered the bout in alternating periods.

With the tremendous match reaching its boiling point, Pillman found himself paired off with Vicious. Sid positioned Brian for his powerbomb finisher, the aesthetics of which looked ridiculous, as the cage roof wasn't that far away from the top of Sid's head to begin with. Vicious leaned forward, clasped his hands around Pillman's waist and hoisted him upside down in the air. Sure enough, Sid wasn't able to rotate Brian and the back of Pillman's heels smashed into the cage roof on the ascension. This caused the momentum to switch in the other direction, with Sid incapable of opposing gravity's wishes, driving Pillman to the canvas high on the back of his neck and shoulders. "Oh Jesus!", screamed Dusty Rhodes on commentary, horrified at the devastating impact. Landings like these have had career-ending results, and it was a scary moment for the pride of Norwood. Brian was knocked for a loop in the ring, but had the wherewithal to continue with the planned finish, which was for Sid to repeat the move. This time, the two were more cautious and Brian was dropped correctly, flat on his back. As Pillman sold on the canvas, El Gigante, a 7'5" former basketball player that was once drafted by the Atlanta Hawks (also owned by Ted Turner), came to ringside and requested the match be stopped due to the injury to Brian. Gigante was positioned as a babyface and a friend of Pillman's, and the bell rang to signify the end. As fate would have it, the blown powerbomb added a certain gravity to an ending that could otherwise have weakened Brian.

Having started the bout, courageously held his own with the storyline injury and losing upon an outsider's instruction, it was an acceptable out and a great showcase for Pillman. He was booked to be and was the star of the match, and had managed to gain in defeat. Elements of it could be questioned, certainly. Coming off like a match of this magnitude was out of Pillman's depth was risky, but the nature of the finish meant it was all in the follow up. If the right aspects were focused on, Brian's position as the main event underdog hero had legs.

Brian went to the hospital but was released that night, diagnosed with muscle and ligament strains to his neck. He returned to the hotel in a neckbrace with no major long-term damage done. Rather, as the cobwebs cleared, Brian started to realize how great things had gone. More than any other time in his WCW stint so far, it was looking like a genuine run on top was within reach.

Two days later, when taping the WCW Saturday Night show, Jim Ross interviewed Pillman about what happened in War Games. Giving a fiery response, Brian declared that while he appreciated everybody looking out for him, he never surrendered. He also said that he didn't care about the size difference, he was targeting Sid Vicious. Vicious retaliated in an interview with Paul E. Dangerously on the same show, saying he was sorry for what he did – sorry Pillman was able to walk out the hospital, and that he didn't go the extra inch to finish the job.

The following day at the Worldwide tapings, an angle was shot where Sid arrived at ringside during a Barry Windham match with Ricky Morton. As the two heels attacked Morton, Pillman sped down the aisle fighting off both Vicious and Windham, knocking Barry out the ring and dropkicking Sid over the top rope to the floor with the crowd going crazy. They'd put Brian in the position to run off two significantly bigger heels and the audience bought into it completely. The natural revenge story was writing itself, and it looked as if Brian was going to have his first hot issue as a solo star since the Luger matches in '89.

In classic WCW fashion, things took a different turn only a week later at the tapings for WCW Pro. They began promoting a "Revenge Tour" of TV matches in the coming weeks, as Brian looked to even the score by taking on each member of the Four Horsemen in separate matches. Pillman's quest immediately stumbled, as he found himself losing to Barry Windham when Barry grabbed the tights for the pin. Though the fight continued after the match, it was Barry who repeatedly got the upper hand. The scene ended with El Gigante showing up and saving Brian.

On the road, Pillman and Owen had a dry run of their proposed tag team in a series of matches with the Fabulous Freebirds. On television they were kept separate, as Hart was given victories over lower card wrestlers and Brian continued to cut promos vowing retribution for Sid trying to end his career at War Games. WCW were nothing if not inconsistent and the lack of focus wasn't encouraging, with many seeing Brian in the middle of the card as a sign that the push was stalling.

Brian eased his mind by instead focusing on a huge show coming up at the Tokyo Dome on March 21st. WCW was doing a joint show with New Japan Pro Wrestling, where a number of the biggest names would face off in interpromotional matches. The Dome was the most prestigious venue for wrestling in Japan, and with 64,500 fans set to attend, it was easily the biggest crowd Pillman had wrestled in front of. More importantly, for a student of the game like Brian, he knew the implications of getting over in Japan, both to the fans and the company – make an impression on a big stage and you open the door for a return down the line. His first brief tour hadn't offered an opportunity like this, and Brian was looking to seize it.

It wasn't just a good performance on the show that Brian wanted out of the trip. Pillman had been talking to Mike Graham a lot, angling for WCW to start a Junior Heavyweight Division just as New Japan had, that Brian could be the star of. No matter how hard he worked or how well he got over, the fallout of WrestleWar had convinced him that even if WCW pushed him, they'd do it in such a way to portray him as the little guy. Brian saw how much the light heavyweight style could get over, and having watched Tiger Mask and Dynamite Kid engage in a series that elevated them both to the level of genuine stars by doing things nobody else could, Brian viewed that as his way to break out of the pack and make big money. And he had just the guy that could be the Tiger Mask to his Dynamite.

Keiichi Yamada, the promising, stocky young kid that Brian had seen back in Stampede had returned to his native land and been transformed into Jushin "Thunder" Liger. Debuting the gimmick (based on an anime character of the same name) at the Tokyo Dome back in April 1989, Liger was an immediate hit. He was quickly the top star of the division, beating fellow Stampede alum Hiroshi Hase for the IWGP Junior Heavyweight Championship only a month later. Liger had been having excellent matches as champion, including a series with Chris Benoit who was working under as mask as Pegasus Kid. Pillman thought that between the costume, ability and charisma, Jushin could be huge in America. Brian pitched the idea to Liger and to Dusty, and went about preparing for the show.

As he often did, Brian went out to the squared circle in the empty arena and tested it. It was a different ring, so Brian got familiar with his surroundings by running the ropes, looking for sweet spots on the canvas. He felt that a lot was riding on this show and wanted to be ready. He was slated for a six-man tag, teaming with Tom Zenk and Tim Horner against New Japan stars Shiro Koshinaka, Kuniaki Kobayashi and Takayuki Iizuka. When putting the match together with the other five, Brian took the lead throwing out a million ideas, keen to spotlight his abilities as much as he could. There was more at stake for him than simply a match on the undercard – he wanted to shine enough to entice Liger.

The match ended up being a hit. Designed to showcase the American contingent, both Pillman and Zenk stood out and seemed to win over the immense crowd, using a lot of their double team moves perfected the year prior. Brian lit up the audience with a crossbody from the top rope to the floor on Iizuka, before Koshinaka went on a rampage of hip attacks, allowing Iizuka to pin Horner with a dragon suplex. Though not the best match on the card, it accomplished its objective.

Further to the point, WCW got to see Jushin Liger in person on the same show against Akira Nogami, and after being very impressed, serious talk began circulating within the office about putting together their own division. In the face of the success of a lighter weight category in several other countries, wrestling in North America had indoctrinated in the audience for years that bigger was better. As a result, it seemed like a gamble. It could either revolutionize the game, bringing an extra level of excitement to the product, or the audience could reject it, deeming it a preliminary title featuring guys not good enough to hang with the big boys. All was to be determined, but the idea was on the table.

Upon returning to the States, Brian was booked to continue his Revenge Tour and wrestle Ric Flair at a TV taping for WCW Saturday Night in a non-title match. Enthused at having another chance to work with Flair, Brian went hell for leather, delivering a match that was arguably even better than their famous bout the year before. Flair sold a tinge of fear by backing up early on, as Jim Ross and Paul E. Dangerously on commentary talked about how Brian was one of the toughest men to ever step in the ring. The dialogue from Ross and Heyman perfectly complimented the match as Flair threw everything at Brian, but Pillman stayed alive, chopping Flair so hard he drew blood from

Ric's chest. It was treated as a genuine grudge match and delivered in spades. After 12 minutes of superb action, Flair ducked a Pillman dropkick attempt, which ended up knocking the referee out cold. Brian hit a top rope crossbody for the visionary pin, before Arn Anderson came to ringside. Flair chopblocked a distracted Pillman and caught him in the figure four, with Arn illegally helping add pressure to the hold by grabbing Flair's hands from ringside. Once again, El Gigante appeared on the scene to attack Arn Anderson and apply his clawhold finisher to Flair, prompting a disqualification. It was almost tragic in that the match was so good on all fronts, a tremendous production from the company, before the Dusty-booked finish muddied the waters. Brian was made to look strong, but the audience was denied a clean finish, the focus was once again placed on El Gigante, and Pillman was now 0-2 on his quest to destroy the Horsemen.

The next day in Perry, Georgia, WCW taped matches for Pro and Power Hour, including another stop on the Pillman Revenge Tour as Brian wrestled Arn Anderson to a time limit draw. After the match, Barry Windham ran in for the sneak attack. Windham and Anderson delivered a spike piledriver, leaving Brian dead to rights, until El Gigante once again ran in to scare off the Horsemen and check on Brian. Following the great match and being made to look so good against Flair, the decision to book this match with another Pillman beatdown was troubling. But the true test was yet to come, as Brian had another showdown with Sid Vicious at the Meadowlands coming up.

Sid had been the subject of many issues over the previous week after giving WCW his notice at the end of March. Though he was under contract until September, he'd notified them of his intention to quit in order to renegotiate his contract. Sid told WCW that he would be leaving the company at the end of May unless his demands were met. His demands were an extra $100,000 added to his contract (bringing him to $350,000 per year, closer to the Lex Luger/Sting level he saw himself at), and to have June and July, which just so happened to be softball season, off. On the same day that Flair and Pillman tore the house down, Sid came to a verbal agreement with WCW - he would sign a new three-year deal for $350,000, but wouldn't get the time off.

As Brian arrived at East Rutherford, New Jersey, it was hard not to think about his match with Sid in the same building back in January. This, it seemed, would be a good barometer to judge how serious this new push was. He walked into the Meadowlands and was aghast at what was lined up.

In the midst of what was supposed to be Brian's big push, the match was designed to be almost exactly the same as January, with Sid going over in 5 minutes and dominating the entire match. Brian was livid. The nature of how the match was designed illustrated that the last four months of being involved with the Horsemen didn't mean a thing. Brian couldn't make sense of it, having gone neck and neck with the World Champion days before, to now being treated as a glorified jobber. With all the television time and momentum imploring WCW to treat Pillman with a shred of credibility, it was asinine to sacrifice him to anybody at this point. The fact it was Sid only rubbed salt in the wound.

Pillman tried to negotiate a better outcome when putting the match together, but Vicious was having none of it, saying it wasn't realistic or believable for him to go fifty-fifty and sell for Brian given the drastic height difference. With his temper triggered by the size issue, Pillman was quick to counter, saying he'd knocked people bigger than Sid on their ass for real in the NFL plenty of times. Sid stuck to his guns, saying it would look ridiculous and nobody would buy it. Brian knew how much harder working and how much better he was than Vicious, and it bothered him to be treated so poorly by all involved. With the company doing their best to appease Sid before he signed his new contract, the match went ahead as laid out. As a matter of principle, Brian refused to take Sid's powerbomb for the finish. Vicious caught Pillman coming off the top rope with a crossbody, delivered a backbreaker and pinned him clean after selling virtually nothing the entire match. El Gigante lumbered out to the ring to run Vicious off and save Pillman from further punishment one more time. It was a total squash, and Brian was outraged.

"I was at that show", reflects Dave Meltzer. "It was terrible. Sid really was so much bigger and when you saw it from a visual standpoint it did look tough, but you could still give Brian certain things and make a match out of it, and he did not do that."

Days later, Sid backed out of the verbal agreement with WCW in order to sign with the WWF, and told WCW his last date would be May 19th at the Superbrawl pay-per-view. Any movement towards a potential Sid/Pillman feud stemming from WrestleWar was abruptly dropped.

The same week, Owen Hart and WCW agreed to part ways, as Owen's abundance of dates elsewhere meant he wouldn't be around enough to justify the time and effort to push him. The proposed Wings team never saw the light of day on WCW television, and Brian's backup plan was also out the window.

After coming out of WrestleWar with the momentum to be a hot babyface, WCW had fumbled the ball in miserable fashion. The Revenge Tour matches began airing on television, dedicating a lot of time to Brian without him winning a single match in his run against the Horsemen. Similarly, Brian was being jobbed out on house shows, and with Sid on his way out and being lined up to lose to El Gigante at Superbrawl, Pillman was now being paired off with Barry Windham. Inexplicably, the television shows began attempting to spin the narrative that it was Windham who had injured Pillman back at WrestleWar, not Vicious, despite video evidence, replays, and their own promos to the contrary. Within six weeks Brian had been cooled off dramatically, and while a series with Windham had potential, it no longer looked to be the opportunity it promised to be on that February night in Phoenix.

"I don't know what happened there", responds Dave Meltzer when asked about the failed push and decision to veer away from a program with Sid. "He was in main events and then he wasn't in the plans and stuff again. He was always like that. He'd be doing well, but then there would be a booker and they just wouldn't see him as a top guy. He really wanted to be a top guy, and would have done anything to be a top guy. Some bookers just didn't see him at that level for whatever reason. They just didn't."

Making matters worse, the rivalry with Windham seemed designed to establish Brian's place low in the pecking order rather than elevate him. After the television built up a Taped Fist match at Superbrawl to continue Brian's blood feud, the match instead only went six minutes, hardly the length of time appropriate for such a grudge match. While the action was good, with Windham bleeding within moments and the crowd eating up the wild fistfight, Pillman was superplexed and pinned decisively, again looking out of his league against a key player.

In the aftermath of Superbrawl, Dusty went a bizarre direction with the program, as Windham's matches were constantly interrupted by a man dressed as various animals. Whether disguised as a rat, a chicken or a gorilla, the mascot shook his ass in Windham's direction and served as a general nuisance with its inane hijinx. A couple of weeks later, after Barry Windham defeated an enhancement talent, the man in the rat costume returned, unmasking as Pillman before attacking Windham again. The angle was completely illogical with no reason ever given as to why Brian took this approach, and only served to kill any remaining credibility or thread of seriousness the angle had. But as Brian would later go on to tell Power Slam magazine, "One of the hallmarks of WCW is its absurdity."

In reality, the rationale behind the de-emphasis of Pillman probably made perfect sense to the booker, Dusty Rhodes. With the introduction of Dusty's son as "The Natural" Dustin Rhodes to WCW in February, it was clear who the "Magnum push" originally promised to Brian was really going to. Dustin hadn't taken a single defeat since his debut, always got the pin in tag matches and was regularly fighting off the heels by himself no matter what the odds. Ric Flair was even referencing Dustin during guest stints on commentary, talking about how he'd be defending his championship against "The Natural" far sooner than people expected. When going over instructions with Dustin's opponents, Dusty would often remind them - "Make the kid look good out there, he's the fruit of my loins." It dawned on more than one babyface in the company that they were downplaying any opposition for Dustin on the good-guy totem pole.

Dusty's run as booker wasn't going smoothly. House show attendance and television ratings had actually dipped since the start of his regime. At the start of June, the higher ups instructed Dusty to reduce his own presence on the shows, and questions were circulating about the long-term stability of Dusty's position.

With the booker's priorities elsewhere Brian continued to suffer, and the true extent of his push became clear. Pillman's goofy antics led to another match with the Horsemen, this time teaming with El Gigante against Windham and Anderson at Clash of the Champions XV. A stipulation was added where the person that lost the fall would be forced to leave WCW. Much to Brian's chagrin it was decided he'd be pinned by Barry Windham again, and this time in just three minutes. While WCW tended to overbook the Clash shows, cramming in so many matches that none had time to play out, this was an inexcusable burial, intentional or not.

After castrating Brian's promising run, Dusty's idea was for him to be cast out of WCW and return under a mask as The Yellow Dog. With the costume not doing a good job of concealing his face or distinctive voice, everybody in the world would be in on the joke that it was Brian Pillman, and Windham would be incensed that Brian had found a way around the "Loser Must Leave" stipulation. The name itself was a nod to a gimmick that Windham himself had done in Florida Championship Wrestling, going under a mask as the Dirty

Yellow Dog when he'd lost a Loser Leaves Town match. The most famous incarnation of this type of charade up to this point was, of course, Dusty himself, who had multiple runs as The Midnight Rider when the situation called for it.

Almost as soon as the Yellow Dog began, with Barry Windham putting out a bounty to anybody who could unmask him, it stalled amidst WCW's regular maelstrom. The angle was weak to begin with and suffered from a major lack of focus, as Pillman's run against the Four Horseman had pretty much come to an end. While the Yellow Dog found himself wrestling a mixed bag of opponents without much rhyme or reason, Dusty had made the call to break up the Horseman unit. Brian's angle had also taken a back seat to the biggest story in the company since his arrival.

Jim Herd and Dusty Rhodes decided they wanted the WCW World Title off Ric Flair, and with Sting having gone down as a failure the prior year, Herd wanted to anoint Lex Luger as the new top dog. The company was building to a match between Flair and Luger at the Great American Bash. It was intended to be the night that would finally, after countless false starts, be the passing of the torch to Lex, which Herd and Rhodes hoped would bring WCW to new heights.

Jim Herd wanted to not only move Flair out of the top spot but to cut his salary in half, from $700,000 a year to $350,000. Flair's current deal had almost a year left on it, and the company wanted to essentially rip up the current contract to start a new, three-year deal with the lower figure and reduced dates. After being used for so long as a champion that made everybody else look like a star (with his own marketability sacrificed), Flair saw it as a slap in the face to be 'rewarded' with such a steep drop. Worse yet, since the man earmarked to take his place, Luger, was earning $600,000 a year, Flair felt slighted that he'd be working alongside a man who, irrespective of his A+ physique, wasn't in Flair's league as a personality or performer, but would be making far more.

Flair began leveraging his impending title loss to try and get the figure to a more favorable level. The pay cut was indicative of Herd and Dusty's regard for Flair's value going forward, and the widespread talk was that Ric, after losing the title to Luger, would be feuding with (and putting over) Dustin Rhodes. Flair was looking at a major demotion, both financially and in terms of position, and dropping the title was the only bargaining chip he had. Inside the WCW offices, it was openly discussed that they feared Flair would hold the company up for a better deal and refuse to lose the title unless the new contract was more to his liking.

In an attempt to avoid the impending showdown, the call was made for Flair to instead drop the WCW Title before the match with Luger at the Bash. The new plan, which Ric was told about only days in advance, was to have the Nature Boy lose the belt to Dusty's family friend, Barry Windham (who was, in the ultimate irony, uncontracted) at a house show in Macon, Georgia on July 1st. Flair was sticking to his guns on wanting to resolve the contract issue before dropping the title. Herd, known for reacting quickly and explosively, blew up. Hours before the show in Macon took place, when it was clear Flair wasn't going to attend, Herd faxed a termination notice to Flair's attorney, Dennis Guthrie. The World Champion and top star, Ric Flair, had been fired and stripped of his title. WCW, which suffered a huge public black eye in how they dealt with the Flair situation since fans empathized with Ric, backpedaled within days. As it turned out, WCW had no legal basis to fire Flair and only a week after being sent his termination, the TBS legal department ended up making Flair an offer to return for $750,000 a year. Flair turned the offer down and took his chances in the WWF.

The domino effect of all this was to Pillman's detriment. Windham was moved to the main event of the Great American Bash to wrestle Lex Luger to crown the new WCW World Champion. As chants of "We Want Flair" drowned out the match (and the entire show), Luger won the belt with assistance from Harley Race and Mr. Hughes, turning heel in doing so. Barry Windham was turned babyface in the process. In the fallout of Flair's departure, Pillman's rival was now on the same side of the fence as him and the story was lazily left unfinished. With turmoil abound, WCW was its usual absent-minded self when it came to Brian's storyline, continuing the bounty on the Yellow Dog's mask while neglecting to mention who put the bounty on it to begin with. It was about as far away from Dusty's grand vision of a megapush as could be, but Brian saw a beacon of hope on the horizon.

With the shambolic angle occurring stateside, Pillman was given a break from the nonsense with a brief tour of Japan. Scheduled for a show at the start of August in Nagoya and three more at Tokyo's Sumo Hall, Pillman was more than happy to return to New Japan Pro Wrestling. While the first three matches were of little consequence, it was the final night, August 11th, that Brian had his eye on. For on that night, he was scheduled to wrestle Jushin Liger for the first time.

10 - AERIAL ATTRITION

As Brian's WCW theme music played, the fans in Sumo Hall clapped to the beat of the song, a respectful response indicating a growing familiarity. The place positively lit up when Jushin Liger's music began, the established superstar of the division swiftly making his way down the aisle. Liger climbed to the second rope to engage the audience, then hopped down and turned directly into a Pillman dropkick, with Brian getting the jump on Liger before his entrance music had even stopped playing. The fans uncharacteristically booed Brian, but were quickly wowed by a crossbody from the top rope to the floor by Pillman. As he re-entered the ring the fans roared with approval, the hot start energizing the crowd.

Liger returned to the ring and a leg lariat later, Pillman himself wound up on the arena floor, with Liger barreling off the ropes to return the favor. When Brian moved, Liger feigned the dive, and the fans in Sumo Hall exploded as Liger gestured to them.

The match rolled on, with Brian looking to escalate the excitement by removing the thick blue mats that sat around the ring for protection and executing a crippling piledriver on the floor. With Brian's offense putting the favorite in jeopardy, loud chants of "Liger!" echoed from the rafters of Sumo Hall. Jushin worked his way back into the match, hitting a tombstone, flying headbutt and Liger Bomb, with Pillman kicking out of each before finally falling to a gourdbuster and top rope headbutt to the back of the head. While not an instant classic, the chemistry between the two was obvious for all to see. Brian knew that going all-out on a bigger stage, they could make magic together.

Seeing that the Yellow Dog direction was going absolutely nowhere, Pillman had lost faith in the idea of being pushed as a true top guy and continued to campaign for WCW to institute a light heavyweight division. Finally, Dusty and Herd began putting plans in motion. In music to Brian's ears, it was soon confirmed that WCW had made an agreement for Jushin Liger to come in at the end of the year for a short run. Liger had the potential to be a revelation in the States, and Pillman would be right there with him, hoping to elevate himself without having to interact with those that the booker would be inclined to protect. Even in the early stages, the plan was to get to Liger Vs. Pillman for the title by the end of the year.

On the August 24th episode of WCW Saturday Night, The Yellow Dog was taken out back and put out of its misery, as it was announced that Brian Pillman was reinstated and would be part of the new WCW Light Heavyweight division. Early indications weren't encouraging about WCW's attitude towards the new project, as the lineup for the seven-man championship tournament amounted to a rogues' gallery of undercard luminaries such as Joey Maggs, Johnny Rich and Mike Graham. Other participants included the criminally underused Terry Taylor, the ill-conceived heel Ricky Morton, and Brad Armstrong under a mask as Badstreet, none of whom were knocking crowds dead in their current roles. Safe in the knowledge that he was booked to win and that Liger was coming in soon, Pillman chose to think positive. He had a chance to set the tone with his first match in the new division, a bout with Badstreet booked for Clash of the Champions XVI on September 5th.

Armstrong, while never displaying the type of extroverted charisma that could click with the audience, was well respected for being a performer with ability beyond his position. The Badstreet persona was one of many attempts by WCW to give Armstrong a role to shoehorn personality into his act and allow them to use his in-ring talents.

Pillman took to the ring with a chip on his shoulder after months of poor treatment. After a lackluster beginning to the new light heavyweight endeavor, the two put on the type of match that was exactly what people were hoping the new division would be. The bout was filled with unique highspots, such as Badstreet suplexing Brian from the ring apron to the floor, Pillman coming off the top rope with a dropkick only to be met in mid-air by a Badstreet dropkick, and Brian launching himself through the top and middle ropes with an insane tope that saw him overshoot his target and crash into the barricade, his legs bouncing off the concrete on impact. Pillman hit his top rope crossbody to conclude what was easily the best match on the show. More encouraging yet, the crowd ate it up, giving no excuses to the bookers to second guess the direction.

Regrettably, Pillman tore a muscle in his back on the tope and was limited in what he could do until Halloween Havoc, where he was set to face Ricky Morton in the tournament final. Pillman still made the house shows, however, showing up with his arm in the sling, citing it as the reason he couldn't wrestle. This would allow a heel to show up and attack him, then stomp on the faux injury so they could enter their match with some built-in steam. It was a fairly easy gig, but it was on this loop that one of the most remembered backstage incidents of Brian's career took place.

The crew had done a show in Greensboro on October 13th and were set to fly out to Alabama on the 15th via Atlanta, giving the guys a night at the Ramada Inn close to the airport. With many of the guys drinking at the bar, the recently departed Sid Vicious dropped in to say hello. After a few beers, Sid couldn't help himself. He was more than happy to talk down to the wrestlers in the company he'd left behind for the WWF about how much greener the grass was on the other side. While the WWF was having its own problems at the time, nobody could really argue that 1991 had been a disaster thus far for Turner's ensemble.

One person who took exception was Mike Graham, who suggested that Sid should shut his mouth. Instead of heeding the request, Sid kept up his obnoxious tirade and responded that he'd drawn more money in the last week than Graham did his entire career. With Graham being close to Brian and with things getting heated, Pillman found himself involved. Brian's ear perked when Sid began his rantings and he couldn't resist joining in once Vicious mentioned drawing money, given his less than stellar track record. Sid was all too eager to extend his attention to Brian, saying that the reason the WWF is where it is and WCW is where it is, is because they have the correct, more believable approach of keeping the big guys away from doing programs with the little guys. The flashbacks to their previous issues and ixnayed program crossed Brian's mind, and combined with the fact he had to listen to this same mentality for as long as he could remember, he'd heard about enough. Sid then delivered the line that Pillman would never make it in wrestling because not only was he a pretty boy, but he didn't know how to work, which was tantamount to Adolf Hitler preaching equality to Martin Luther King Jr.

Pillman aggressively rose out of his seat with fire in his eyes, ready to fight. Brian had no intention of backing down or letting the comments slide. Just as it seemed the two were to come to blows, it was Sid who declined. Pulling up his shirt to reveal a band-aid on his forearm, covering a scar from a recent surgery for a torn bicep, Sid cited it as his reason for not fighting. As Sid left the bar, the guys began to cool down somewhat, the tense situation seemingly diffused. People had just about got their hands back on their beers when Sid re-entered, menacingly holding a squeegee (the plastic windshield cleaning device) in his hand as if it were a deadly weapon, challenging both Pillman and Graham to bring it on. Without much effort, Graham took the squeegee away from Sid as the other wrestlers held Pillman back. Vicious then left the bar for good. Pillman and Graham, despite staying away from Sid's weapon of mass destruction, managed to come out of the entire incident squeaky clean. Indeed, Pillman left the encounter as a locker room hero for backing down Sid, and the comedy value would be parodied for years.

At a house show in Greensboro on November 17th, 1991, with word having traveled of the incident, a number of ringside fans were armed with cardboard squeegees. Upon Brian's arrival for his match, he took one look and offered up, "You've got to be 6'8" and have no balls to carry one of those." On the same show, Cactus Jack and Sting would do battle in a cage match in the main event. As Sting mounted a flurry of offense against Cactus, forcing him into retreat, Jack reached towards the corner. Putting his hand under a strategically placed towel under the bottom turnbuckle, Cactus turned around, holding a squeegee before him as if engaging in Olympic fencing. Sting sold it with great fear, with Cactus chasing him around the ring with the foreign object before it was confiscated by the referee.

When Sid left the WWF months later, noted cartoonist Bret Hart mourned his departure with a sketch on the locker room blackboard. The drawing depicted a bent-over Sid clutching a squeegee as Brian Pillman, sat on Mike Graham's shoulders, shoved a dozen farewell roses up his ass.

Unfortunately, during this period of time a couple of less publicized situations occurred that impacted Pillman's private life greatly. Brian and Rochelle were driving around their home base of Atlanta late one night and stopped by an ATM. Attempting to deal with his ailing back, Brian reclined the seat all the way to gain some relief by laying supine, leaving Rochelle to withdraw some cash outside. A few moments later, Pillman noticed a couple of guys approaching her from behind, loudly threatening her for money. With Rochelle clearly intimidated, Brian leapt out of the car and went into action, knocking one of them to the deck before tackling the other and essentially bodyslamming him on the concrete. The police were called and the two men were promptly arrested, though the assailants did attempt to press charges on Brian in the aftermath, accusing him of initiating the damage.

Shortly after, with Brian on the road, an even more serious situation occurred in their own home. The groundskeeper for the apartment complex the two were living in broke into the house and assaulted Rochelle. After a brief struggle, the intruder stabbed her with an ice pick. The attacker was caught and went to jail, but while the physical wounds healed, the already fragile Rochelle lived in fear following the traumatic incident.

∞

With the tournament final on the horizon, WCW's inability to frame or position the Light Heavyweight division effectively was an ominous sign. Commentators on television would frequently talk about how the division was giving a chance to the smaller wrestlers who wouldn't have a chance to be champion otherwise, portraying them as out of their depth against top heavyweights. The unimpressive field was bad enough, but the company seemed oblivious to the message being sent when they talked about the new title being Joey Maggs' chance to shine, as he was being battered by Lex Luger with ease. Indeed, the new championship was appearing to determine the King of the Jobbers, rather than segregating a crew with a different style. Clearly, this would be an uphill climb.

Pillman won the championship at Halloween Havoc against Richard Morton (using the elongated version of his name since joining the York Foundation) in a match that largely failed to show what could make the division special. It wasn't a poor match, but Morton's style wasn't conducive to putting on the spectacular showcase that the division sorely needed to differentiate it. Jim Ross on commentary was keen to note, "I'm sure the great Jushin Liger is watching this match closely", laying the groundwork for the rivalry Pillman was banking on to break him out of the pack.

By this point, WCW under Herd and Dusty was bipolar at best. With Ric Flair gone and the company banking on Lex Luger, house show attendance dropped to its lowest point in the year, with November doing an average turnout of only 1,130 fans. It seemed as if for every good decision being made there was a bad one to match. Since the first joint show with WCW and New Japan Pro Wrestling back in May was a success, the two sides agreed to collaborate for a second one at the Tokyo Dome on January 4th, 1992. However, one of the major hits of the first Supershow, Pillman, was not on the list of talent used. Instead, WCW took El Gigante, Bill Kazmaier, and requested a match where Dustin Rhodes could wrestle in a tag match alongside his father, the booker, Dusty.

In contrast, it was announced that the first encounter on American soil between Pillman and Liger would take place at the Omni in Atlanta, the building that the company held in the highest regard, on Christmas night. The two were booked to work together for the entire run of post-Christmas shows. Four dates, back to back, that would allow the two men to perfect their act together and demonstrate just how much the WCW Light Heavyweight Title could mean. They'd settled for a pretty good match at Sumo Hall, but both men wanted to create something special.

Brian was constantly chasing perfection with his work and wasn't one to settle knowing he could do better. Though it seemed a risk lobbying to work with a virtual unknown in the States, he was willing to gamble thinking it could bring him closer to his best. "He took chances and wanted to be different", says Bruce Hart. "Most of the good talents like Bret, Brian and Dynamite, they were never quite satisfied. Even when Brian had by most terms an ass-kicker, an awesome match, he was never satisfied with his performance."

As much as Pillman fantasized about this series being his way to revolutionize wrestling in the States and reap the benefits of being on the crest of the wave, it meant every bit as much to Liger. Long before Keiichi Yamada worked Stampede Wrestling all those years ago, he'd wanted to break into the American market and hit big. Most of the iconic, legendary wrestlers in Japanese history had runs in the States and got over well, and Liger wanted to add his name to the shortlist. With lofty expectations on themselves, they looked to reach for the stars, starting on December 25th.

As the match took to the ring at the Atlanta Omni, it didn't take long for the audience to grasp that they were witnessing something special, far beyond the measures of an ordinary spot show. Pillman and Liger were holding nothing back, throwing caution to the wind by exchanging dives to the outside. Liger kicked out of Brian's signature top rope crossbody and picked Pillman up for a tombstone, but Brian kicked his legs to send Liger backwards, allowing him to reverse the move and execute the piledriver. A charging

Pillman leapfrogged Liger, Liger leapfrogged an incoming Brian, and the two collided in mid-air as they both attempted to outsmart the other on the rebound. Finally, Pillman left his shoulders down on a belly-to-back superplex and the match and championship were awarded to Liger. The post-match embrace and endorsement of Liger from Pillman cemented the two as equals, and Brian looked every bit the star in losing.

The reviews were overwhelmingly positive. A live report called it the best non-Ric Flair match they'd ever seen live, and multiple accounts rated the bout highly. Not looking to be a one hit wonder, they poured every bit as much into the following three nights. In Dallas on the 26th the crowd responded unexpectedly, booing Liger and getting fully behind Pillman with vociferous chants of "U-S-A!" The pair tweaked some of their twists and turns from the previous night and added some ringside brawling to heat up the action to the tastes of the live crowd. Again, the match was raved about, as the two men went through their series of big moves and dramatic near falls.

The next night they took the match to the Meadowlands in New Jersey, the site of two of Brian's biggest embarrassments of the year. The contrast in opponents between Sid and Liger was as striking as can be, and once again the pair pushed the limits to create a classic. Borrowing from the night before, the two brawled around ringside at one point, with Pillman bringing a steel chair into play. This time, it was Brian that earned some boos. Liger responded by hopping up to the apron, jumping up to the second rope and flying off backwards, hitting an Asai moonsault to the amazement of the fans. It bears mentioning here that while WCW had its share of talented workers, such effort and risk was rarely seen on the house shows, and the crowd reacted accordingly. For the third night running, Pillman and Liger not only had the best match of the night, but also generated the most heat from the fans in attendance.

Their final match on the loop was much the same as the pair took their refined war of aerial attrition to Baltimore, where the fans again bombarded the ring with the loudest cheers, gasps and groans of the evening. Liger got the win all four nights, but the standing of both men had risen, with it seeming like Pillman Vs. Liger was everything people had dreamed it would be. It was in WCW's hands to run with it. "Brian and Liger had phenomenal matches", states Dave Meltzer. "Those matches really put Liger on the map in North America too. It definitely put Brian at a higher level and that was the first time a lot of people would have ever seen Liger. It was two guys both trying to prove themselves and Liger was one of the best in the world. He was just an incredible talent."

The following night, WCW aired their annual Starrcade pay-per-view. Dusty Rhodes had devised a new creation called "Battle Bowl" for the event, which saw a "Lethal Lottery" take place to pair 40 wrestlers off into chance tag teams that would do battle in random matches. The 20 winners would advance to a battle royal at the end of the night to determine the winner of the competition.

The idea of building an entire show around intrigue was questionable and the random combinations too frequently served no purpose, often making people look worse than they were. Case in point, Jushin Liger, fresh off his blistering series with Pillman, was paired with the inept Bill Kazmaier against Mike Graham and a very inexperienced Diamond Dallas Page in his first televised encounter. Within the first minute, Liger had problems working with Graham, attempting a handspring back elbow that Mike was out of position for, resulting in Liger gracelessly crumbling to the mat to the laughter of the crowd. Jushin returned to the dressing room furious.

Brian was only a shade luckier. Pillman's tag match opponents, Sting and Abdullah The Butcher, were feuding, and the match was more about Pillman helping his opponent, Sting, fight off Abdullah and Brian's own partner, Bobby Eaton. The peak of the match was Pillman entering the ring and bodyslamming the 350-pound Butcher, following it up with a sensational top rope splash. As only WCW could, the camera missed the bodyslam. Though his team went down in defeat when Sting pinned Eaton, Pillman celebrated as if victorious. The Christmas matches with Liger, which were truly state-of-the-art compared to the styles featured in the WWF and WCW during that era, had gotten people talking. On pay-per-view, however, neither was given any special consideration when it mattered most.

It would come as no surprise for WCW to produce what turned out to be a largely irrelevant Starrcade under normal circumstances. Yet, as the book closed on 1991, it was very clear internally that circumstances were anything but normal.

Under the booking philosophy of Dusty Rhodes and leadership of Jim Herd, things had continued to move downhill for World Championship Wrestling. With the three years of losses under Turner ownership inching towards the $20 million mark, TBS ordered a report on the wrestling division to get to the root cause of the issues. After talking to people at all levels of management, the common denominator cited as the main problem was the Executive Vice President, Jim Herd.

At the same time, Herd was frustrated with Dusty, and felt he deserved the lion's share of the blame for the struggling operation. After a poor twelve months and with TBS now looking for answers, Herd pointed the finger towards the man they'd fired once before. Since Dusty had been hired by Herd's superior, WCW President Jack Petrik, Jim was insistent that he was handicapped by the cards he was dealt. Herd wanted Dusty gone, and vowed to leave unless he was removed. On the back of the negative report that outed Herd as a temperamental leader with a lack of knowledge in the field, Petrik made his decision. On January 8th, 1992, Petrik requested that Herd take a position in TBS syndication and leave his WCW duties behind. Herd refused, and instead decided to resign from TBS altogether.

Petrik immediately appointed a new leader at the helm of WCW. Failing to learn from his mistakes, the replacement had even less knowledge of pro wrestling than Jim Herd. The man was Kip Frey, who was hired by TBS to be an attorney in April 1991. In his late thirties, Frey was a graduate of Duke University Law School that had privately practiced law in North Carolina and California before entering Turner's doors, and was given a six-month contract in the role of WCW Executive Vice President. On the surface, it was a doomed assignment if there ever was one.

Nevertheless, Frye had a positive attitude and went to work, trying to immerse himself as quickly as possible to understand what WCW needed to prosper. Surprisingly, Frye's untainted attitude, optimism and aggressive mentality yielded some good early results. Recognizing that WCW had presentation issues, he ordered new graphics and intros for the television shows and hired Jesse "The Body" Ventura, the former iconic WWF commentator and future Governor of Minnesota, to lend his talents and credibility to the WCW broadcast booth. Frye instituted a bonus system for the best performances on big shows to provide extra incentive for the talent to excel. He also started aggressively looking at WWF talent and began talks with a number of key players to try and lure some of them to WCW. On top of that, Frye was making generous offers in contract negotiations with existing WCW talent. With Pillman's contract coming up shortly, the timing of the replacement at the top couldn't have been better.

Eager to impress his new boss, Pillman put in a tremendous shift at the first Clash of the Champions in 1992. Teaming with Marcus Alexander

Bagwell against Terry Taylor and Tracy Smothers, the four men worked hard to light up the crowd. Though there was no relevant issue between them, the match was still a success, with Pillman and Bagwell going over in impressive fashion. What followed, in WCW's latest schizophrenic booking, was a bizarre promo to hype a match for Superbrawl, WCW's February pay-per-view.

It was announced previously that Brian Pillman would get a rematch for the WCW Light Heavyweight Title on that show against Jushin Liger. Justifiably so, as the series had generated enough discussion to get the match seen by a much broader audience. As Pillman stood on the podium with third-string announcer Eric Bischoff and Johnny B. Badd, he unleashed a peculiar tirade that seemed out-of-character for the smiling, white-meat babyface that Brian was often portrayed as. "It goes much deeper than armdrags and hiptosses for me, and I say that with the most utmost respect for the Japanese people", started Brian. "But all I can remember since I was this high, a little kid growing up, all I've watched - Japanese industries buying up neighborhood communities and turning them into high-rise office towers. Seeing close friends of mine, former classmates, looking them in the eyes and seeing their despair because they've lost their jobs at the auto plant thanks to a rebate, courtesy of a Japanese automaker. Well, I can assure you of one thing Thunder Liger – there's one thing I'm not gonna' watch, and that's you taking that belt back to Japan, because February 29th, 1992, Superbrawl, I'm bringing that belt back where it belongs: the United States of America!"

The xenophobic promo was totally out of left field and seemed particularly out of context with Badd trying to steal the scene beside him with exaggerated reactions. The interview earned a lot of negative reviews, though the live crowd got behind the fired-up speech. Badd, who was in the midst of a babyface turn, ended the interview by planting his red lips sticker on Pillman's cheek. Brian turned to Badd and yelled "Kiss that!" before punching him in the face, leaving the previously excited audience silent, completely unsure what to make of Pillman's conduct. Whatever the design or theory of the interview was when conceived by Dusty, it was a total misread and was never referred to again.

With the Clash being treated like it never really happened for Brian, he looked ahead to Superbrawl where he and Liger were longing to tear the house down in front of the entire world. But fate, it seemed, wanted to test their convictions before granting them their wish.

Liger had gone back to Japan after Starrcade and suffered a fairly serious rib injury. Rather than rest up before returning to the States, New Japan requested he gut out the remainder of the tour. In addition, the back injury that Pillman suffered against Badstreet the previous September had returned, and he was pulled from shows for a couple of weeks before Superbrawl. With both men in questionable condition, fears arose over whether the big showdown on pay-per-view would live up to the almost mythical underground reputation the initial run of matches had acquired.

In the meantime, Kip Frey had decided he wanted to lock down his roster and called Pillman to talk about his new contract. In the prior weeks, rumors were flying that Frye had come to a deal with WWF Intercontinental Champion Bret Hart (which almost came to pass, though Hart's contract had rolled over preventing the deal from being finalized), and was also looking to steal Marty Jannetty from the WWF to form a new tag team in WCW with Shane Douglas. In response, WWF was looking to retaliate, and had sent feelers to Pillman to gauge his interest in jumping ship. Before things got too far in that direction, WCW made a big pitch directly to Brian.

Frye was a big believer in Pillman and saw keeping him as a major priority. In his early impressions on the business, Frye was a fan of the light heavyweight division and the possibilities it presented, and saw how valuable Brian could be as the linchpin. Beyond that, he felt that as good as Pillman already was, at 29-years-old his prime was still ahead of him. Thinking long term, he perceived Brian as a future top guy and had no intention of losing him. Almost to make a statement about how serious he was, Kip made an offer of a two-year deal for $200,000 for the first year and $225,000 for the second, guaranteed. Additionally, incentives would be built in so that as Brian progressed and got close to main-eventing the major shows, he could make as much as $75,000 more.

After over two years of seeing the company struggle, Brian knew how good the offer was and took it while he could. The WWF wasn't in the habit of offering guaranteed money, hoping that wrestlers would flock to them for the greater fame and potential high earnings if they caught on with the crowd. With WCW figuring him to be valuable enough to put that type of offer on the table, surely, he thought, they'd be doing their best to get a return on their investment. It seemed illogical to do anything but stay – the deal was almost too good to be true.

Concern still lingered about his back, and a trip to the doctor the week of Superbrawl saw Brian get the thumbs down for wrestling at the pay-per-view.

But listening to medical advice hadn't been Pillman's way for a long time. With the chance to steal the show with Liger in his fingertips in front of a new regime that he felt believed in him, he drove up to the Mecca in Milwaukee bound and determined to work. Thankfully, Liger's ribs had healed enough that he too could perform at the level he was capable of.

Superbrawl II hit the air as Pillman stood behind the curtain. Finally, a true chance to shine that was all his. As the first match on the show, both men would have an eager Milwaukee crowd to work in front of, and much like their first match back in Sumo Hall, they opted to start fast.

Liger quickly escaped a wristlock by rolling and flipping out of it, as the two light heavyweights hit the ropes, traded leapfrogs, and both went for a dropkick at the same time. The early stand-off earned an excited round of applause, the audience rising with a Pillman headscissors and Liger moonsault within the first minutes. Knocking Brian to the floor with a leg lariat, Liger ran off the ropes to execute a dive, but as Pillman moved out of the way, Jushin hit a handstand against the ropes, rebounding to his feet and doing a back handspring, coolly and calmly daring Pillman back in. At last, the style many had envisioned when the division was announced was on full display, and Liger whipped up the crowd further, their spirited enthusiasm growing.

The match temporarily went to the ground, with Jushin kicking at Brian's knee, looking to apply an upside-down surfboard and settling for a figure four leglock. While in the hold, a dose of intensity was added. Pillman fired a hard slap to the face of Liger which was quickly returned by the Tokyo native, the two exchanging strikes as the crowd began shouting "U-S-A!" to encourage the Cincinnati kid.

After a flying headscissors from Pillman, Liger tipped Brian over the top rope. He then climbed the turnbuckles and hit a breathtaking somersault dive all the way to the floor, awe rattling through the Milwaukee Theatre as they fell to the ground. Brian responded with his springboard clothesline, then suplexed Liger from the apron to the arena floor. This was no regular opener, and it certainly was a long way from the preliminary match aura that had surrounded the championship on previous pay-per-views. Not one prone to hyperbole since his credibility was important to him, Jesse Ventura offered the perfect soundbite on commentary, saying, "This is the greatest aerial match I've ever seen in my career."

Pillman hit his own big dive, a crossbody from the top turnbuckle to the floor, but was quickly foiled when he tried a similar attack off the ring apron, crashing throat-first on the barricade. The continued swings in momentum were captivating, as Liger jumped off the top rope only to be caught by a dropkick. Brian went for a top rope dropkick, only to be met in mid-air by Liger throwing his own with both men catching nothing but air, a favorite Pillman big-match spot.

The two went into the home stretch with big moves that would typically be seen as finishers to the American audience in 1992. Pillman's top rope crossbody, a powerbomb by Liger, a DDT from Brian, a superplex from Jushin, all garnering a two count with each one closer than the last, the crowd in a veritable frenzy as the match reached its apex. In the end, Liger went for his top rope headbutt, but missed. Brian hooked his feet under Liger's arms, rolled him onto his shoulders and executed a Backlund bridge for the victory.

The bout was an unmitigated success, earning a standing ovation from the crowd. In recognition, Frye issued $2,500 bonuses to both Pillman and Liger, and the revolutionary match was the talk of the business. In the 1992 Observer Reader awards, it was the highest voted North American bout for Match of the Year honors. So pleased were the company with the reaction to both men that the idea was discussed for the two to form a tag team upon Liger's return to WCW later in the year.

A steeper price may have been paid by Pillman for working against doctor's orders, however. In the process of putting on an instant classic, he aggravated his injuries and ended up being extremely limited in what he could do for the next two months. He worked his way through matches for television shortly after Superbrawl, but the pain was chronic and he was forced to ride the bench for a few weeks.

In his absence from action, Brian found another way to contribute to the promotion in a way that spoke to one of Kip Frye's newest and most newsworthy agendas. In 1991, the WWF had come under fire for their involvement with Dr. George Zahorian, who was convicted of illegally distributing steroids to their wrestlers. Among the names scheduled to testify at the trial was the biggest star in the industry, Terry "Hulk Hogan" Bollea, before a plea to the judge removed his name from the line-up. With the media on the chase, Hogan appeared on the Arsenio Hall show to "clear the air" regarding his history with steroids. Instead of taking the high road and squashing the story, Bollea proceeded to lie to the nation in a misguided act of self-preservation. Claiming he'd only used steroids three times to repair an injury, Hogan painted an even bigger target on himself and the WWF.

The bad press and scandals continued, while WCW got off relatively clean due to their mainstream irrelevance. Sensing the need to be proactive amidst the heat, Frye drafted a steroid policy for WCW, one that included a 10% salary bonus for wrestlers who voluntarily complied and offered themselves for testing. After the problems Brian had with steroids in the past (he blamed his Bengals hamstring tear and Stampede tricep tear on his use) and knowing the difference they made in others stationed ahead of him, he hated them. Pillman immediately supported Frye's approach, seeing himself as an obvious beneficiary of a crackdown on the drug. A general downturn in the size of the average wrestler could potentially translate to the "you're too small" criticism being a thing of the past, and Brian was all too happy to contribute. Several WCW wrestlers did public service announcements to air on television, and Pillman's thirty second warning was played frequently.

"It's decision time for all you young athletes", began Brian. "Take steroids or not to take 'em. Well let me tell you something, I talk from experience. I've seen throughout my career what steroids can do. I've seen the record bench presses. But unfortunately, I've seen the injuries, I've seen the illnesses, and I've seen the heartbreak and despair when a young athlete and his family have to go through a career ending suspension thanks to steroids. Make the right decision – don't do steroids."

With his back bothering him, it was difficult to capitalize on any momentum Brian was able to gather from the match with Liger. Tom Zenk was named as Pillman's challenger for the upcoming WrestleWar show on May 17th, and an angle was filmed to air 24 hours before the pay-per-view to ramp up last minute interest. The conflict with Zenk flirted with the idea of Brian as a heel, speaking to the general lack of direction for Pillman from booker Dusty Rhodes. Without a follow-up planned, there was no depth or meaning other than creating false drama for an undercard match.

Pillman continued to take it easy, only wrestling once in May before WrestleWar to heal up. In the interim, Brian started hanging out with Scotty Flamingo, a newcomer to WCW that would later go on to greater fame as Raven. Flamingo was earmarked to work with Brian in the near future, and with their similar personalities and lifestyles they quickly formed a friendship. "He just loved having a good time", remembers Raven. "He was a man's man in every sense of the term. He was tough, he was athletic, he was good looking. He was the guy that every girl wanted to sleep with and every guy wanted to hang out with, which is why he was such an over babyface. The definition of a babyface in the old timer days was exactly that, it's what bookers used to say. But he was *exactly* that."

As the two began hanging out, there was an incident in an Atlanta club that showed Flamingo that there was more to Pillman than met the eye. "One day I got in a fight with three guys", begins Raven, "And so I didn't win, it was three guys. Two guys were 275 and the one guy that started it was my size. Luckily, they didn't do any damage because I covered up. I went back to the club with Brian one day and I remember I was in the bathroom peeing, and the guy who started it was peeing next to me. And he says, 'Hey! How's it going?' I'm like, 'You motherfucker'. He knew I was going to beat his ass because he didn't have his two buddies around. He hurried up and jumped out before I finished."

Looking for revenge and a fair fight, Raven approached Brian and asked him to watch his back in case the guy's friends tried to get involved. Pillman's answer, however, caught Raven by surprise.

"Brian just goes, 'No'", he details. "I go, 'Whaddya mean, no?' And he says to me, 'You're trying to earn your spot at WCW. You get in a big fight, it's gonna get out and you're probably going to ruin your shot. So what's more important - your career or the fight?'"

Caught off-guard, Raven saw sense and agreed to let the grudge simmer. "I really respected that. It's not what I expected, but it was more valuable. Because Atlanta's a small town, even though it's a big city. Everybody's business was everybody's business. It showed his intelligence, it showed his grace and his poise, and it showed his friendship. Because let's face it, nobody wants to go get in a fight. Well, some people do, but most people don't. Brian's certainly not going to back down from a fight, but I totally think he made the right call looking back. I knew at the moment it was the right thing, but then, for like a week, you question your judgement. Was it really the right thing? Of course it was the right thing. If I told you that story but didn't tell you the answer, you would have thought that he backed me up in the fight, right? But no, it goes the exact opposite way, but it goes the right way. So, we just went out and did more drugs."

During this period there were more internal changes within WCW, ones that would rock it to its very core. Back in April, WCW President Jack Petrik had been removed from his position and replaced by Bill Shaw and Bob Dhue. The new figureheads immediately began looking for a long-term leader to replace Kip Frey, and at the beginning of May, got their man.

11 - NEW SHERIFF, OLD STORY

It was Tuesday morning, May 12th, to be exact. The usual 11am executive committee meeting was about to take place, as Kip Frye, Jim Ross, Bill Shaw, Bob Dhue, Jim Barnett, Dusty Rhodes, David Crockett, Magnum TA, Sharon Sidello and Keith Mitchell all piled in to a TBS conference room. There, rather than the usual discussion on strategy and approach, they were introduced to the new Vice President of Wrestling Operations - "Cowboy" Bill Watts.

Watts, a former wrestler who had successful runs in Florida, San Francisco, St. Louis and New York, had more relevance as the promoter of Mid-South Wrestling (later the UWF). Based mainly out of Oklahoma, Mississippi, Louisiana and Arkansas, Watts had a sterling reputation when it came to producing top-notch wrestling television. With intriguing angles, well promoted personalities and tremendous conflicts in front of red-hot crowds, Mid-South was considered the cream of the crop as it pertained to dramatic action. Watts' territory was on fire in the early eighties on the back of pushing Junkyard Dog as the top star, peaking in 1984 with an influx of new talent. Even with the concentrated region he worked in, the Cowboy was able to pack twenty to thirty thousand fans into the New Orleans Superdome for his biggest shows.

The biggest criticism of WCW since the Turner purchase was that they'd never had anybody at the top of the food chain who was a "wrestling guy". Jim Herd and Kip Frey had never been responsible for promoting in a way to draw money like Watts had, and didn't have the understanding of what worked. Watts had a track record. He was also well known for being a bully and a dictator, demanding a lot out of his talent and insisting on things being done his way.

The potential clash between the corporate culture of TBS and generally uncouth Cowboy was interesting to say the least. Watts had been interviewed by Jack Petrik to work under Herd in 1989, but both came away from the meeting thinking it was a bad idea. In the three years since, a lot of money had been lost, which did an awful lot to change perspectives. Bill Shaw and Bob Dhue, in meeting with Watts, had focused on WCW's awful financial situation and stressed that the primary objective was to get the bottom line looking better, no matter what. In an interview with the Pro Wrestling Torch newsletter shortly after his assignment, the Cowboy had put it bluntly – "This son of a bitch is in worse shape than I thought."

Watts was paid $7,000 per week to replace Frye, overlooking Dusty Rhodes who stayed in the position of booker. The final say on Dusty's booking now went to Watts, and the company waited in anticipation at the changes he'd bring. Pillman, however, was given a heads-up as to what he should expect.

"The day after Watts got the job, I was on the phone with Watts for 2 hours", Dave Meltzer recalls. "And it was not a conversation, I probably got five words in in two hours, Watts was just going on and on and on. I'm listening to Bill and I had never thought of this; how much wrestling changed, because when you're watching every week it's gradual to you. But when I'm listening to Bill and what he's talking about it, it was like, 'Oh my God, wrestling has changed so much in five years, talent and everything'. I got off the phone with Bill and the first thing I did was call Brian."

Initially excited by Watts' appointment, Meltzer relayed the details of the call with a more accurate assessment. "After that conversation I go, 'Oh my God Brian, this is not what I expected it to be. He ain't gonna turn this thing around'."

With another regime change in full swing, the roster turned up to impress at WrestleWar on May 17th. The main event, a War Games match pitting Paul E. Dangerously's "Dangerous Alliance" of Rick Rude, Steve Austin, Arn Anderson, Bobby Eaton and Larry Zybysko against Sting, Nikita Koloff, Dustin Rhodes, Barry Windham and Ricky Steamboat was a bona fide classic. Underneath, Pillman and Zenk outperformed expectations, mixing up matwork and highspots in a way that brought the crowd out of their seats on several near falls. Pillman was given the victory and looked like he'd not missed a beat following the injury, incorporating a lot of the spots that worked with Jushin Liger at Superbrawl and tweaking them slightly to suit the larger Zenk. The size difference made for a good dynamic, though it did lead to a heated exchange on commentary between Jim Ross and Jesse Ventura, perfectly summarizing the cynical nature of Brian Pillman in a big man's world.

Ross: "The year Pillman was a second team All-American at nose tackle…"

Ventura: "Nose tackle?"

Ross: "The first team All-American was William Perry, the Refridgerator. Pillman was second team All-American…"

Ventura: *"Nose tackle!?* Now wait a minute…"

Ross: "I know they don't play football much up in Minnesota, Jess, the guy that plays over the center defensively."

Ventura: "That's exactly what I'm questioning, Jim Ross. Up in Minnesota our nose tackles usually weigh 250."

Ross: "Pillman weighed about 245 at the time, but he's down to his best wrestling weight…"

Ventura: *"Nose tackle!?* Wasn't Ron Simmons a nose tackle?"

Ross: "Yes he was."

Ventura: "Well, there's your more traditional nose tackle in my opinion."

Seeing that trying to use Brian's background in football was a lost cause, Ross dropped the issue and went back to calling the action. Hearing the doubt over his size always riled Brian since he'd heard it forever, and it wasn't the first time Ventura had been flippant on commentary towards the division. On television, Jesse had once said, "It gives guys with the short man's complex a chance to wrestle instead of walking around with a grudge all the time because they're short." Certainly, WCW weren't about to win any awards for their presentation of talent.

It could have caused concern for Pillman knowing Watts was in charge. Though Bill had success promoting the Rock and Roll Express and Midnight Express as top acts in 1984, Watts' bread and butter was in backing the large, thick-set, barrel-chested types that physically resembled a young version of himself.

It didn't take the Cowboy long to make broad changes to WCW. When the day arrived for Bill Watts to run his first television taping on June 1st, he released a set of rules that the locker room was expected to obey going forward. The new laws became known as the Cowboy's Ten Commandments.

1. Wrestling outside the ring is discouraged.
2. If you do wrestle outside the ring, use of the ring posts or crowd barricades is strictly forbidden, and will result in the referee calling a disqualification if it occurs.
3. Talking on the microphone on shows is prohibited unless specifically instructed. In addition, lewd hand gestures or audible foul language is banned.
4. Low blows are outlawed. If one is performed, the offender will be subject to a fine. On the same note, the wrestler receiving a low blow is expected not to sell it as such.
5. Wrestlers must be at the building one hour before the start of the show, or be subject to a fine.
6. The babyfaces are no longer allowed to publically or socially associate with the heels. They may not travel together, eat together, train together, or make public appearances together.
7. Injured wrestlers will still make their scheduled appearances so as not to false advertise. The only exception is if the injury makes them medically unable to travel.
8. Missing a scheduled appearance is considered a breach of contract, unless it has been prevented by an act of God.
9. Wrestlers will be given a maximum of two comp tickets each. Any other friends or family beyond the two comps will have to pay for admission.
10. No family or friends may enter the backstage area.

Watts also insisted that wrestlers stay until the end of every show and study the matches. He rehired everybody's least favorite curmudgeon Ole Anderson to be an on-screen referee and off-screen road manager. Obviously seeking to institute a greater sense of discipline, Watts placed Ole in charge of handling fines for disobeying his doctrine.

Wanting to create a greater element of danger to the show, Bill removed the mats from around the ring that would typically protect a wrestler on landings and moves to the floor. He was also darkened the arena lights so as not to show the crowd during matches, feeling it was more of a distraction than a benefit. The aesthetic standard of major league wrestling was the WWF. While the argument could be made that Watts had come in to cut costs and was only serving his masters, it downgraded the vibe of WCW shows when it was so easily compared to the slick production of Vince McMahon. Most controversially of all, Watts declared that moves off the top rope were now banned, cause for an immediate disqualification.

Watts had a method behind the move. He believed that top rope moves had become so commonplace that they were no longer seen as dangerous by the fans. By making them illegal, it would add an aspect of suspense when it would happen in carefully chosen moments. But regardless of the psychology and logic behind the decision, to the fans it was eliminating one of the most exciting elements of modern wrestling. With a light heavyweight division that needed the unique moves to stand out of the pack, it certainly did them no favors to subject them to the same law and remove one of their selling points.

To demonstrate the rule Watts wasted no time, using it in a match taped on June 2nd to air after the upcoming Beach Blast pay-per-view. During a six-man tag with Pillman, Badd and Zenk against Morton, Tracy Smothers and Sgt. Buddy Lee Parker, Flyin' Brian was chosen to come off the top rope with a clothesline to Tracy. The troubleshooting referee, Ole Anderson, disqualified Brian. Given that WCW was the only company in the world that felt top rope moves were too risky, it was hard to see the decision as anything but poor judgement.

Even if the concept was a winner, the execution guaranteed failure. WCW and the National Wrestling Alliance were working together to crown new NWA Tag Team Champions, and ran a tournament featuring teams from all over the world competing on WCW events. After an initial backlash to the ban, it was decided that the tournament matches would be held under "NWA rules" and allow talent to take to the top rope. Right as it was supposed to be established that the moves were prohibited, WCW promoted matches that showcased how asinine it was.

The first round of the tournament took place at Clash of the Champions 19 on June 16th, and Pillman was teamed with Jushin Liger to go against two men they'd worked with years back in Stampede – Chris Benoit and Biff Wellington.

The match was a tour de force, with everybody throwing caution to the wind to have the best match on the show. With no mats around ringside, Liger still hit his Asai moonsault on Benoit and a crossbody from the top to the arena floor on Wellington. Brian hit an exhilarating belly-to-back superplex that turned Benoit inside out, the crowd coming out of their seats for the incredible offense on both sides. Finally, Liger hit a moonsault from the top on Wellington to score the pin, the fans erupting despite Benoit and Wellington being complete unknowns, thrown out with no hype or promotional build, a great achievement.

Days later at Beach Blast, Pillman lost the WCW Light Heavyweight title to Scotty Flamingo in another quality bout. Positioned as the opener, the pattern of good Pillman matches taking place in front of hot crowds continued, but the idea to put the belt on Flamingo was a surprise. Furthermore, the finish was booked for Brian to lose totally clean, even after Flamingo protested to Dusty, preferring a win shrouded in controversy. "What a horrendous finish", Raven remembers. "A really bad idea because I didn't cheat. I'm a heel, I should have heeled the win!" Pillman still lost in dramatic fashion, leaping over the top rope to the outside at Scotty, who sidestepped, causing Brian to land face-first on the wooden ramp. Although handcuffed with the inability to use the top rope, Pillman and Flamingo delivered big.

As it turned out, the Scotty Flamingo reign was a short-lived stopgap, as he ended up losing it a couple of weeks later to Brad Armstrong. Armstrong, a perennial undercard wrestler, wasn't given anywhere near the appropriate build for such a win, and did more to underscore the title as a low-level championship. For Pillman, it was clear that the loss to Flamingo was ultimately to replace him in *his* spot with Armstrong, who Watts had booked previously and supported. In the UWF, Brad had been given the North American Heavyweight Title by Cowboy Bill, and it was expected that the division was going to be built around him, not Brian, or even Liger.

The reversal in fortunes for Pillman following Beach Blast was both drastic and startling, losing regularly on television. Further emphasizing their place on the totem pole, Pillman and Liger lost to Ricky Steamboat and Nikita Koloff in an underrated match at the Great American Bash 1992, eliminating them from the NWA Tag Team title tournament. At house shows, Pillman found himself losing to the likes of Dan Spivey, Dick Slater, Super Invader, Barbarian and Greg Valentine. By this point in his career, Brian knew the pattern and was readily aware of what was happening. His value was being intentionally sabotaged.

Meanwhile, cuts were being made to the roster in line with Watts' goal of balancing the budget. Terry Taylor's $156,000 per year deal was dropped. The Freebirds were offered lump sums to scrap their existing contracts altogether. Talk began circulating around the locker room that the Cowboy was targeting the guaranteed deals, which he'd been openly opposed to upon his arrival feeling it bred laziness. Ironically, Watts was one of the first promoters to offer guarantees in the waning days of the UWF, an effort to prevent talent from jumping to the WWF. The initiative to target them now sent a message – it was more important to Shaw, Dhue and Watts to save money than it was to keep and cultivate a great roster capable of taking on McMahon's empire. Once Watts had killed the guarantees, he planned to institute flat fees and nightly deals without so much as a guaranteed number of dates. To everyone who'd been in WCW for any length of time, it was the reign of Ole Anderson all over again.

The news, combined with the effects of Bill's commandments, led to morale plummeting. With his position on the card falling, Pillman was subsequently being denied his incentive bonuses. "Watts just came in and crapped on all of us", recalls Raven. "Brian was disgruntled because he wanted the money and he knew how much more talented he was than like, Lex Luger. He always used to complain about Luger, and getting Luger money. For some reason he focused on Lex. I guess it was because Luger really wasn't the greatest worker but he was the biggest moneymaker, and Brian felt like they'd given Luger a million shots to be the top guy but he never came through. Brian had everything Luger had, *and* he was athletic *and* he could work, but he couldn't get his spot. Luger was his Moby Dick, I guess, in many ways."

Pillman developed a dislike for Watts early. The booking treatment was one thing, but Bill had way too many of the obnoxious traits that Brian had dealt with for years from big guys that looked at him condescendingly. It became tough to discern where legitimately founded worry ended and paranoia began, but there was certainly an expectation that a showdown was forthcoming with Watts and his locker room.

Brian did receive a brief distraction in August when Kim Wood sent him a loose-leaf copy of Lou Thesz's upcoming autobiography, titled *Hooker*. Though there were few books published on pro wrestling at the time, Pillman was a veracious reader of anything he could get his hands on. He'd previously poured through *Fall Guys: The Barnums of Bounce*, the 1937 book by Marcus Griffin that attempted to uncover the secrets of the business. Brian was fascinated by the history of wrestling and was eager to read Lou's work.

Thesz, widely considered among the more legendary wrestlers of all time, filled the pages with anecdotes and tales from his incredible career, a run that saw him hold the NWA World Heavyweight Title for a combined total of ten plus years. Thesz was proud of his image as the ultimate tough guy, and Pillman devoured the book in the space of a weekend, making annotations throughout and committing it to memory. Looking to substantiate some of the stories in the book he felt he saw through, Brian got on the phone to the man he deemed the ultimate authority, Stu Hart, and read him the passages for a second opinion. When Stu confirmed the inaccuracies, Pillman boldly sought out Lou. "Pillman would call Thesz up and get into some verbal piss fights with him", says Kim Wood. "It ended up that Lou Thesz was pissed at Brian for being an asshole, for being a wise guy."

On screen, Pillman was on a collision course with Brad Armstrong for the Light Heavyweight Title at Clash of the Champions 20. A spanner was thrown in the works, as Armstrong had gone on tour with New Japan shortly after winning the title and blew out his knee. Instead, as Clash 20 hit the air on September 2nd, Bill Watts announced that due to the injury Armstrong was being stripped of the WCW Light Heavyweight Title and his match with Pillman was off. Furthermore, a new champion would be crowned in a tournament held at a later, unspecified date.

A follow-up interview segment would take place later in the evening that marked a significant milestone in Brian's career. For the first time since he entered the business, Pillman was going to get a chance to have a run as a heel.

As Jesse Ventura talked to Brad Armstrong about being stripped of the title, Brad expressed his disappointment. Armstrong talked about how he felt he'd let his family down on such a big occasion (Brad came from a wrestling family, with his father Bob raising four sons in the business). Suddenly, a sharply dressed Brian Pillman sauntered onto the scene, his demeanor noticeably different. As Ventura asked why Brian had joined them, he launched into a verbal assault the likes of which he'd never had a chance to unleash before.

"You know Jess, the more I think about it", he started, "The more I realize what a total disgrace this whole situation is. Tonight, millions of my fans were supposed to witness me regaining the world light heavyweight title. Rejoice in my victory, but *nooo*! We've gotta stand here and watch our former world champion hobble out here like some broken down, pathetic piece of garbage and announce to the world, 'I'm scared, I'm a coward, my knee hurts...'" Brian's words dripped with sarcasm, his delivery instantly drawing boos. Jesse interrupted to add, "But Brian, the man's hurt. The doctor says he can't wrestle."

Undeterred, Pillman continued. "Yeah, you know who else is hurt? Your daddy's hurt. Because your poor father is sitting up in the VIP room right now, hanging his head in shame because his son has no guts." After Brad made an appeal to Brian's better sense of judgement, Pillman added the exclamation point. "You make me sick, Brad. To sit here and watch a gutless coward like you? I don't know what to say. Frankly, I'm quite embarrassed for you. You're scum, just to look at you makes me wanna puke!" With that, Pillman slapped Armstrong across the face and stormed off the set. The turn was complete.

The move was done without any real planning and in the context of Brian's run, really didn't make any sense. After the recent stretch of losses, alienating his fan base without a build-up only served to cool him off further. The great irony was that it was easy to see from the beginning that it was a completely natural fit. Though he hadn't explored every possibility as a babyface and few people would have chosen to execute the turn in this manner, it was clear that Pillman was born to be a heel. As Brian would find out, it wasn't a decision born out of creative thinking. None of the recent calls regarding him were.

Very early into Watts' run, Bill looked at the existing contracts to identify the most exorbitant, and among the ones he found most appalling was Brian's. To the Cowboy, who had readily and almost proudly declared that he hadn't followed the business since he'd previously gotten out in 1987, Pillman was just a lower card wrestler making far too much money. Bill felt it was an outrageous sum to promise somebody relative to Brian's size and spot, based on the pure dollars and cents that WCW was (or wasn't) bringing in at the time. Rather than see the deal as an investment in Brian's and WCW's collective future, he wanted to find any way he could to cut the figure and bring him and his contract back down to earth. The constant losses and abrupt heel turn were calculated moves to lower Brian's stock and momentum. Strategically, mere days after Brian was turned, he was called to a meeting with Watts.

Bill had a proposal. He made no bones about the fact he thought Brian's guarantee was ridiculous and had an extra bone to pick with the incentives.

Watts told Pillman that he was at a point in his career (after being freshly turned heel) where it could go either way for him – it could go up, or it could go down. Much like he did to the Freebirds, Bill offered Brian an upfront sum of cash, this time in exchange for dropping the incentives from his contract. Watts also wanted to cut his guarantee down to $156,000 per year. The amount Pillman would get would be far below what he was giving up. Watts explained that since it would cost WCW money to push Brian, it currently made no business sense to do so. But, Bill vowed, if he dropped the incentives and lowered his salary, Pillman would get a push in return. The alternative, Watts said, was that Brian could keep his current deal and be made meaningless for the duration of the contract.

It was a horrible position to be put in, and Brian left the meeting disgusted with the tone of the ultimatum. The nature of the offer got around the locker room quickly and became the hot topic of the week. Some wrestlers even urged Brian to cave to Bill's demands. Others told him not to, partly due to the fear that if Brian backed down it would set a bad precedent for the rest of them.

The same week, Rick Rude was also given a similar offer for a restructure. Watts presented Rude a lump sum amount to cancel his current guarantee (which clocked in close to $400,000), and instead work for a flat $1,000 per show. Rude shot it down quickly. When asked about the delicacy with which the two situations were handled, Watts told Pro Wrestling Torch, "The only place people are created equal is in the constitution. Not in life or in business. Everybody's not the same. Pillman's not a Rick Rude. Pillman's not a Sting…Business is not a democracy. People are a commodity and they have value…We've got a lot of guys. Brian Pillman is a fine young athlete, but he's not a proven commodity in any way, shape or form as far as drawing money."

Bill continued, speaking flippantly to Brian's place in WCW. "If Brian Pillman is with this organization or not with this organization, it's not going to mean a hill of beans." It was this tone that Pillman couldn't stand, and he wasn't about to let it defeat him.

"Brian just said that it was ridiculous, which it was", remembers Mark Madden, a Torch columnist at the time whom Brian had recently befriended. "People praise Bill Watts, and there's no doubt he was a creative genius when it comes to wrestling, but he was a bully of the worst kind. If you take over a wrestling company you take over the contracts too, and that's just such a cheap way of doing business to say, 'If you don't take a pay cut I'm going to bury you'. 'Okay, well then bury me. Fuck you, I signed a contract and you have to live with it'. There was some consternation between Brian and Watts with that, and you're not going to bully Brian."

While those encouraging Brian to play ball felt that taking the cut was a wise move long-term (with a push, Pillman's value may be greater when it came time for renewal; without it he was taking two years of good money but the jury is out from there), eliminating the guarantee in favor of a gamble is a preposterous notion. "Say you take the pay cut right?", asks Madden. "There's no guarantee he's gonna' push you then. Or maybe he pushes you for a month and it's not working in his mind, so he gets rid of you then."

Besides, it was the principle of the entire situation, being publicly backed into a corner by someone with such little regard for his talents, that galled Pillman the most. "Really that whole thing with Watts exposed Watts on what his priorities were", details Madden. "Because again, you hear about what a genius this guy was with talent, but he was willing to intentionally bury quality talent to try and bully them out of money. Now what kind of wrestling booker does that?"

On Friday, September 11th, Brian Pillman approached Bill Watts at a house show in Chicago and informed him that he was turning down his offer and keeping his current contract. Living up to his promise, Watts ordered Brian to lose to Brad Armstrong that night and for the rest of the week's events. Pillman began joking to the locker room that he was happy to be the highest paid job guy in wrestling history.

"He was one of the guys where, if he could have made Lex Luger money, but as a jobber, he would have done it", says Raven, who goes on to explain the mentality most wrestlers have and how Pillman was the absolute wrong guy for Bill to pull such a move on. "Everybody in the business says that, but most people wouldn't, let's face it. They'd rather have the Luger push. Like now, would you rather have the Randy Orton spot, or the Orton money but be a piece of crap on the card? To me, I never wanted to be a piece of crap on the card because it's no fun. I always wanted to be high on the card because you had more fun, you had more freedom, more creativity. The point is, you talk to a hundred wrestlers and say, 'We'll give you $5,000 a week but you have to get jobbed out on TV like a piece of crap, or we'll pay you $3,000 but you're in a good spot, I say 95% of the business would claim the one, but take the other. But Brian would take the money for sure."

The standoff generated a lot of debate, and on September 20th at the

Omni, Watts and Pillman met once again to talk over the situation and settled the issue with a handshake. The next day at the television taping, Brian was put over Brad Armstrong. On the surface, it seemed as if Brian had gone toe-to-toe with Watts and come out on the better end of it.

WCW continued on shaky ground under the leadership of the Cowboy. The average ratings for the programming were falling to record lows. Morale took another hit when Watts announced that all medical coverage was being removed, telling the Wrestling Observer that, "If they want insurance - they make enough money, they can get their own." WCW's workman compensation premium was more than $400,000, and it was an easy, seemingly guiltless cut for Watts to help his end game. Watts then fined six of his top wrestlers $1,000 for their work not being up to par, vague as that criticism was. In another decision that raised eyebrows, Bill's son Erik started on the road with WCW as a wrestler, honoring the truest tradition of wrestling's nepotistic nature.

Brian's immediate future was thrown another curveball when it was announced that the proposed tournament to crown a new Light Heavyweight Champion was postponed indefinitely. As it turned out, the tournament never saw the light of day, and the potentially revolutionary division that once had such promise went out with a whimper.

Feeling that Pillman was too small to get heat on his own, Watts had the idea to put Brian in a tag team. The person originally earmarked to be his partner was Chris Benoit, who had won a number of people over back at Clash of the Champions 19 and was getting rave reviews for his work everywhere he went. Benoit was scheduled to come in at the end of September, but his debut was pushed back due to his New Japan commitments. As a potential solution, an idea was kicked around for Pillman to form a team with "Stunning" Steve Austin under the management of Paul E. Dangerously.

Austin, who had come into WCW in 1991, was a sensational talent with an incredible engine between the ropes. After the demise of the Dangerous Alliance, Austin was at a career crossroads of his own, but his potential upside was obvious. Having not been sacrificed in a way many of his counterparts had been by negligent booking, the option to elevate him was very much available. Talk started to circulate that Austin would be paired with Harley Race (who was also managing top heel Big Van Vader at the time), be given a run with the United States title and groomed to be the next top heel. Suddenly, that plan was history and Steve was being put in a tag team.

Austin went to Dusty and Watts to see what had changed. Dusty spoke of the need for a new heel tandem, which didn't appeal to Steve's singles aspirations in the slightest. Austin was forthcoming with his feelings that the move was undercutting his potential, that he was being screwed with and wasn't happy. Rhodes explained that at the very least, the duo would be needed as a short-term fix. On that basis, Austin agreed to team with Pillman, but was unyielding in his objections to forming a regular combination thinking it was a lateral move at best. The fallout of Brian's showdown with Watts was fresh in everybody's mind, and being paired with Pillman could have meant bad things for Austin by association.

Besides, Brian wasn't the only one in the proposed unit that was currently in the doghouse. Much like Pillman, Paul E. Dangerously was immediately in the Cowboy's crosshairs due to negotiating his own big money contract with Kip Frye weeks before Watts arrived. Heyman had signed a two-year contract approaching $250,000 per year, registered as an employee rather than an independent contractor like the rest of the talent.

In his first weeks on the job whenever Watts would encounter Heyman, Bill would flippantly remark, "You make too much money for a manager." Paul was later told he'd need to renegotiate the figure or face being completely phased down and eventually out. Like Pillman, Paul stuck to the deal that was already on paper. Watts kept his promise, breaking up the Dangerous Alliance, feuding him with Madusa and taking him almost completely off television. Before long, he was gone from WCW. Alas, working with Brian wasn't to be just yet.

Austin and Pillman randomly appeared on television as a tandem to challenge WCW Tag Champions Dustin Rhodes and Barry Windham to a future match. Brian and Steve were merely bystanders to the story of a Windham heel turn, with Dustin accepting the challenge without consulting Windham first, creating on-air tension between the two.

Pillman went his own way for a singles match with Ricky Steamboat at Halloween Havoc in what was easily the best match on the show. The event, while a surprising financial success due to the build up to a match pitting Sting against Jake Roberts, was an artistic disaster, and to say Pillman and Steamboat stole the show would imply petty theft at best. The good buyrate for Halloween Havoc was clearly an anomaly as well. Business was so bad that when WCW went back to Cincinnati Gardens on October 23rd, they drew under 900 people to the 10,500 seat arena, even with large ads in local papers and sending Pillman to do a couple of local radio interviews.

With a heel team badly needed, and with Benoit still held up hammering out contract and visa issues, Shane Douglas turning down the spot and Austin so strongly rejecting the idea, Pillman was paired with Windham for a short time to go opposite the new champions, Ricky Steamboat and Shane Douglas.

Meanwhile, Austin was totally absent from the November Clash of the Champions and Starrcade, and was very audibly displeased with his position. Putting himself at risk even further, on a house show in Greensboro, North Carolina on December 13th, Austin refused to lose to the son of the Cowboy, Erik Watts. Erik had received an outrageously strong push out of the gate, beating the likes of Bobby Eaton and Arn Anderson with his STF finisher to the obvious displeasure of the die-hard fans. Though nobody had anything bad to say about Erik from a personal perspective, the transparent nature of his success bred a growing resentment in wrestlers and viewers alike. Austin took a stand, hoping it would lead to Dusty and Bill taking his concerns seriously.

It worked to a degree. The following morning at the television tapings, Austin met with Watts and Rhodes to discuss what happened the night before and to vent about what he felt was a lack of interest in using him in a prominent way. The United States title push he was originally promised for 1993 was scrapped, now earmarked for Rhodes' son, Dustin. With Austin turning down the pairing with Pillman he'd effectively removed himself from the picture. Rhodes again began to sell the team with Brian to Austin, and sensing that if nothing else, it would put him back in the game since there were no alternatives on the tag team front, Austin agreed to it. That night, Pillman and Austin taped matches to air in the new year.

To wrap up the team with Windham, Pillman tagged with him one last time against Steamboat and Douglas in a hot match at Starrcade at the end of 1992. With plans for Windham to move up the card, a backstage segment was taped for television where Barry introduced Pillman and Austin as a full-time team. As the two men spoke in the segment about creating an unbeatable machine, it was easy to think that the new tandem would be the latest in WCW's assembly line pairings, destined to be used and discarded to make way for the next one. Everything about the combination felt utterly makeshift on first impression.

It wouldn't take long for that to change.

12 - IT'S A GREAT DAY TO BE A BLOND

With little depth in the tag ranks, the first major match was right around the corner, as Pillman and Austin squared off against the champions, Steamboat and Douglas, at the Clash of the Champions on January 13th, 1993. The pre-taped matches spotlighting the new team were starting to air, and the respective work ethics and drive to succeed made the combination intriguing. It was the contest at the Clash, however, that revealed that the thrown together duo was more than just the sum of its parts, and getting to work with a premier performer like Steamboat and a hungry Shane Douglas was almost idyllic for the new team's inception.

With little to no build to "Stunning" Steve and "Flyin'" Brian as contenders, the crowd was almost cold to the encounter early on. Through hard work, a frenetic pace and some clever spots, the crowd got progressively louder, and by the end were biting hard on the final near fall, gasping as Douglas saved the titles with a last second kickout. With the design of the match being to begin the series rather than end it, it broke down into a disqualification finish with Austin blasting Douglas with a title belt and busting him open. Pillman came off the second rope with another belt shot to the bleeding face of Douglas, later whipping Steamboat with it when he covered his defenseless partner. The shots to the legendary "Dragon" earned Brian a tongue-lashing backstage, with Steamboat feeling Brian was more careless than he needed to be. Pillman apologized, saying he got caught up in the moment, and understandably so. The bout had offered a glimpse at the world of potential that a series between the two teams boasted, and Brian was excited at the possibilities.

"The one thing that struck me with them was that, almost immediately, they had a chemistry", says Shane Douglas. "That sometimes takes time to forge. When you first get put together in a tag team there's a learning curve for you to each learn each other's mannerisms and timing. With Brian and Steve, it was a matter of days, maybe a week. You could tell very quickly with both guys that their chemistry was tight."

For the next few weeks, Pillman and Austin rode together to the shows, and their personal chemistry blossomed almost as quickly as their in-ring synergy. Brian knew there was a spark and wanted to devote himself entirely to making the new project work. "As soon as they were told they were going to be put together, Brian's mind was just, 'tag team, tag team'. All he was coming up with was ideas for the team", recalls Dave Meltzer. "He wanted to watch tapes of Pat Patterson and Ray Stevens. Unfortunately, there were no tapes around, but he had heard about them and how good they were as The Blond Bombers."

On the road, Brian and Austin talked incessantly about how to refine the act and what they could do to turn the provisional plan into a top-level, big money pairing. They honed their skills at the live events throughout January and February, opposing Steamboat and Douglas on almost every show.

Both the enthusiasm for the feud and pride in their craft is perhaps best exemplified in a story Ricky Steamboat told years later about a Friday night house show at a high school in North Georgia. The Blonds were scheduled against Steamboat and Douglas in the final match of the sold-out show. In the middle of the event, an unexpected blizzard hit the area and by the time the pre-main event intermission came it was looking dangerously like everybody would be snowed in. WCW made the call to notify the fans about the ongoing storm during the break, but neglected to tell the wrestlers.

As the two teams took to the ring for the main event after intermission, they were floored to see less than twenty people sitting in the stands. The four men stood in total confusion until the referee smartened them up, alerting them that the entire crowd had left, afraid they'd have trouble getting home in the treacherous conditions. All except for the families that lived across the street, who decided to stay. Regardless, the two teams still wrestled hard for forty minutes in front of the miniscule crowd, determined to put on a great show and enjoy themselves.

A televised rematch of the Clash encounter took place at the end of January at the storyline request of the champions, a non-title encounter built as a grudge match. This time, it was Austin and Pillman coming out on top in another exciting effort. Jesse Ventura was quickly becoming a vocal supporter of the team on commentary, something he'd only do when he personally enjoyed watching a heel act flourish. The quality of the series was paying off, as the houses for cards headlined by the tag match were well above the monthly average for the company.

"We all followed Ricky's lead", reflects Shane Douglas when asked about the construction of the matches. "The thing I loved about working with Ricky was that he wanted input from all three of us. We all would have ideas and typically Brian, Steve and I would talk. Ricky had this sort of ritual he did. He'd get a cup of coffee, then he'd sort of meander around the dressing room and walk around the hallways of the building, then after 20-30 minutes he'd come over and talk about it. When the three of us would fire out an idea he didn't just automatically go with it, he would say, 'Well that won't work because…', and he'd explain the psychology and the reasoning. Then he'd say, 'What if we work that in here instead?' That's why all three of us liked working with Ricky so much. He's a fountain of knowledge of course, but he was also very accommodating to all three of us. It would have been very easy for Ricky to say, 'Hey guys, follow me'. But Steamboat was the one lone top-tier guy who was willing to have that openness with other guys to have input."

With momentum building, Pillman was desperate for the team to have a name and a look, recalling his prior experience co-creating Bad Company in Stampede. As Brian and Steve would spitball different ideas for finishing moves, jackets, tights and whatever else came to mind, Scotty Flamingo, who regularly rode with them, would offer suggestions of his own. Austin, originally from Edna, Texas, was always billed in WCW as being from Hollywood, California. Without ever committing all the way on a Tinseltown-based theme, "Stunning" Steve would sport a jacket that read "Lights, Camera, Action", and it was suggested to go further in that direction. Flamingo proposed the name "The Hollywood Blonds", used by Jerry Brown and Buddy Roberts in 1970 when they teamed up in NWA Tri-State, managed by Sir Oliver Humperdink. "I always liked that name", recalls Raven. "I just thought that was a cool name and they just ran with it." The moniker had been copied a couple of times after that, but never with the type of prominence or national stage that Pillman and Austin had to work on, and Brian liked it.

"Steve and I literally built the Hollywood Blonds from scratch", Brian would later tell Power Slam magazine. "We'd drive up and down the highways, thinking of what the gimmick should be, what our interviews should be like. You know, we came up with everything, and that's why we were so proud of it."

Though Austin was very smart and strong-minded, especially for his level of experience, it is fair to say that Brian was the leader of the team, to the point that Steve himself would later call Brian the "guiding force" of the unit. Pillman convinced the thrifty Austin to cough up for new boots, tights and jackets to give the combination a distinct look, and proposed they both wear matching gold chains around their neck in interviews.

The promos themselves went from standard heel antagonism to a more enjoyable, sarcasm-laden cockiness that really stood out on the otherwise sterile television show. Regularly referring to themselves as "The Team of the Nineties" and "The Big Blond Machine", Steve and Brian organically bounced off each other. At first, Austin would thoughtfully rub his jawline or hold his head high as Pillman spouted off at the mouth. Before long, their real-life comedic senses bled over and they'd be increasingly ambitious behind the microphone. "The thing that people don't remember is that Brian was the personality of that team", adds Dave Meltzer. "Steve had not yet come to grips with his personality. Obviously later he did, but I think Brian from a personality standpoint made the team."

As the unit was beginning to evolve, WCW was undergoing yet another change in leadership, as "Cowboy" Bill Watts officially resigned from his position on February 10th, 1993. Turner bigwig and all-time baseball great Hank Aaron had made a cameo for WCW back at Starrcade 1992, prompting Mark Madden to fax Aaron some racially insensitive comments Watts had made in the Torch the prior year. The Cowboy had his fill of the corporate TBS environment and was happy to go when asked to leave. To say the office employees and wrestlers were glad to see the back of Watts would be putting it mildly.

Any enthusiasm for Bill leaving his post was tempered by the news that Ole Anderson would be his replacement. Even more out of left field was for Eric Bischoff, an unproven third-string announcer at the time, to land the new position of Executive Producer of WCW Television, which would turn out to be the most prominent spot of all. At least the new regime would reap the benefits of Watts' last big move before his resignation – luring Ric Flair back to the promotion.

Setting aside the anarchy behind the scenes, WCW produced a fantastic pay-per-view show a few days later, Superbrawl III on February 21st. Following up on their progress as a duo, Pillman and Austin were given a win over Erik Watts (who was quickly moved down the card) and Marcus Bagwell to build them towards another match with the champions. With the matches pitting Brian and Steve against Douglas and Steamboat having lit up the house shows and the new heel team having caught on, the decision was made to go all the way with them.

On Worldwide, Pillman and Austin pleaded for one final match for the titles, billed as their last opportunity at the belts. The match, taped on March 3rd, was the best of all the televised encounters. After Douglas and Steamboat took the early advantage, the heels turned the tables with a trick they'd developed at the house shows that had gotten some serious heat. As Austin kicked out of an O'Connor roll sending Shane into the ropes, Brian was waiting with their new trademark – the terrible towel, which he wrapped around the throat of Douglas as the crowd came unglued. After several close escapes that brought the audience louder and louder, Douglas finally tagged in the Dragon, who delivered a classic comeback. After his finishing crossbody block from the top rope on Pillman, Steamboat made the cover, moving out of the way at the last second so that Austin's top rope elbow, meant for him, hit Pillman. The crowd exploded as Brian kicked out on two. The action continued, as the referee moved Douglas back into his corner, allowing Austin to hit Steamboat with one of the title belts. Pillman made the cover, and WCW had new tag team champions.

It was a moral victory for Brian, who had been fighting to maintain prominence for almost two years through bad booking, neglect, and the encounter with Watts. The next day at the television tapings the team was officially christened The Hollywood Blonds. Finally, after being given a half-baked idea as a tag team, the collective efforts of all four men had breathed new life into the scene and created a hot commodity that WCW could bank on for years to come.

∞

At this important point in Brian's career, his real life saw some drastic changes too. In typically theatrical fashion, Brian had seen a picture in Penthouse magazine of a stripper named Melanie Lawrence, and vowed to others that he was going to find her. As fate would have it, Lawrence was no stranger to the wrestling business and had dalliances with a few individuals in the industry already. Most notable among them was the Ultimate Warrior, Jim Hellwig, who had lived with Melanie in 1990 before the combustible relationship fell apart.

Born September 23rd, 1965 and originally from Lawrenceville, Georgia, Melanie was introduced to Brian through a mutual friend who was dating another wrestler, and the two quickly hooked up. Pillman was still with Rochelle at the time of their introduction, but things progressed at a breakneck pace. As daring and audacious as Brian was known to be, Melanie was similarly aggressive in going after what she wanted and it led to a fast-moving courtship. Unfortunately, it also led to heartbreak for Rochelle in the process.

"Melanie was pushing her way in, and Rochelle didn't fight it and just kind of let her", remembers Linda Pillman. "She wasn't that type of person, to stand up and fight for it. Melanie was a pushier and stronger personality than Rochelle was."

The brazen approach that Melanie took worked to win Brian over. Melanie was even so forward as to call the house and ask for Brian when Rochelle was the one answering the phone. With Rochelle's lifelong self-esteem issues, it wasn't in her nature to battle tooth and nail for Brian's heart. "She had a very low opinion of herself", elaborates Linda. "She was a beautiful girl, a real head-turner. But she didn't think she could compete with Melanie, and she was so much prettier and better than Melanie. Melanie just had that personality. She's just very bold. Whatever she wants, she goes for the throat." Rochelle was jilted by Brian, and was really never the same.

The topic of women is a complex one with Brian. Throughout his adult life, his preposterous tales of liaisons with the fairer sex were celebrated as a source of humor and revered in the locker room. "Remember Penthouse Magazine?", asks Kim Wood. "They'd have the Penthouse Letters, right? And you'd read them and know a couple of things. You'd know that the same guy wrote all these letters, and the second thing is that he made it all up. So what we would say was, well you're half right. Pillman wrote all the letters, but he actually did everything. And that was Brian."

"The boys loved it, they loved his stories", states Raven. "He was a showman, he was so popular. He was loved, people were jealous of him, they wanted to be like him. I'm telling you, he was a showman. He would have been a great P.T. Barnum."

Some friends say that part of Brian's womanizing came with an undercurrent of mistrust. After being burned in an early relationship and hurt emotionally, Pillman's approach to girls ever since was almost nonchalant. It was no secret that he had a propensity for getting with beautiful women on a regular basis, and in fact it was almost something of a psychological calling card. It has even been said that if a gorgeous girl was introduced to the business or to the wrestlers in general, Brian almost made it a point to be the first one to sleep with them. The flip side was that Brian was never particularly concerned with whatever emotional damage occured. Without him to explain the reasoning, those close to him imply that it was something he just didn't let bother him, since he'd previously been hurt himself and considered it part of the deal. Unfortunately, the indifferent mentality and recklessness would come with major ramifications in time.

By January, not long after they'd met, Melanie had become pregnant with Brian's child. Pillman then proposed at the Grand Canyon and the two officially married in a private ceremony on March 17th, 1993.

"They either got engaged or married way too quick", says Dave Meltzer. "Nothing against what happened, I just know it was a real quick thing. It was like, he was with Rochelle and then all of a sudden he's married to Melanie. It was just like, 'Whoa, okay'."

Like Brian, the new Mrs. Pillman brought two children from previous relationships, Alexis and Jesse, into the marriage. Conscious that he would be responsible for four children with a fifth on the way, Brian began reading finance books when on the road for WCW, looking for ways to invest wisely.

"Austin would drive, I'd sit in the passenger seat and Pillman would be in the backseat reading his power vocabulary books", remembers Raven. "He was a reader, he was so enamored of intelligence and proving his intelligence. He was always either reading power vocabulary books to improve his vocabulary, which he had a masterful vocabulary, or he was reading tax books on how to save money."

The three riding partners had developed a bond with their similar sense of humor, to the point that they nicknamed themselves 'The Comedy Trio'. Pillman already had a reputation for being the king of the locker room promo, breaking up the wrestlers with sensational diatribes. "Let's say somebody did something stupid", begins Raven. "He would cut three or four-minute promos off the top of his head obliterating whoever he was talking about, but so funny. And not necessarily mean. My favorite thing was he always dropped the F bomb, which he told me was his bridge. So it would be, 'You fuckin' stupid fuckin'…', and he put that in while he was compiling the promo in the back of his head. It's like when a wrestler goes, 'Let me tell you something' - that's them thinking of the next line they're going to say in a promo. But with Brian, it just made it funnier because it's such a funny word anyway."

Austin and Pillman would go to watch movies together looking for a bad joke, which was their cue to erupt in exaggerated, uproarious laughter as everybody else in the theater sat in confused silence. As they took turns looking to one-up each other, the laughter would grow so obnoxious and ludicrous that they would end up cracking for real. The appreciation for goofy humor saw the group grow to include Kevin Nash, Tex Slazenger, Shanghai Pierce and Mick Foley, and become a full-blown comedy league.

"We would break down comedy to its essence", says Raven. "It just kept building and building. Then we decided we were going to have a heavyweight champion. We made Nash the champion, but then we had to strip him of the title because he didn't wait for us to go into the Cobo Arena or something. We had contenders for the title, it was just ridiculous. Anything to occupy time, you know?"

Steve and Brian's nascent friendship led to the team becoming more creative on-screen. Pillman began bringing a director's clapperboard to the ring, while Austin would sometimes wear a camera around his neck. Both would taunt opponents by moving their hands as if turning the handle on an old film camera, pointing it at their fallen foe. They routinely talked of giving their opponents a "brush with greatness", and stuck with using the towel as a gimmick in matches to the point WCW even merchandized Blonds towels to sell at the arenas. So impressive was their ability to feel like a complete act that at the end of March, talk started to circulate that the tag champs would soon be working with the returning Ric Flair and Arn Anderson in a headline feud.

This isn't to indicate that all was perfect in the world of Brian Pillman. Though the career was going as well as it had in some time and he was enjoying married life with his new bride, Brian had a distressing scare in early 1993. A trip to the doctor had flagged that Brian's fast lifestyle and love of partying was catching up to him in a major way. After a full examination, the doctor diagnosed Brian as an alcoholic and warned that if he didn't stop drinking, he'd be dead within a few years. Hearing that, and with things going so well elsewhere, Pillman went cold turkey on the booze, at least for a while. When he and Austin hung out at a bar, Steve would be the only one drinking.

The matches with Douglas and Steamboat continued, with the two teams going to a 45-minute draw in the main event at the Atlanta Omni in front of 5,200 fans. The rivalry still had legs and the decision was made to prolong the series, this time with the babyfaces chasing. A new storyline was created, starting on an episode of Saturday Night, when Tony Schiavone conducted an interview with two suited men wearing lucha masks and sombreros. The team was accompanied by an interpreter who explained that they were "Los Dos Hombres", who had come to America with only $19 in their pocket, hoping to wrestle the Hollywood Blonds so that they could take a tape back to Mexico City and show they were worthy competitors. In the middle of the interview, Ricky Steamboat walked in and wished the new team the best of luck, but warned them not to trust the Blonds.

Later, Pillman and Austin came out and took the microphone. "It's a great day to be a Blond", started Brian, who went on to announce the start of the 'Brush With Greatness Tag Team Tournament'. They vowed to take on unknown stars from the best federations around the world, before Austin threw out a line foreshadowing upcoming events saying, "Someone once said, 'To be the man, you have to beat the man'", alluding to Ric Flair's famous phrase. "Well to be the team, you have to beat this team."

Austin continued, giving some background on tonight's opponents, "One of these wrestlers has a triple moonsault off the top rope that is cur-razy! He makes Jushin Liger look like he's moving in slow motion." The other, he said, was in demand all over Europe and a big name in Japan. They then introduced the illustrious duo – Sgt. Buddy Lee Parker and Joe Cruz.

After Pillman and Austin picked up the quick win with their "Atomic Blond" finisher, a double splash off the top rope, Tony Schiavone asked about Dos Hombres and the challenge was accepted. By this point, the Blonds were eager to get in as much shtick as they could, with Brian saying, "Speaking of Mexico and Tijuana, Tony, I know you did a little recruiting of talent yourself down there of the non-wrestling variety." As Schiavone blushed and turned away, Pillman followed up with, "Hey, don't sweat it – the charges were dropped, weren't they?"

From a personality perspective, both men were really starting to come into their own. "I had never really found myself as an entertainer", Brian told Power Slam magazine. "With the Blonds I was finally able to do that. I really found myself as an entertainer...as a heel."

Beyond that, the matches were red hot to boot. The same day, May 8th,

WCW Worldwide was headlined by the Blonds wrestling 2 Cold Scorpio and Marcus Alexander Bagwell to a noteworthy time limit draw that tore down the Municipal Auditorium. The combination of old school cheating and dirty tactics with hot action sequences was paying dividends, the crowd at a fever pitch as Scorpio tried to beat the champions before the final bell.

"I thought the Hollywood Blonds, my God, they could have got over as a tag team in any territory, in any time period", says Jim Cornette, speaking to how well-rounded the duo were. "I was actually a fan of watching their shit."

The next day on Main Event, the champions squared off in a non-title match with Dos Hombres. Clad in full body suits and doing a comedic hat dance, the new duo weren't taken too seriously as Pillman and Austin looked on bemused. The Blonds paid for their arrogance, promptly losing every single exchange, growing more and more frustrated with their inability to get the advantage. After a slingshot splash by the masked duo that looked remarkably familiar, Pillman rolled out the ring, screaming the obvious – "That's Ricky Steamboat and Shane Douglas!" Austin stood bewildered beside him, exclaiming, "That ain't no Dos Hombre!" The preposterous story was played to the hilt as the match continued. Finally, after one Hombre did a press-slam on his partner dropping him onto Pillman, another trademark of the former champions, the Blonds bailed up the aisle claiming the jig was up. Before they reached the curtain, however, Shane Douglas showed up casually dressed, sending the Blonds recoiling in disbelief. Austin and Pillman continued bumping for Dos Hombres in the ring as the show ended, with Schiavone screaming that we were suddenly out of time.

It was a fun angle, with Steamboat and Brad Armstrong being the two men under the hoods. As it turned out, it wouldn't be the only time somebody would fill in for Douglas. It was later announced that the Blonds would wrestle Shane and Steamboat inside a cage at Slamboree.

Before then, Pillman and Austin would appear on Ric Flair's talk show, called "A Flair For The Gold". Since returning in February, the "Nature Boy" had been doing live interview segments on house shows and television which weren't doing much to keep him hot. The production felt cheap, the audio was often lousy, and worst of all, Flair himself had little to say, cast as a babyface without a match to build.

Ric's return to the ring was impending, and the call was made for it to take place against the Blonds at the Clash of the Champions in July. Falling ratings for the TBS specials were a concern, and it was felt that Ric Flair's first match in WCW in two years, with the hottest new heels in town no less, was the answer. As the latest episode of the hokey talk show began, with Arn Anderson in the Ed McMahon role, Flair introduced the tag team champions as his guests.

Immediately, the Blonds began railing on the host with a barrage of age related gags. Austin flippantly referred to Flair as "old man" to get things rolling, before confusing Arn Anderson with an antique statue. Pillman asked for Flair's autograph on behalf of his great-grandmother and said that at Slamboree, which was also advertising a reunion of wrestling legends, "We're flying in all those has-been, washed up old timers, these so-called legends who have fallen on hard times, and we're going to bring a nice, hot, home cooked meal to them. And I've got to believe your right-hand man, old Double A, is gonna' be first in line at the buffet."

Flair and Anderson eventually rose to the insults, with the Blonds leaving the scene untouched. Watching the segment, Austin and Pillman felt like the future of the company and held their own in an angle designed to move them towards the top of the promotion. Before the feud was to get underway, there was the issue of the cage match at Slamboree and a minor problem that had cropped up in the prior week or two - one of the participants was no longer going to be there.

Shane Douglas had suffered a shoulder injury in April and had missed some dates. In a somewhat related issue, Douglas' contract was going through a renegotiation. Douglas later said he was being paid $350 per shot at the time, and after working with Austin, Pillman and Steamboat in a successful (by WCW standards) house show series, Shane was looking for a better deal to move him a touch closer to the level of the other three. Unfortunately for Shane he was having these negotiations with Ole Anderson, who was more than happy to keep Douglas on the same money. Whether the injury and upcoming Slamboree appearance were being used as part of the negotiation depends on perspective and opinion. Even if Shane didn't intend it, the WCW office was convinced it was part of the game. Ultimately, Douglas would not be wrestling on the pay-per-view and ended up leaving the company.

One week before Slamboree, Dos Hombres pinned the Blonds in a non-title match on Main Event. In a post-match interview, Steamboat took his mask off and said that he and "Shane", who didn't unmask for obvious reasons, would do it one more time in the cage. As it turned out, Steamboat and his partner came to the ring at the pay-per-view dressed in their Dos

Hombres outfits, with "The Dragon" claiming he and Shane were wearing the costumes for good luck given their prior success. Of course, it wasn't Douglas under the mask, it was Tom Zenk. The match itself was less heated than expected until a blistering final sequence, where Steamboat unmasked at the top of the steel structure and leapt off with a crossbody. The referee counted 2, but the timekeeper rang the bell. The screw-up added an energy that was largely missing from the show for the final minute, before Austin pinned the masked Zenk.

Elsewhere on the show, Ric Flair announced his return to the ring, promoting a match against Pillman and Austin in three weeks at the Clash of the Champions. With little time to build, a couple of quick angles were shot to heat things up, the highlight being when Brian and Steve were given a chance to unleash on the June 5th WCW Saturday Night. It was there that one of the most memorable skits of the year took place, a Blonds parody of Ric's talk show that they called "A Flare for the Old". As *Also Sprach Zarathustra*, the theme song of the "Nature Boy" began to play, Pillman hobbled out from behind the curtain on a walking cane, sporting a grey wig and hand-me-down robe. Accompanying him was a heavy-set redhead named "Par-tay", a take-off of Flair's maid Fifi. Pillman introduced "Stunning" Steve, leading to the two going back and forth, focusing on the age of the Horsemen. From Brian falling asleep to needing his medication halfway through ("Keeps the old pencil sharp", Pillman quipped), the two were wildly entertaining. An unimpressed Arn Anderson gatecrashed the scene, leading to Steve looking at Anderson with a mocking contempt and saying, "The last time I saw a body like that, it had an apple in its mouth and it was roasting over an open flame." The fight was on before Arn was outnumbered and Flair made the save.

The promos in the following weeks continued pushing the idea of the old versus the new, the eighties versus the nineties, the Horsemen versus the Blonds. To spotlight the classic theme of Flair's comeback, it was announced that the match would be two out of three falls, meaning the bout would likely get considerable time in addition to its headline position.

While the segments were good in isolation, it bears repeating that it was taking place in a promotion that was struggling more than ever. Things were looking bleak for WCW, with house show business bordering on disastrous. After April had drawn an average 1,520 fans per show, May plummeted to only 490. Shows in major cities like Philadelphia and Baltimore were doing the lowest attendances in company history. WCW only managed to pull 300 fans to the over-6,000 seat Pepsi Coliseum in Indianapolis, and one show in Alabama drew less than 100 people. Shows in the first week of June were continuing the low trend.

Television ratings the week before the all-important Clash were approaching record low levels, with the June 12th WCW Saturday Night barely managing a miserable 2.0, Main Event doing a 1.7 and Power Hour doing a 1.0. The overall product and presentation of the company was highly flawed, beside some of the talent on the roster or segments on the show.

So it was, as Clash of the Champions 23 hit the air on June 16th. The Norfolk Scope housed a little over 2,000 paying fans, with 4,000 more entering with free tickets on the night. As the main event prepared to go on, WCW once again proved their inability to create drama or execute the simplest of touches, as Ric Flair entered the ring to a generic Horsemen theme song, side-by-side with Arn, as opposed to drawing out the excitement of Flair's first match with his signature entrance.

Between the ropes, the match was a success, generating by far the most heat of anything on the show. The crowd seemed to want nothing but Flair all night long, and Ric was on fire playing the crafty veteran schooling the young punk upstarts to the delight of the fans. The Horsemen took the first fall. The match continued, with Flair putting the figure four leglock on Austin. Just as the belts looked to change hands, Barry Windham ran in for the disqualification giving the match to the Horseman, but keeping the belts with the Blonds on a technicality. The show ended with Flair and Windham brawling around ringside, and Austin and Pillman, who did a stellar job as stiff competition with an aura of overmatched cowardice, faded into the background. Notwithstanding the focus not being on them, the feeling when the show went to black was positive for the Blonds.

The rating came in bearing bad news. The Clash did a 2.6 rating, a 4.7 share and an audience of 1,549,000 homes, all figures that set the record for the all-time low for Clash specials. The show started with an abysmal 1.7 rating, indicating that interest in the product in general was at a rotten level, but grew throughout, peaking at a 3.6 for the main event. Still, even that came with the distinction of being the lowest rated headliner in Clash history.

The 2.6 generated talk in the office that the Clash concept may not be long for the world. While the numbers across the board were calamitous, TBS paid special attention to the Clash ratings due to the more prominent spot on the schedule. For boss Eric Bischoff, booker Dusty Rhodes and Operations V.P.

Ole Anderson, a scapegoat was needed to justify why things had taken a drastic plunge. The truth is that the company was demonstrably colder than it had ever been; a result of years of bad booking, mind-boggling office decisions, a sterile presentation and general inability to provide what fans were looking for. Acting in their own best interests, that reality wouldn't be reported to the higher-ups.

The obvious person to blame would be Ric Flair, who had been out of the ring for months to build up a return on a show that failed. However, Flair was held in high regard by people that mattered and had a track record as the biggest ratings draw in the company from years past. From there, the outcome was obvious, and the blame shifted to Brian and Steve.

"It stunned all of us", reflects Dave Meltzer when asked about the initial reaction. "It was a terrible rating for a Clash. Somehow, they got the blame for it which made no sense at all. It wasn't like Austin and Pillman were flopping as a team, they were doing about as well as you could do considering the state of that company."

Clash 23 was poorly promoted and with business being what it was, it had the makings of an imperfect storm for Pillman and Austin going in. With a fair analysis, one could argue that maybe the Blonds on top hadn't been treated seriously enough for a long enough period. Perhaps the team didn't have enough heat or credibility to be seen as a main event level threat. But clearly, Flair's return meant nothing for ratings either. The real conclusion was obvious – the entire promotion wasn't over.

In the face of excelling throughout the year, the Blonds were victimized based on the one bad rating, and plans for them to continue working with Flair were dropped. Ric didn't exactly lobby against the decision. Dusty Rhodes made the determination to ice the team, claiming that the number showed that while they were entertaining, they couldn't draw. Only a week later, WCW hired the Nasty Boys, Brian Knobs and Jerry Sags, with intentions of making them the new top heel team in WCW. After a three-year run in the WWF, the Nastys were seen as more viable in the position than Austin and Pillman. It didn't hurt that Jerry Sags just so happened to be the brother-in-law of the booker, Dusty Rhodes.

The fate of the champions, so promising just two months prior, was sealed.

13 - THAT'S A WRAP

The decision was made to get the belts off the Hollywood Blonds. It just didn't work, surmised the powers-that-be, so it was time to do something else. In a company scrambling in the dark, one of the few bright lights of 1993 was about to be snuffed out. Looking at what happened in the seven days after the Clash, however, provides great insight into the mindset of the people in charge.

On the June 19th WCW Saturday Night, the company unveiled an $80,000 mini-movie to promote the upcoming Beach Blast show that was among the most embarrassing efforts in the history of major league wrestling in North America. The vignette, featuring a midget blowing up a boat in an effort to kill Sting and Davey Boy Smith, was widely lambasted and the concept was never revisited.

Three days later, a new team was to be introduced at a television – the Posse (later Harlem Heat). Sid Vicious, who had returned to WCW earlier in the year, proposed an angle where a rich southern character named Col. Robert Parker would introduce the two black men in shackles and chains, on the premise they were escaped convicts. Ole Anderson and Dusty Rhodes both signed off on the idea. The offensive act was about to go through the curtain when Eric Bischoff saw it and immediately nixed it. Not only was the idea hideous, but mind-numbingly tone deaf considering what had happened to Bill Watts less than six months beforehand. In the middle of all of this, the Hollywood Blonds were deemed to be the major cause of WCW's problems, and action was quickly taken to put them back in their place.

Bischoff had struck a deal with the MGM Grand Studios at Disney in Orlando, and was hoping to upgrade the quality of the television shows and save significant money. His idea was to shoot 12 weeks of television at once over a four-day span, and so the booking direction from August to October was about to be revealed in one fell swoop. At the first day of the tapings, footage was shot with Arn Anderson and Paul Roma holding the WCW Tag Team titles. In the shows airing later, the Nasty Boys had the gold, and Pillman and Austin's road to ruin was now etched in stone.

Fate dealt WCW a funny hand, however. It was unheard of for so much to be openly revealed at one time at the tapings (revealing months of pay-per-view outcomes), and news quickly broke in the underground newsletters of the impending results. Bischoff was incensed, and was surrounded by old school, out-of-touch types who hated such revelations coming to the forefront.

The Blonds were being advertised to wrestle Arn Anderson and Paul Roma at Beach Blast, and all signs pointed to the tag title switch based on the Orlando tapings. In an attempt to surprise the insider audience and stay ahead of the newsletters, the call was made to put the Blonds over. Tony Schiavone even subtly alluded to the nature of the outcome on commentary, saying, "They stunned a lot of people, a lot more people than you and I really know, Jess, by retaining the titles." Of course, they would have to lose the titles eventually anyway, since it had already been taped. But the booking committee determined that they could simply postpone the title change until the next Clash of the Champions on August 18th, and were irrationally proud of one-upping the sheets.

Of course, WCW handcuffing themselves by committing to such long-term plans backfired. Nine days before Austin and Pillman were supposed to lose the tag titles, they taped a television match against Mark Starr and Frankie Lancaster. During the babyface comeback, Pillman took a monkey flip out of the corner from Lancaster and over-rotated, coming down awkwardly and severely twisting his left foot. Brian was taken to hospital that night and diagnosed with bone chips and torn ligaments in his ankle, and was going to be out of action for about a month.

Since the titles had to change hands, Lord Steven Regal was randomly inserted as a substitute in the Blonds team against Anderson and Roma, allowing the belts to move to the Horsemen as Pillman stood on crutches at ringside. After rescuing the tag team division, creating a new image and showing main event upside, the Hollywood Blonds lost the belts in as unceremonious a fashion as you could imagine.

As the summer ended, Brian and Steve couldn't help but wonder what was next for the act they'd worked so hard to cultivate. Greg Gagne, a member of the WCW booking committee, approached them backstage to bluntly give them their answer. "Well", Gagne began, "We're going to break up the team because, you know, you're just not over."

"I remember Brian telling me they were breaking the team up", begins Dave Meltzer. "I thought he was just trying to see my reaction. And I'm like, 'Yeah right, sure'. But it was actually true! And I go like, 'How can they be so stupid? You guys are such a great team!'"

Brian and Steve were adamant that the team stay together, but their requests fell on deaf ears. Dusty's priority wasn't the Blonds, but instead to use Austin in a feud with Dustin. After not wanting to team up initially due to the promise of a United States title run, Austin was now being told he was getting exactly that. Contrary to his feelings in 1992, Steve was sour on it. The team with Brian was such an obvious hit and one bad rating didn't justify killing it for good in Austin's mind. Pillman was again given the stigma of "too small to push", and after a short series with Steve, there were no plans for him. Both men hated the decision, but had no way to prevent it from happening.

"Steve wasn't happy, and Brian was absolutely furious when they broke the team up", adds Meltzer. "Number one, it was back to doing nothing with Brian. And number two, they were hot. They were getting great reactions every night and they were a great team. I heard it was off that rating, but it's like, one TV rating? TV ratings are funny, you can't overreact to one rating."

"I still think to this day the Hollywood Blonds are the best team of that era certainly, and one of the best teams ever", states Mark Madden. "Not that you could have kept them together indefinitely, because I think those guys had so much to offer individually, and both proved that after the team did get broken up. I thought at the time the team was broken up prematurely, and it really frustrated Brian."

At television tapings on September 7th, WCW had Austin receive a proposal from Col. Robert Parker to drop Brian and become a singles star under his guidance. It became a recurring theme over the course of several weeks, with Pillman at one point knocking Parker to the deck for trying to break up the Blonds. At the October 4th tapings they shot the angle where, after Brian once again drilled Parker, Austin turned on Brian and left him laying. The "Team of the Nineties" had come to an end.

Ten days after the split aired, Austin beat Pillman at Clash of the Champions 25, thanks to Parker's interference. Brian immediately became secondary, sitting on the sidelines for Starrcade in December, watching as his former partner won the United States title.

As quickly as the two men burst into the limelight, got over and shocked fans and the company alike, they were beaten, broken up and disposed of. Another idea thrown by the wayside, another instance of Brian dejected at the state of his career and his employer. Not surprisingly, business continued on the downward trend for WCW throughout 1993.

In the middle of an extremely sour professional life, Brian had an injection of happiness in the real world, as his first child with Melanie was born on September 9th, 1993. Pillman was thrilled to learn that the newborn was a boy (having had two girls previously), even giving him his own first name - Brian Zachary Pillman. The household now had an element bonding the two sides in blood, and were about to enter a new life as a burgeoning family.

With Austin now holding the United States title, Brian was embroiled in a comedy feud with Steve's new manager, Col. Robert Parker, based around Pillman's desire to put Parker in a chicken suit as retaliation for breaking up the tag team. It was an uninspired scenario and as 1994 began, it became obvious to everybody that a change was needed at the top. Dusty Rhodes was ousted as booker and replaced by Ric Flair. Whether this would be a good or bad move for Brian's future was unknown, but he didn't find himself in the best spot on the card as Flair took control.

Pillman being involved in low card hijinx and clearly being the lesser priority in the Blonds split was unnerving, since the sweetheart contract he'd signed with Kip Frye in 1992 was set to expire on March 13th, 1994. Given the situation, Brian was optimistic in hoping to keep his current contract. In their initial offer, WCW was looking to take Brian's deal down to a flat $190,000 per year, eliminating all the incentive bonus clauses in the process. The new, lower figure was right in line with Steve Austin's contract. Austin's deal was also coming up, and the Texas native was lobbying for a raise on his own $190,000 deal, but was also offered a cut.

As luck would have it, the two would work together on the February 27th edition of WCW Main Event in the feature match. The show, built around the two of them, did the best rating of any WCW show that week (2.6), and the highest for Main Event since late 1992. It still didn't matter. After being the best tag team in the business in 1993 and with all the obvious positives the two had, WCW had no inclination to seriously invest in either of them. The low offers were doubly insulting in that, while WCW was a money losing operation, they were still making key offers and expenditures elsewhere.

Knowing that, Pillman and Austin began considering their options. Brian called Scotty Flamingo, who was now in the WWF as Johnny Polo as well as was working in the office, to gauge interest. Curiosity from the WWF quickly came, and both of them were flown to Connecticut to meet with Federation officials.

Brian began talking to independent promoters, and contact was made with All Japan Pro Wrestling as well. The WWF seemed the obvious preferred destination, but while both were sought after (particularly Austin), McMahon's contracts at the time offered very little on paper. Typically, a WWF booking contract would offer in the region of ten dates at $150 a shot, guaranteeing the bare minimum. Any additional dates were at the will of the company, and for those dates they could pay whatever they felt. For Brian and Steve, they were offered the same as everybody but the top guys – the "opportunity" to make more.

Another drawback with the WWF option was the more grueling schedule, which was tough on families and had turned many on the roster into zombies in years past. With so much time on the road, it became a lot easier to turn to the kind of vices Brian was trying to stay away from at the time.

As the sides went back and forth in negotiations, Brian's contract actually expired. He wasn't going to accept a lowball offer without a fight, but it started to seriously look like the sun was setting on his WCW tenure. Pillman was pulled from all shows and removed from all future publicity and merchandise. The stance softened soon after, as a program over the WCW Television title was underway between Pillman and Lord Steven Regal to build to the Spring Stampede pay-per-view. Brian agreed to fulfil his previously advertised dates during the no-compete period of his expired deal. Mentally, WCW figured that Pillman was done, and he was off the booking sheets as of April 17th.

With Spring Stampede fast approaching, the expectation was that an agreement wouldn't be reached. As late as the Thursday before the event, it was planned for Pillman to be replaced in his match by The Patriot. But as crunch time drew closer, Bischoff had a change of heart and opened up the purse strings to Austin and Pillman after all. Austin was given a raise and

Pillman was kept at the same as his previous deal, both signed for two more years.

At the pay-per-view, Pillman and Regal wrestled to a draw, with WCW not wanting to job out their fresh investment, but not wanting to give him the Television title either. Talk again began to surface of turning Brian heel, this time to pair him up with Sensuous Sherri – played by the former Sensational Sherri of WWF fame. They shot and aired a number of matches with Sherri scouting Pillman, referencing her desire to manage a new, championship level wrestler. As per WCW form, the angle was dropped on a dime and never referred to again, once new booker Ric Flair decided he'd take Sherri as his own manager to help him with his upcoming heel turn. Flair was moving towards that side of the fence for seemingly good reason – Eric Bischoff had made an acquisition that would completely transform World Championship Wrestling.

14 – LANGUISHING IN MEDIOCRITY

A landmark signing hit WCW in May 1994, as Eric Bischoff hired the biggest wrestling star of all, Hulk Hogan. Hogan, who had left the WWF the year before, had spent his time shooting the abominable "Thunder in Paradise" show and working occasional matches in New Japan Pro Wrestling, where he was able to command top dollar. Bischoff made an enormous play to bring in Hogan, a huge offer that included complete creative control of his on-screen character (something previously unheard of), as well as a percentage of pay-per-view revenue and a massive guaranteed amount per year. For all the issues WCW had for years fighting off the minor league stigma, signing Hogan was a gigantic move. In his first WCW match, Hogan beat Flair for the World Title on July 17th at Bash at the Beach, and dominated the rest of the feud to boot.

More than just the power afforded to Hogan over his own character, the overwhelming influence he wielded on every move WCW made was quickly evident. The entire company immediately shifted to Hogan's vision, as the elements that made up WCW in years past quickly went by the wayside. Hogan brought in a cascade of former WWF stars he'd worked with during his most successful run. His real-life manager Jimmy Hart came aboard, as did best friend Ed Leslie (previously Brutus Beefcake). Hacksaw Jim Duggan entered the company at Fall Brawl and pinned Steve Austin for the United States title in 35 seconds. The former Earthquake, John Tenta, came in as Avalanche and was immediately pushed as a headlining heel. At Halloween Havoc in October, Hogan beat Flair in a retirement match, supposedly ending his career, in a match officiated by Mr. T (who was attached to Hulk Hogan's hip in 1985 when Hogan's mainstream star was born). Immediately after the match, his opponent for Starrcade was revealed – Hogan's best friend, Ed Leslie, now going by the ring name of The Butcher.

During this period, Pillman and others of his ilk were merely bit players, helping facilitate Hogan's vision at best, or relegated to the role of prelim guys at worst. Brian spent his time on house shows working with other low-level performers that were far away from Hogan's orbit, trading wins and losses with Bobby Eaton or Jean Paul Levesque. There would be weeks when Brian wouldn't be used at all, and truly for the first time since his arrival in WCW, Pillman was floundering, mired in obscurity. Following his match with Regal at Spring Stampede, Brian, despite his record for delivering in big matches, wasn't used on WCW pay-per-views or Clash specials for over a year. During this period of professional dissatisfaction, he picked up drinking again.

The first real use the Hogan regime appeared to have for Brian was to help elevate another one of Hulk's incoming friends, the Honky Tonk Man. Honky had a run in 1987 as WWF Intercontinental Champion and drew big money in a feud with "Macho Man" Randy Savage (who also entered WCW shortly after), but he'd been jobbed out, devalued and was considered a WWF washout by 1990. Returning to feud with Johnny B. Badd for his TV title four years later, it was felt Honky needed some wins on the house shows to gain traction. Sadly, it was Brian who had to lay down repeatedly.

"I remember WCW came out here", says Dave Meltzer. "And we went to a house show where he was in the first or second match and he lost to Honky Tonk Man, and oh, he was *so* livid. Honky Tonk Man was a great personality of course, but in Brian's mind his era was over, and he's out there putting over the Honky Tonk Man in a six-minute match. And he wasn't happy to do that."

When it came time for Honky to finally wrestle Badd, he was ordered to lose. Honky refused and walked out of the company, leaving Pillman damaged for no reason.

Brian was but a pawn on the chessboard with little in the way of options. The only silver lining was the memory of signing a new contract in April – while his position wasn't guaranteed, the money was. But Pillman and Austin weren't happy with the lot they were handed in light of Hogan's changes. They weren't the only ones, as more and more of the prominent talent of 1993 began to get phased down. One of these individuals was Lord Steven Regal, who had become good friends with Pillman and Austin in the last year.

"Regal was one of the few guys in the business that Brian both genuinely liked *and* genuinely respected", says Kim Wood. Seemingly out of the blue, Regal was selected along with Brian to represent WCW in a very peculiar crossover.

TBS was pouring a lot of advertising into "CyberBrawl '94", an attempt to create an annual video game awards show, anchored by Leslie Neilsen and Jonathan Taylor Thomas on November 5th. With WCW Saturday Night being the highest rated show on the station and the awards show airing directly afterwards, it was considered a good idea to play the corporate crossover card and use WCW wrestlers to convince fans to stick around.

The show was an overproduced and poorly put together fiasco, with cockamamie skits and alleged "comedy" breaking up illogical awards. Among the ridiculous segments was a scene where Brian and Regal would be calmly playing on the WCW Superbrawl game, while Leslie Neilsen did a slapstick speech about violence in the genre to the tune of "Battle Hymn of the Republic". Of course, the friendly game would turn into a wild fight behind Neilsen. The producers, looking to ham up the show at every opportunity, wanted midgets riding unicycles to join the fray before a pair of greased up bodybuilders arrived to manhandle them all. As Regal tells in his excellent memoir *Walking a Golden Mile*, Brian was quick to point out the ludicrousness of the scenario.

"Hang on a minute", Regal quoted Brian, "This show is only on because it follows our show, which gets the best ratings on this channel, so you can get some of its viewers to watch you. We are two of its stars and you want these two nobodies to throw us off the stage?" As it turned out, Regal and Pillman beat the hell out of each other trying to instill some legitimacy to the skit. Brian repeatedly chopped Lord Steven's chest hard, slammed him on the wooden stage, then slammed a midget on top of him for good measure. No matter how hard they tried, the audience giggled their way through the routine. Finally, Neilsen pulled a pistol from his holster as gunshots played over the P.A. to break it up. The bodybuilders were nixed, after Regal helpfully offered his opinion: "If those two wankers come anywhere near me I'll fucking kill them." To the surprise of nobody who watched, there was no CyberBrawl '95.

Knowing that his career was on a treadmill, Brian sought entertainment in other ways. At a Worldwide taping at the Disney MGM Studios in Orlando, Pillman was hanging out in a heel locker room with Regal, Rip Rogers, Buddy

Wayne and Frank Andersson, shooting the breeze and drinking a coffee with his colleagues. Brian seemed to have no real point of conversation, instead just lingering and chipping in to the discussion here and there. Three hours later, Regal, Rogers, Wayne and Andersson woke up. As it turned out, Brian had dropped a halcion into the coffee pitcher after he'd poured his own. There was no malice involved; he just loved to sit back, watch things unfold, then deny all involvement after ribbing people.

Another bizarre opportunity came up in November for Brian, as he ended up making his first appearance for ECW. Since Paul Heyman had left WCW, he'd taken up the book for Tod Gordon's Eastern Championship Wrestling, and was in the early stages of rebranding the company Extreme Championship Wrestling. Based out of Philadelphia, the fledgling company would routinely fill its primary location with some of the most hardcore, passionate wrestling fans around. In front of an audience of newsletter reading die-hards, Heyman would shoot innovative angles, promote hot new characters and create a television show that felt far more dynamic than anything the WWF or WCW had to offer.

Following the issues surrounding Heyman's dismissal, Paul E. frequently preyed on the anti-WCW sentiments that spoke to his audience of fans disenfranchised with the state of major league wrestling. On one night, however, Heyman was to gain the services of a contracted WCW performer - Steve Austin. WCW had recently been promoting an upcoming lucha libre pay-per-view called "When Worlds Collide", an event featuring the stars of AAA and IWC. The name of the event had been used six months earlier by ECW and as part of a settlement, Heyman requested the use of Austin for a show. Steve suffered a knee injury late in the game, and Heyman's second choice, Pillman, ended up getting the nod.

On the night, ECW did its best attendance ever up to that point to watch Shane Douglas and short-term manager Sherri Martel introduce their surprise partner, Brian Pillman. As Brian walked through the curtain, he received a hero's welcome from the Philly fans, decked out in his Hollywood Blonds jacket and doing the old camera pantomime he was known for with Austin. Together, the two teamed to lose to Ron Simmons and 2 Cold Scorpio. Though the focus of the match was on Douglas and Sherri Martel, Brian put in a solid effort and was affirmed to know his standing with the most avid wrestling fans was intact. That knowledge would come in handy before long.

Although there was obvious unhappiness with his current WCW status, it was more Brian's nature to figure a way out of the hole he'd been dug into, rather than lament his situation. "Brian was often frustrated because he always thought he could be used better", details Mark Madden. "He never, to me anyway, complained very much. Now if he was mad at somebody he'd talk about what a despicable son of a bitch so-and-so was, you know what I mean? But he wasn't a crier, so to speak. He wouldn't talk about trouble so much as he would try to talk to you about things that were going on that would solve the problem. He always had a plan. Brian was wrestling's Wile E. Coyote. I'm not sure if he ordered products from ACME but that would certainly be in keeping with his M.O."

Brian went to work on his latest idea. After some convincing by Pillman, Bischoff had agreed to bring back the Light Heavyweight division, rechristen it the Cruiserweight division, and base it around a heel Flyin' Brian. Bischoff had his eyes and ears open to talent around the world, and wanted to bring in hot prospects Chris Benoit and Sabu from ECW. Additionally, he was looking to bring in a number of Mexican and Japanese talents to give the new championship a distinct feel. But while Bischoff had his perfect world idea, it was a low priority and not a lot of time, effort or attention was put to making it happen.

In the meantime, a friendship that Brian had struck with one of Hogan's crew led to a surprising opportunity. Pillman had become friends with Jimmy Hart, who liked and saw potential in Brian with a different image. Through Jimmy and WCW, Pillman was given the opportunity to film a cameo for Baywatch, which at the time was on fire as the world's most popular internationally syndicated show. Highlights of the appearance would later be shown on WCW Saturday Night in January 1995, where Brian's appreciation for California and way-too-short shorts was spotlighted. As Brian approached the director he was referred to as "California Brian", to which Pillman responded, "That has a good ring to it."

The idea was to repackage Brian completely, complete with new name, colorful new tights, hair extensions and a fresh theme song titled "Blonds Have More Fun". To go along with the renewed push he looked to find a new finishing move, first toying with the Octagon special before finally watching a tape of Eddie Guerrero performing his second rope swinging DDT. Respectfully, Brian called Guerrero up, telling him that he was sorry but he had to steal the move - it was too good not to use.

An "Up Close" video feature was also recorded of Brian, going into

Pillman's real life background, and a series of squash match victories were taped for television. While Jimmy Hart was gung-ho on the new Pillman, others got cold feet. The first match that saw Pillman go by his new name of "California Brian", taped for the Saturday Night show against George South, was redubbed to remove the name and stick with Flyin' Brian. In addition, the launch of the new Cruiserweight division, originally set for March 1995, was postponed when WCW couldn't come to an agreement with AAA on talent, Chris Benoit turned them down flat, and Paul Heyman wouldn't allow Sabu to work any WCW events.

Pillman was downtrodden. His stock had never been lower and there was no sign of any kind of turnaround. With zero direction, a meaningless win here or there and jobs to pushed commodities, it was difficult not to be bitter. Just two years before, Pillman was viewed as one of WCW's upcoming headliners, and certainly was performing at the level that would be expected with such plaudits. As time passed, he'd simply found himself waiting for a future that never seemed to come. Similarly disgruntled was former partner Steve Austin, who would be offered constant promises only to see them fall through time after time. Talk that Austin and a heel Dustin Rhodes would join Ric Flair and Arn Anderson in a new Four Horsemen came apart, and he too had nothing in the pipeline. Brian and Steve would often get together to vent about their situations.

Colin Bowman, who had been working with WCW since the early nineties and at this time was the editor of the WCW Magazine, was a friend of Brian's and happened to be privy to many of the conversations between he and Steve. Through osmosis, it was almost bothersome to witness their angst. "Eventually", begins Colin, "I would sit with him and Steve and I'd go - You know what, I'm running a story. Here, let me take a picture of the pair of you sitting here. I'm going to run this and say, 'Are the Blonds getting back together?' Of course, WCW would then go apeshit and ask, 'What the fuck are you doing?' I just said, 'You guys didn't give me anything to work with this month so I'm just trying to fill up pages.' They just didn't know how to repackage either of them after they split them up."

To make matters worse, there were rumblings that Eric Bischoff was under the gun to make substantial cutbacks to the budget and was looking to eliminate disposable big contracts. Back in March, Bischoff had been given orders by TBS to free $500,000 from the company budget and fired Dustin Rhodes, Blacktop Bully, Mike Graham and Paul Roma for disciplinary reasons soon after. With Eric looking to slash some contracts, Pillman and Austin were the first two rumored to be on the chopping block.

With his career struggling, it didn't help Brian that his home life had become equally difficult as well. With the marriage to Melanie and multiple children with different mothers, the inevitable clash between Mel and Brian's ex-girlfriend Rochelle was growing more painful. Rochelle was struggling with drug issues that were compounded by the pressures of an impending custody battle for Brittany, and it was turning nasty.

In one instance when Brian was on the road, Rochelle went to the house to see Brittany, but Melanie wouldn't allow it. Rochelle was forced to look at her crying daughter through the window, having been denied the ability to spend time with her. Both sides began throwing serious accusations at the other, from charges of drug use back and forth to claims of child kidnapping and sexual abuse. Brian would leave the dismay of his failing WCW run and be mired in a brewing personal drama. It was mentally doing a number on all sides.

Brian's fortunes in WCW appeared to change, albeit briefly, after an incident at the Worldwide tapings in May. As part of Hulk Hogan's vision for WCW, he brought in an inexperienced unknown by the name of Rio Lord of the Jungle as "The Renegade", a cheap carbon copy of the Ultimate Warrior, who was always being chased for a return by Hogan. In line with what got the Warrior over so strong in the WWF in the eighties, Renegade was given quick squash wins on television to rush him up the card. The strategy hit a stumbling block when the name on the board opposite The Renegade happened to be Steve Austin.

Austin outright refused to lose to the green, overpushed newcomer in such circumstances. After the mishandling of his own career in the last two years, "Stunning" Steve felt that until WCW showed a genuine effort to do something with him – a plan, a direction, a feud, *anything*, that he could no longer cooperate with WCW burying him in such a manner. Booker Ric Flair went to Austin to try and convince him otherwise in front of the crew, but Steve had had enough, packed his bags and left the building.

It was a gutsy move by Austin, and it appeared to all that he quit the company. Telling the booker "No" in front of the other wrestlers put WCW in the tough position of having to back Flair to save face, or undercut their own booker by siding with Austin. When Bischoff met with Steve the next week and explained the situation, Austin stood firm – he would lose to The

Renegade on the provision that WCW showed they had a legitimate plan to use him, and it wouldn't be a squash. The plan Bischoff and Austin agreed upon was to reform the Hollywood Blonds and give Brian and Steve another run as WCW Tag Team Champions.

Brian was thrilled. At last, something. The team had six weeks to wait before it relaunched, as both men had back-to-back tours with New Japan Pro Wrestling to fulfil. But as a morsel of promise found its way to Pillman's professional life, things were getting worse at home.

On May 26th, Rochelle was supposed to pick up Brittany for the weekend, but was nowhere to be seen. Attempts to contact her failed, and it was as if nobody knew where she was. A planned meeting with a custody representative a couple of days later saw Rochelle no-show again, and Brian began to get concerned. By the evening of the 30th, it was a full-blown panic. When Brian's questioning caused enough of a stir in the family, Rochelle's mother reported her as missing to the police. As they searched Rochelle's house, cops deduced that she hadn't packed for a trip and were suspicious as to the nature of her disappearance. Brian was scared. A missing ex-girlfriend in a custody battle with a high-profile personality would almost certainly raise eyebrows in his direction if the story got out.

"He was frickin' frantic because she disappeared and he didn't know if she was dead or alive", says Dave Meltzer. "He would just go like, 'I didn't do anything to her, I promise. I'm not O.J. And I'm going to be O.J. if they find her dead."

Having drank too much and fearing the worst, Pillman initiated his own detective hunt for Rochelle. Driving erratically around the worst parts of Cincinnati, Brian would stop outside clubs and ask the bouncers if Rochelle was inside. Having no luck, he found his way to the Main Street District, which back then was known to be riddled with crime as panhandlers, pimps, prostitutes and drugs dealers filled the sidewalks. "Instead of hiring somebody to look for her or letting the police do their job", recalls Mark Madden, "Brian drove around every crack house in Cincinnati to look for her, and he called me from every stop. 'Well, she's not here...well, she's not here...well, she's not here', and it just went on and on all night. At one point, because he was a person of interest, he left a message on my machine in the middle of all this saying, 'Rev up the white Bronco, A.C., I think we may have to take a ride.'"

Since it was no secret within the city that the area was rough, patrol cars would frequently roam around to make sure nothing broke out. With Brian's car blocking traffic as he attempted to gather information and suspecting that he may not be of sound mind, police decided to search him. Pillman was wearing his fanny pack at the time, inside which sat a single blue pill with no bottle to be found. On that basis, he was arrested for carrying a controlled substance. When he was taken in, Brian refused to take a breathalyzer test and thus was given a DUI charge as well. After spending the night in jail, Pillman plead not guilty to both charges at an arraignment at the Hamilton County Courthouse the next day.

It turned out that the illegal drug possession charge fell through, as Pillman was able to provide the pill bottle and prescription for the anti-inflammatory tablet. The two real issues were that Pillman's arrest got a ton of publicity, with stories in local papers, reports on the news featuring his mugshot, and even a story in USA Today. With the standard reporting only explaining the bare minimum – 'pro wrestler arrested for carrying illegal drugs', it was a blow to Brian's reputation. "After he got arrested", remembers Linda Pillman, "People drove up our street one time and yelled 'Drug Addict!' We had our front window open and Mom said, 'What did they say?' And I just had to say, 'I don't know, I didn't hear them'."

People's reactionary nature was bad enough, but given Bischoff's budget directive and recent habit of releasing people from their contracts for discipline issues, it was reasonable to fear that WCW could use the incident to cut bait with Brian. Thinking proactively, Pillman volunteered to take a drug test to clear his name, the results of which came back negative. After a meeting with Bischoff where Pillman explained the entire situation, Eric assured him that the arrest wouldn't be held against him, or the planned Blonds push.

The other issue was that Rochelle still hadn't turned up. It came to light that her sister knew where she was all along, but wasn't telling anybody. She ended up being found days later in a car in Fort Lauderdale, surrounded by gentlemen known locally for being involved in illegal activity. But concerns about a worst-case scenario were assuaged, at least for now.

The flurry of bad luck continued when Brian heard that Steve Austin had torn his tricep during his New Japan tour and needed surgery that would keep him out of action for months. The proposed reunion would have to wait.

In the meantime, Brian was given a chance to shine for the first time in a while. He returned to pay-per-view at the Great American Bash in a match against Alex Wright, a 20-year-old German that booker Ric Flair was high on.

Pillman's role was to put him over and play subtle heel throughout the match, but it didn't play that way at all. The event was held in Dayton, Ohio, where Pillman's grassroots following wouldn't allow him to be the bad guy, cheering every cheap shot he threw. Wright, while a good wrestler, was having trouble getting over in his role of youthful heartthrob and was booed heavily at points. Still, the two put on a fantastic opener, seemingly a throwback to the Pillman pay-per-view efforts of old that hadn't been seen in far too long.

Brian set off for his three-week stint in New Japan, where he participated in their annual Best of the Super Juniors tournament. Working with the likes of Eddie Guerrero, Chris Benoit, Dean Malenko, El Samurai, Shinjiro Ohtani and Gran Hamada was a welcome change, reinvigorating him at a time he sorely needed it. Working with the cream of the crop, however, gave Brian a shot of perspective that planted a seed for what was to come. Dave Meltzer got a late-night phone call on the subject. "It was just like 'Oh my God, these guys are so good'", starts Dave. "And I'd say, 'Brian, I know they're good', and he'd say, 'No, you don't understand. When you work with them, these guys, technically, they are *so good.*' To him it was like a different level to the guys in the United States."

When he returned, things had changed in WCW. Ric Flair had been removed from his booking position after disagreements with Eric Bischoff and Hulk Hogan over the direction of the company. In his place was Kevin Sullivan. To Brian's dismay, Sullivan had no interest in reuniting the Hollywood Blonds and the planned title run was completely dropped.

Sullivan had a different vision for World Championship Wrestling. On top, Hulk Hogan and Randy Savage would work with a parade of over the top cartoon characters just like in the WWF days. Underneath, he'd shore up the card with talented workers who could put together the type of great action that Hogan couldn't. Sullivan was closely connected to Paul Heyman at ECW and had his eye on picking up Chris Benoit, Dean Malenko and Eddie Guerrero. Additionally, he pushed for Bischoff to bring in Sabu to fit this category. Around this time, plans were being put together for WCW to launch a new show called Monday Nitro on TNT, head to head with the WWF's Raw. The belief was that WCW needed to stockpile talent to provide great television matches that the WWF couldn't compete with.

Rather than see this as a benefit, Brian saw it as threatening to his position. He was flagging in the midcard as it was. Without a push, a feud, or something to showcase his personality, his biggest attribute was his ability between the ropes. After working with most of the newcomers in the Best of the Super Juniors tournament, Pillman felt that he was about to take a few steps backward on the list of WCW's best in-ring talent, making him more expendable than ever.

With a body that had seen its fair share of abuse from years as an undersized guy in football and wrestling, his cripplingly painful back issues had flared up again, preventing him from doing any training in the gym. "In his mind his body was looking like hell, but he was getting a great tan so people wouldn't notice it as much, that's what he would tell me", laughs Dave Meltzer. With his back in such bad shape and seeing that the quality of the in-ring product was about to escalate, the Japan tour served as a catalyst for change. "That was where the mentality first came for what he changed into", adds Meltzer. "He would tell me, 'Physically I'm not going to be able to do this for a long period of time, the Flyin' Brian thing. I can't be Flyin' Brian any more. I've got to be something else'."

As a student of the business, Pillman had his eye on a man he thought was going to catch on huge - Rey Mysterio Jr. Brian would talk to Rey throughout 1995, concerned about the potential risk of injury his death-defying style brought with it. Seeing that Mysterio was a different level of daredevil and acrobat, Pillman knew he couldn't be Flyin' Brian once Rey landed in WCW or the WWF. "It was just the fear of having all the kids, because that was a big thing, having all the kids and thinking that his body wasn't going to be able to stand up to all the flying", summarizes Meltzer. "So he had to do a character, a strong character."

While Brian began searching for a change, WCW's first Monday Nitro broadcast on September 4th was a testament to the new company philosophy. As Hulk Hogan main evented with Big Bubba Rogers (who he'd successfully headlined with in the WWF), Brian was placed in the very first match to air on the show against Jushin Liger, who made a rare WCW appearance for the event. Time constraints didn't allow it to reach the peaks of their prior bouts, with only six minutes allocated to the men who'd previously had one of the best series of matches in WCW history.

The most newsworthy event of the show turned out to be the return of Lex Luger, who had been working for the WWF without a contract and expressed interest in returning to WCW. Bischoff was cold on the idea, initially only offering $1,000 per shot with no guaranteed number of dates to Luger. As the first Nitro grew closer, Bischoff fell in love with the idea of firing a major shot at Vince McMahon, who clearly had his guard down in 1995. When Vader was fired after a backstage fight with Paul Orndorff, his large guarantee was suddenly on hand to use. With nobody aware of Luger's ability to jump ship, his perceived value suddenly jumped in Bischoff's eyes. A two-year guaranteed deal was agreed at a significantly higher figure and Lex Luger, after a failed WWF run, was back in the fold. Once again, he'd positioned his way into the type of big contract that Pillman longed for, and Brian was in disbelief.

The personnel news got worse a couple of weeks later for Brian when his closest friend, Steve Austin, was fired from WCW. Bischoff cited the amount of time Austin had been off injured (WCW had a 90-day injury cycle in their contracts that voided the deal if the talent was incapacitated for a longer period) as the reason for the firing. In reality, Steve and WCW had been at odds for a while, and the headstrong Austin found it difficult to exist in a company monopolized by Hogan and the handpicked few.

On the flip side, Brian found himself in the best position he'd been in for some time, seemingly out of nowhere. One of Sullivan's early decisions was to reunite the Four Horsemen, and Pillman got the nod from everybody involved to be part of the newest incarnation. A couple of days after Austin was fired, Brian Pillman opened the WCW Fall Brawl pay-per-view against Johnny B. Badd in a match to determine the number one contender to Sting's United States title.

For all the talk backstage of Pillman and Badd as two of the guys in the midcard that would be providing great matches in lieu of Hogan, people within the WCW inner circle were keen to put Pillman and Badd in their place early. The match was given almost thirty minutes, typically way too long for a babyface match with no heat going in, in an attempt to expose the two as being incapable of carrying a key position on a major show. Instead, the two men tore the house down in a match that blew away expectations, filled with twists, turns, big moves, classic Pillman spots and some new ones thrown in for good measure. Though he lost the match, Brian was a big winner in his performance.

Moreover, later in the show Pillman hopped onto the ring apron during a heavily promoted Arn Anderson Vs. Ric Flair match and kicked Flair in the back of the head, assisting Anderson to victory and forging a new alliance. The plan was ultimately for Flair to join the crew, but the run-in was easily the most newsworthy event for Pillman on-screen in almost two years.

The following night on Nitro, Pillman wrestled Ric Flair in the main event, losing clean to the figure four in five minutes. Not exactly a red-hot start to Brian's heel run, and it only served to send a message that despite the better spot, there was no real intention of elevating Brian.

The week after, Pillman and Anderson cut a live promo alluding to their desire to form a new Horsemen, in which Brian showed trace elements of a more aggressive act. WCW later taped matches with Arn and Brian together as a team at Center Stage, the two looking to be featured prominently in the immediate future.

Then, out of nowhere, things took a drastic turn for the worse.

After the tapings, Pillman stayed over at Joey Maggs' house in Atlanta, where he got a phone call on October 13th bearing some terrible news - his ex-girlfriend Rochelle was dead.

The custody battle for Brittany had ended in favor of Brian and Melanie, with Rochelle's disappearance at the end of May playing a major role in the final decision. The downward spiral had continued since, and the situation was too much for Rochelle to deal with. Without any sense of self-worth and with mental health issues to begin with, losing Brian, losing custody of Brittany and struggling with drug addiction, Rochelle saw no other way out. She committed suicide in dramatic fashion, shooting herself in the head while on the phone to her mother, after failing to get Brian on the phone to witness her death as her final revenge.

Upon hearing the news, Pillman lost control, utterly devastated. Maggs told friends that it was as close to a nervous breakdown as he ever saw Brian have, and had to pick him up off the floor several times. He was crushed that somebody he was once so close to, albeit with flaws in the relationship, was gone. He felt awful that Rochelle's mother, who he'd become close to, had to witness her daughter die on the phone. He was distraught that Brittany would grow up without her mother. But worst of all, while Brian could justify that Rochelle's drug problems were so bad that she couldn't be saved, he still blamed himself for not handling such an obviously delicate situation better.

He was very friendly with Rochelle's family, but they all shared the same perspective. While the issues weren't one sided and her problems pre-dated Brian, between Brian shifting his home life from Rochelle to Melanie and the volatile custody fight, it was perceived that he had heaped mounds of despair on somebody who wasn't equipped to cope with it all. In some respects, it was difficult to see it any other way. "I think he felt a lot of guilt over that", shares Linda Pillman. "And rightly so. But it was what it was."

It shattered Brian, who told his closest cohorts that he didn't know if he'd be able to go on. He continued the only way he knew how, by going back on the road. He didn't miss any dates for WCW, even wrestling in the Nitro main event just three days later, teaming with Arn against Sting and Flair and having a hell of a match. With Ric and Sting standing tall at the end, the storyline of Flair earning the trust of his long-time nemesis over several weeks was complete, right in time for Halloween Havoc on October 29th. With Flair outnumbered since Fall Brawl, Sting had finally forgiven the Nature Boy, opting to back him up against his newfound enemies.

Of course when the pay-per-view came, Ric Flair aligned with Pillman and Anderson, turning heel on Sting and reforming the Horsemen as planned. The energy in Detroit as Flair decked Sting and the three collectively pounced was electric, a heated mix of boos and cheers filling the Joe Louis Arena. In a company otherwise barren of genuine emotion, the sight of Flair, Arn and Pillman standing as one seemed to light up the entire show.

"There were two times when he called me after a show and told me it was the greatest night of his career", mentions Dave Meltzer. "The first was when they turned on Sting. And it's because he's in the Horsemen, he did an angle with Sting and he felt like he was in *the* main event angle. So he called me up that night and he was really on a high."

After almost two years of terrible booking, Brian was elated to be part of Flair's group, hoping this would finally be his ticket to the top. Shortly afterward, an old buddy from Stampede, Chris Benoit, was announced as the fourth member of the group. On the surface, it seemed that Pillman was back in the mix in a big way.

Underneath, the scars of the recent personal tragedy were deep, permanent and extremely difficult to deal with. Seeing that he was in a decent spot for the first time in a while and sensing he needed to evolve professionally, he decided to throw himself into his work 100%. Mentally wounded, Brian would soon feel that escapism was the best remedy.

15 - CONCEPTION OF A LOOSE CANNON

With around five to six months left on his existing contract, Pillman, at 33 years old, started heavily thinking about the future. Looking at his current deal, which promised him $225,000 per year, Brian was uncertain what realities his next negotiations would bring. With his spot in the Four Horsemen, the fear he may have had at one point that WCW would spit him out for good was erased. But Brian was still in the position of losing fairly regularly, including a clean defeat at the hands of Eddie Guerrero on the November 20th Nitro, and eating the pinfall in a tag match against Sting and Lex Luger on the following week's show. Brian could see the writing on the wall. With the company still keeping his profile low and his Horseman spot not providing nearly the political protection he expected, it was more likely that WCW's Executive Vice President Eric Bischoff would offer him the same $156,000 per year that Bill Watts offered back in 1992. In a best-case scenario, maybe he could get another extension on his current deal. But Brian saw through WCW's efforts to keep him on ice and wanted no part it. He'd settled for mediocrity long enough.

As November turned to December, his brain started working overtime, surveying the wrestling landscape, looking for an opening. This wasn't just a financial matter to Brian; he wanted a run as a top guy, a chance to main event shows and be everything he always knew he could be in pro wrestling. He also knew he wasn't going to get it by simply existing within the current system, especially one dominated by the looming presence of Hulk Hogan. Pillman didn't want to wait two or three more years and hope that his body and career were in a position to leverage a better deal down the line. He knew that it was his time to act. The only question was, what could Brian do that he hadn't done for years before?

It had to be something different. Something drastic. With this in mind, he sat down with Kim Wood, the man responsible for getting him into the wrestling business all those years ago, at Kim's kitchen table. It was here that the pieces came together.

Brian believed that in WCW, if the money was in place, the push would come along with it. Even though that hadn't served him well previously, if he could somehow land a deal in the neighborhood of $450,000 to $500,000 per year, surely WCW would have to treat him like a top guy in order to justify the contract. Doubling his money seemed unfathomable at that exact point in time, but as Wood states, "I said to Brian, 'We gotta' think this out, because we gotta' do something here that makes it so that you go into that contract negotiation hotter than heck'."

The talk turned to Brian's character. Kim saw Brian's real-life credentials as an NFL alumnus with a rep as a street fighter; an alpha male who, with the things he would say and do, gave off an air of being insane. Using this as a base, Wood recalled his own experiences with several other wrestlers. "I was always impressed with the Road Warriors", he says. "Whenever I'd go backstage, they would always still be in character. And the one guy was just a goofball, that Hawk. But they were like that – they refused to lose and they would fuck with everybody, and it worked out for them." Indeed, the Road Warriors, or Legion of Doom in the WWF, were one of the more legendary tag teams of all time.

Originally put together in 1983 by Ole Anderson, Mike "Hawk" Hegstrand and Joe "Animal" Lauranitis quickly became a sensation. The team was a hit based on their freakish physiques, explosive destructions of lesser opponents on television, selling for nobody, and the ability to play the part convincingly. They were a favorite of the magazines, frequently adorning the covers, and booked to steamroll even the most credible of stars in minutes when a territory would bring them in. Between the spiked shoulder pads, face paint, over the top aggression and careful booking, it was an iconic act. But they were very aware of their value, and due to how popular they were throughout the States as well as in Japan, they often balked at the idea of losing. Animal, in particular, was never keen to take a pinfall defeat. The promoters, not wanting to lose the ability to use the Road Warriors, would have to work around their demands.

To compliment this dynamic, Hawk's reputation for having a short fuse created an element of fear to the combination in real life. While Hawk would sometimes be amiable to autograph seekers, there were instances of him hitting fans who caught him on the wrong day. He had incidents sucker punching Eddie Guerrero and Randy Savage in separate arguments. He once tried doing the same to Too Cold Scorpio, but Scorpio dodged the cheap shot and rattled off a series of punches that left Hawk's face a bloody mess.

Hawk's drug use, for recreational and bodybuilding purposes, wasn't exactly a secret inside the business either. He once bragged to Bill Watts that he'd began shooting monkey hormones for his physique, and woke up every day wanting to kill someone. As a partier, he was as wild and over the top as anybody.

To say they weren't easy to deal with puts things lightly, but the team was lucrative for years, and how they conducted themselves in real life was key to that. "They weren't tough guys", says Kim Wood. "Well, Joe (Lauranitis, aka Animal) might have been, but Hawk wasn't. But they would act like tough guys to the troupe, so after a while people were thinking they were tough guys. Then they refused to lose and they walked out on places. Like Bruiser Brody. He'd walk out on places and people would go 'Oh Wow', you know. And he parlayed it into making a lot of money."

Brody was another classic case. Born Frank Goodish, "The Intelligent Monster" was as memorable a character as the business has ever seen. Between his caveman appearance, scarred forehead, crowd chasing and chain swinging antics, Brody drew attention in spades. His brawling style and bloody battles served as the prototype for many big men, with a distinct interview style that could sell tickets like they were going out of fashion. He was also a ruthless strategist behind the scenes. After he hit it big in All Japan Pro Wrestling, ran by Shohei "Giant" Baba, Brody was very much aware that he was dealing from a position of power to American promoters. He was enough of an attraction to merit his use and would be built up as a superstar by a territory upon his arrival. It often paid off financially for the company, but as soon as the booking appeared not to prioritize Brody's best interests, he'd leave and go somewhere else.

A great example, in fact, of the two entities Kim Wood cites as inspiration for Pillman's character is when Bruiser Brody and the Road Warriors crossed paths in All Japan Pro Wrestling in 1985. TV-Tokyo would air tapes of American promotions on their World Pro Wrestling show, and footage of the

Road Warriors in their element captivated the imagination of the Japanese audience. Baba saw this and offered them contracts for $10,000 per week, money that was as high as anybody was earning at that time. On the Road Warriors' first night in, Brody saw how hot the act was and spotted the similarities to his own. Eager to not look secondary, Brody made a huge deal with Baba's promotional rival, New Japan Pro Wrestling. The contract with New Japan offered Brody $14,000 a week for 1985, $16,000 a week in 1986 and $18,000 a week in 1987, for 16 weeks per year, as well as a six-figure signing bonus. The deal was not only the most lucrative ever signed by a pro wrestler up to that point, but it cemented Brody's position as the number one foreigner on Japanese soil.

At a legitimate 6'5" and 280 pounds, Brody was a fearsome presence and a true outlaw, his reputation as a cunning businessman backed up by his impetuosity. There were many instances of Brody being uncooperative in the ring or changing plans mid-match, and he was no stranger to locker room incidents himself. Unfortunately, this rebellious nature ended in tragedy for Brody when Jose Gonzalez stabbed him several times in a bathroom at a show in Puerto Rico in 1988. It seems sadly ironic that the methods that made him a success in wrestling ultimately contributed to his demise.

The blueprint for their success was clear to Kim Wood, and this perspective became the foundation of what would become the "Loose Cannon". Kim and Brian discussed cultivating an unpredictable personality that would act the same when there were no cameras on him at all as he would on television with millions watching. Like Hawk and Brody did behind the scenes, the idea was to unsettle enough of the wrestlers with his bizarre behavior that, not only would some of them genuinely believe he had gone nuts, but more importantly, he'd be the center of attention and they'd all be talking about him.

The conversation went back and forth, as the depth of the plan went far beyond morphing a wrestling persona and fooling his colleagues. "The idea became to con the conmen, fuck the fuckers", Wood would go on to say. "The thing that Arthur Jones taught me that I taught Brian is - nobody is easier to con than a conman."

As talk turned to the impending negotiations, Brian had told Kim about how Eric Bischoff had photos of himself as a kickboxer on the walls of his office. He explained how when wrestlers would go in to talk with Eric for contract negotiations, Bischoff would take out his false teeth, put them on a plate that sat on his desk and crack his knuckles before starting the conversation. This not-so-subtle gesture was to indicate that while they were there to talk business, he was the boss, and was willing to fight if things weren't going to his liking. In a world built on deception, Bischoff was keen to present himself as real to the wrestlers.

Whether Bischoff was genuinely a tough guy or not is completely irrelevant, the point is that he went out of his way to project that he was. Kim heard Brian loud and clear, and saw the opening Pillman was looking for. "When somebody is telling you that they're a tough guy, they're sending you a red flag that they can be fucked with", Kim explains, "And we knew that Bischoff was a mark for himself."

With the desire to create controversy with a character that would remain intact 24 hours a day and generate notoriety among the wrestlers, the approach was discussed. "Get tight with this guy Bischoff and make him part of it", said Wood. "Let him be an insider, and he'll be thrilled to death that you're pulling this rib on the boys together." Being offered the theoretical position of the mastermind puppeteer of this scam would appeal to his ego. It would hone in on and exploit the part of Bischoff that wanted to be, on some level, above the wrestlers in the same way his negotiating tactics did.

Bischoff getting in on the ground floor would serve a dual purpose. For starters, working closely with Eric in an effort to work everybody would allow Brian a great deal of creative freedom and direct control over his destiny, something almost nobody else in the company had. This added freedom would allow him to do things that would draw far more attention to himself than he'd get by simply playing along with whatever plan WCW cooked up. Besides, stealing the spotlight at this crucial time was exactly what this was all about. With the inside track on Pillman's antics as co-conspirator, Bischoff would be too happy playing along and reveling in the rush of working the boys, the newsletters and the internet to notice what was really happening. He would be, in the process, adding a significant amount of interest to the name Brian Pillman right as the weeks, days, minutes and seconds were counting down to the end of his contract on April 17th, 1996. The other purpose of being close with Bischoff would come out in due time.

A world of possibilities began to flow around the kitchen table for what Brian could do as the rogue employee within WCW with the covert backing of the boss. One of the main things batted around was something that never happened, but was generated based on the knowledge of Bischoff's desire to be seen as a tough guy. After weeks of supposed brewing turmoil, Eric and Brian would get into a very heated, very public argument. Tensions would rise, and before an audience of employees only, Brian and Eric would fight. Surely, they mused, Bischoff would go for it because it was important to him that the wrestlers thought he was a fighter. "If Brian could have beaten up Bischoff", elaborates Wood, "Bischoff would be a part of it because he wants to increase his credibility with everybody that he's a tough guy and was actually in a fight." Pillman was even willing to allow Bischoff to give him as many shots as he would give in this proposed scenario. "People knew Bischoff was prepared to fight. Great, let's get into a fight with Bischoff in front of everybody. But that never came off", states Kim Wood.

What's key to note is that it was the current lay of the land that made the timing of Pillman's expiring deal rather fortuitous. In fact, it was the real crux of the scheme. With the dawn of the Monday Night War, the hyper-competitive atmosphere between WWF and WCW was at a fever pitch. Eric Bischoff was regularly knocking the competition's show, on occasion revealing the results of their pre-taped Raw broadcasts on the live WCW Nitro in an effort to keep channel-surfing to a minimum. But it also bled into the way the companies ran their day to day dealings, as evidenced by the Luger jump. Indeed, both sides were looking for any edge or chance to upstage the other. American wrestling soon became a nuclear arms race for talent, and Brian saw that it had never been easier to play both sides against the middle. Furthermore, his deal was coming to an end at a time where he could be one of the first names since the inception of the Raw Vs. Nitro showdowns to have the chance to create a bidding war. At this point, Bischoff had the reputation for leaving contract negotiations to the very last minute, which Brian was counting on. In discussing the approach with Pillman, Kim was steadfast about WCW's plan to keep his salary low, saying, "There's no loyalty here Brian, they're gonna' fuck ya'."

By hooking Eric in, by creating a character that would naturally get attention and generate controversy, all the interest and intrigue in becoming the talk of the wrestlers and the insider audience might not mean so much to ratings, buyrates and live attendance. Those would be the obvious metrics a promoter might typically be looking for if he were to hand out a raise. In truth, those metrics would only ever mean so much to the office since the money made or lost wasn't Bischoff's, it was Turner's. Brian had discovered throughout his run that the only currency that was evergreen in the running of WCW was ego, which he was banking on big time in catering to Eric. For Pillman, even if there were no hard stats in his favor, by creating constant news and discussion around himself, the added interest would transform into value as soon as it appealed to the real target. "Really the game was played on one guy – Bischoff, to work another guy - Vince", explains Wood.

The plan was to make as much noise in WCW with the secret support of Bischoff, in order to create a perception of value that would appeal to Vince McMahon. Or at least to enough of his closest confidantes (including Jim Ross and Jim Cornette at that time), that Vince would want to buy him, perhaps to spite WCW as much as truly wanting Brian.

In years past, Vince had gone out of his way to hire people to spite competitors. During the national expansion of the WWF in the early-to-mid-eighties, Verne Gagne's AWA in particular felt the brunt of Vince's malicious signing practices. McMahon scooped up not only prominent wrestlers, but television announcers and even production staff to impede Gagne's progression. It was the biggest signing from the AWA, Hulk Hogan, that ultimately made all the difference and serves as a reference point for the McMahon hiring ideology to this day. Hogan was on fire in Japan and the AWA, hitting the silver screen in 1982 with his appearance as "Thunderlips" in Rocky 3 opposite Sylvester Stallone. Vince saw the value, and thus, made the investment to make this already hot commodity his very own.

In late 1995, with the WWF/WCW rivalry growing more spiteful by the week, the belief was that if Brian could get Vince's attention and lure McMahon to swoop in, the bidding war was on. And that's where the other purpose of getting close to Bischoff came in.

By making Eric part of this character he'd be more emotionally connected to it, and thus more invested in not losing it to the competition. The numbers proposed for Brian Pillman's next contract would only escalate as a result, and the collateral damage on either side was irrelevant. "Don't forget", says Kim Wood, remembering the example of Brody and the Road Warriors, "You can fuck over people in pro wrestling and they forget about it. There's no pride!"

The plan was in place. As always, Brian's academic approach led to him delving deeper. He watched the 1987 film House Of Games, directed by David Mamet and starring Joe Montegna, and fell in love with the movie. The film sees the main protagonist Dr. Ford, a published female psychologist, stumble upon a quiet establishment with a bar and some backroom gambling after a patient tells her that he owes the House money. Ford tries to clear the issue up with the owners to aid her patient.

She encounters the guy at the top that simply goes by "Mike" (Montegna), who vows to wipe the debt clean if Ford helps him catch an opponent's tell in an ongoing poker game, which she agrees to do. The plan appears to backfire and ends up with Dr. Ford, at gunpoint, offering to help pay a hand that Mike loses, before noticing the gun is a harmless water pistol. She realizes the poker players are really working together in an effort to con her, and reneges on her $6,000 check. Rather than be appalled, with no harm successfully done she finds the crafty, good-natured charm of the conmen strangely endearing, and wants to know more about their world.

Ford gets closer to Mike and begins to revel in the thrill of the score as she watches the conmen do their thing to others. After insisting on going along with a big scam to witness it in person, it goes horribly wrong. Dr. Ford discovers that the proposed mark in the con is actually an undercover police officer about to bust her newfound friends, and in her panic to escape, accidentally kills the officer. Desperate to flee the scene, the conmen leave $80,000 in cash, borrowed from the mob to entice the mark, at the scene of the crime. Guilt-ridden and desperate not to make the situation worse, Dr. Ford dips into her savings and gives Mike $80,000 to pay the mob back and save their lives, before they all go their separate ways.

Fearing that her role in the murder will come back on her, Ford goes through a great deal of personal turmoil and distances herself from what happened. Then, by circumstance, she discovers everybody from Mike to the police officer that was "murdered", even to the initial patient that led her to the House of Games at the beginning, sitting at a diner talking about working together on their long con – her. "Poor Brian was never the same after watching it", jokes Wood. Pillman saw that in his plan, Bischoff was Dr. Ford, somebody who would go along with his scheme as long as he knew something everybody else didn't.

"He was so sure that the one thing Eric would want was to make it look like he was in control all along", adds Dave Meltzer. "But to do that he has to go back to Bischoff and Eric has to resign him, but then he has leverage to get real money from Eric."

Eager to learn more, Brian began to study con man literature. He dived into *The Big Con* by David Maurer, a book detailing the con games used in the early 1900's. The scams all attacked from the angle of convincing the mark that they'd stumbled upon people with an inside track on a way to make guaranteed money. The mark would get taken to "the big store", a building set up to resemble a bookmaker's establishment, but was actually occupied by fellow conmen working as extras for the express purpose of the ongoing scheme. It was here that the mark would see the money-making method pan out with their own eyes. Intoxicated by their surroundings as they saw big money changing hands so frivolously, and with the temptation to join in too great, they'd hand over tens of thousands of dollars to get a piece of the action. Ultimately, the plan would blow up in their faces and the mark left without a penny, oftentimes thinking his cohorts had suffered the same fate. Reading it cover to cover, Brian became obsessed with the art of manipulation and the psychology that allowed the mark to melt like putty in the hands of the charismatic swindler.

Brian read the autobiography of Yellow Kid Weil, one of the more prolific conmen of the early twentieth century, and a 1946 novel by William Gresham called *Nightmare Alley*. Gresham's book, based on the traveling carnival (the very circuit from which the wrestling business originally spawned), offers tremendous insight to the nature of human psychology and the willingness to be manipulated, both of which were fundamental to Brian's objective.

Feeling prepared, Pillman went to Eric Bischoff with the idea not just to transform his character, but to collaborate on a piece of theater that would get everybody talking. They'd fool the wrestlers, they'd fool the newsletters, they'd have the fans asking questions and intrigued at what would happen next. Regardless of how bizarre Brian's idea was, his conviction was compelling and he was persistent in his argument. "Brian was the kind of guy", says Mark Madden, "Where when he wanted to do something, depending on who he was pitching, it was sometimes easier to just let him do it than to battle it. He would wear you down."

In this case, it immediately appealed to the boss. In his book *Controversy Creates Cash*, Bischoff revealed, "I like keeping storylines secret. I know it was next to impossible in my own organization to keep things secret." As anticipated, Eric was keen to work his own guys, relishing the idea of playing master manipulator. Beyond that, he also saw the potential upside to having such a character around on a live broadcast every Monday. The ratings battle with WWF Raw was only going to grow fiercer, and this new gimmick played into the vibe that Eric was looking to cultivate on his show. "It went directly to the philosophy of doing things differently and continually surprising the viewer", wrote Bischoff. With the endorsement of the Executive Vice

President, Pillman went to work, starting with his look.

Brian grew in his goatee and began wearing more and more eccentric clothing. He'd wear, in addition to his regular Horseman T-shirt, shirts bearing the image of pop culture icons such as James Dean and Marilyn Monroe. The subconscious allusion of the shirts being that in a WCW world that had become a cartoon with the Dungeon of Doom on top (that featured outdated characters such as Shark, The Zodiac and The Yeti), he was to be associated with the real world and with controversial figures. More often than not, said shirt would feature a square cut out over his left pectoral, another creation from around the kitchen table. "We were trying to create a fashion", says Wood, "It was that he had no heart. That there was just an absence there." Other staples of Brian's would be a cane with a horse's head on the end and Nehru suit jackets to further distinguish him from the pack.

He studied the interviews of wrestling's most convincing madmen, in particular Bruiser Brody, Roddy Piper and Terry Funk. He observed their wide-eyed delivery and unpredictable speech patterns, the inflection changing as the promo went on depending on the message articulated. Adding little elements of their work to his already impressive speaking skills would only enhance the character he was looking to portray.

The Rogue Horseman was given its first glimpse of life on the December 11th episode of Nitro. With the group introduced for an interview by Gene Okerlund, the focus of the segment was completely on Brian, who took the opportunity to go off on a rambling tirade. Erratically transitioning from point-to-point and scolding Okerlund for trying to cut him off, Brian mocked Hulk Hogan's recent pseudo-heel turn. He insulted announcer and former Chicago Bear Steve McMichael, talking about finding pictures of him with the American Males, a Chippendale-esque tag team. Saying of the pictures, "Can't comment on their content, but I'll say this McMichael - for a big guy, you're pretty flexible!"

He turned his attention to the Dungeon of Doom and then to Paul Orndorff, deriding his lame new gimmick (after a boost of confidence from Gary Spivey of the Psychic Network in an atrocious backstage skit). Shortly after, Orndorff walked down to confront Pillman. The scenario resulted in the Horsemen piledriving Orndorff on the concrete floor with Pillman front and center in the attack, the commentators teasing possible paralysis. For the first time since his initial heel turn, Pillman was given some real heat. In its formative stages, the amped up character stood out, a work in progress.

16 - GOING ROGUE

Brian boarded a plane to Calgary to wrestle at the Stu Hart 50th Anniversary Show on December 15th, 1995. The standalone event would see an extremely rare co-mingling of WCW and WWF contracted talent, as well as regulars from the old Stampede circuit. The gathering, put together by Bruce Hart, was to commemorate Stu's efforts in the business and local community. Brian was in a heavily featured spot, as he and Bruce reformed Bad Company to go up against Terry Funk and Dory Funk Jr. in the penultimate match on the show. "It was a dream come true for both of us", said Bruce Hart, "I'd been a huge fan of Dory and Terry since before I'd even got in the business. Dory was the quintessential World Champion, maybe ever, for the NWA. Terry was the same. I was organizing the show and Dory called me up and said, 'You'd better include us.' I was honored and delighted. It was almost too much for me to ask them because they were such big heroes of ours."

Typically speaking, a show of this kind has its tropes. With goodwill being the vibe in the air, you'd expect a series of straight up, hard-fought matches, usually with the babyfaces going over to make the crowd happy. With a sterling group of wrestlers on the card, such as Bret Hart, Davey Boy Smith, Chris Benoit, Owen Hart and 1-2-3 Kid, and the fact it was a tribute to Stu, it appeared to follow that traditional pattern. Terry Funk, however, had other ideas.

"I remember getting with Terry before the match with Brian and Dory. Terry's saying what he wanted to do. He wanted to have an old school, hardcore bloodbath, which is almost kind of a radical departure from the tone of the whole card", says Bruce. "We went out brawling in the crowd, Terry was covered in blood, I think I was covered in blood, Brian was...it was fun, you know." Bruce can't help but laugh as he recalls the match, saying, "I remember my Dad and a bunch of these dignitaries like the Prime Minister, the Mayor and the Premier, they were in the front row and had blood on them. We'd have never dared to ask...like if I was booking the card, I wouldn't have had the audacity to say, 'Okay, Dory and Terry, we need juice, nut shots, and a brawl in the crowd with tables and chairs.' I'd expect somebody to say, 'That fucking idiot Bruce. He wants to do a tribute to his father and he wants juice and fucking hardcore.' But that's what it became. Given it was the Loose Cannon and the King of Hardcore, it almost suited the situation. Brian was on good form that night."

Funk was a one-man show from the second he stepped through the curtain, whipping his towel at fans and ringsiders, seemingly moments away from punching his hecklers, grabbing camera equipment and ringside furniture to keep all eyes on him. The match received positive reviews and for Brian, the chance to work with the insane Terry Funk in the middle of his own transformation was akin to learning from a professor.

With Brian's mind racing a mile a minute and obsessed with the con, he saw this special show as an opportunity. Indeed, the novelty of seeing WWF and WCW wrestlers interacting (including a Chris Benoit Vs. Rad Radford match that pitted WCW and WWF talent against each other), when those worlds had always refused to co-operate, was huge. He believed that people would be desperate to see it because, after all, the promotional rivalry was the talk of the business. Excited, Brian called his mentor. "He says to me", starts Kim Wood, "'I got this tape. We wanna' duplicate it and sell it on the black market. I don't legally own this – I stole it. But it's in the United States and it would be three or four years before they could stop it'." Chuckling as he remembers the conversation, Kim states, "He stole it from Bruce Hart! These are his best friends! His best friends in life, and he's saying to me, 'You know how we could do it - by beating the copyrights. It would be like a short-term deal, but we could score fifty to a hundred grand.' And I'm saying 'Get outta' here!' He was a lovable rascal, but he was a rat."

If nothing else, Pillman took the opportunity of working the Stu Hart Anniversary Show to get close to Terry Funk. Brian added him to the list of folks he'd phone, at whatever time of night it happened to be, to spitball ideas on the best way to play the game and get the most out of his ambitious new character. One idea in particular that the two batted back and forth stands out.

"Pillman comes to me, and it was one of the last times I said, 'Brian, I'm not gonna' do it'", recollects Kim Wood. "He was hanging around Terry Funk, and the Super Bowl was going to be in Sun Devil Stadium in Phoenix, Arizona. I would get Super Bowl tickets, because I had access to them, that he would give to Jim Ross and he had got some for Funk. All those guys are crazy football fans. And Funk gets the idea, 'Kim Wood can get you tickets'. This was before 9/11 and everything so there wasn't a whole lot of security going into the Super Bowl. The end zone was such that you could drop down to it. He was going to go wrapped in chains and chain himself to one of the goal posts."

With the largest television audience of the year watching, the disturbance would get huge media attention which would only intensify when it was uncovered that the person doing it was a high-profile professional wrestler. With the philosophy that his value was directly tied to his ability to attract attention and publicity, there would be no greater way to jump start that perceived value than by having the entire nation talking about the crazy guy at the Super Bowl. But it wasn't to be, as Kim explains, "The key to the scam was getting the tickets, and I wouldn't do it…because *I* would get in trouble."

Determined to make it happen, Brian sought an alternative means to the end zone. The Super Bowl that year was to be contested between the Cowboys and the Steelers, and seeing an opening, Pillman dialed his Pittsburgh connection. "Brian called me up", remembers Mark Madden, who was covering the game for the newspaper. "He goes, 'Look, here's what you need to do. You need to give me your press pass, and then I'm gonna' sneak on the field and chain myself to the goal posts. That'll get on TV everywhere, it'll really help this gimmick out a lot, it'll make me a lot of money.' And he was serious about that. So I said to Brian, 'That's a great idea. But if I did that, I couldn't cover the game, I'd be fired by the Pittsburgh Post-Gazette, I would never work in my industry again.' And there's like a long, thirty second pause. Then Brian goes, 'Look, I can't be the only one making sacrifices'."

Pillman closed out the year with an appearance at Starrcade, an event pitting the WCW wrestlers against the crew from New Japan. Instead of wrestling against a member of the New Japan roster he may have been familiar with, he was lined up for a run-in during the main event of Randy Savage versus Ric Flair for the WCW World Title. Despite constant company efforts to diminish Flair, the belt found its way back to "The Nature Boy" after interference from the Horsemen. But the post-match scene was stolen by Brian, who spat on the camera lens in his rabid celebration, then proceeded to rip the championship belt from Flair's hands and lay into the fallen Savage. "Look at this loose cannon!", uttered Tony Schiavone, a tag Dusty Rhodes on commentary was happy to repeat.

With the little time he was afforded, Brian seized the moment. Going along with his side of the scam, Bischoff told people that Pillman wasn't even scheduled for Starrcade but showed up anyway. Intimating that Brian was written into the show late in the game, Bischoff feigned disgust with his improvised antics.

As 1995 bled into 1996, Brian had his end game in mind and the embers of a method to achieve it. He began putting on a show wherever he went, whether it be in hotels, restaurants, strip clubs or locker rooms around the country. He began calling dial-in radio shows in character to rant and rave, or contacting local newspapers to harass them about their wrestling coverage. He began showing up late for television and would disappear for hours at an event. When he did show up, he'd be in character the whole time. It didn't take long for word to get around, the gossip queens on the roster all too happy to talk about what was going on with Brian. One person Pillman didn't stay in character to, however, was Dave Meltzer. To the contrary, Kim advised him to avoid talking to Meltzer for a few weeks, hoping to keep him out of the loop without having to lie to him.

On the January 1st, 1996 episode of Nitro, Pillman was given another chance to cut his teeth with the new persona. After Arn Anderson and Chris Benoit lost their respective matches, Brian hit the ring to verbally run down his Horsemen teammates. Following his rant, where he once again mentioned the Dungeon of Doom as a target, two of its members, Kevin Sullivan and The Zodiac, began walking down the aisle. The Giant, another member, followed them out and dragged them to the back, not wanting the two sides to collide. Storylines aside, the talk among the wrestlers had become strong enough that in Dave Meltzer's review of the show, he wrote, "Pillman only said one thing to nearly cost him his job in this interview when talking about how well Benoit performs with naked women in the limo."

Brian got a kick out of working everybody and would constantly perform little put-ons and moments of erratic behavior, just to gauge reactions and the psychology of those around him. With his new attitude, he was getting noticed. It helped that Bischoff was playing along with the mock conflict to whoever he talked to as well, keeping everybody he worked with, including top star Hulk Hogan and head booker Kevin Sullivan, in the dark.

The following week, Pillman and Bischoff built the tension further. On the January 8th Nitro, Pillman accompanied Chris Benoit to the ring for his match against Alex Wright. Watching Brian at ringside was captivating as he interacted with fans and honed his quirky gimmick, a powder keg ready to explode in any direction, embodying many of the qualities Terry Funk exuded doing the same thing. Any time the director in the production truck cut to a shot following Brian, Bischoff on commentary urged them to get the camera off him. When the match was finished, Pillman stood over Wright and spat on him, prompting Eric to say, "Don't be surprised if you don't see Brian Pillman in WCW a whole lot longer", as the scene wrapped up. The combination of Bischoff's off-kilter comments, Brian's character and the backstage whispers were creating the desired effect. Without being wise to the scheme, Meltzer wrote, "The irony on Pillman is that the more out of control he gets, the better he is as a heel and he's probably the best heel in the business right now, but everyone is afraid of him because they think he's out of control." The newsletters all reported that Brian's WCW tenure was looking shaky, and "The Rogue Horseman" personally rejoiced at his ability to create talk. Eric did too, and was eager for more.

A match was scheduled for the next episode of Nitro between the Horsemen and the Dungeon of Doom. Rather than go ahead with the announced match, every member of the Horsemen and the Dungeon called a truce in the ring, vowing to stay on neutral terms. But the segment, which included all the top heels in the company, was really all about Pillman, who was addressed by Sullivan as the cause of all the problems between the two sides. Arn Anderson, who was doing the talking on the Horsemen's behalf, was interrupted by Brian in his now typical off-beat pomp, and responded by slapping his Horseman cohort hard across the face. Pillman's expression changed, as Bischoff on commentary made a point to mention, "Watch Benoit!", who was visibly unhappy with Arn's strike.

The infighting storyline with the Horsemen had seeds planted from the beginning of Pillman's change in character, but the slap made a point to emphasize it. The long-term plan being kicked around by Pillman and Bischoff was for the Horseman to break in half, with Brian taking Benoit with him as his "enforcer", much as Arn was to Flair. From there, Pillman would rebuild the group as the leader, adding two more names to his stable before feuding with Flair and Anderson. Brian kicked around names like "The Apocalypse" and "The Generation X Horsemen", wanting his team to represent the next evolution of the classic unit. He also pitched names like Eddie Guerrero, David Finlay and Chris Jericho as possible candidates to round out the group. It was an idea Brian kept in mind as his elaborate scheme continued.

Pillman was now being figured into the plans going forward. He was scheduled to get a couple of wins over Dean Malenko and Eddie Guerrero on television to set him up for a shot at the WCW World Title against new champion Randy Savage on the February 5th Nitro. But two unplanned incidents that occurred within the space of a week really threw gas on the fire.

The matches with Malenko and Guerrero were to occur on the Janaury 22nd Nitro and January 23rd Clash of the Champions respectively. Both events were held at Caesar's Palace in Las Vegas, strategically timed to coincide with the annual convention held by the National Association of Television Program Executives (NATPE). Both the WWF and WCW would regularly host a booth in an effort to rub shoulders with television bigwigs and raise their profile in the industry. It wasn't unusual for the wrestlers themselves, typically in costume, to be brought along by the company to garner attention. With so many high-profile people in the same location at the same time, it was the place to be for a guy like Brian.

Pillman headed to the Sands Convention Center in full Loose Cannon regalia. "Pillman had a scam where he'd carry a camera around with him", recounts Kim Wood, "He'd take people's pictures and wouldn't say anything. He just had a thing going on, and he'd meet girls that way and take pictures of anybody official looking." Pillman took his camera on this particular trip and since he didn't have a press pass, wasn't allowed to enter the booth area. Instead, he was drawing attention to himself and taking pictures of pretty girls among the thousands of regular attendees. One person who did have a press pass, however, was Brian's good friend, Dave Meltzer. He bumped into Brian and since he was leaving, he offered him the pass. Pillman gladly took it and sauntered in, for this gave him direct access to the real target in his entire game – Vince McMahon. Brian seized the moment and made a beeline for the WWF booth, which was being manned by Vince and Jim Ross. In character, he launched into an outrageous display of praise for the WWF, ending by yelling "I love you, man!" in McMahon's face. Clutching the camera hanging around his neck, Brian began snapping pictures of Vince, who clearly had no idea what to make of the situation. Pillman handed his camera off to a nearby girl, asking her to take a picture of Vince and Brian together. Pillman then turned to his old friend Jim Ross, who couldn't help but be unnerved. Brian lunged forward and hugged him enthusiastically, making sure to whisper in his ear, "It's all a work", before saying goodbye.

McMahon was totally ill at ease, but Brian had made a distinct impression with his audacious approach, as Ross clued Vince in on Pillman's quiet message. Meanwhile, Pillman faxed the photo of him and Vince to Kim Wood. Kim promptly faxed it on himself – to Dave Meltzer, and also Wade Keller (Pro Wrestling Torch editor). "The reason we faxed the picture, it was like, let's give them the pearls but they've got to supply the string. We're fucking with them too", says Wood. Indeed, the more conversation about a defection, or just talk about what he was doing in general, the better.

Sure enough, people were biting. When Pillman arrived at Nitro, he proceeded to vanish once again for several hours and a number of WCW personnel began to panic, thinking Brian had left the building to board a plane to Stockton, California, the site of that night's Raw. While the one-hour flight made it a possibility, it wasn't the case, and Brian appeared in time for his match with Dean Malenko.

Brian created even more news when his match at Clash of the Champions against Eddie Guerrero took place. His matches with Malenko and Guerrero fell short of in-ring expectations based on time constraints and Pillman's focus on playing his character rather than putting on a wrestling clinic. Case in point, Brian rolled to the arena floor during the early moments of his match with Guerrero to hassle the fans. When he went to do it again, Eddie Guerrero jumped to the top rope as if to dive on Brian on floor. Spontaneously, Brian ran behind Bobby Heenan, who was commentating at ringside with Tony Schiavone. Pillman started pulling at Bobby's jacket from behind, causing Heenan to yell out, "What the fuck are you doing!?", live on TBS. Heenan had suffered severe neck injuries during his time wrestling and managing, even having to undergo surgery to correct the issues. With Bobby paranoid that either a ringside fan was going for his neck, or that it was the man whose reputation for unpredictable conduct was growing by the day, he slipped up. Heenan moved away from the desk and started walking up the aisle, clearly rattled. After considering heading backstage, "The Brain" regained his composure and returned to the announce booth, apologizing for losing his cool and blaming Pillman.

Brian ended up riffing off the incident in a promo later in the evening with Eric Bischoff, threatening to use "the seven words you're not supposed to say on TV". He followed up by looking at Eric and saying that if he did, "You'd be fff….in a lot of trouble." Bischoff closed the segment by stating that Brian was on "thin, thin ice".

When the F bomb turned out not to generate much static with TBS, Bischoff was happy to tell his employees that the heat was falling on Brian. In the Observer, Meltzer wrote of the incident, "Not sure what the status is of Pillman as it appears to change by the minute." Wade Keller wrote in the Torch that, "While there are legitimate roots of Pillman having problems with management, this current on-air bashing of Pillman by Bischoff is so believable and effective, it pretty much has to be a work. Otherwise, why keep featuring him on TV?" Though onlookers had their suspicions and their theories, nobody knew for sure.

The incident created a lot of noise, attracting the attention of several in the WWF booking committee. "The first thing I remember was when he went by Heenan and grabbed his neck", recalls Jim Cornette, who was working on the committee at the time. "I remember watching that in Knoxville and thinking, 'Ah *fuck*!'. He looked to me like he was Kurt Cobain, which I'm sure was an influence. I thought it was a great fucking gimmick because, just the look on his face, it was convincing. It was believable that he was a maniac, and the fact he jostled Bobby into doing that made every viewer think that even the Brain, that knows everything and knows all this shit is supposed to be fake, *he's* scared of this guy or doesn't trust him, so he must be nuts. It was great!"

People were being fooled, and Brian invested himself even deeper into the character. He got a gig with Bill Cunningham's radio show on 700WLW in Cincinnati to allow him to be the Loose Cannon even more, playing a right wing shock jock, interacting with callers and taking pot shots at Hulk Hogan at every turn. It originally started as a one-time gig as a guest stand-in back in December, but he did well enough to be invited back. Alex Marvez, who at the time was working for the Dayton Daily News, remembers his personal introduction to Brian during this period.

"Through Kim, I got to meet Brian", begins Alex. "I liked the guy, but he also was very secretive as to what was going on. He didn't want anyone to know whether this was a work or a shoot. At the same time, and I don't think this can be understated, he was really becoming a mainstream media personality in Cincinnati, and had the chance to truly become part of the fabric of that city way outside of pro wrestling with what he was doing on WLW."

Marvez recalls getting an invite to appear on Brian's show alongside John Harbaugh, where Pillman had a couple of surprises for his guests. "The first is on John, which is that he calls John's dad, who's the head coach of Western Kentucky at the time, and has the coach start telling stories about John as a kid, which was just fabulous. You could just see John getting redder and redder in the face as things go on. The other thing is, Melanie comes in wearing a leopard print onesie. And you can just imagine, I have no idea what's going on here, just the shock value. But Brian was fabulous, he had great personality, dealt with topics in and out. It wasn't even a wrestling show, per se. He would talk football, some wrestling, but also just mainstream stuff."

The response to his show was strong, and there were people at the station trying to convince Brian that with his presentation, he had a future in the world of radio. However, it wasn't what he really wanted.

He was tunnel-visioned in his efforts to channel the hostility of Bischoff Vs. McMahon for his own gain, and was using every trick in the book to advance his standing within both hierarchies. With McMahon's known love of bodybuilding, it was an easy move for Kim Wood to send Vince Hammer Strength jackets and equipment. Meanwhile, Ted Turner's uncle, who raised Ted, lived across the street from Kim. Through this connection Pillman would send Turner, a big fan himself, various wrestling memorabilia.

With the ongoing storyline with the Horsemen and Dungeon of Doom, Brian pitched his next idea. The boss, Bischoff, was already playing this to the hilt. Kevin Sullivan, the leader of the Dungeon, was the head booker, so it naturally fit for Pillman to oppose him based on the image he was hoping to perpetuate in real life as anti-WCW office. The backstage gossip and talk amongst newsletters and fans in the know would only amplify, and the rebellious aura surrounding Pillman would as well. With that in mind, Pillman approached Sullivan and confided in him a portion of his plan, telling him that everything he was doing was to create a buzz and convince people he was legitimately crazy. Much like Bischoff, Sullivan was going to be a part of the scheme, and so the manipulation seemed appealing. Plus, Sullivan deduced, if the wrestlers buy it, the fans will too. Similar to his original plan to fight with Bischoff, Brian was willing to let Sullivan be the aggressor to appeal to his ego and earn the supposed respect that would come from the other wrestlers as a tough authority figure. Pillman and Sullivan started talking about the things they could do to create a faux tension between them backstage, as they looked to embark on one of the more bizarre storylines in years.

On the January 29th Nitro, with Sullivan and Hugh Morrus in the ring, Arn Anderson and Brian Pillman stormed the scene to talk about the tensions between the groups. Anderson turned to Brian and began to lay blame at his feet, vowing more tough love while taking off his belt, saying, "This is going to hurt you more than it does me." But as Pillman pleaded with Arn to reconsider, Sullivan and Morrus attacked. Pillman ended up on the floor as the Dungeon members double-teamed Arn. The camera strategically cut to Brian on the outside, who instead of storming the ring to save Anderson, was cowering behind the apron. Sullivan spotted him, ran to the outside and began whipping Pillman with the belt. In the ring, Arn made his own comeback against Morrus, then ran outside to aid Brian. The first strike had been made by the Dungeon, as the two Horsemen returned to the ring to vow revenge. Brian closed the segment saying, "I got us into this mess, and I'll get us out!"

WCW's next set of tapings were on February 1st. The regular setting of the Disney MGM Studios was pre-booked on this occasion, and instead Eric Bischoff made a deal with Universal Studios to use them as a base for 13 weeks of tapings. On the first night, Pillman was part of another ridiculous story that occurred at the Residence Inn. Just after midnight, a woman was thrown out of her hotel room naked, and the man responsible ended up taking her hostage and barricading himself in his room. The SWAT team was called in to deal with the situation and their first move was to evacuate all the rooms. As the WCW crew was staying there, wrestlers and officials filled the hallways. Brian, in character and wearing his Horsemen shirt, decided this was the perfect time to make a scene and started telling everybody, "Don't worry, the Horsemen are here to save the day!" Pillman started barking orders at the police and acting as if he was about to go in the room and apprehend the guy himself, having to be held back. Even in the middle of a tense stand-off he didn't drop character, opting instead to steal the scene. "The cops didn't know if the guy in the room was armed or not", says Mark Madden, who was now working for WCW. As it turns out, he wasn't, which allowed the SWAT team to tear-gas the man out of the room and promptly pound him into oblivion. "When the cops were done beating the shit out him", adds Madden, "They were about to take him down to the station, and Brian insisted that the cops allow him to pose for a picture with the guy. So there's this picture somewhere of Brian with this huge cheese-eating grin and his arm around this guy who had been beaten within an inch of his life."

Part of Brian's plan to be promoted better by being on the inside with Bischoff and Sullivan was already working. He hadn't lost a single match since the inception of the Loose Cannon and the plans for him were only getting bigger. His scheduled match with Randy Savage on the February 5th Nitro was pulled, and Benoit was put in Brian's place to lose. Instead, the plans now had Savage Vs. Pillman for the WCW World Title at the Uncensored pay-per-view, a huge step up. With that match rescheduled, Brian was booked on the February 5th Nitro to team with Arn Anderson against Sullivan and Morris, in what turned out to be the latest act of the Loose Cannon's twisted theatre.

The match began as per usual in an exchange with Pillman and Morrus, but took a turn when Sullivan tagged in. As Pillman shot Sullivan into the ropes and met him on the rebound with a clothesline, Sullivan opted not to sell the blow, barely registering it. The two continued, with Sullivan Irish whipping Pillman into the ropes and catching him as he returned with a right hand that Pillman, in kind, didn't sell. Pillman and Sullivan exchanged a flippant verbal exchange as both men tagged out to their partners, seemingly frustrated.

Things continued with Sullivan out of the ring, as Anderson and Pillman worked over Hugh Morrus. After a clunky spot in the corner, Pillman barked at Morrus to tag out, bringing Sullivan back in. Pillman charged him as he entered, both men swinging wildly at each other as the crowd's excitement started to rise, the blows being thrown unlike your typical pro wrestling punch. Sullivan picked Brian up and hung him in the corner upside down for his trademark running knee. Upon making contact, Pillman immediately rose, again not selling the move, and threw another wild punch. Sullivan double-legged Brian to the ground and got on top of him, as Anderson and Morrus, sensing the match was falling apart at the seams, got in to separate the two. Pillman lunged back in for a front facelock but Sullivan slipped out, grabbed Brian's head, and started digging his fingers into Pillman's eyeball (an old school wrestler trick for real life fight situations), prompting Arn to grab Sullivan and yell, "Not the eye! Not the eye!", pulling him away. It appeared to anybody inclined to think deeper that this fake pro wrestling match had broken down before their very eyes. Bischoff on commentary spoke softly, saying, "This match is officially out of control. Trust me when I tell you that."

Arn splintered off with Kevin for a spot in the aisle as Pillman fought with

Morrus. With the planned finish being Sullivan whipping Pillman with the belt, Sullivan fired off two shots to Brian's back before "The Loose Cannon" rolled out the ring and walked off, a furious look on his face, with Bischoff again ordering the production truck to keep the camera off Pillman.

As chaotic as the scene was in simulating a total lack of communication, the show didn't end when the cameras cut to commercial. Brian immediately got into a huge argument with Sullivan as soon as he walked through the curtain, in front of a number of the wrestlers, about how Sullivan wasn't selling for him. The two went back and forth before Brian stormed out of the building, leaving eyewitnesses with the impression he was done with WCW. Bischoff, in the following segment, off-handedly mentioned that he doubted that Pillman would be in WCW by Superbrawl that coming Sunday. Certainly, the opinion going around was that the altercation on live TV was unplanned and legitimate, as the Wrestling Observer wrote that, "It may finally be the straw that breaks the camel's back when it comes to Pillman's tenure in WCW."

The next day, WCW went back to Universal Studios for more TV tapings. Bischoff called a meeting with all the wrestlers in the dressing room. As the assembly got underway, stumbling in through the door, acting as if he were under the influence, came Brian Pillman. As Eric began to go over the do's and do not's of working at Universal, Brian blurted out, "Does that go for the booker man too?" The boss and Pillman argued for all to see, just as Brian and Kim had laid out at the kitchen table weeks before. Bischoff told Pillman he was very lucky to still be employed after what happened on Nitro, and hinted to everybody that he probably wouldn't be for much longer.

After the meeting wrapped up, a number of wrestlers pulled Sullivan aside, talking about what a jerk Brian was being lately and that he should probably kick his ass for speaking out of turn. Sullivan would later joke that the same wrestlers would go to Pillman and praise him for speaking out against the booker, and tell Brian he should kick Sullivan's ass. Kevin and Brian laughed over the phone later that night at the two-faced nature of the guys.

For the rest of the tapings, Pillman was kept away from everybody else, dressing in a different trailer, which management told people was due to the heat between Pillman and Sullivan. Brian only caused more of a stir when it came time to film his matches, as he and Benoit went to the ring to wrestle Renegade and Dave Sullivan. Dave had taken to carrying his pet rabbit Ralph to all his bouts, placing him in a cage during the contest. Playing his crazed character to the hilt, Pillman grabbed Ralph's cage, with him inside it, and booted it into the air. Reckless as it was and as much as it freaked a number of folks in WCW out, Brian wasn't about to miss a chance to be the topic of conversation.

Jim Ross, Bruce Pritchard and Jim Cornette in the WWF were watching and hearing the chatter about Brian and loving every second of it. "The best thing was", explains Jim Cornette, "He was able to do it himself within the context of not only how they were booking him at the start, but even when he pitched to be more and more nutty and Kevin was in on it, the shit he was able to get away with while still doing, in principle if not in letter, what they asked him to do, it was like somebody getting the lead role in Death of a Salesman on Broadway and playing it like the Rocky Horror Picture Show, and nobody complains. It was amazing."

Sullivan and Pillman was booked for Superbrawl in a "Respect" Strap Match, a take-off of the "I Quit" match, where the only way to determine a winner was to punish your opponent enough to force him to utter the words "I respect you". Of course, after what happened on Nitro and his antics at the Universal tapings, there was plenty of second-guessing over whether the match would even take place. Pillman, playing his part, opted not to talk to most of the people he regularly spoke to, instead calling people from all over the country that he wouldn't talk to frequently, insisting the situation was a shoot. All week long, Brian was saying that he thought he'd be done in WCW imminently because when you clash with the booker, you have to go elsewhere. Privately, he was just planting seeds for his real next step.

Brian would constantly refer back to the man who devised the scam with him, Kim Wood, on what to do next to propagate the impression of unpredictability. With Brian already getting a reputation as an outspoken outlaw, Wood imparted some knowledge to Brian that would help the illusion tremendously. "I knew the guy that did the TV for Paul Heyman - Steve Karel", says Wood. "I knew through Karel, and this is something that they'd all deny, that both Vince and Bischoff were paying Heyman to keep ECW going. Both were, without the other one knowing it."

In the almost 18 months since Brian's first ECW appearance, the promotion had exploded as an underground phenomenon. From bringing in talent like Rey Mysterio Jr., Psicosis and Juventud Guerrera to introduce Lucha Libre to American wrestling, developing a glut of cutting edge characters like Raven, The Sandman and Sabu, through to featuring some of the best promos in years from the likes of Steve Austin and Cactus Jack, ECW was the best television product in American wrestling. Given their strong anti-WCW mentality it seemed unfathomable for the two sides to be working together. But as Wood found out, there was a connection.

This covert association was the perfect thing to exploit to spotlight the Loose Cannon. Armed with this information, Brian talked Bischoff and Sullivan into creating a scenario where he'd leave WCW in dramatic fashion and show up in ECW while under WCW contract. Surely, everybody would believe he was fired if he showed up in the anti-WCW promotion, spewing venom in their direction. Plus, he said, he'd be hotter than ever when he came back because he'd have become the ultimate rebel, and everybody would believe in the animosity between the two sides. Bischoff and Sullivan salivated at the thought of such an elaborate charade and began putting things in place to orchestrate the move. After speaking with Kim Wood, Steve Karel went to Paul Heyman, who jumped at the opportunity to use Pillman at a time when he was generating so much talk. Brian didn't even get paid by ECW for the appearances, instead being paid his WCW money under the table. Heyman, in exchange, would give him carte blanche to do whatever he wanted for his character, since he was getting the benefit of Brian Pillman on his television show. The set-up was mutually beneficial, and the plan was in place.

The night before Superbrawl on WCW Saturday Night, the company ran the full, unedited skirmish between Pillman and Sullivan from Nitro, and ran an inset promo from the leader of the Dungeon. Sullivan began by holding a pencil up to the camera and breaking it in half. The booker of a territory was sometimes referred to as "the pencil", and the insinuation from Sullivan was, for the people that knew he was booker (a very small percentage of the audience), he was no longer acting under that guise. "Now that we've got that out of the way", started The Taskmaster, "You want to be a free agent? You want to be a loose cannon? Me and you in St. Pete, I'm gonna' make you a free agent!"

It was surreal. The notion of airing the Nitro match as it was and then airing a promo like that, deliberately playing off backstage machinations, prompted Dave Meltzer to finally call Brian. "At first, I was like everybody else wondering what the hell is going on and I was kind of worried", says Dave. "But when Kevin Sullivan did the interview it's like, okay, it's got to be an angle because he would have never done this interview. And then I talked to Brian and he was really mad that I knew. He was just mad because it was supposed to be this secret. I go, 'Well Kevin did that interview'. And Brian was almost like, 'Well he wasn't supposed to do it like that and give it away!' And I go, 'Well, most people still didn't see through it." But I knew Kevin would never do that interview in that way if it was real, he would have ignored the subject. Because it wasn't a spontaneous live TV interview where you go, 'Well, it's live TV', you know what I mean? It was taped." Keeping his cards close to his chest, Pillman still didn't divulge his entire plan at this point.

To fans that lived and breathed wrestling, and sought out every bit of news they could, Sullivan's promo was an acknowledgement of the inner workings that hadn't been seen before. Today, references to real life elements of wrestling are somewhat commonplace, but in February 1996, everybody was talking about what this was…or wasn't. There was enough intrigue with the new ground being broken that people were eager to see the next chapter of this unfolding saga. "The type of theater that wrestling is, it's all tied to mystery", articulates Kim Wood, explaining the allure of the angle. "People love mystery."

Pillman got in a rebuttal to Sullivan's pencil-breaking promo the next night on WCW Main Event, which doubled as the Superbrawl pre-game show. Chris Cruise conducted the interview, even after being told by officials that he didn't have to if he felt uncomfortable, since Pillman was crazy enough to punch Cruise on a whim. In building up the Respect match, Brian's words spoke to those who knew about his political conflicts in years past and served as an explanation for the shift in demeanor.

"Boy, how times have changed", said Brian. "Remember the good old days? The power of the pencil? The dominance games?" To the fans savvier to the business, it was played as if the years of having the rug pulled out from under him by bookers had created the new Pillman. "You want to make me a free agent?", he continued, "Moron, I'm already a free agent. I'm an independent contractor which simply means - I can work for whoever I want, whenever I want. I can say and do whatever I want. My suggestion to you, Kevin Sullivan, is to take that pencil and erase my name from the card." As Pillman went to continue, the video faded back to the arena. Whatever was going to happen, based on the build-up alone it promised to be unique.

The bout was listed on the Superbrawl format sheet as a 12-minute match, starting with the referee hooking both men by the wrist to the leather strap. But the theatrics were playing out all day long as Pillman pulled a vanishing act, with Sullivan loudly panicking that nobody had seen him to give him the planned finish. Even further, Brian had stolen the strap that was to be used.

When it came time to get underway Pillman charged the ring wielding the strap, with he and Sullivan immediately tussling in much the same manner they did on Nitro. Sullivan went for a double leg takedown, while Brian began whipping the rawhide against Sullivan's skin, including a vicious shot across his face. As Kevin got to his feet, he fired off a great looking punch to the jaw, sending Pillman to a knee. Brian got up and started chasing after referee Jimmy Jett, who was clutching the microphone in order to capture the magic words that would result in victory for either man. As Pillman took control of the mic, he looked back at Sullivan, and famously proclaimed, "I respect you...booker man."

Pillman dropped out the ring and walked to the back, holding a middle finger in the air to the audience before the camera cut away from him. The match had ended in one minute and thirty-six seconds, apparently by forfeit, as the backstage area went into a complete panic. The production team flipped out at the meticulously timed out show being thrown off-kilter. The announcers were completely jarred, not knowing a thing and without a clue how to react at the exposé. Pillman walked backstage and immediately got into an argument with Eric Bischoff in front of the wrestlers with both men furiously swearing at each other, before Pillman in his acerbic tone said, "Sorry about your 12-minute strap match!" In the middle of the chaos, with the wrestlers awestruck by what was happening, Disco Inferno was the only one to offer up a conflicting opinion. With everybody else spellbound, Disco asserted, "They're working the boys."

Disco later clarified why he said it in an interview with Bryan Alvarez, saying, "I just knew whatever Brian's doing is a work. Whatever it is, it's a work. It's got some plan to it because I know this guy. Whatever he's done or whatever he's doing has resulted from hours and hours of phone conversations with people to figure out the best way to do it." Ignoring Disco's rightfully-placed cynicism, the rest of the locker room was too caught up to consider it, including a confused Hulk Hogan asking, "What's the deal with Pillman?"

After the argument with Bischoff, Pillman caught up with Chris Benoit and left the building. The incident took on a life of its own immediately, as whispers of parking lot arguments and Pillman jumping in a car and crashing into another vehicle in his hasty exit made the rounds.

On the live pay-per-view, Arn Anderson had to be brought out by Jimmy

Hart for a completely on-the-fly, improvised strap match that went to a non-finish. But it didn't matter for Brian, Eric and Kevin's plan, which was to fool everybody. To the die-hard fans, Brian used a taboo, inside term from the closed world of pro wrestling, outed Sullivan as booker and "legitimately" fucked with a WCW pay-per-view for the world to see. To the casual fans, they had no idea what a "booker man" was and just left thinking Pillman was a nutjob who walked out on a fight. Regardless, all the talk amongst the communities Bischoff and Sullivan were listening to was about the Brian Pillman situation. In the Observer, Dave Meltzer wrote, "It was either the most highly calculated and hard to logically explain ruse in the recent history of pro wrestling, or the end of Pillman in WCW."

Brian flew home the next day, the only reference to him on that night's episode of Nitro coming in a Superbrawl recap video package, when Eric Bischoff simply said, "Pillman, he left the building, he's history", before quickly moving on. All of his matches recorded at the Universal tapings were pulled from broadcast. That Thursday night, February 15th, WCW publically announced the firing of Brian Pillman. Responding immediately, Pillman stated that he'd hired Reuven Katz, the same lawyer that famously represented Pete Rose, and was suing WCW for wrongful termination.

ECW was running its big monthly show at the ECW Arena two days later, and Brian was to fly to Philadephia for the event titled "Cyberslam". As much fun as it was to work the world, it was at this point that Pillman had a conversation with the only other man who knew the ultimate purpose, Kim Wood, who felt the need to clue in one more person. "Once the thing got going it was like, Brian, we've got to tell Meltzer. We can't keep him in the dark, he would misinterpret anything else. The other guys, fuck 'em, who cares", explains Wood. "So I called Dave and I told him everything. So there were only three people that really knew what was going on."

Pillman showed up backstage at the ECW Arena wearing a La Parka mask and speaking to others in broken Japanese to throw people off the scent. As the event began, Joey Styles stood in the center of the ring to record the opening for Hardcore TV. Just as he vowed that the show would be "one of the most extreme hours of wrestling", the lights in the building cut out. It was a typical ECW trick, usually leading to a surprise appearance, and this was no exception. A rush of excitement surged through the crowd in anticipation, and when the lights came back on, standing in the middle of the ring holding aloft his familiar cane with the horse head on the end, was Brian Pillman.

17 - THE LONG CON

The fans erupted, a cascade of fists passionately pumping into the air to greet the sight of the antihero that embodied the frustrations they had with World Championship Wrestling. Brian slowly rotated, his seemingly calm manner juxtaposed perfectly by the chaotic reaction, which eventually morphed into a chorus of "Pill-man!" chants. As Joey Styles interrupted the scene, asking "What are you doing here?", Brian moved towards the microphone and began the most memorable promo of his career.

"Haven't you heard?", started Brian, who launched his speech against the backdrop of the fans singing in unison – "Bischoff takes it up the ass, do-dah, do-dah! Bischoff takes it up the ass, all-the-do-dah-day!" Indeed, there was an obvious direction for this promo to go, and Brian was going to give them what they wanted. After clarifying his situation by saying "I…have been fired…by Eric Bischoff!", the boos began to thunder throughout the arena. Pillman let the response linger, joking that not only was Eric popular with the fans, he was popular with his legal department as well, before bursting into an aggressive, "Bischoff, or should I say – JERKOFF!" The audience loudly cheered. Bashing WCW's head was nothing new to them. It had been done countless times on ECW shows, but the fresh wound of Pillman's apparent exodus made it relevant, with the delivery of Brian's words adding an extra sting to the tirade. After stating, through his psychotic laugh, that the "former coffee gopher for Verne Gagne is now leading the show in the big time!", Pillman shot his piercing stare at the camera as he fearlessly proclaimed, "You…are a piece…of *fucking shit!*"

Moving away from the microphone after a deafening roar of approval for his profane statement, Joey Styles began his typical throw to a commercial break. "A bombshell has been dropped, Brian Pillman is in the ECW Are-", when Pillman cut the voice of ECW off before he could conclude. Indeed, this wasn't the conventional segment. After giving the cliché anti-WCW rhetoric, powerful as it was, it was time for the real fun to begin. "No no no, Joey Styles, you're not running this interview, I am. 'Cos I'm Brian…Fuckin'…Pillman!"

With the fans eating out of the palm of his hand he grabbed the microphone again, taking the segment in a direction befitting his unpredictable moniker, his eyes growing wider, his pacing more erratic. "You know what Eric Bischoff is? Eric Bischoff is each and every one of these motherfuckin' smart marks rolled up into one giant piece of shit!"

The response this time was different. In the building, the sound system began to falter, which Brian picked up on. "I guess you guys didn't get that. *Smart marks*!", said Pillman, his voice dripping with his unique twinge of condescending sarcasm. He was pandering no longer. Instead, he was turning his venom on the people. "What's a smart mark? A mark with a high IQ?", Brian wondered aloud, aiming his question at the front row of regulars. One of these regulars was known as "Sign Guy", due to his proclivity for bringing placards with inside references that encapsulated the niche mentality of the ECW live crowd. As luck would have it, the fan had brought a sign bearing the message "Pillman – Don't Work Me", and was holding it up at this precise moment. A number of surrounding fans began chanting "Read the sign!" Brian chuckled for a second, then returned to his derisive tone, "Okay, *smart marks*, okay!" After explaining that a mark was a guy that spends his last twenty dollars on crack cocaine and believed that O.J. Simpson didn't do it, he vowed to do "the only appropriate thing Brian Pillman should do – I'm gonna' yank out my Johnson and piss in this hellhole!"

As Brian dropped the microphone with a thud on the canvas, he began unbuttoning his jeans to the astonishment of the crowd. ECW's on-screen Commissioner Todd Gordon, real life booker Paul Heyman and Shane Douglas set the land speed record in hitting the ring to stop Brian committing the heinous act, with both Heyman and Gordon proclaiming, "this wasn't part of the deal!" The scene was tense and captivating, as Pillman replied, looking right into Heyman's eyes. "Deal? I do whatever I want, whenever I want, and I don't give a fuck about you or your smart marks…*booker man!*"

ECW's powers-that-be ordered security to eject Pillman from the building, which led to a standoff of back and forth insults off-microphone, right there in the middle of the ring. Finally, as a pair of uniformed officers began to escort Brian out, the scenario apparently all but completed, it was time for it to take another twist. To say that Pillman's verbal spear to the fanbase was completely effective in forcing them to hate his guts would be a lie – they were caught up in the wildly entertaining spectacle. They were even chanting "Let him piss" when it looked as though Brian was to be hauled out. But Pillman broke free and held four fingers in the air, the Horseman symbol dating back years, as his attention turned to the same front row fans he'd insulted earlier. Pillman launched a wad of spit at one of them, gesturing to the fan to take a free shot at him. After a couple of seconds, the fan threw a punch, which Brian ducked underneath, dragging him over the guardrail and onto the concrete floor. The audience gasped with legitimate disbelief, not an easy response to elicit from such a jaded crowd. Pillman pulled the fan into the ring and reached into his boot, pulling out a fork. As the panicked voice of Joey Styles could be heard frantically yelling "He's crazy!" over the P.A. system, Brian lunged forward, stabbing the fan repeatedly in the neck, until Shane Douglas returned to the ring to run him off to the back.

The rest of the scene played out perfectly. Some fans stood in shock not knowing what to make of it. Others, feeling that what they'd seen was amazing to behold, began their familiar battle cry of "E-C-W!" The "fan", actually a trainee and member of the ECW ring crew named Chris Krueger, was surrounded by medical personnel as security pulled a wild Pillman back through the curtain. With him fighting every step of the way, they dragged him around the ring, through the crowd and out through the front door, as the fans serenaded him on the way out with a loud "Na-na-na-na, na-na-na-na, hey heyyy, goodbye!"

When all was said and done, it was an excellent angle and a masterful play to debut in a manner you couldn't ignore and still had people guessing what was real and what wasn't. The vibe in the air was infectious, and Pillman stayed in character long after the show was over.

With the night's event concluded, the entire crew went to the Travelodge where ECW routinely stayed, and where the company's fans would gravitate to hang around the wrestlers. Unlike others who were happy to socialize with the fans and enjoy the positive attention, Brian walked into the lobby with Stevie Richards looking to make a scene. "There was this woman who came up to him with this scrapbook, asking for him to sign it", remembers Mike

Johnson of PWInsider.com, a regular at the ECW events. "Brian's kind of looking through the pages of it, then he just screams, 'Fuck you!' in this woman's face and tosses the book in the air."

When Sabu walked through the lobby, Pillman began cutting a promo on him in front of everybody. Calling Sabu every slur under the sun, Brian looked ready to fight, as a dumbstruck Sabu stood in confusion at Pillman's claim that he'd ducked him in WCW in 1995. "Sabu is standing in the lobby, wide-eyed, in sheer terror not knowing how to react to this", says Jeremiah Evans, a longtime Pillman fan who witnessed the encounter. "So of all the guys for Pillman to pick, he picks the guy whose gimmick is he doesn't talk or react, he's a savage. He just totally shrunk Sabu into a terrified child right in the lobby in front of everyone."

Sandman reached his Singapore cane around Pillman's chest, pulling him into an elevator and off to his room, leaving the fans in the lobby feeling like a tornado had just blown through. "Everybody in the lobby goes back about their business", adds Mike Johnson, "Suddenly, the elevator doors open again, and there's Pillman looking completely normal for about one second, like he's laughing to Sandman. Then he realizes where he is and he immediately jumps out and starts again, 'I'll fucking get you, Sabu!'"

Finally, the doors closed and the lobby was safe. Funnily enough, one of the people Pillman saw on the way up to his room was his old buddy Colin Bowman, the editor of WCW Magazine, who had come to town to meet friends and watch the ECW show. Terrified that people would connect the dots and interpret a WCW presence at the event as a sign that Brian wasn't really fired, Pillman snatched Bowman into the lift and away from prying eyes. "When I was pulled into that elevator I didn't know if I was going to get the shit beaten out of me or what", says Bowman. But alas, Brian just shot him a wink and dropped him off on a different floor.

After escaping the view of the fans in the lobby, Brian met up with his old pal Raven and indulged in a late-night cocaine binge. While Pillman wasn't exactly clean prior to the Loose Cannon, it started becoming easier to rationalize poor judgement as just being part of a fictional character, merely progressing his agenda. The thrill of manipulation he'd hoped to instill in Bischoff had bled over to his own life, his grasp on the line separating fact from fiction gradually slipping.

"He definitely, as the years went by, became more and more the character", agrees Dave Meltzer. "It went from at the beginning he was Brian Pillman playing this character in the world for everybody else, to where he was playing that character at one in the morning. He was that guy all the time all of a sudden."

Perhaps the best insight on the process of morphing into a self-created character comes from Raven himself, another victim of the syndrome. "Brian was so deep into the character that he felt for it work he had to be somewhat true to it, and then it just kept getting more and more true to it", he explains. "Because in his mind it started out as a work too. He didn't plan to be that, he only wanted to be perceived as a Loose Cannon, he didn't want to be the Loose Cannon. I think what happened is, and I remember reading this about Cary Grant, that first art imitates life, but then life begins to imitate art. And I always applied that to my character because it happened to me."

After transforming himself into a brooding, self-loathing miscreant on ECW television, the personality of the real-life Scott Levy began mirroring the successful gimmick over time. With introspection, Levy draws parallels with himself and Pillman. "Raven was based on me", he says. "I'm a goofy bastard, but the traumatized person who wasn't happy with himself was real. So art imitated life. But then unfortunately, the more I became the character, the worse my drug use became and everything else because life started to imitate art. I think it happened to Brian first, and it was happening to me at the same time but I didn't even realize it was."

When watching footage from this period it's easy to understand why Brian consumed himself with the character - Pillman was having the time of his life.

"The only time that Brian was really fulfilled and comfortable with what he was doing was when he did the worked shoot", says close confidant Mark Madden. "He was very comfortable with that because he was totally in charge of it. Whatever he wanted to do, he just did. And that's what Brian wanted, in real life and in wrestling, was to act how he wanted on the spur of the moment."

The man that showed up at the ECW Arena was such a jarring contradiction to the Pillman people knew for years before that everybody took notice. "He was always the smiling, happy Flyin' Brian", reflects Jim Cornette. "Smooth, trying to get along with everybody, fun, laughing, witty, smart ass or whatever. When he completely changed into Charles Manson, it was like, 'My God, what has happened to Brian?' But it stood out." The reaction to the sensational appearance fed on itself, swelling the conversation about wrestling's sudden hot commodity.

Interestingly enough, after being clued in on the scam, Dave Meltzer's coverage was very different. In reporting on Brian's ECW appearance the Observer stated, "There are claims he's still on the (WCW) payroll as there are indications the company is going to great, and even laughable lengths to try and get everyone to believe it's a shoot." Without going into great detail on Pillman's true motive, there was no illusion portrayed by Meltzer once he knew. But it almost didn't even matter. In the same issue, Meltzer wrote, "The Pillman story was the subject of more wrestling conversation in the past week than any wrestling angle in recent memory. There was more of a reaction on both the Hotline and Internet than to the Shawn Michaels (collapsing) angle or the Lex Luger and Madusa jumps, largely because of people not being sure whether it was a shoot or a work. I'm just not sure how that translates into making money in wrestling other than from Monday through Wednesday of last week on hotlines."

Taking note of the interest and not wanting to miss a single trick, Brian started his own hotline the following week to monetize the insider interest he was gathering. He began doing as many radio interviews as possible plugging the new venture. Fans dialing in to 1-900-288-PILL were treated to a profanity-laden, insult-based tirade about the WCW office and Hulk Hogan. He designed and had printed a new T-Shirt, pocketing all the money himself rather than being handed down a small percentage of the revenue. He managed to convince ECW to advertise it on their television show, and would carry them around and sell them while playing the Loose Cannon in strip clubs and outside shows.

Pillman made another appearance in ECW days later, attending the February 23rd show in Glenolden, PA, walking to the ring during a Shane Douglas match with Raven. Smoking a cigarette and sporting a press pass around his neck, Brian had his trusty camera with him, snapping pictures of Shane Douglas and starting another heated pull-apart. The early interactions between Douglas and Pillman were designed to set things in motion for an eventual match. Thinking independently, Brian was keen on the idea of creating a videotape of his character's uncensored thoughts on the wrestling world, combined with his ECW segments and bout with Douglas, and selling it in order to make a tidy profit for himself. But it would be less than honest to say that the ECW venture was simply to set up a major match, or a quick score selling a video.

There was an urgency to Brian's actions since the death of ex-girlfriend

Rochelle in October. While it is perfectly understandable why somebody might throw themselves so hard into their work in the fallout of such a tragic situation, there was more to it than providing a distraction to the cruel real world by living in a realm of fantasy. The reason tied in to why Brian saw ECW as such an appealing option in the first place.

Right after Rochelle's suicide, Brian, fearing that his own health problems and wild lifestyle for years were going to come with a price, looked to take out life insurance. After undergoing a battery of tests, Pillman was only allowed to purchase $135,000 of insurance. As part of the entire Loose Cannon scam, he was looking to rectify that.

Pillman had met a man named Elliot Pollack at the NATPE convention back at the start of 1996, and made a deal to use Pollack as his agent going forward. Contrary to many people's understanding, however, Pollack wasn't a sports agent. Instead, he was a disbarred New York attorney that dealt with individuals in the movie industry. While he was looking to enhance his position within the wrestling business and get the biggest contract he could, Brian had another major objective.

"The real plan for Pillman was to go to the movies", says Kim Wood, when asked about his long-term aspirations. "One of the great scams in pro wrestling is to somehow get into movies and get a SAG (Screen Actors' Guild) card. Because none of the wrestlers have insurance and don't get it. But if you have a SAG card, you get the best medical insurance for the rest of your life. That was his goal." With life coverage being one of the other perks of membership, Brian was earnest in his wish to acquire it.

With that in mind, ECW became an excellent vehicle for him. Not only were they over the moon to have somebody with Brian's reputation and momentum on their show, but they let him have free reign over what he wanted to do. Pillman and Pollack filmed a series of vignettes themselves and sent them to ECW for Heyman to use on his show – which Paul E. was more than happy to do. More than just a blank canvas, Brian looked at everything he did in ECW as a means for something bigger. With the ability to do whatever he wanted and be as creative as he could be, he viewed every vignette he filmed as a demo tape for Hollywood.

On the first March episode of ECW Hardcore TV, three of these videos aired. The first one, opening the show, was the famous scene of Brian Pillman screaming in a living room, the camera racing to find him, before spotting him talking to a six-foot pencil. "You want me to do what? A job for…I don't think so booker man!", yelled Brian, before slapping the pencil to the ground and diving in to wrestle it. At one point it appeared the pencil was turning the battle around, choking Pillman, before he got back on top and threw a few punches, stopping to look at the camera. "I always end up fighting with the pencil", said Brian, before clutching the neck of the giant piece of stationary as if to strangle it, holding four fingers, the Horseman salute, in its imaginary face to close the scene. The play on words of "fighting the pencil", the inside term for the booker, wasn't lost on its intended audience. Funnily enough, the idea came from Brian sleeping at Pollack's house in his child's bedroom. The infant had an oversized toy pencil in the corner of their room and the idea popped into Pillman's head to use it. The next day, Pollack himself was holding the camera as the piece was put together.

That same day, they filmed another vignette in Elliot's house that aired on the same episode, this time closing the broadcast. A naked Brian Pillman sat alone on a couch, addressing Bischoff aloud as his eyes moved around the room. "Congratulations Eric – you've stripped me of everything", started Brian. After detailing what the WCW boss had taken away, Pillman stated that he'd also given him "the greatest gift of all. Freedom…to be me. In other words Eric, you've given me the fucking ace!", as Pillman held his four fingers to a painting behind him, depicting a giant Ace of Diamonds.

On a roll, the two took a ride in Elliot's limousine next to film a scene with Pillman and Pollack going over his ECW contract. As Pillman smoked a cigar, largely uninterested, Elliot brought up a section that caught his eye. "*Early termination.* Now that's an Extreme concept. You're screwed", said Pollack, which cause Pillman's head to jolt in his direction. "Well I guess I'd better wear a rubber", offered Brian, as he turned his attention to the camera, "Because I know where they've been." As his now familiar maniacal laugh ended the scene, it was hard not to be entertained at the oddball delivery and creative use of language.

All three bits were brilliant for the show, and Pollack went on his mission of getting them around to showcase his new client's range. The promos got rave reviews, with the pencil promo still being a cult favorite to this day. "Heyman loved it because it was really creative stuff", details Dave Meltzer. "It was so different, and everybody talked about it. Every segment that he did, everybody was talking about it because it was just so bizarre and weird and everything."

Indeed, the ECW move was perpetuating the image that Pillman played a superb crazy heel. While his in-ring talent was never in doubt, it was becoming obvious that the potential in the Loose Cannon was astronomical. In the meantime, with Elliot working his magic in acquiring auditions, Brian kept playing the character nonstop, even more engrossed in it now than ever. Wondering what the next step was in his masterpiece, he made a call to Kim Wood.

"He called me up", remembers Kim, "And he said, 'This is working, I talked to Meltzer, this is working. What do I do next?' And it had gotten so bizarre, and the stuff Meltzer had written was so awesome and it was so set up, that I forget what triggered me saying it but I said, 'I'm out of this Brian, I don't know what the fuck's next.' He said, 'What's coming next?' I said, 'Leave me out of it, I don't know what's fucking coming next. You can get this far, but you're on your own from now, kid'. Because all of a sudden, we've hit so many bullseyes in a row, thanks to Vince, thanks to Heyman, thanks to Bischoff, things fell so well into place, he said, 'What do I do now?' I said 'That one I don't know. You're just going to have to wing it from now on'."

Left to his own devices and determined to find the perfect play, Brian would stay up all night, talking on the phone and falling deeper into the persona he was hoping to convince the world was real. Pillman had recently become fond of the internet and would spend countless hours on America Online. Brian made the effort to set up his own folder in AOL's Grandstand wrestling section and would frequently check in to drum up his support (dubbing his supporters the "Cannon Cult"), spread his anti-WCW propaganda and harass other users. A few others, such as DDP, Marc Mero and Alex Wright had also set up folders, but Brian and Melanie were by far the most active, using it for social media purposes before such a thing existed.

"We did a lot of crazy stuff online to drive people nuts", says Colin Bowman. "Back in the old days with AOL chat rooms, we'd take turns on which one of us would get banned. We'd just be messaging each other privately and we'd be setting up our next AOL chat room angle. 'How about if I say this, where is this going to go?' Back then your flame war would be so mild compared to the ones today."

At the time, AOL was able to police the smaller internet community rather tightly, but Brian didn't care. He was trolling people for the fun of it and to cause any havoc he could. At one point, Brian went into the German-born Alex Wright's folder, asking him, "How many Jewish deaths was your father personally responsible for?"

"I remember after that, he got the message from the moderator to kind of stay in line, or else he'd get banned", says Mike Johnson, who got to know Brian online during this time, citing him as the first wrestler to talk to him as a peer, rather than a fan. "And Pillman just says, 'Hey moderator – fuck you!' So his account got shut down. It was Melanie's account, and back then you literally had to call AOL up and plead your case for why your account should be reinstated."

"We'd get kicked off for a week or two weeks or whatever", Bowman laughs. "You get that little thing – 'You're in violation of your terms of service, please review it here'. And it's almost like, 'And please think about where you are going in your life. Make good choices in future'."

It bears repeating that the timing for Brian to pull off this elaborate scheme was pivotal to its success. The internet as we know it today was in its infancy in 1996. At a time before either WWF or WCW had established any kind of real online presence, Brian saw that it was becoming a hub for the most passionate wrestling fans and identified it as yet another tool to promote himself. While there were always fans more die-hard than others, the mid-nineties saw pockets of these fans coming together in greater numbers, with ECW being an obvious early gathering point. Newsletters and hotlines had existed for years, but the world was right at the beginning of becoming a smaller place in early 1996. With the internet age looming, accessibility to insider information was opening up. Wrestling hotlines with real life scoops (and made up stories, for that matter) were being promoted on television and generating real money.

The wrestling business had been struggling since the early nineties and at this stage in the war, neither company was exploding in popularity yet. As a result, with the number of casual fans dwindling, the more serious, hardcore fanatics were able to congregate and make their common voice far more powerful than before. A classic example of this was at the WWF's King of the Ring 1995 pay-per-view in Philadelphia, when the fans responded to an awful show (more specifically a Mabel Vs. Savio Vega tournament final to crown the next King) with an impossible to ignore "E-C-W!" chant.

"All of the stuff Brian did was very avant-garde and struck a chord with a fanbase that really, to me, hadn't been tapped", says Alex Marvez. "It was actually the perfect gimmick for the perfect time because, with the beginnings of the internet, people were starting to find out pro wrestling secrets. So when you put something like that on TV it's like, 'Holy crap, is the guy for real or isn't he?'"

The number of these knowledgeable insider fans was relatively small by percentage of the total audience population, but they carried a lot of weight. Promoters could see things were failing and this segment of the audience, unhappy with the state of the business, was importunate in telling them why. Bischoff was enticed by the idea of working all of them with the Pillman character, but Brian was taking advantage of the zeitgeist of the time and getting over like nobody else in wrestling with this small, yet powerful voice. He knew that even if Bischoff and McMahon weren't completely listening to these fans, they could still hear them.

Pillman would play to this segment constantly, having as much fun on AOL as possible. He'd regularly go into the WWF's chat room and create a commotion, and noted how much more intrigue there was when he crossed over into their world. It was then that he came up with another idea that was sure to garner attention.

Madison Square Garden has always been considered the WWF's "home arena", with roots dating back to Jess McMahon (grandfather of current WWE owner Vince) being appointed MSG's boxing matchmaker on October 30th, 1925. The venue would become the centerpiece of Vincent J. McMahon's Capitol Wrestling and later the WWWF, the company that would be sold to his son Vincent K. McMahon in 1983.

In 1996, the company still considered Madison Square Garden to be holy ground and it was often considered a good barometer for overall WWF business. The next WWF date in "The World's Most Famous Arena" was a house show on March 17th. In the middle of his masterpiece, Brian quietly purchased fourth row tickets to the event and was planning on attending with Elliot Pollack. The plan, as he devised it in his mind, was to wear his trusty La Parka mask to the show and when Shawn Michaels came out, he'd hop the barricade, jump into the ring and unmask. With MSG fans being some of the most avid in the country, they'd know who he was, and their shocked reaction would make Pillman look like a gigantic star right in front of Vince's eyes. Even knowing he'd likely get arrested or given a fine of some sort, Brian believed it would be worth it for all the talk it would create, that a presumably fired WCW wrestler, who was tearing it up in ECW, showed up unplanned at a WWF show and got arrested. But most of all, it would demonstrate to McMahon how "his fans" perceived the Loose Cannon, which was only going to be positive. Brian kept it quiet, knowing he was onto a winner.

He kept his eye open for other events that looked like the place to be and became drawn to them, looking for any opening to create news and enhance his value further. One such event was the Arnold Classic, held on March 2nd in Columbus, Ohio.

The Arnold Classic was an annual bodybuilding event traditionally held at the Greater Columbus Convention Center. It served as something of a melting pot, luring agents, pornstars, hustlers, fans and wannabe stars to one venue with its gravitational pull. "If you like fake tits that's the place to go", jokes Kim Wood. "It's a cesspool, there's drug dealers…you just wallow in the sleaze."

Pillman's visit was dual-purpose – in addition to hanging out at the expo, he was filming a commercial to plug his hotline to air on Hardcore TV. ECW's television crew Stonecutter Productions, headed by Steve Karel, put it together with Brian. In what would become an unfortunate, ironic twist of fate, it was Karel, the same man who told Kim Wood about the WCW-ECW connection which led to Pillman becoming the talk of the industry, that took Brian to the Arnold Classic. Of course, a lot of the attendees were wrestling fans and with Brian in character, he was getting almost as much attention as Arnold himself. Brian and Karel took the sleaze a step further, going back and forth between strip shows and nude woman contests, when Pillman came across a model that caught his eye. In this case, however, it wasn't a female.

One of the sponsors of the Arnold Classic was Hummer. Schwarzenegger fell in love seeing a fleet of military Humvees roll past the set of Kindergarten Cop in 1990 and wanted one of his own. Arnie finally convinced AM General to produce them, and it was Schwarzenegger himself who purchased the first Hummer off the assembly line. Since then he was linked with them and with the bodybuilding expo bearing his name, it was only natural to have a number of floor models on display. Pillman loved the look of one of the Hummers in particular and since the ones being showcased had to be gotten rid of, Karel, with his connections, was able to get Brian a pretty good deal if he wanted to purchase it there and then. Despite all his hard work being with the goal of cashing in and making it out on the other end financially better off, Pillman's focus lapsed amidst the intoxicating vibe of working everybody and living his character. Against his prior instincts, he bought the vehicle.

ECW hosted a two-night extravaganza, dubbed "The Big Ass Extreme Bash", with an event on March 8th at the Lost Battalion Hall in Queens, New York, and another on March 9th, back at the famed ECW Arena in

Philadelphia. With the Loose Cannon on a roll, he participated in a pair of memorable angles to further his storyline with Shane Douglas.

The first night kicked off with Joey Styles bringing "The Franchise" out for an interview, while Brian Pillman sat calm and reserved in the front row. As Douglas got going, Pillman rose, clutching at the barricade separating the fans from the ringside area and jumping up and down, screaming at the crowd and drawing everyone's eye. Shane quickly spotted him and dismissed the situation, saying, "Brian Pillman, I'm not gonna' waste an ounce of sweat on your little ass tonight." After taking a moment to contemplate the situation, Douglas leaned back in and yelled, "The hell I'm not!" After jumping to the floor and getting within touching distance, Shane challenged Brian to jump the barricade and fight him, or risk being dragged over. As Styles turned the microphone over to Brian for a response, he insisted that since he couldn't be Brian Pillman in ECW, that "I'm just here with my agent, my cousin Debbie and her beautiful boy. I have a ticket."

Douglas jumped in, saying he was going to give Pillman until the count of three before the decision was made for him. As Brian goaded him, Shane got to three and reared back to punch him, but Pillman had pulled his cousin, and more importantly the young child, right in the line of fire to protect himself. Shane stopped the punch short of the child, as Styles became indignant at Brian's actions. Pillman grabbed the mic again. "Shane, why don't you just quit? Like you quit everything else! You quit the WWF, you quit the Dynamic Dudes! I'm a real man, I don't quit, I get thrown out of town!" As the provocation continued, Pillman reached over the child and pie-faced Shane, causing him to swing a chair in their direction. An army of people appeared to stop the blow and frantically try to gain a measure of order. The red-hot pull-apart progressed the story nicely and further established that Pillman was the heel, sinking to deplorable levels to use a child as a human shield.

"What I loved about working with Brian, and it took some time to get used to, but he was so off the cuff it sort of forced you to be organic out there", points out Shane Douglas. "It looked so real and believable because we didn't sit in the back and say, 'Okay, you say this and then I'll say this and I'll count to three'. We just went out and performed. One thing about him was, especially as a heel, you knew Brian was always going to lob some bomb out there that you could respond to."

The rivalry continued the next night in Philadephia, as a suit-clad Pillman walked to ringside in the middle of a match pitting Bad Crew against Damien

Stone and El Puerto Ricano. Flanked by Pollack and Philadelphia Eagles' offensive tackle Harry Boatswain, Pillman strolled right into the ring, threw a couple of blows at the participants and took control of the microphone. As Joey Styles joined him in the ring, Brian began verbally laying into Douglas until Shane's voice cut off his tirade. With Shane situated on the staging area, he declared his willingness to be sued and blackballed from Hollywood to beat up Pillman, and made a move to the ring. Meanwhile, Brian checked his watch and opted to leave, determined to show no redeeming qualities.

He made a second appearance backing that up further. A match pitting Taz, an MMA-inspired character portrayed as a legitimate bad-ass, against Chris Jericho ended with Taz refusing to break his Tazmission choke sleeper. As underneath wrestlers began trying to help, who should hit the ring wearing a cut-off shirt and an oversized pair of jeans held up by rope, but Brian Pillman. Displaying a babyface fire reminiscent of his Stampede days, jumping up and down, Brian was ready to fight as Taz broke the hold upon his arrival. Styles on commentary told the story that Pillman helped train Jericho at the Hart Dungeon (which wasn't true) and was coming to defend him. Taz turned around and delivered a devastating suplex to Damien Stone, dropping him high on his neck and shoulders. Pillman's demeanor immediately changed, as he looked at the hard camera and dropped out of the ring in retreat. As he stood telling the camera he wasn't stupid, El Puerto Ricano started to run down the aisle to hit the ring, but was intercepted by a Pillman clothesline. Ricano, a smaller, lower card competitor, was routinely used as a punching bag in ECW due to his ability to take good bumps. Suffice to say, cheapshotting him was hardly the act of valor his original Jericho save looked to be. Shane Douglas arrived back on the scene chasing Pillman, who once again ran away from the fight, jumping over the barricade into the waiting arms of Harry Boatswain who was perfectly positioned in the crowd. Together, they exited the building in record time. Brian's cowardice and gutless nature underscored his intentions – he saw himself as a main event heel, and running away from real battles was sure to keep him on that path.

"With that angle, again, he never ever said to me, 'This is how we're going to cap this off, this is where I'm going to make my exit'", Shane remembers. "Which I think sells that as coming off completely believable, because I didn't know what he was going to do. He's playing his side, I just had to play my side, and how would I react as the Franchise of ECW to a guy that's saying and doing these types of things."

Pillman filmed another couple of vignettes for ECW TV, his creativity leading him to seek free reign of a restaurant. When he found the perfect location, he donned a chef's outfit and filmed a promo from the kitchen under the premise of being out of work in the wrestling business. The camera moved up to Pillman, wielding a pan and saying to himself, "I guess Bischoff thought I was just some dumb jock. Well that really burns me." Seconds later, his pan went up in flames, as Brian tried desperately to put it out. As the fire calmed down, a voice off camera called "Chef Pillman! The Juster table is waiting for their salad!" The person referenced was Gary Juster, who worked in WCW's legal department at the time and doubled as a local promoter. "Mr. Juster's here? Oh well", offered Brian, before working up and launching a huge wad of snot and spit onto the plate of food. "Courtesy of Chef Pillman", he concluded with a laugh.

A second scene was shot where a cameraman arrived to pick up Brian in the restaurant, where he sat alone at a table at the end of the room. As the camera moved towards Pillman, a waiter entered the scene and asked Brian for an autograph. Acting completely rationally and showing no signs of the character, Brian humbly asked, "How are you doing tonight, sir? Who's that too?" After signing the autograph, the waiter thanked him, "You seem like a very nice guy." "It's all a work, you know", responded Pillman, "I'm not really the Loose Cannon." As the waiter exited the screen, Pillman began to glare in his direction, raising his fork and absent-mindedly jabbing it into his own forearm. His eyes rolled towards the camera, his raspy whisper proclaiming, "It's all just their perception...of reality." The clever shots were spliced into ECW's TV show immediately, and he was mastering the role more with each performance.

ECW was dealing with a limited viewership, and Brian was in constant contact with Eric Bischoff back at WCW. Bischoff had told everybody that would listen that Pillman was legitimately gone from the company, but was as zealous as Pillman to continue playing it to the hilt. They agreed the time had come to shoot another atypical angle, where Brian would come to that week's episode of Nitro and cause a disturbance in the crowd. Due to the live nature of the broadcast, the image of the fired outcast causing an unplanned disruption would surely keep the ball rolling.

On the March 11th WCW Nitro, during the opening contest pitting The Giant against Jim Duggan, a pair of white banners appeared in the first few rows opposite the hard camera reading "Call Brian – 1-900-288-PILL". The live crowd rose and immediately reacted, as Bischoff on commentary alluded to something happening at ringside. While the cameras cut strategically to shots not revealing what was happening to the folks at home, Bischoff blurted out, "Pillman! It looks like Brian Pillman down at…I'm going down there!" Giant clutched Duggan in a bear hug in the ring, as a wide shot revealed Pillman being held back right behind the barricade attempting to get to Eric. It was a fleeting shot, only a few seconds, but it was enough to draw the attention of the arena to him. A closer shot failed to catch a glimpse of what happened as Brian was escorted out. The intrigue of what WCW apparently didn't want you to see furthered the mystique of the entire angle. His hotline numbers jumped through the roof and did big business for the next few weeks, scoring him some quick cash.

Back inside the arena on March 11th, however, Bischoff was dealing with the consequences. As it turned out, their play for headlines threatened the entire scam.

Watching on as Pillman lit up the crowd by acting like a lunatic was Hulk Hogan. While everybody had told him that Pillman was on the outs, Hogan knew an angle when he saw one and was furious that he was lied to. He immediately approached Bischoff's personal assistant, Janie Engle, and told her to tell Eric, who was live on the air, that he could go to hell. He watched on as a nervous Engle left to pass on the message, repeating those words verbatim to Eric while Nitro was on a commercial break. To Bischoff, Hogan's words meant a great deal.

When the show was over, Eric felt he had to answer to Hogan for the situation. Since the Nitro era began, Hogan was as hands-on as ever with the creative end of the company. He would routinely get the original formats faxed to him to glance over and would often show up on Monday with changes in mind. Hogan knew that Bischoff and others saw him as the golden goose and even with his popularity waning, his influence on the company direction was enormous. Feeling obligated to come clean with his star attraction, Bischoff told Hogan the entire idea as it has been pitched to him. Hogan had sat idly by and seen the groundswell of interest in Pillman developing, and the thought hadn't crossed his mind that he could do anything about it. Now, he could.

At this point, WCW was advertising the main event for the upcoming Uncensored pay-per-view as a preposterous one versus four contest, set to take place in a triple-decker cage, pitting Hogan against Ric Flair, Arn

Anderson, Lex Luger and Kevin Sullivan. Hogan was becoming insecure with his position in recent months due to fans booing him at the live Nitro tapings, his merchandise numbers falling to miniscule levels and an upswing in house show business without him based on a hot Randy Savage Vs. Ric Flair rivalry. If he wasn't on Nitro, it wasn't certain ratings would suffer as a result, and his response was to insist on being booked stronger than ever.

After leaving Nitro in a bitter mood, Hogan sat for a couple of days and thought about what to do. That Wednesday, he told the company the new direction – the cage match would go from being one versus four, to two versus eight. Randy Savage would be his partner, and he was bringing in more people for him to defeat. Among them were actor Tiny Lister, who had a short run as a Hogan opponent in 1989 in the WWF as Zeus, and Jeep Swenson, an enormous bodybuilder best known for playing the role of Bane in the 1997 film Batman and Robin. Most of all, Hogan wanted the talk of the business, Brian Pillman, brought back to television to kill this outsider storyline off, and added to the cage match to be pinned with Hogan's patented legdrop.

That exact same day, as coincidence would have it, Brian Pillman was on the operating table and going under the knife. Since he was off, he figured he'd pencil in a routine operation at Vanderbilt University on his throat to scrape his vocal chords once again. When he found out the plan, he saw Hogan's power play for exactly what it was – an attempt to kill everything Brian had worked to cultivate and use it to benefit himself. Even with WCW believing the aim of this ruse was simply to bring Pillman back for a major angle down the line as a figure of controversy, they were throwing it all away on a whim. While Pillman raised his concerns and fought the idea, they fell on deaf ears. Hogan had made the call, so that was that. Brian was to return to television on Monday.

It was a potentially crushing blow. Brian hadn't lost sight of the real destination and knew that squashing his momentum when his contract was up in a month was the kiss of death. He raised the subject of the new deal with Bischoff and was offered a renewal of his existing contract at $225,000 per year. Pillman shot high and asked for $500,000. With the gap far apart, Bischoff said they'd come back to the subject.

Things weren't looking good, and Brian knew it. He dreaded the thought of the match to begin with, telling many that he expected it to be a debacle. He had no legal right to refuse anything Bischoff asked him to do, so if the request was made to come back, he had to do it. But he wasn't going to give this gambit up without a fight. There was no way he was doing that match.

His first move was to let as many people know, via his constant phone calls, internet marketing and his hotline, about the throat surgery as a prelude for what was to come. Gene Okerlund, on the WCW hotline, claimed that Brian's surgery was a work of fiction, saying he'd personally called the hospital and they had no record of Pillman's procedure. Knowing what was at stake, Pillman was adamant about maintaining his credibility and immediately had a legal letter and patient discharge sheet sent to Okerlund, demanding he make a retraction on Nitro. Gene missed the show, but later made the correction on the hotline.

Timing wasn't on Brian's side either that week. A situation arose with one of the kids at home, forcing him to cancel his plan to attend the Sunday night WWF show in Madison Square Garden. "I ended up sitting in the seats Pillman bought next to Elliot Pollack, who told me the whole idea", utters Mike Johnson. "The barricade was open, three rows ahead. When Shawn Michaels was in the ring, I just kept thinking to myself, 'This show would have been so much better had Brian Pillman shown up'."

With his mind racing and undoubtedly anxious about the next seven days, Brian was caught off-guard when he was sent a bill by ECW and Stonecutter Productions for $7,600 for the filming and editing of the Pillman hotline commercials that had been running on ECW TV. The adverts would begin promoting "Quagmire Ribs", a supposed eatery that was an inside reference to his torment of Bill Kazmaier, before static would cover the screen. It cut to a quick spiel from Brian followed by the phone number. Pillman wasn't too thrilled to pick up the bill, saying he felt that part of his agreement to go to ECW for free was for them to promote his hotline. He later got into an argument with Paul Heyman at 4am on Sunday night regarding the bill. It's likely that the impending return to WCW and canceled MSG plan had put him in a sour mood, but when the phone call was over, Pillman was so rattled that he'd quit ECW. Or at least, he told people he did to explain the events of the next day.

Pillman made the trip, as instructed, to Chattanooga, Tennessee for Monday Nitro. The main event was scheduled as Hulk Hogan and Randy Savage against Ric Flair and Kevin Sullivan. The layout of the show-closing angle was for Pillman to return only to have Hogan beat him up, before Tiny Lister and Jeep Swenson would come in the save him, backing Hogan down.

Brian was bound and determined to have things work out in his favor, but he had to act wisely.

As the match took to the ring, it very much seemed to be the standard WCW fare. Hogan made his trademark comeback on Ric Flair, when out of the corner of the screen came Brian Pillman, running through the crowd and hopping over the barricade. Clad in a white shirt bearing his hotline phone number, he and Arn Anderson attacked Savage on the floor. The cameras were too busy focusing on Hogan to even catch the return until Hulk ran over to interject. "The psychopath is loose!", screamed Bobby Heenan. A wild brawl ensued, with Pillman focusing on Savage and staying clear of both Hogan and Sullivan, the man that was supposedly his legitimate nemesis. Sullivan, in an attempt to keep his own angle going, swung a chair in Brian's direction right as Pillman did the same to Savage. Hogan came over and grabbed Pillman to lead him to the ring for the planned ass-kicking, but Brian pulled away. They later had a brief exchange with neither man selling, before Pillman again returned to trading blows with the Macho Man. The melee continued until Jimmy Hart led Lister (who would be renamed Ze Gangsta) and Swenson (who would be billed at first as The Final Solution in a remarkably color-blind decision, before being rechristened The Ultimate Solution) to the ring. As soon as the oversized heels approached, Pillman moved off-camera, turned around and jumped right back over the barricade and disappeared. When Hogan and company backed off to leave the heels in the ring, Pillman was supposed to be among them. As the villainous collective were interviewed by Tony Schiavone, Brian was all but forgotten, with only Arn Anderson pointing out his return.

Though not exactly doing what he was told and getting another hotline plug in to boot, the return still destroyed any suspension of disbelief that Pillman wasn't on the WCW payroll. The wrestlers who had bought into it realized they'd be worked, and by advertising him on the pay-per-view as part of an army of heels, it greatly lessened the drama that was building for a later return. Though WCW had been more than happy to facilitate Pillman's creation, they were unable to see it through to their own benefit.

The next day, Paul Heyman called Brian to confirm there were no issues, with both agreeing to continue the angle with Douglas. But knowing that full participation on the WCW pay-per-view would destroy the image of being an outsider, Pillman made his move.

WCW pre-taped their Saturday Night television show on Wednesday, where they recorded interviews building up Pillman's spot in the cage match. The next afternoon, Brian called the WCW office and told them that he'd suffered an infection in his throat following the surgery and would be unable to wrestle that Sunday. WCW's response was amazingly (and yet unsurprisingly) ignorant. They encouraged Brian to reconsider, and even after being told outright he wouldn't be appearing and having 48 hours to make edits to the broadcast, they decided not to make any changes to the WCW Saturday Night show that heavily advertised his participation. In their arrogance, they believed that when show time came, Pillman would be there. After all, he had built his reputation as somebody that would go no matter what and he'd surely worked through worse. The truth was that he had, and if it were any other time Brian would most likely have sucked it up, been the company guy and done his best to put on a good performance. But this wasn't any other time.

After WCW Saturday Night aired, Brian again took to his AOL message board and began openly burying his own employer. Insisting that he wasn't going to appear at Uncensored, Pillman declared that the company was knowingly false advertising and that their efforts were simply propaganda incited by Hulk Hogan and WCW to try and squash all the talk about the Loose Cannon. WCW neglected to correct themselves the next night on their own pre-game show, live from the Tupelo Coliseum, where they absolutely knew he wasn't in the building. When Uncensored went on the air, Brian Pillman was nowhere to be seen, just as he'd told them to expect.

On the live broadcast, Eric Bischoff made the public excuse that Pillman wasn't going to participate because he refused to team with Kevin Sullivan. As Brian predicted, the eight-on-two cage match was an absolute shower of shit, as Hulk Hogan threw horrible punches before a silent audience to an assembly line of abysmal villains. Criminally, with the wide array of talentless bums in the match to do the job, Ric Flair was still the man anointed to take the pinfall, demonstrating that WCW's stupidity wasn't just limited to their dealings with Pillman.

Regardless, people within WCW, Hulk Hogan and booker Kevin Sullivan in particular, were furious, and pinned the blame on Brian for how the entire incident made the company look. The WWF, on the following night's Monday Night Raw, couldn't resist taking a potshot at WCW for their bait-and-switch tactics, and the entire situation left them with a black eye. Talk within the top circles was that Brian had buried himself with his actions. There was a prevailing opinion from the WCW side, perhaps one that allowed Bischoff to grant Brian so much free reign all along, that Vince McMahon wouldn't be interested in signing Pillman due to the size issue he'd dealt with his entire life. If so, Brian would ultimately be the one to come crawling back to WCW if he got low-balled on offers elsewhere.

Pillman still stayed in close contact with Eric Bischoff, insisting that he'd given them the heads up well in advance. Everybody in the company could think whatever they wanted, so long as he had Eric's ear, he was still in the game.

In the face of what he heard from his cronies and stars, when Bischoff would speak covertly with Brian he was charmed into seeing the same thing he found appealing in the first place. That exhilarating rush that came with manipulating everybody and knowing you did it. It was too hard to deny, and Pillman's fervor was contagious. He also had an idea to take things to the next level. Without question, people had surely stopped believing in any real numbers that Brian was a free agent after the past seven days. Rather than focus on the negative, Pillman opted to use this new controversy to make the angle more real than ever.

Afraid that his momentum would sputter and that Hogan and Sullivan would find more ways to cool him off at this critical stage, Brian wanted to keep his destiny out of their hands. Insisting that they needed to go over the edge to encourage the idea Pillman was fired, Brian made a bold suggestion to Bischoff just before Uncensored – why don't you actually draw up a written contract release? Pillman theorized that any time anybody questioned Eric, he could pull out the release notice and people would believe it. If Brian was sent a copy as well, he could do the same. Pillman told Eric that, with the paranoid nature of the wrestling business, it would eventually come out from the company headquarters that he was still in WCW. Contending that they had to fool the office staff so that word would get back to the crew, Bischoff agreed and offered to send a mock termination across. Brian pushed it even further, telling him it had to be legitimate. After what took place with Hogan meddling with the angle, anything less than perfection would be doubted.

Whether he felt a measure of guilt for allowing Hogan to damage what he and Pillman had worked on for months or was caught up in the idea of working the boys, Eric agreed, and went to the WCW legal department to get to work on it.

Brian couldn't believe it. With around three weeks left on his WCW contract, he was sent a legitimate termination notice. The brilliance in the move was that he would be completely free to legally negotiate with anybody he wanted while he was currently on fire. Though negotiations with contracted talent through intermediaries were commonplace, there were limits to how brazen Pillman could be in approaching the WWF and using them for leverage as originally planned. In addition, Brian had no right to refuse any demand Bischoff made previously and was subject to the whims of Hogan. But now, WCW had sent him the golden ticket via fax.

"It's one of the greatest things in the history of wrestling", states Dave Meltzer. "It's so unbelievable. He didn't tell me ahead of time he was doing it, but as soon as he did it he told me what he had done. And I was like, 'No way'. He goes 'Yeah, everybody thinks I'm released because they sent me a real letter of release. They don't believe it, but it's a real letter! I told him we've got to fool the secretaries, we've got to fool everyone', and he goes into this whole speech. 'We've got to make this look real. You know the way everyone talks in wrestling, if you don't give me a release they're going to go, 'Hey, he's still under contract'.' And Brian just goes, 'You know, now there is no way Eric is going to want it to look like Vince took their hot guy, so Eric for sure is going to give me a good deal'."

It was time for Brian to test the waters. After being one of the biggest talking points in the industry for months, he sent feelers to the WWF to see what their interest was. Pillman was dismayed to find out that Vince McMahon seemed cold to the idea. Not for lack of interest, but with all the talk and outside the box maneuverings, as well as remembering his own experience with Brian back at the NATPE convention, Vince was reluctant to bite. As it turns out, Pillman was almost too convincing a maniac for his own good, and Vince didn't know what to make of him.

"Vince wasn't going to say, 'Hey, we've got to get this guy from WCW', about pretty much anybody", says Jim Cornette, who goes on to explain the process of McMahon's approach during the period. "He was going to wait until one of his people said, 'Hey, so-and-so's contract in WCW is coming up and I think you ought to take a look at him'. Well Brian, until he started being nuts, would probably not have been high on the list of hills people were wanting to die on, based on the way he was being used. If a big star came up, yes, but Brian had to be nuts first. But I don't know that Vince got the whole thing at all to begin with."

Luckily, Pillman had allies close to Vince's ear who went about campaigning the virtues of the potential signing to the WWF don. "Once I found out they were going to talk to him I was like, 'Fuck yes! Please! Brian Pillman is great!'", recalls Cornette. "Once Brian had created that whole thing, then a lot of Vince's people, whether it be JR or Bruce Pritchard or me, whoever started it, were all over it. I remember when he had just been talking to Brian, me and Bruce telling Vince at one point, 'He's a great guy, a great talent and he's not a gimmick, but in a good way. He's nuts, but in a good way, it'll be fine'."

Brian began racking his brain on how to eliminate any doubt about his potential upside. While everything he'd done had turned him into a hot heel and a bigger star with a certain audience, there was nothing to point to from a pure numbers standpoint that could justify the main event money he wanted from his next contract. Remembering that it was more about creating the illusion of value than anything else, he came up with the idea of going to Mexico. In many ways, differences in persona aside, a lot of the qualities Brian was mastering as the Loose Cannon were reminiscent of the late Art Barr – over the top, constantly drawing your eye and generating a ton of heat by constantly being the center of attention. Barr had drawn big money in Mexico's AAA promotion as one half of La Pareja del Terror, teaming with Eddie Guerrero as a pair of pro-USA mega-heels. Together, with Guerrero supplying the body of work in the ring and Barr's incredible facial expressions, charisma and personality, they became the hottest ticket in Mexico.

Pillman saw himself fitting in well as a main eventer in the same mould, so he picked up the phone and called his old friend Konnan. Though Konnan had recently started working for WCW, he remained with AAA at the same time, helping book the promotion and serving as the AAA Americas Heavyweight Champion. In hearing Brian's idea, Konnan told him that there wasn't much money in headlining Mexico at the moment, especially compared to the money he was making at WCW. Indeed, the peso had crashed at the end of 1994 and had made it very difficult to earn a full-time living. But Pillman didn't care, telling Konnan, "Fuck that, I just want to show people I can be a main eventer, and I know I can in Mexico."

Meanwhile, Brian's agent Elliot Pollack called with good news – he'd gotten Brian some auditions, and one of them was big. With Pollack shipping tapes around of his ECW vignettes, casting director Todd Thaler was wanting Brian to come to the Northeast to read for a supporting role in the movie that became "Cop Land", starring Sylvester Stallone, Harvey Keitel, Ray Liotta and Robert De Niro. With the end of his contract growing ever closer, it was a massive shot of confidence for Brian that a major goal, the SAG card, was in touching distance too.

Not only that, but word got to Brian that Vince McMahon was softening on his previous stance. The WWF, which was struggling to make new stars that made a difference to the bottom line, was now becoming a victim of the same issue that they had created for so many promoters in the eighties. Back then, every major talent move was in their direction, which painted the WWF as the place to be and the local territory as a dying institution. With WCW in acquisition mode in 1996, they compounded this modern twist on the perception game by signing Kevin "Diesel" Nash and Scott "Razor Ramon" Hall, two of the WWF's biggest stars. Huge guaranteed money and reduced schedules were offered and accepted, leaving major voids at the top of the cards. Realizing it was a major blow, Vince felt he had to show that the roster changes weren't just in one direction. With his aides still insisting that the Pillman antics were the work of genius rather than insanity, he re-opened dialogue with Brian.

Though he did send Pillman a termination notice, it would be somewhat unfair to portray Bischoff as completely naïve to Brian's intentions. After the shenanigans at Uncensored, there were whispers in WCW that Pillman was using the company for his own gain and began questioning who was really working who. But Brian was so slick in his patter that he never let Eric feel like they weren't collaborating and moving toward their original plan. Bischoff was keen to come to a deal with Brian and publicly commended him for being a professional in business dealings. In part, that was because many believe Brian never actually wanted to leave WCW.

"At the end of the day he was hoping, for sure, that WCW won the bidding", offers Dave Meltzer. "It's not like he closed his mind on going to the WWF, but his mentality was definitely to get the guaranteed contract from WCW because with Vince, I think one of the things was - you're going to do however well Vince wants you to do. Whereas with WCW, all those key guys were always on top, year after year after year, because they were making the big money and that's the way it was always justified to corporate. And he really wanted to be a main eventer."

WCW had the reputation as being a great place to end your career, due to the reduced workload, guaranteed pay and reserved attitude that many on the roster had. Even if Brian left, it was still in his best interest to keep Bischoff sweet rather than burn a bridge on the off chance he could get one more contract for good money at the end.

Kim Wood has the impression that the real mark was McMahon, with the WWF being the ultimate destination. In all likelihood, Pillman himself was going back and forth on the pros and cons of both sides daily. A lot had changed in the two companies since this game had begun. The WWF was now severely depleted at the top with Hall and Nash jumping, combined with perennial top star Bret Hart taking an indefinite hiatus. With a smaller than usual new WWF Champion in the babyface Shawn Michaels, the landscape seemed perfect for Pillman to slide in with his new character and be an opponent. It was a perfect contrast and the matches promised to be top-notch. The question was whether the WWF would go that far with him or give him the leeway to get over the way he had done in recent months.

Staying with WCW, if he could get the big contract he wanted, would be more secure, but with Hogan's ever looming presence and now Nash and Hall coming in as big money players, the room for upward mobility was looking thinner. Bischoff had told Pillman that he planned to use him in a hugely promoted match at the Great American Bash in a couple of months, where he'd team up with Ric Flair to face renowned NFL players Steve McMichael and Kevin Greene in their first pro wrestling match.

It was a lot to weigh-up, and time was growing closer for those all-important financial numbers to be discussed. One thing was for sure, no matter what the end result, nobody could say Brian didn't explore every avenue to achieve his goal. In the process of doing so, he'd figured out how to be the complete package like he never quite had before. Never was his creativity, his charisma, his presence, his interviews and his personality so on point at one time. His ring work was established, but after seven years in World Championship Wrestling, he'd truly found himself.

"It was all a work, but it was actually consistent with Brian's real-life personality", says Bruce Hart, "He had that slightly off-the-wall Loose Cannon mindset in the beginning anyway, it's part of what made people like him or hate him. It wasn't *that* much of a stretch."

"Brian Pillman on TV, especially in the latter days, was as close to Brian Pillman off-camera as possible", states Mark Madden in agreement. "I don't know if he grew into that persona or if it was always basically there and trying fully to get out. But there's no question that Brian the TV character merged with Brian the real-life persona over the course of time."

Kim Wood lends further credence to the point, stating, "The thing with Brian, he really wasn't the Loose Cannon…but he really kinda' was."

Whichever side got him, the potential for what could be done with this incredible talent was irrefutable, coming at a time when the business was looking for that one special act to break out of the pack and lead either company ahead in the ratings battle. The negotiations continued, as Brian began thinking about what he could do to generate more buzz at the next ECW Arena show on April 20th. He was scheduled to run-in during the main event to cost Shane Douglas the ECW World Title in his match against the champion, Raven. Joey Styles on Hardcore TV announced that Pillman would only be allowed back to the company if he agreed to wrestle "The Franchise". Costing Shane the title was the perfect catalyst for what had been brewing and the angle was building to its natural crescendo.

In understanding Brian's motivations for the last six months of shenanigans, his mentor Kim Wood re-emphasizes Pillman's objective. "In reality, it was the tail wagging the dog", begins Wood. "But why did he do it? Because it was the only way, in the spot he was in, that could actually get him more money. He didn't do it for art, he did it for the money."

Mark Madden adds his own perspective, offering, "Brian saw the business for what it was - a business. I always have too. Maybe it's why we were good friends." When asked about whether the money or a top spot was at the true heart of Brian's mission, Madden elaborates. "He wanted both", he says. "I think he wanted both. Because if you get one you're going to get the other. And Brian was such a mercurial character that I think that what he wanted would change from day to day and minute to minute sometimes. Brian wanted to be a star. I think that was, more than anything, what he wanted to be."

"He definitely wanted to be a main eventer", says Dave Meltzer in summary. "There was a feeling about being a main eventer that was a big, big deal to him for sure. But supporting the kids was number one."

Looking at the big picture, Brian could sit back with a smile. He'd managed to do what he set out to do at Kim Wood's kitchen table. He'd created enough of a stir to achieve his goal of becoming a red-hot free agent with exceptional timing, incredible creativity and a spot of good fortune. Everybody wanted him. Both sides felt they needed him. Crunch time was about to commence.

Then, on one idle Monday afternoon, his entire life changed again. And not for the better.

18 - ONE IDLE MONDAY

On April 15th, Brian Pillman hopped into his new Hummer and drove around his hometown of Walton. After turning onto Kentucky Route 338, the story becomes murky, with only one person knowing the real truth. Pillman himself later gave multiple versions of what happened. In one, Brian claimed he was mailing some dubbed copies of the Stu Hart Anniversary Show to some personal friends, that one of the tapes slid down to the gas pedal and when he went to grab it, he lost control of the vehicle. In another, Pillman claimed that he was coming back from handing in his tax returns (which were due that day), and after working on them all night, fell asleep at the wheel. Others have speculated that given Brian's habits of being wired and staying up all night, his body caught simply up with him. Or maybe that he'd simply had too much to drink before turning the key in the ignition.

What isn't debatable is the end result. For whatever reason, while driving 60 to 70 miles per hour in a 45 mile per hour zone, the Hummer veered off a road which didn't have any shoulders. The vehicle rapidly approached the stump of a large oak tree which had been cut at a wedge angle, serving as a ramp and shooting the automobile high into the air. The Hummer came down nose first and upon impact, Pillman, who wasn't wearing his seatbelt, was launched with such force that he pierced the convertible top, being hurled 40 feet through the air. As the Hummer did two end-over-end flips and crumpled into a pile of wreckage, Brian brutally landed in a field, his body much the same.

EMTs arrived on the scene. With blood covering his face and his leg clearly destroyed, the medics stabilized Brian and told him that given the state of his ankle, if he had the ability to handle extreme pain, it would be best to force it back into the socket right away so it didn't set incorrectly. Pillman agreed, and endured the excruciating agony of having his foot twisted back into place.

He was taken to St. Luke Hospital West where he was diagnosed with a badly broken ankle and multiple lacerations. Furthermore, his face was destroyed on the landing, breaking his nose, eye socket, and cheekbone. He was transferred to University Hospital where he was listed in critical condition, but upgraded to fair and then stable condition by the end of the day.

It was devastating. The truth is he was very lucky to even be alive. Had he been wearing his seatbelt he'd surely have died, as the Hummer was flat as a pancake. A different landing in the field could also have had fatal consequences. "I went to the ER and they gave me his clothes, and he had been wearing a padded Harley Davidson leather jacket", recalls Brian's sister Linda. "He had no internal injuries, and he was thrown 40 feet through the air! But when they gave me his clothes and I pulled that jacket out, that jacket was shredded. I believe that jacket saved his life. Because he had injuries to his head and ankle, but he had no internal injuries or bruising to his chest or torso at all."

As it was, his left leg was ruined. "I think they really wanted to amputate his foot the ankle was so messed up", says Bruce Hart, remembering conversations with Brian. He refused, and underwent an operation to reconstruct his ankle with bone from his hip. The doctors inserted steel pins in his ankle that attached to an external rod, and told him that he'd also need surgery to fix his face, which was virtually unrecognizable. "I went to see him, it was in the General Hospital here, University Hospital", says Kim Wood. "I went in there and I never saw anything like that in my life. He had tubes going everywhere, his head's the size of a beach ball. I mean…his face was *gone*."

Pillman was originally placed in the burn unit at University Hospital, placed on a special mattress that elevated him so that his skin wasn't touching anything since they didn't know the full extent of the issues. "The nurse told me that his foot was hanging off the table because the bone was so shattered", recollects Linda Pillman. "The orbits around his eyes were broken, and one of the doctors when I walked in had Brian's teeth and he was moving them around inside his mouth. I asked, 'Is he going to lose his teeth?' He said, 'No, the teeth are in the sockets good, those are his gums that are shattered.' The doctor could actually move his teeth around. So, they had to wire all his gums and jaw shut and build up around his eyes."

Brian left the hospital on April 19th, returning the following week to have the facial surgery where four titanium steel plates were drilled into his skull, with the skin pulled back over the top. The scope of the damage on Pillman physically was immense.

As he lay in bed at the medical facility, he was crestfallen. Everything he'd worked for, everything he'd consumed himself with for every minute of every day for the last four months was within his grasp. With one lapse too many, his entire career was now jeopardized.

"It's really too bad, because he was 33 when the crash happened", explains Dave Meltzer, when asked about Brian's mindset. "So he was going to have seven really good years. That's what his mentality was, to go to 40. He really wanted to make money for seven years. The whole thing with having the kids was always a big pressure thing for him – 'I have to make money and I have to support the kids.' That was overriding. That was number one, before anything else, was supporting those kids. It wasn't that he always talked about them, but when it came to the motivation when we talked about business stuff, at the end it was like, 'I have five kids, I have to have big years. I *have* to'."

Doctors told him that his ankle was so badly damaged that he'd never be able to run again. Which meant he'd probably never wrestle again. While he'd made an entire life out of turning "No" into opportunity, Brian knew his body and knew just how grave the situation really was. He told everybody that he was given a timetable to return in late July, but deep down knew that wasn't the case. Here he was, in hospital without a contract, fearing the worst in terms of what this had done to not just his market value, but his very existence in the business. He'd put himself in the most horrible position, professionally and personally, and took it extremely hard feeling he'd cost himself everything.

Amazingly, that wasn't the case. Believing Brian's condition to be serious but temporary, both WCW and the WWF were eager to negotiate and lock in the deal to bring the Loose Cannon to their television shows. WCW was particularly aggressive in contacting Brian to discuss terms, with Eric Bischoff issuing a very public 'get-well-soon' sentiment on commentary during the April 22nd Nitro.

"The interesting thing was that when he had the accident, there was no next step", explains Kim Wood, when questioned about the desire to sign

Pillman. "There was no next move for Brian to make after that. You just wait for somebody else to do something." When pushed further about how proactive Pillman had been in the build-up to his WCW deal ending compared to this point, Wood elaborates, "What I'm saying about Vince and Bischoff - these aren't creative active minds, they're very passive people. They've got a structure that's impossible for people to express themselves, but they're waiting for somebody else to do something." Luckily, Brian had figured that out long before, and even with what should have been a major spanner in the works, he was able to reap the benefits of still being highly sought after. He couldn't believe it.

"At this point in time, Brian was really one of the most talked about guys, maybe *the* most talked about guy in the whole industry right before the wreck", says Meltzer. "Because when he had the wreck, everybody thought it was a publicity stunt because he was doing all these things to get talked about." In one of the more ridiculous examples of locker room gossip, murmurs began circulating WCW (started by Sullivan) that Pillman was actually having plastic surgery to look like Shawn Michaels in preparation for a run in the WWF.

In the fortnight following the crash, Brian rested up and downplayed the injuries, insisting he was ahead of schedule in the healing process. While the wreck had put his acting ambitions on hold, he was still eager to complete his primary objective. In typical Pillman fashion, he'd joke about the Hummer on WrestleRadio USA, "And you're wondering why we're having trouble going toe-to-toe with the Croats and the Serbs? That's a military vehicle? The thing is totaled. I'm still here. It's supposed to be able to take on a landmine!"

But what seemed like good fortune, with his leverage intact and positive verbiage minimizing his condition, was really a smoke screen for the real underlying problem. His left leg was ruined, and now he was playing a game of getting to the finish line of signing a new contract not knowing what he'd even be capable of once he got it. "He was never right after that", says Wood, solemnly.

After taking some time to let his ankle rest and the swelling in his face to go down, Brian started to engage both sides. The fact that Vince McMahon was interested meant Pillman could do exactly what he wanted all along, which was use him to up his price. He started spreading rumors and getting stories out that he was leaning towards the WWF, which instantly made him more appealing to Eric Bischoff.

Eric made an offer and felt pretty comfortable about his chances of coming to an agreement. After all, WCW's money was guaranteed, and the WWF traditionally offered little more than "an opportunity", a low guaranteed sum that served as a prelude to the company paying whatever they wanted depending on the ebbs and flows of business and political favor. For a father of five, guaranteed money was certainly more appealing, without even taking into consideration the injuries. But Pillman wanted more, and contacted the WWF.

In response, Vince McMahon requested that Brian and Melanie meet with him at Titan Towers on May 23rd to try and lure him to the company. Hoping to be able to manipulate an ideal situation, Brian also agreed to meet with Bischoff on May 28th where he'd inevitably relay the outcome.

Upon arrival in Stamford, Pillman and McMahon sat down to talk about what it would take to put together a deal. WCW's guaranteed offer came up, as Pillman stressed the importance of knowing what he'd be getting. Brian also raised the issue of the WWF historically taking key talent with a reputation from elsewhere and repackaging them under a new alias, as had recently been the case with two other WCW alums. The man once known as Cactus Jack was transformed into Mankind, and Brian's old partner Steve Austin was given a new name upon his arrival, becoming The Ringmaster. When Austin requested a new moniker, he was faxed a barrage of ridiculous names to choose from (most famously Ice Dagger and Chilly McFreeze), prompting him to immediately call Brian to read them to him over a speakerphone, sending Pillman into hysterics. Brian had no desire to leave his name or gimmick at the door as they had.

McMahon surprisingly agreed on both counts, both massive breaks in WWF protocol that established that not only did McMahon want him, but that it was so important to Vince to land this deal that he was willing to do it on Brian's terms. Understandably so – since Pillman's Humvee wreck, two more WWF stars, Jeff Jarrett and Ted DiBiase, had left the company to accept deals with World Championship Wrestling, and the perception game was one that Vince was losing badly. After talking with Pillman at length, McMahon was taken by his intelligence.

Brian left the meeting very happy and let everybody know it. It didn't take long for word to travel to WCW's headquarters in Atlanta, and Eric was quick to pick up the phone and find out what it was going to take to keep him. The originally planned meeting for May 28th had fallen through, but Bischoff still considered Brian a top priority and was in constant contact. Pillman was making a lot of requests, some of which he was more serious about than others. Maintaining control of his merchandising and being granted first class airfare for his scheduled appearances were minor issues of debate, but the conversation centered around the per year dollar figure. Pillman was still shooting high at $500,000, while Bischoff was having a hard time getting past the tipping point that Brian was looking to budge him over. Eric was determined to keep him in the fold and vowed to get back to him on the asking price.

In the meantime, Pillman headed to the ECW Arena in Philadelphia, where he was set to make his first public appearance since the car wreck. Brian was still privately declaring his intentions of wrestling Shane Douglas and doing interviews on ECW before either returning to WCW or debuting with the WWF, and saw this as a chance to get people talking about him since he'd been out the limelight for over the month. On the morning of the show, June 1st, Pillman got another call from Eric Bischoff who quickly threw the magic numbers at Brian - $425,000 per year, for three years. While there were still particulars to work out, Pillman tentatively agreed. Through everything, it was looking like he'd managed to get to his destination.

Keyed up and looking to create news, Pillman entered the ECW Arena in his wheelchair with a microphone in hand, interrupting a match between Rob Van Dam and Mikey Whipwreck. The audience rose with excitement as he rolled down the aisle, still keen to be reviled, yelling, "Each and every one of you scumbags wants to bow down to a real God? Get on your knees right now and pay homage to Brian Fuckin' Pillman!" The crowd still cheered, before Brian urged Whipwreck to confront him if he had a problem with the disruption. In typical ECW spirit, Whipwreck replied in the affirmative, slapping Pillman across the face. As he turned his back, however, Brian drilled Mikey with his wooden crutch, rising from his chair and repeatedly hitting Whipwreck in the back as he fell to the concrete. The match ended shortly thereafter, with Rob Van Dam joining Pillman at ringside as Joey Styles approached them for an interview.

What followed was a vulgar, obscenity-laced rant that was even shocking and shameless by ECW standards. "It's been great therapy for me to come back here", started Brian, looking at the fans before continuing, "Not to look at you pieces of shit!" After extolling the merits of RVD, he fired his hail of bullets liberally at random ECW personalities. He referred to The Sandman as "some bumly drunk", mocked the promiscuity of Missy Hyatt and insulted

Sabu, screaming, "He sucks, and so does each and every one of you pieces of shit in this fucking building!" Most shocking of all, however, was referring to the tag team of The Gangstas, New Jack and Mustafa Saaed, as "those Niggaz Wit' Attitudes wannabes", a sense of unease overwhelming the crowd as the words left his lips.

"You've got to understand, the ECW Arena was like everybody's happy place, where you had all these people that would never hang out together in normal life", explains Mike Johnson, who was sat in the front row. "You had bikers hanging out with nerds, white guys hanging out with black guys, a real wide demographic brought together by a love for ECW. As soon as Brian said that, the black fans got angry, which made everybody else angry because it felt like insulting family. It wasn't the kind of heat that made you want to see him get his ass kicked. It was, 'Ugh, Brian Pillman, why are you ruining our happy place?'"

New Jack happened to be on the stage watching the promo, and sections of fans turned to face him in disbelief. The other wrestlers and staff surrounding him all did the same. New Jack, the real-life Jerome Young, had his own well-deserved reputation for volatility and was absolutely livid. Pillman wrapped up his promo and succeeded in his goal to be despised, a biting tension in the air as Van Dam wheeled him to the back. The genuine heat was tangible, as fans leaned over the rail to yell and point in his direction, audibly screaming, "Get the fuck out of here!" in disgust. But that was nothing compared to what was waiting on the other side of the curtain.

Confronted immediately, Brian was asked by New Jack to repeat what he said. Paul Heyman saw what was coming and grabbed him around the neck to pull him away. Pillman brushed it off, saying it was all a work and he was just trying to get heat, but New Jack wasn't accepting that as an explanation, yelling that they weren't working together so there was no reason for it. Other wrestlers quickly got between the two to try and prevent anything physical, moving New Jack to the other side of the locker room. The situation was extremely tense with New Jack going ballistic at the slur, at Pillman, and at ECW for allowing it, asking, "Why are you all protecting this motherfucker? He's messing with everybody!" Heyman tried to calm New Jack down by telling him the issue wasn't worth it, saying that starting anything physical would be a detriment to his career. New Jack responded by punching a hole in the wall and returning back to the stage. For his part, Brian was quite non-plussed about the drama. But it was questionable whether New Jack would even do his scheduled match, as he insisted that Heyman allow him to cut a promo in response to Pillman first.

New Jack talked for ten minutes about nothing but Pillman, saying that when he came to ECW he was told to leave the heavily racial element of The Gangstas gimmick in Smoky Mountain Wrestling (where they were strong heels for that reason), but the company just violated that themselves. "Leave that piece of shit out of ECW!", he yelled, the crowd cheering as he went on to challenge Brian to repeat his comment to him in the ring. The public nature of New Jack's response and challenge raised people's eyebrows as to whether this was another Pillman work of fiction, but the actions in the aftermath indicated the opposite.

The offending line from Brian was edited out of his promo when it aired on television, and New Jack's response was never mentioned again. Pillman insisted in the fallout that he was comparing The Gangstas to rap group N.W.A, but most that witnessed the event live felt that Brian used the band's name simply for the shock value of the offensive remark.

After the whirlwind of his ECW appearance, he returned home and began dealing with his WCW offer. One of the points of contention that still remained was a standard clause in WCW's contracts that allowed the company to terminate the agreement every 90 days. This quarterly period of review was built in to ensure that if a talent was incapacitated for an extended period of time, the company wasn't bound to pay the full guarantee amount, since they would theoretically be unable to get the desired return on the investment. Pillman had asked around and discovered that in some cases, typically with top stars who Bischoff had lured with big money deals, the 90-day cycles had been removed. Brian knew enough to know that his injuries were going to affect the rest of his career, whether he admitted it to anybody or not. With a family of five children, signing with WCW was a sure thing if it was guaranteed for three years, unless McMahon topped the amount. But if it was only guaranteed for three months, Brian was less certain he'd get the full sum of money, over a million dollars, knowing how bad his situation was. Bischoff felt the cycles, like the other issues, were not deal-breakers.

Eric felt confident enough that on the June 3rd episode of Nitro, pieces were put in place to hint to his return. He was mentioned by name by Kevin Sullivan, as a clip of Pillman's match with him at Superbrawl aired. Sullivan had moved on to a feud with another member of the Horsemen, Chris Benoit, built on the premise that Sullivan saw Benoit as a threat to Ric Flair and Arn

Anderson, much as he viewed Pillman. The promo was to create movement on the Old Horsemen Vs. New Horsemen storyline that was teased at the beginning of the year, and Brian's name and face was reintroduced on the belief he'd fit right in to the angle.

Pillman, however, had other ideas. He took WCW's offer and relayed it to the WWF, who quickly negotiated a series of terms that seemed very attractive to Brian's cause. While they wouldn't match the $425,000 offer, they offered a full three-year contact. They also offered a new type of deal, which featured a downside guarantee - a minimum amount that was absolutely assured every year in a worst-case scenario. It still operated under the previous "opportunity" incentive-based system, where if the pay issued based on the success of the shows and position on the cards surpassed the downside guarantee figure, Brian would earn the higher amount. The downside number thrown at Pillman, guaranteed for three years, ranged between $250,000 and $400,000, depending on who you talk to. To sweeten the deal, Pillman requested he keep his hotline number and independent merchandising separate from the company, which they agreed to. The option of working independent shows was also approved, meaning he had the opportunity to return to ECW to supplement his income if needed.

Brian's situation had transformed completely. What started out as a method to earn the money, respect and position of a top guy had become, out of necessity, about guaranteeing a job and an income. If Pillman couldn't overcome the odds this time, he would at least be somewhat secure.

With the WWF making an offer that had the potential to come close to the WCW figure, Pillman called Bischoff to hash out the obstacles standing in the way of the big guarantee. Eric had come so close to providing the perfect deal for Brian, but no matter what points of negotiation he conceded, he wouldn't remove the 90-day clause. While Bischoff didn't know the full truth, he was aware of the possibility of Brian not being 100% and didn't want to be tied down to such a big contract in the event Pillman was incapacitated for the long haul. WCW had callously fired Ricky Steamboat at the end of 1994 shortly after suffering a back injury in their ring, based on it being career-ending. WCW took a lot of criticism for the move but it wouldn't stop them from doing it again, and Brian was well aware. Weighing up the situation and with guilt coursing through him, he realized that with Bischoff not budging on the 90-day termination cycles, his decision had been made for him. On June 7th, he signed his contract – with the World Wrestling Federation.

19 - NEW YORK STATE OF MIND

Brian wasn't really in any kind of shape to be getting involved right off the bat. Not only was his ankle far from healed, but he'd suffered a bad infection in the area that forced him into hospital for another surgery. Coming out of it, Pillman was hooked up to intravenous antibiotics. The WWF soon came calling, looking to reap the benefits of the signing. Far too eager to get involved, he'd unhook himself from the IV and travel to the events, then hook himself back up when he returned home.

Mere days after the deal was signed, Brian Pillman was rushed on to WWF television, appearing on the June 17th episode of Monday Night Raw. A faux press conference for his signing, emanating from Titan Towers in Stamford, Connecticut, showed a tearful Pillman thanking his audience for the chance to sign with the WWF. While only the emotional first minute of the angle aired on Raw, Pillman immediately snapped and went into a classic tirade, only highlights of which were ever shown on the weekend television shows.

McMahon was all too happy to throw Pillman on the air, hoping the groundswell of momentum he'd built would give his show an added boost. Wartime hostilities were at an all-time high, with Kevin Nash making his WCW debut the previous week and Nitro going to a two-hour format.

"If the wreck had not happened, I think he would have made a lot of money, probably real quick", says Jim Cornette. "Not only on the guaranteed contract, but he would have got over in a top spot. That's the worst thing, really not being able to get started. He had a lot of buzz, a lot of fanfare, and then of course that made him feel more pressure to try and get back quicker."

But while WWF officials were thrilled with their latest acquisition, members of the WWF locker room didn't share the same sentiment. Pillman's contract earned him a lot of jealousy from his peers, many of whom had the minimum possible guarantee on paper. One of them, Paul Levesque, playing a pompous aristocrat named Hunter Hearst Helmsley and struggling to get over, was vocal in his objections to Brian's contract. On an AOL chat later that week, Helmsley would sound off. "They made a big deal of his contract signing on Monday, I say big deal. Who cares?", he began. "I am sick and tired of this war with WCW allowing for guys to come in the door thinking they are something because they made a little name for themselves someplace else. If you have never been to the big dance and proven yourself there, then when you come in the door of the WWF, which no matter what anybody says is the big dance, then you start out on the ground floor. Just like everybody else. And until these people, including Brian Pillman, and we all know everybody else who I mean...until these people prove themselves as main event draws that bring people to the arenas, they have proven nothing to me. They should start out where everybody else starts out. They should be forced to prove themselves before being given what is not known."

Another person who wasn't particularly thrilled was the Undertaker. After leaving Ole Anderson's WCW in 1990, Mark Calaway had been given a top spot and a tremendous gimmick by the WWF and never looked back. The way the WWF operated was being forced to change by the war and those who weren't the immediate beneficiaries had sour grapes. After six years without a guaranteed deal, Undertaker wasn't thrilled to see newcomers like Pillman and Marc Mero walking in the door with a financial safety net. It was made worse by a personal dislike that dated back to their WCW days.

Undertaker's demeanor was generally a cool, calm reserve that commanded respect, and eccentric types could rub him the wrong way. Pillman's personality clashed with his, and Brian didn't particularly care for him at all. With Pillman's credibility as a street fighter and NFL alumnus, he saw a vast contradiction in Undertaker, who Pillman deemed a "fake biker". Brian saw him as a man without any reputation as a credible fighter but still carried himself as if he should be feared, whose athletic background was as a tall basketball player with Texas Wesleyan University that never made it to the pros. In many ways, Pillman thought Calaway a phony. As mentioned, they'd had words after a match at a Clash of the Champions and never had any regard for each other personally after that. But Undertaker had gone from a green, colorless big guy in WCW to a major player and bona-fide star in the WWF, and it was in nobody's best interest to be on the opposite side politically to Taker.

That Sunday, Brian made his first live appearance at the King of the Ring. Pillman hobbled down the aisle on crutches for an interview with Jim Ross. Since his first outburst never aired on Raw, Pillman held nothing back with a fantastic diatribe. "How's my extended family doing, Jimmy?", he started, mocking his words from the press conference. In a little over two minutes, Pillman mocked the Milwaukee crowd saying that it was easy to see why Jeffrey Dahmer tried to eat the entire state, called Jim Ross a "stupid son of a bitch", and vowed to "rape, pillage and plunder this entire Federation!" With his hyena-like laugh, questionable verbiage and psychotic expressions, it was the perfect introduction. "While you're crowning a King of the Ring – the leader of a new revolution ascends to his throne."

Good as it was, it wasn't the best promo of the night. That honor went to Brian's friend Steve Austin, who won the tournament and cut the now-famous Austin 3:16 promo that helped put him on the map.

The following night, Pillman approached McMahon at the announce table on Raw and asked, "Who in the hell I've got to talk to to get my Goddamn money!" With Brian unable to wrestle, the WWF opted to place Brian in random spots to keep his name alive. From trying to attack Savio Vega with a crutch, to marching with then assaulting the Bushwhackers, there was very little he could do but serve as a pest. He spent most of August rehabbing, as more talk circulated around the locker room of Pillman making money while contributing little. "That guaranteed deal was another reason why Brian felt a ton of pressure, and I'm sure a ton pressure was put on him", states Jim Cornette. "It was one of the first ones and one of the bigger ones at that time. I remember Vince was more often asking for updates on him. 'What's Pillman's condition, what can we do here?'"

Brian himself was looking to stay as hot as he possibly could. One funny idea came up to maintain a WCW presence while under WWF contract. Pillman called up Colin Bowman and pitched the idea of doing a back page monthly column in WCW Magazine under the pen name of 'The Yellow Dog'. "We were going to drop enough hints that people would maybe guess that it was him", laughs Bowman. "I'm not sure what WCW overlords would think when they'd leaf through to make sure everything was fine. In truth, they wouldn't have got anything. I could have probably said it was by Brian Pillman and put a picture of him there and they still wouldn't have figured out, 'This isn't something we should be doing'."

The WWF started to get more focused in September, as Brian was able to walk on his own volition again. With a tentative target date of November for Pillman to start up as an active wrestler, they started integrating him a little more with the key names in the company and throwing out ideas on how to use him. There was talk of starting a heel stable with Pillman, Austin, Helmsley and Mr. Perfect, but McMahon shot it down. A pitch was made to give Brian his own interview segment, akin to "Piper's Pit" that Roddy Piper had used so effectively in years past. In a dummy run for television, Pillman did an interview with Shawn Michaels to hype up a match with Mankind that was pulled before it ever aired. Instead, the WWF settled on an angle where Pillman would buddy up with Owen Hart, vowing to bring Bret Hart back to the WWF for an interview on the Mind Games pay-per-view.

The backstage interplay with Brian and Owen was humorous in how blatantly disingenuous it was, making it clear that neither of them had ever spoken to Bret while claiming they'd pulled the coup of the century. At the big event, Pillman endeared himself to Philadelphia by calling it "a cesspool of drug abuse, battered women and welfare recipients". He brought out Owen, claimed Bret had bailed on the return and introduced Steve Austin to insult Bret even further. Austin had been handpicked for a feud with Hart. While he'd turned heads at King of the Ring, it wasn't until the feud with Bret that Austin started gathering main event level momentum, as he used his cutting wit to run down a top tier player. With Brian laughing along, Austin proclaimed that, "If you put the letter 'S' in front of Hitman, you've had my exact opinion of Bret Hart!" After challenging Bret, Austin claimed that, "I'm the best there is and that's the bottom line, because Stone Cold said so!" Closing out the segment, Brian comedically got the last word stating, "And Philadelphia sucks, because I say so!"

The Austin feud, being set up for Hart upon his return, was quite a risky move. The match was being teased at a time when it wasn't certain Bret Hart would be coming back at all. Similar to Pillman, Bret had found himself with his contract expiring at a wonderful time and was batting offers from both WCW and the WWF. Since the WCW debut of Kevin Nash, launch of the New World Order angle with Hulk Hogan shockingly going heel and Nitro becoming a two-hour show, Raw had been getting beaten every week in the

Monday night ratings. For the first time, Vince McMahon's product had the public perception as the number two promotion in North America. Not wanting to lose one of his few remaining stars, McMahon pushed the boat out and eventually offered Bret a twenty-year contract, at $1.5 million for the first three years, in order to keep him.

With the battle for the Hitman dominating the headlines, a WWF policy change snuck under the radar, only earning fleeting discussion due to the breakneck pace of the business. In mid-October, the WWF issued the following communication to the wrestlers:

"This memo is to advise of certain changes in our drug collection and testing efforts, and to reiterate our position on the use of illegal and performance enhancing drugs. As each of you know, the Company instituted systematic drug testing years ago on a group basis. Additionally, the standard talent contracts contain provisions strictly prohibiting the use of illegal and performance enhancing drugs which subject any offender to termination of their contract.

As a result of our drug testing program, the incidence of use of illegal and performance enhancing drugs is so slight that group testing is no longer cost effective or necessary. Thus, we are, effective immediately, suspending drug collection and testing on a group basis. In doing so, we wish to reiterate that the strict prohibition against use of such drugs remains our policy and that any person caught violating our policy will be dealt with strictly. Additionally, we reserve the right to test any individual, at any time, for the use of illegal substances. If any individual tests positive for any prohibited substance, appropriate sanctions up to and including termination may be imposed."

The switch in stance was emblematic of the fight for survival on Monday nights, which was only becoming uncannier. In January '96, Vince McMahon publicly decried Ted Turner on Raw for not having any kind of drug policy in WCW, insinuating that it showed a lack of care for the talent. Only nine months later, McMahon was abandoning his own policy. Financial reasons were very much part of it, but the public heat on the steroids-in-wrestling issue was all but gone, washed away by the constant churn of soundbite news. Seeing WCW stars with physiques most likely obtained with chemical assistance, and with McMahon's mind drawing back the eighties when the large bodies contributed to his company's success, it had to bother him tremendously to have to play by the rules. Especially at a time when he appeared to be losing. To the WWF, there seemed to be very little reason to keep regular testing in place, and so it was eradicated.

In the meantime, a trip to the doctor for Brian in early October brought back poor results. His ankle hadn't healed correctly, the result of Pillman traveling around the country to do shows, putting weight on it when he shouldn't have. The infection had also done a number on the ankle's ability to restore itself, and Brian was dejected to hear the doctor tell him that it would need to be rebroken. The healing process would need to begin all over again. Worse, the ankle was in such bad shape that the only way it could be repaired would be to permanently fuse the ankle into one position. The restriction this would place on his movement would be significant. He was again told that he wouldn't be able to run any more, but there were no other options.

To deal with the situation on screen, the call was made for Steve Austin to savagely attack Pillman and get the heat for taking him out of the picture. On the October 21st episode of Raw, Bret Hart made his return, announcing he'd re-signed with the WWF and would face Steve Austin at Survivor Series. When Bret stated his intentions, the camera cut to a number of wrestlers, including Austin and Pillman, watching on a monitor backstage. Pillman jumped with the glee of a schoolboy as Bret declared he was staying, earning him a dirty look from Austin.

The following day, the WWF taped Superstars in Cincinnati, the perfect place to vilify Austin. In conducting an interview with Steve, Brian began touting Bret Hart's return in a babyface manner, earning him the scorn of Stone Cold. Austin even acknowledged that once upon a time, he and Brian had been a tandem, stating that he'd once "carried him to a world championship in the bush leagues". As the interview came to a close, Pillman referred to Bret by his often-said handle of "the best there is, the best there was, and the best there ever will be", but was attacked by a rabid Austin. As Pillman rose to his feet, Austin took Brian's own cane and broke it over his ankle. Steve followed it up by taking a steel chair, threading Brian's ankle through it and stomping on the seat, providing the visual effect of crushing or snapping the bone. It was a powerful angle, so much so that the technique used is, to this day, called "Pillmanizing" as part of wrestling parlance.

24 hours later, Brian was on the operating table again. Talk started going around that the ankle was destroyed and there was a possibility that there would never be a full recovery. Brian was quick to diffuse it, telling everybody that he'd be back in early 1997. "He was always telling me he was going to be

able to come back, he always said that", mentions Dave Meltzer. "Even though I don't know that it was as sure as he would lead everyone to believe."

The Pillman injury and the focus on heating up Steve Austin presented a unique opportunity, one that got McMahon's gears whirring. Since Nitro had gone to a two-hour format (8pm-10pm), they had a one-hour lead-in before the head-to-head battle with Raw began. The decision was made to move Raw from 9pm to 8pm by the WWF and USA Network, to prevent TNT from having the extra time to establish an audience and build up to the competitive hour. In doing so, McMahon was looking for something big to shock the audience into breaking their current habits and tune in to Raw.

With the perfect hotheaded characters in Pillman and Austin, McMahon proposed a scenario to Bonnie Hammer of the USA Network where Steve Austin would break into Brian Pillman's home in Walton, Kentucky, but Brian would be waiting for him with a gun. Brian would shoot twice at Austin but the feed would cut out, leaving the viewer wondering what had happened. They'd spend the entire show on the unfolding saga, treating it like a news story. This would eventually lead to Austin returning to the house, a melee ensuing, and Brian's wife Melanie getting thrown down in the chaos as they went off the air.

Hammer nixed the on-air gunshots and Melanie getting hurt, but gave the okay for the gun to be teased and to add a more real-life vibe to the show. Given the green light, the angle and commentary would be recorded live, with taped matches and angles interspersed throughout the show.

The entire November 4th episode of Raw was based around Austin and Pillman's ongoing drama, opening on a shot of Brian's house. In the middle of the first match, a phone call with Steve Austin broke in, confirming that he was on his way to Walton. Kevin Kelly played an on-the-scene reporter, interviewing Brian and Melanie inside the house. Pillman set the scene talking about their deep-rooted history as a team when McMahon cut in, asking if Brian felt like a hostage in his own home, the verbal cue for the peak of the promo. "Steve is a dead man walking, because when Austin 3:16 meets Pillman 9mm glock, I'm gonna blast his sorry ass straight to hell!"

With that, he pulled out his firearm, the announcers going into an immediate panic, as Bruce Pritchard (who produced the segment) off-mic screamed, "Steve Austin's out there now!" In a move that demonstrated the WWF's difficult balancing act, the scene then cut to the next segment – the Milton Bradley Karate Fighters toy tournament.

We returned to see footage directly outside of Brian's house, where Austin was beating up a couple of Pillman's friends (students of Les Thatcher, who was also there for the taping). After trying to drown one in a kiddy-pool and pushing a car door on the head of the other, Steve walked around the side of the house, looking to gain entry as we cut away.

After the next match finished in the arena, the show went back inside Brian's home, where Pillman was tightly clutching the pistol. Suddenly, the sound of glass breaking set off Melanie's screams, the camera catching Austin opening the door and barging in. Jerry Lawler screamed "Don't go in there!" on commentary as he turned the corner, where Brian was waiting with gun pointed. Suddenly, static covered the screen and the show went to commercial.

Coming back, the show returned to the arena for a Shawn Michaels debate with Sid, talking about their upcoming WWF Title match at Survivor Series. The segment, which wasn't much to begin with, was completely secondary to the conversation between Vince and Lawler about what was happening in Kentucky. McMahon explained that the power had gone out and nobody knew what had actually happened. Mid-segment, Vince talked over his champion, saying they'd got the feed up and running and were going to cut away, before backtracking and saying it wasn't ready.

The main event went to the ring as background noise, the focus now on a phone call between McMahon and production member Kerwin Silfies. After being asked if he heard any gunshots, Kerwin said he'd heard explosions, but didn't know what they were. The drama continued to play out with McMahon asking if the authorities had been contacted and Jim Ross getting into an argument with Vince about egging on the situation for television ratings.

Finally, to close the show, the feed was restored on the sight of Pillman being contained by his friends, with Kevin Kelly saying that Austin saw the gun and left, and that nobody was hurt in any of the "explosions". Suddenly, a cry of "Oh my God he's back!" broke through, as Austin charged towards Pillman screaming "Shoot me!" While Steve was restrained and pushed out of the room, Brian, still sporting the enormous cast from his surgery, hopped on one foot, wildly pointing the gun. "Let him go! That son of a bitch has got this coming! Let him go! I'm gonna' kill that son of a bitch! Let him go!"

As Kevin Kelly screamed for somebody to call the police, Pillman continued his outburst. "C'mon, get out of the way! Get out of the *fuckin'* way!" The camera then panned to a crying Melanie to send the show to black.

The angle was the hot topic in the business. Thrilled with their performances, the daring nature and the fact that they were the most featured acts on the show, Austin and Pillman were desperate for the ratings to come in. Hoping that this would be the night that broke Nitro's streak of victories, Brian was after every bit of information on the demographics and quarter hour breakdowns he could get his hands on.

When the numbers came in, both men ended up disappointed. Nitro won once again, doing a 2.9 in the head-to-head hour to Raw's 2.3. Raw's rating was only slightly up from the previous week's 2.0, though some credit should be given for improving the rating in a new timeslot, when traditionally there is an initial decrease while viewers adjust their habits.

Analyzing the figures, Raw started soft, only doing a 2.0 for the first two quarter hours (opposite Nitro's 2.7 and 3.0 quarters), up to the point Pillman pulled out the gun and pointed it at Austin. The intrigue surrounding it was positive, as Raw jumped to a 2.8 for the third quarter as they speculated on what had happened, tying Nitro which also did a 2.8. The shows were neck and neck heading into the final segment. The bad news was that the Raw main event match, the fake Razor Ramon versus Marc Mero, wasn't enough to hold viewers until the closing scene, the rating falling to a 2.5 as Nitro grew to a 3.2.

When Brian and Steve looked at the figures, it told a tale that none of the key demographics were impacted enough to stay. 125,000 kids, 11,000 teenagers, 63,000 men aged 18-34, 49,000 women aged 18-34, 105,000 men aged 35-54, 20,000 women aged 35-54 and 12,000 women over 55 all tuned out. Men over 55 held even on Raw, staying until the end. In reality, despite being one of the more memorable moments in Raw history, and to this day it is lauded as a key angle in the Monday Night War, it was tough to call it a success or a failure. It did elevate the rating in a new timeslot, but only marginally. One of the bigger failures was that, due to large switchover of children, Nitro was able to claim victory in the kids demographic, typically a WWF stronghold, at a crucial time. Though there was an obvious desire from McMahon to experiment with a more risqué direction throughout 1996, it was results like this that prevented him from adjusting his product completely – if the adults didn't flock to it, the risk of losing the children to WCW would leave him without a key base to market to.

It wasn't the outright success Austin and Pillman were hoping for, but did help to ramp up Austin as he approached the biggest match of his life.

Interestingly, the fallout of the angle looked like the biggest potential negative of the entire thing. With Brian's screaming, "Get out of the fuckin' way!", which wasn't approved by anybody, and the general public concern about a gun being pulled in a live setting on a show heavily marketed to kids, the USA Network distanced itself from it. The station issued an apology vowing it wouldn't happened again and sent representatives to Raw in the following weeks to "monitor content". The WWF volunteered itself as the sacrificial lamb, knowing the USA Network would be happy if they deflected any bad publicity, offering an apology for the skit. The angle even got some press in TV Guide, asking if it was really appropriate for children.

From there, Brian was left at home where he was given the time to rest and rehabilitate. McMahon seemed to understand the cause for Pillman's prolonged absence, even commenting on it in a press conference in Toronto. "We brought him back too soon", started Vince. "He was too eager and too anxious to start back into competition. Brian just had another operation and we are not going to make the same mistake this time. When Brian Pillman comes back this time, he will really be ready. He has a huge heart and a great pride."

Indeed. But as the age-old, time-tested expression goes, pride comes before a fall.

2**0** - FULL CIRCLE SUMMER

Brian was kept out of the loop until a house show appearance in Cincinnati on Valentine's Day, 1997. Pillman showed up in the front row, distracting Steve Austin. He still wasn't close to being ready to return, but the opportunity to get involved was a welcome change for Brian, who was growing weary sitting on the shelf for the past four months.

His ankle wasn't feeling particularly great to say the least, but being sedentary wasn't a fond option for somebody of Brian's history and disposition. Life at home was becoming more difficult without the business distracting him from the scars of his past, piling more pressure on his shoulders. "At that time, his relationship with Melanie was all going to hell too", states Linda Pillman. "It wasn't a good environment to be trying to heal, when you're sick and you've got your wife not doing anything to help you get better. She wasn't caring for him. He was coming to our house and eating. He couldn't drive, so he was taking taxis from Kentucky over to where we lived, and that was probably a good thirty to forty-five-minute ride. He would come to our house to eat, sometimes he would spend the night there."

Multiple family members state that Melanie had a controlling nature during this time, making them schedule appointments to see the kids rather than extend an open invitation. When the couple would argue, it is said that she would bring up her past relationship with the Ultimate Warrior (who Brian hated with a passion) and rub it in his face, using one of his biggest insecurities as ammunition.

What's more, the time off had really let Brian stew in the perils of his situation, which had a major effect on his attitude. "This injury made him vulnerable for the first time in his life", says Alex Marvez. "It's like that with professional athletes who make their living through their body. Then, if you can't rely on that body to help get you through, what do you turn to next? In Brian's case, he was smart enough, wily enough, and perceptive enough to continue to reinvent himself and do different things in wrestling, but that was something that I don't think he could comprehend."

In early March, Brian was walking around and finally ready, in his mind at least, to try getting back in the ring. One of the hopefuls that hung around Brian was a man named Chip Fairway. Pillman had directed him to Les Thatcher's training school in Cincinnati to learn to wrestle, and through Chip, contacted Les asking to use his ring to get back into shape and see what he was capable of. When Pillman arrived at Thatcher's gym, it didn't take long for Brian's heart to sink, sensing his limitations. He couldn't run, and it took everything he had to shuffle awkwardly around the ring. He tried doing some of the things he used to do with ease, but failed time after time. "It was sad, it really was", remembers Les Thatcher. "It was frustrating for me, realizing his passion for the business and how good he was, and that he was never going to be that good again regardless. I could see his frustration."

Brian started trying on different boots and shoes, desperately trying to figure out a way to work around his fused ankle. Before long, he was getting exasperated with the students. "In one way, it was good for the kids that I was training to be able to get in the ring with him", says Les. "But then I would see him get frustrated with them a little bit and I'd say, 'Well, Brian, give that kid a break and we'll give you somebody else.' And I did that simply to keep from having a major problem."

"It really bothered him a lot though that he was never going to be able to work the way he did again, and he knew that", offers Mark Madden. "I always thought that with Brian's personality and his promos he should have adopted the philosophy, at least after a certain point of his career, where less was more. It wasn't worth taking the risks and it was better to just use his creative thinking and influence the process that way. Because the WWF at that point weren't having five-star matches, nor did they care about it."

"He had set a real high standard in the ring", adds Alex Marvez. "He was very proud of his in-ring performances and should be, and now Flyin' Brian was grounded. That's what it came down to."

While he was in no condition to return, Pillman insisted to WWF officials that he could and would. There was no such thing within the company as "medical clearance" at the time, and no legitimate doctor would have signed off on Brian getting back in the ring with his ankle in such condition. The company was under the impression he'd be returning to the ring after WrestleMania and had it in mind to give him a substantial push. Brian was given a new role in the WWF in the interim – co-hosting Shotgun Saturday Night with his old friend Jim Ross.

Brian took the job seriously, preparing hard and looking to incorporate as much of his act as possible. With his gift of gab and remarkable intellect, JR told Brian the position could be permanent if he wanted it to be. "I think it probably would have been smarter for him to become a television announcer", mentions Dave Meltzer. "Maybe it was his football background or whatever, but he felt that he wasn't serving the team well. He was getting such a good contract from Vince he felt he needed to earn it, and as a TV announcer he wasn't earning his money and he wanted to. To him, the only way to earn his money was to be in big programs as a wrestler."

It turned out that the duo were a lot of fun in the booth, with Brian walking a fine line with a variety of verbiage that would be dubious in any era. The run ended up lasting three and a half months and produced a litany of humorous moments.

∞

Highlights of Brian Pillman Commentary

JR: "ECW stands for Extreme Championship Wrestling. They're a small regional wrestling organization based in Philadelphia."
Pillman: "Boy that's being magnanimous. They operate out of a bingo hall for Christ's sake."

JR: "Jerry Lawler and Ahmed Johnson. What a mismatch this is physically as far as Ahmed Johnson is concerned."
Pillman: "It's an even bigger mismatch mentally as far as Lawler is concerned. You could almost call it a handicap match."

On Venom Vs. Hysteria: "These two are great athletes. I mean you gotta be, to swim across the Rio Grande."

On Marlena: "She only weighs ninety pounds, and twenty of it is silicone."

On Doug Furnas and Philip Lafon:
Pillman: "They're not very pepped up or excited about being here."
JR: "Are you questioning the level of charisma?"
Pillman: "I'm questioning the level of caffeine I've got in my mug right now."

Sunny: "Who wants to get under the covers with me?"
Pillman: "Who hasn't?"

During an eight-man lucha match: "You know, these futuristic costumes they wear are certainly blithe to the fact that they live in such a backward country. When asked about these elaborate headgears and costumes, they didn't really care for them either, they just love irony."

Mankind: "The cream always rises to the top. But around my house there's a filthy pond, and I know for a fact that sometimes the scum rises too."
Pillman: "I'll say - look who's in the White House."

On Bret Hart traveling to South Africa and Kuwait: "The international superstar that he is, out on tour lining the coffers of the WWF with gold, yet this organization would soon as spit on him. Shawn Michaels gets a chest cold and we all gotta go walking around with black armbands on for a week. Gimme a break."

JR: "We'd like to congratulate Tony Randall, aged 77, and his wife Heather, aged 27. They were married last November and they expect their first child April 9th."
Pillman: "They said he was through, hey - the guy's still an up and comer!"

On April 19th: "Are you aware there's been three major tragedies on this date? Waco, the Oklahoma City bombing, and me having to sit through another one of Furnas & Lafon's matches."

JR: "Most ECW bouts are in the Northeastern part of these here United States."
Pillman: "Standing room only of about 118 people."

During a tag match: "If they cut that apron off, Lawler will be out of a job."

As Tommy Rogers performs two forward rolls at the start of a match:
Pillman: "What is Rogers doing? He just fell to the mat twice for no reason."
JR: "I think he's loosening up a little bit."
Pillman: "My God."

On movies: "Sunny was up for the 007 role, but unfortunately they've already used the character Pussy Galore."

"How about that new movie Ross – 'Eight Heads in a Duffel Bag'. Reminds me of the front office of a company I used to work for."

Ross: "Hey, did you see Sable's spread in the Raw magazine?"
Pillman: "Yeah. I saw her pictures too."

On Faarooq using his belt on Ahmed Johnson: "Faarooq whipping Ahmed like the Uncle Tom that he is."

During a Leif Cassidy Vs. Jesse Jammes match:
JR: "A battle of two underrated competitors..."
Pillman: "How do you define underrated? Calling these guys underrated."
JR: "Well, I think they're underappreciated somewhat."
Pillman: "Certainly by me they are."

Pillman: "You think Ahmed is any relation to Michael?"
JR: "I don't know."
Pillman: "Definitely not, Michael's too good of an athlete. But they do have one thing in common."
JR: "What's that?"
Pillman: "They're Johnsons."

On HHH's female bodyguard: "You don't think Eddie Murphy may have extended an invitation for a ride home to Chyna, do ya?"

On the Bret/Shawn backstage fight: "Michaels left without his smile, and apparently without a lot of his hair as well."

On Abismo Negro: "Quick translation, he's abysmally black."

After Mankind applied the Mandible Claw to Jim Ross: "I'll tell you what, you just created a new Slammy category - the Linda Lovelace Award. Because Ross, you just got deepthroated!"

JR: "Are you questioning Ahmed Johnson's judgement in accepting a 3 on 1 challenge with the Nation?"
Pillman: "Well, it's going to be God awful to have to sit through three Ahmed Johnson matches."

Pillman: "Are they going to be recruiting new referees for this Light Heavyweight Division? Quicker, smaller, more agile?"
JR: "You looking for work?"
Pillman: "No, I got my hands full now carrying your ass through these broadcasts. Should see the size of my traps now."

Pillman: "Look at that sign - Gang Bang. That's got no place here."
JR: "No, *Bang Bang*. That's an old catchphrase of Cactus Jack."
Pillman: "These fans are sick. When would Cactus Jack have been invited to a gangbang? That ugly S.O.B."
JR: "No, BANG BANG!"
Pillman: "Oh."

On JR putting over Sid: "Ross, am I gonna have to take a squeegee to that rose-tinted window you're looking through?"

∞

As he prepared to return, things were changing in the WWF. McMahon was still looking for the answer to his WCW problem and in searching for it, turned Bret Hart heel and Steve Austin babyface to freshen up the scene. Making both moves in one night, Austin and Hart had arguably the best match in company history at WrestleMania 13. With Bret forming The Hart Foundation group with Davey Boy Smith and Owen Hart, and Austin being the storyline reason for Pillman's absence, Brian had a natural slot to fall into for his ready-made comeback.

Pillman was handpicked by Bret to join the group, which McMahon approved. Though Brian and Bret were friends and had a mutual respect, it would be fair to say that Pillman was closer to Owen and Bruce, so the nomination was a compliment to his talent. "We used to joke about Bret, in the sense that Bret took his stardom very, very seriously", says Dave Meltzer. "Later when I knew Bret I figured out that's why he was, because he wouldn't have been a star if he didn't take it so seriously. Bret and Bruce didn't always get along and Brian was close with Bruce, so I think there was something there. Brian didn't dislike Bret, but there were certain things that Bret would do that he would find funny."

Though he was excited to be brought back at the top of the mix, Brian had some reservations about the angle he was returning to. Bret was lobbying for a storyline where he and his collective would be the top heels in the United States, playing on anti-American sentiments, but continue to thank his fans and play as babyfaces to the rest of the world. It was something that hadn't been done before and while Pillman was usually fond of such ideas, he wasn't 100% sure it could be pulled off. Moreover, he thought that Bret playing a pseudo-babyface would sabotage the Foundation's impact as heels in the States, and that Hart was lobbying for it out of self-interest.

"We both talked about this and we were both so wrong", recollects Dave Meltzer. "Brian's like, 'I don't want to be this babyface in Canada, you can't do this, you've got to be a heel!' And Bret was so adamant because he was such a big star he didn't want to give up Canada, so he contrived this way of how he was going to do this. And I was just like, 'You can't be a babyface in Canada and a heel everywhere else.' I mean, now you could do it easily, but then I didn't think you could do it."

In addition, Pillman questioned whether it was the right move for him to return as part of a group. "Brian didn't like to be caught in the crowd, he thought that obscured him", says Mark Madden, remembering discussions with Pillman on the subject. "I think his first exposure to that was when he was in the Four Horsemen, because he really didn't gain anything from being in the Four Horsemen until he split from them. Brian was much better as an individual."

Consequently, Pillman going forward would frequently state that he wasn't a member of the Hart Foundation, just an affiliate, which tied into his solo aspirations and desire to break away if the situation presented itself. "I don't think Brian saw much value in being part of a group", confirmed Madden. "I can understand where he's coming from because groups generally benefit one person, or two people at the most. The rest of the group is there to protect those one or two people, and I think Brian saw through that pretty early." As it turned out, it seemed as if Pillman was one of the few who would be protected.

Brian reemerged in the final moments of one of the all-time great episodes of Monday Night Raw on April 21st, 1997. With Bret Hart about to go under the knife due to a knee injury, a story was concocted where Austin would challenge him to a street fight, targeting the injured knee to play into reality. A show-long game of cat and mouse between Austin and Bret began, with Davey and Owen spending the show looking for vengeance. During the final segment, an interview in the ring with Austin, Davey and Owen finally ambushed Stone Cold, pummeling him until Shawn Michaels made the save by chasing them off with a steel chair. Steve rose to his feet alone inside the ring, using the ropes for assistance. Just as it looked like the show would fade to black, Brian Pillman hopped the guardrail having come through the crowd, rushing Austin from behind. As Pillman swung a chair at Steve's back, Ross captured the moment with the perfect callback to their controversial angle, bellowing, "It sounded like a gun going off!" Eventually, Pillman opened up the chair and threaded Steve's leg through in the same way Austin had done to him back in October. Before the act of revenge could be committed, Shawn Michaels reappeared, running Brian off, as Raw closed on the sight of a grinning Pillman exiting the same way he came.

The scene was manic, and a hot show was desperately needed since Nitro had been extending its lead over Raw in the previous months. As thrilled as Brian was with the quality of the angle and the fact he was so prominently featured, he was openly in extreme pain after the show went off the air. As high-ranking officials gathered around Pillman and saw how badly he was hurting, it raised concerns that his ankle was still nowhere near fully healed. The idea of him joining the Hart Foundation was, in part, to help fill in for Bret Hart on the house shows as a series of six-man tags were originally planned for the May loop. After seeing him struggle to walk after Raw, people weren't so sure if he was ready for the squared circle.

Brian's pain continued throughout the rest of the week, so the WWF made the call to add another member to the Hart Foundation to help make up the numbers. Still, with the momentum of the great angle and new heel faction, Pillman was thrust to the forefront on the following episode of Raw, opening the show with a live, in-ring interview.

Walking to the ring to a shower of boos, Brian delivered a tremendous promo proclaiming to be a religious man. As such, he wanted everybody to join him in prayer. With one hand raised aloft, Brian prayed for the recovery of Bret Hart, for those who reveled in Austin's recent actions, and "for those across America, this great land, who savor the bloodthirsty violence that pervades our society." Seemingly caught up in the moment, Pillman used his arm to wipe away a mock tear as the fans heckled relentlessly. Eventually, Brian dropped to a knee and prayed for "the complete annihilation and destruction of Stone Cold Steve Austin", stating that he wished him to be stricken down. Austin's image appeared on the video screen as he called Brian's name in his Texas drawl. After he threatened Pillman, Brian proclaimed, "I'm not afraid of the devil. It says in the good book – an eye for an eye, and to turn the other cheek", as he slowly turned and bent over.

Steve made a beeline for the ring, before Davey and Owen appeared from nowhere, attempting an ambush. Austin escaped and left the scene unharmed, leaving the Hart Foundation in the ring. Pillman implored Owen and Bulldog to join him in prayer, as the three collectively sent well-wishes to Bret, with Owen's plea delivered in a hilariously hokey manner. Meanwhile, Austin backstage grabbed an axe-handle and headed back to ringside, clearing the ring as the Foundation scarpered. The angle was the beginning of a show long focus on the Hart Foundation, with several cutaways to Pillman on his own backstage, eyes closed, head bowed, continuing to pray for his teammates wellbeing and for their opponents to suffer.

As the show came to a close it appeared that, after attempting to get to Bret all night, Austin finally had Bret alone and cornered at the top the stage. Right when it looked as though Stone Cold would decimate the "Hitman", Jim "The Anvil" Neidhart attacked Austin from behind, allowing Bret to knock Austin off the stage with his crutch. Steve was wheeled away on a stretcher after presumably falling several feet to the concrete floor. As Austin was carted off, the scene cut back to Pillman in the locker room, still deep in prayer. Suddenly, he shot a look directly at the camera, crowing with his haunting stare piercing the camera lens as the show came to a close.

The group was now fully formed at five, with enough bodies to mix and match on the live events while Bret healed and Pillman eased his way into things. Bret's heel promos were blowing people away, but Brian adding his distinct brand of antagonistic sarcasm was the perfect touch. For the first time in a long time, it felt as though the WWF had a credible top heel act with legs.

"The Hart Foundation run was great because, for one thing, he'd been to Calgary, so they all knew him and they knew how tough he was", says Jim

Cornette. "Everybody wanted to help him; Bret, Owen, everybody. But it wasn't like a pity spot, they wanted a guy like *Brian*. He was the honorary American, they wanted him in it and it was fucking great. He fit with guys like that, not only looks wise because he looked like a fucking star, but even if he was having problems with his ankle, he still was not working at a level that would embarrass the Hart Foundation or Bret would have said something."

"Brian was kind of the catalyst, the ingredient that helped ignite that whole thing", adds Bruce Hart. "Bret had been around there for a while, but that was the hottest he ever really was. Bret was never that dynamic a talker. Nor was Davey, Owen or Neidhart. But once Pillman became that other component in the Hart Foundation, all of a sudden he was doing these cutting edge promos. They sort of took off."

As exciting as it all was and as much as Pillman thrived on chasing that vaunted top position, there was a devastating reality attached that inched ever closer. When May began, his in-ring return was days away, and he knew he was going to have to work twice as hard to even be half of what he used to be. After seeing him in pain after the angles on Raw, officials asked Brian if he was really ready. He didn't deny the pain, but would deflect the issue, telling people that doctors had said it would take up to 18 months for the pain to completely subside. Brian was so strong-willed that he didn't give the WWF much choice, asserting that he was absolutely returning to the ring.

"You could have sat him down and waterboarded him and pulled his fingernails out and he wouldn't have told the office that he was seriously concerned about whether he could wrestle anymore or not", articulates Jim Cornette. "As Chief Jay Strongbow used to say, he was going to get in that ring if he had to go in an iron lung. If it had been three years earlier, I don't think he'd have had that much of a problem with it because he was languishing in WCW. But he'd just gone through all that and done all the Loose Cannon stuff to get one of the first and biggest guaranteed contracts in WWF history, proved everybody wrong again after playing pro football and overcoming this, that and the other thing. And now he's got it? No, he was not about to give that up."

His return to action took place the following week in a dark match after the Raw taping, a six-man pitting him, Owen and the Bulldog against Austin and the Legion of Doom. The match also headlined MSG, Brian's first ever bout in the building, on May 17th. Eager to put on a main event level performance, he went overboard trying to deliver. "That night he was just pinballing all over the ring for Austin, and it looked like he was back to being Brian Pillman again", says attendee Mike Johnson. "Then I saw him leaving with Owen after the show and he was just limping really badly on the way to the car. I remember some fans came up to him wanting a photo and he just yelled at them. You could tell by looking at him, he didn't look healthy at all."

Cosmetically, Pillman's upper body looked much the same as it did previously, the result of human growth hormone (that he'd started taking the prior year) being stacked with a very small amount of anabolic steroids. His lower half, however, was noticeably different, with his legs much skinnier than before and almost no left calf to speak of. Indeed, from the knee down, his left leg resembled a broomstick.

Brian had taken to wearing lifts in his boots to increase his perceived height, but his ankle was too weak and the constant movement and pressure was agonizing. His reliance on painkillers really started to accelerate at this point, and though he relished being part of a top angle, life was becoming more and more difficult. Trying to exist as a pro wrestler with his injury meant there was no point in the day when he wasn't in pain.

"I just remember when he came back and people were telling me how hard it was for him to get through the airport", Dave Meltzer explains. "And he's still trying to wrestle while he can barely get through the airport because he's hurting so bad. He would play softball and couldn't run the bases. He can't run the bases and he's still doing professional wrestling? That was kind of scary, honestly."

With his notoriety as a high profile professional wrestler, it was all too easy for Brian to acquire prescriptions for whatever he wanted or felt he needed. Wrestling had a long history of attracting mark doctors, physicians who checked their ethics and medical responsibilities at the door in order to be friends with famous wrestlers. Brian had gone to a couple who were happy to supply far more medication than required and would do a loop, hitting over twenty different pharmacies near his home to pick up his pills without suspicion.

His first match on Raw took place on May 26th, teaming with Neidhart against the Legion of Doom. While still the workhorse of the match, it was easy to see how tough it was for Brian to do the things he used to. He fell clumsily taking multiple press-slams from his opponents, and worked around his limitations by eliminating much of his offensive arsenal of years past, replacing it with the hallmarks of a classic cheating, biting, punching and kicking heel. Even if it was a style he would have derided years ago, it was the best he could do. In some ways it worked, and was befitting the character. But the days of Brian Pillman being one of the best athletic wrestlers on the roster were over.

"The normal Brian had changed", remembers Jim Cornette when asked about Pillman's backstage demeanor and approach to his work at this time. "He wasn't the fluffy-haired, cherubic smiling babyface because he wasn't that anymore, he'd changed his look. He was more focused and serious, and maybe anxious sometimes about stuff he was doing, wanting to make it good. He wasn't 'water off a duck's back' Brian."

"He had finally figured out wrestling at a real level", says Dave Meltzer, discussing the deeper reason for Brian's concerns. "His understanding of wrestling was way above…I don't want to say anyone's, but it was top tier. Like before, you're trying to learn and trying to learn. I think that he figured out how to get over and then he physically couldn't do it, and that was for sure weighing on him."

Compounding Brian's problems was the fact that his marriage and family life were getting worse by the week. Things had been brewing for a while as the two would clash about things at home, particularly to do with the kids. "Melanie is not a nurturing person", details Linda Pillman. "It was about her. She had kids and that was about it. She didn't do anything to nurture those children, everyone around her did that. Brian wasn't raised that way, and it wasn't what he thought it was going to be. He wanted his kids to have a good life. And when he'd come home, he'd spend time with them and take them places, that kind of stuff."

Between the disagreements and Melanie's concerns of his escalating drug use, the two would butt heads in hostile fashion. It is also important to understand the unique nature of the relationship, with both coming from worlds where exhibitionism and promiscuousness were somewhat encouraged. Adding in the challenges the business throws at married life, it lends itself to the common opinion among friends and family that neither side remained faithful to the other throughout the relationship, and things were coming to a head.

"After Brian's accident", begins Linda, "A couple of friends who were like wrestler wannabes in the local wrestling community stopped by the house to see how Brian was doing. And Brian invites them in because he's bored and wanted to talk to somebody different. They became Brian's flunkies. Since

Brian couldn't get around at the time they were driving him around. He'd say, 'Let's go here!', and they'd take him. Well, then Melanie ended up getting with one of them." The general belief from others is that the wrestler in question was Chip Fairway.

Meanwhile, Brian was involved in a photoshoot in Orlando with Tammy Sytch, who went by the ring name Sunny. Sytch was being promoted as the lead female and sex kitten of the WWF, lauded by the company as the most downloaded woman on AOL. The idea of the beach shoot with Brian was to allude to a secret, scandalous liaison between the two. As often happens in wrestling, fantasy became reality. Pillman, never one to keep a conquest quiet, picked up the phone and called Mark Madden. "He called me in the middle of fucking her", clarifies Madden. "In the *middle* of fucking her, and put her on the phone with me." With both participants under the influence, Sunny began talking to Mark. "She's saying, 'I'm such a pig, my boyfriend is at home and I'm fucking Brian Pillman. I shouldn't be doing this, I shouldn't be doing this'", says Madden. "Then Brian grabs the phone back and with that cackle goes, 'I SHOULDN'T BE DOING THIS! I SHOULDN'T BE DOING THIS! HA HA HA!' and hangs up."

With his life getting harder personally and professionally, Brian's psychological state was deteriorating, and the only solace he could take was in how well things were going in the WWF. Even then, as soon as he stepped through the ropes, the problems began all over again. Depression began setting in, with Pillman telling friends how demoralizing it felt to be capable of so little during the biggest push of his career. "He knew that this wasn't WCW where he wouldn't be given a chance", Dave Meltzer points out. "He knew he had a chance, but then he couldn't perform at the level he felt he needed to perform. He knew mentally he could be doing so well because he was getting TV time and they were allowing him to do his personality, but he couldn't really wrestle by that point."

"It was just a very rough year for him", summarizes Linda Pillman. "In pain, physically and mentally."

The WWF determined that it was time for Brian's first high-profile singles match, a showdown with his old partner and nemesis Steve Austin at King of the Ring in June. Unbeknownst to Brian and Steve, events were unfolding behind the scenes that would drastically change plans for the immediate future.

Real-life tensions had been brewing for months between the two top dogs in the Federation, Shawn Michaels and Bret Hart. The battle for position had led to insecurities revealing themselves, and the emotionally immature Michaels was having a hard time dealing with the pressure. Similarly, Bret would raise an eyebrow any time Shawn made a statement that he interpreted as a personal attack. One such instance occurred in May, when a glassy-eyed and slurring Michaels accused Bret of seeing some 'Sunny days' of late, insinuating a real-life affair with the WWF personality of the same name. Bret and Owen were furious at the comment, with Bret feeling like he had to retaliate. The two were scheduled for a match at King of the Ring, but Bret's knee injury was healing slower than expected, and Michaels' remarks soured him on rushing back to work with him.

Talk began circulating about making Austin Vs. Pillman the pay-per-view main event, but officials were cognizant that Brian's ankle wasn't 100%, opting against putting him in a position to have to carry the show with a great performance in a long match.

As a result, the two top matches for King of the Ring were canceled, as the WWF went with a makeshift Austin Vs. Michaels encounter. Pillman was slated to work with Steve the next night on Raw. It turned out that Austin was hurting too, and ended up being pulled from the Pillman match. In its place, the first ever Shawn Michaels Vs. Brian Pillman encounter would headline Raw. In addition, with the next In Your House event set to take place in Calgary, a ten-man tag was penciled in for the main event pitting the entire Hart Foundation against Austin, Michaels, Sid and the Legion of Doom.

24 hours after King of the Ring, the plans were forced to change once more when the real-life animosity between Hart and Michaels reached a boiling point in a locker room fight. When the two were separated, Shawn had lumps on his face and a large chunk of hair ripped out of his head. Michaels stormed out of the building, vowing never to work with any of the Hart Foundation ever again. With Pillman firmly in the Hart camp, this included him.

"He was just going through the blow-by-blow of that thing with me that night, I think he was right there", remembers Dave Meltzer. "And it was the funniest story in the world where they're in this fight pulling hair and Shawn's trying to get away. He certainly respected Shawn's talent like everybody did, but his story felt to me like Bret was his friend and Shawn wasn't his friend and this thing was just so comically funny. The funniest fight you've ever seen where these two tough guys are pulling each other's hair."

Later, another cog in the Calgary main event dropped out when Sid was badly injured in a car wreck. The major hit in star power forced the WWF, which had little depth to start with, to shoehorn Goldust and Ken Shamrock into the match.

The long-awaited singles encounter between Austin and Pillman served as a narrative function for the ten-man tag, rather than a climactic blow-off of the rivalry. On the June 16th episode of Raw, Brian was forced to wrestle Steve with his Hart Foundation cohorts handcuffed to the ring posts. After a scrappy match that saw Brian get his nose busted open when Austin shoved a steel chair into his face, Bulldog, Owen and Neidhart escaped from their shackles and jumped Austin. L.O.D, Shamrock and Goldust hit the ring to make the save, and the pay-per-view showdown was set.

The pressure and the spotlight was almost entirely on the angle to succeed after the planned WWF Title match, Undertaker Vs. Ahmed Johnson, fell through. Ahmed got injured with only one Raw taping to go and there was little time to prepare a match of significant value. As it turned out, there was nothing to worry about.

In Your House: Canadian Stampede was the first pay-per-view ever held in Calgary, and even the most optimistic hopes of McMahon and the Hart Foundation were exceeded when it came to local interest and publicity. Newspapers featured stories and interviews every day during the week, and the show was promoted as a major part of the annual Calgary Stampede (a ten-day event that typically attracts over a million visitors to witness parades, rodeos and concerts). Focusing on the heritage of the Harts as Canada's first family of wrestling, Bret's first match back from knee surgery and the uniqueness of the jingoistic storyline, it was the perfect whirlwind for the news to report on. To demonstrate the interest locally, a simple autograph session with Bret, Owen and Davey Boy was reported as drawing over 8,000 people.

When the crew flew up to Calgary in preparation for the big event, Brian stayed with Bruce Hart the night before. On Saturday evening, Pillman had gone out and come back to the house messed up, collapsing on the bed at the end of the night. "I remember the day of the show and it was a big pay-per-view", says Bruce, "Bret, Owen and some of the guys were telling me – it's imperative you get Brian to the Saddledome, he needs to be there at 10. I remember getting Brian up, and I was literally having to drag him out of bed, he was barely coherent." As he recalls seeing his friend at his worst, Bruce remarks that while he'd heard stories, it was this trip where Brian's issues really became apparent. "I had been on the phone with him, but I hadn't been around him on a personal basis that much, and it was troubling to see him struggling to get up."

Pillman finally collected himself and showed up to the Saddledome. It almost felt as if everything Bret and the Foundation had been building over the last three months was coming to a head with this one match. With the barrage of injuries and card changes, the only constant in the WWF was the Foundation and Steve Austin at the top of the card, which was now headlining only a four-match event. Going in, eliminating the two constants, it looked to be one of the most underwhelming pay-per-view efforts in company history.

Instead, there was magic in the air in Calgary. The rabid crowd was on fire as every bout delivered on or surpassed expectations, the audience enhancing each match with their unbridled enthusiasm. When it came time for the main event, a palpable buzz flowed through the building, with each of the typically-babyface performers getting a tenser response than usual on Canadian turf. Finally, Steve Austin marched out and proceeded to get booed like a war criminal for the entire duration, flipping off the crowd with his typical salute.

When it came time for the Hart Foundation, they entered one at a time with Brian out first. The Calgary crowd exploded at the sight of Pillman, who tempered his Loose Cannon laugh with mannerisms closer to his younger days as Flyin' Brian. The decibel level seemed to rise with every second, peaking as Bret himself walked through the curtain.

After the Foundation entered the ring, the twenty-five minutes that followed were among the most heated and intense that the WWF had seen in years. The atmosphere was the kind that wrestlers dream of, as every small move and mannerism seemed to tear the house down. Brian was having the time of his life, running in regularly to blindside Ken Shamrock, including grabbing his wrist and slapping Ken's hand off the mat several times, screaming, "He's tapping out!" in mockery of his UFC background. Later in the match, Pillman had an exchange with Austin that saw Steve grab a fleeing Brian by the back of his tights, exposing his ass to the entire world as Pillman sought refuge, getting pummeled in the wrong corner. The battle raged on with all ten men getting a chance to shine, until Owen rolled up Austin for the climactic pinfall to the delight of the Calgary faithful.

The Harts had won in their hometown and soaked up the incredible response. Family members began pouring in, as Bret and Brian helped Stu, at that point 82-years-old, into the ring, with Brian proudly raising the hand of a man he respected so much, elated that he could share such a grand stage.

"It was an opportunity for Canadians to kind of express their support for Canada and underlying disdain for Americans", says Bruce Hart, explaining what he felt made the night so special. "I don't think I've seen anything like that at that level since. It's almost like that moment frozen in time for Canadians when the Hart Foundation went over."

"I was there that night just as a producer", says Jim Cornette, who still believes the match is one of the four best in WWE history. "I went back and forth between watching it live and watching it on the monitor because the fucking crowd was incredible. It was like an old-time territory crowd only instead of Calgary, which maxed out at four or five thousand in the old-time territory days, they had ten or twelve thousand. It was like an old time Mid-South Coliseum or old time NWA crowd. They were wrestling fans and loving every bit of it. They ate that match up."

Despite a whirlwind of turmoil, circumstances had somehow fallen into place to produce one of the best shows in company history, and Brian was euphoric. As he relived the moment in his mind's eye he believed, and told people so, that it was the peak of his entire career. Everything he'd always wanted in professional wrestling – the notoriety, the respect, the heat, the headline position, he got to live all of it at Canadian Stampede.

"He called me up right after and he just goes, 'This was the greatest night in my career. We were so wrong about Bret'", remembers Dave Meltzer. "Because they were such babyfaces in Canada. He thought he would have to be a heel, but he loved being a babyface, loved that crowd reaction, being in the main event, being in an awesome match and everything about it."

The Foundation and Steve Austin were what was making the promotion tick and Brian, regardless of everything going on in his life, was thrilled that he was managing to exist at such a high level.

"That day in Calgary at the Canadian Stampede was like the last hurrah, where it seemed like everything was going as well as it could have", remembers Bruce Hart. "A sold-out crowd, people going nuts, a twenty-minute ovation and everybody being where they all started. They were all Stampede alumni. That kind of made it what it was."

21 - FREEFALL

As the adrenaline of Brian's career peak began to wear off, the crushing reality of the pain resurfaced, and he again found himself reaching for his pill bottles as the night came to an end.

The next day, Brian was to travel up to Edmonton for a Raw taping that began a month-long series of shows going back and forth between Canada and the States. "It was the same kind of scenario as before, I had to literally drag Brian out of bed and drive", states Bruce. "We drove up with my Dad and Brian slept the whole way up there. I initially thought we'd have a good chat, but he basically slept through the whole thing. It was pretty evident that something was going on there."

Brian planned to make the drive back to Calgary with Stu and Bruce, then fly back home on Tuesday. After Raw was over, however, Pillman disappeared for a little while and met back up with Bruce with a new plan. "I remember at the end of the show he came out and looked like he was pretty wasted", begins Bruce. "He said he was going to sleep over in Edmonton at the Coliseum Hotel, which is adjacent to the building where they wrestled. He said he was too tired to drive back."

His trainer would grow more concerned on Wednesday night, as Bruce received a frightened phone call from Walton, Kentucky. "Brian's wife Melanie called me, quite distraught, saying that Brian was supposed to have gotten in some time Tuesday and he hadn't arrived yet. She wanted to know if I had any idea where he was", remembers Bruce. "I told her that the last I saw him was at the hotel, I dropped him off. After a bit of checking, they found him - he was still sleeping. This was Wednesday night at the Coliseum

Hotel in Edmonton, so it was essentially a two day sleep he'd had."

When Bruce called Melanie back to tell her the news, he expressed his concerns about Brian's current condition. Brian's wife asked Bruce to try to talk to him and help him straighten out. They arranged for a three-way call, hoping in some ways to have an intervention and shake Brian up as to just how bad things were getting. "It was pretty much what I had anticipated", begins Bruce, detailing the conversation that went over an hour and a half. "Melanie was saying, 'You've got a problem with drugs, Brian', and he was initially denying it. She was saying that every time he came back from the road, all he did was sleep and take some pills."

Brian defended himself by saying that he was in unbearable pain from the Hummer accident and needed to medicate himself, but the manner in which he spoke was the bigger story. "Brian sounded like he was stoned even then", recollects Bruce. "I had about, maybe, half a dozen of those weird conversations over the summer with Brian and Melanie. At times I thought I was getting to him, and at times he was so incoherent or so far gone that it was troublesome."

Though he wasn't wrestling on television for much of July, Brian was still on the road, struggling through matches early on the cards against Jesse Jammes and Flash Funk. He'd try to get by without taking a lot of risks, electing for brawling-based shortcuts, but running was excruciating. Every night, Pillman was feeling the effects of trying to move on his left ankle and would swallow pills by the handful to kill the pain.

"You go to the ring telling yourself I'll take it easy", says Shane Douglas, who himself battled oxycontin addiction originating from ring injuries. "Then you get out there and the adrenaline starts flowing and it just sort of happens. And once you start taking those pills, it's a cliché, but never a truer cliché, that once you take one and that helps you get over that night's match, now you tell yourself you need it again tomorrow and the day after that. That's an incredibly slippery slope."

On one road trip, Pillman got in a car with Ken Shamrock. The two had ridden together a few times previously, and though Brian really should not have been driving at all given the lack of mobility in his foot, the two would take turns at the wheel. Shamrock offered to drive to the next town, a four-hour trip. "Good", said Brian, who quickly reclined the seat all the way back and took some pills to start the journey. Before long, Brian's body started shaking uncontrollably. Then he began sweating profusely, before dropping unconscious for four straight hours. Finally, he shook it off as they arrived at their destination. Shamrock was horrified by the experience, choosing not to ride with Brian again.

It's important to note that, during this time, drug problems within wrestling were not strictly limited to Brian Pillman. In truth, things had been getting progressively scarier throughout the whole business as the Monday Night War picked up steam. With competition so fierce and with neither side wanting to lose any key commodities, the wrestlers found themselves with a degree of immunity for their actions. Knowing that valuable talent would be afforded the courtesy of a blind eye rather than be fired or taken off TV when star power was at a premium, some wrestlers took liberties. With the WWF having dropped its drug testing policy, it almost invited the type of dangerous behavior that was rampant in the eighties all over again.

Around the time of Canadian Stampede, Road Warrior Hawk created a major scare by passing out on an airplane, becoming unresponsive and needing immediate medical attention. Major stars had shown up for both Raw and Nitro in no condition to perform in the prior weeks, barely making it through live interviews. Arrests were becoming more frequent and red flags were being waved almost every other week to a major problem.

On screen, Pillman was moved to a new feud with Goldust, the former Dustin Rhodes who had undergone a drastic makeover since his days as "The Natural" in WCW. The original mechanics of the feud were kept simple, as the match was randomly announced on Raw with members of the Foundation boldly offering up stipulations if they lost at Summerslam. In Brian's case, he declared that if he were to lose to Goldust, he'd wrestle the following night on Raw while wearing a dress, alluding to the Goldust character's original androgynous tendencies.

Brian barely wrestled on television leading up to the match, instead appearing in the closing moments of a six-man flag match on the July 21st Raw in Nova Scotia. As members of the Hart clan battled Austin, Undertaker and Dude Love, Pillman emerged from under the ring to low blow the Undertaker, allowing his teammates to grab the Canadian flag to signify victory to a thunderous ovation. The following week, back on American soil in Pittsburgh, the faction was soundly booed, a bombardment of debris launched in their direction as they walked to the ring. Undoubtedly, the group was still white-hot. Later in the night, Brian attacked Goldust and choked him with a dress in the final angle before the pay-per-view.

The match itself was a sad exposé of just how far Brian had fallen as a performer. While he worked hard and tried more than he had up to that point, several routine spots were either poorly executed or ended up going painfully awry. Goldust went to launch Brian from the corner to crotch him on the top rope, a favorite Pillman highspot. Brian tried to move the impact away from his left leg and in doing so, missed his intended target and crashed hard onto the ring apron. The finishing spot, a Goldust sunset flip, was badly blown with time standing still as they maneuvered back into position. Brian had to put weight on his fused ankle to recover the spot, allowing Goldust's real-life wife Terri "Marlena" Runnels to clock Brian with her loaded purse to aid her husband to victory.

Later in the show, Bret Hart won the WWF World Title from The Undertaker after special referee Shawn Michaels (whose absence lasted all of a few weeks) accidentally knocked the Undertaker out with a chair. Though Bret, Owen and Pillman celebrated in the ring to end the show with garbage again being hurled in their general vicinity, it drew a line of demarcation under the period where the Hart Foundation were treated as the top heel act in the promotion. Almost immediately, Shawn Michaels turned heel to feud with The Undertaker, monopolizing the headline position for the next two months while Bret, as champion, worked underneath.

By virtue of losing at Summerslam, Pillman was "forced" to wear a dress when wrestling on Raw until he won a match, leading to a series of run-ins and fluke losses for Brian with Goldust getting involved in every bout. After the third consecutive defeat, Pillman took the microphone and made Goldust an offer for a rematch at the Ground Zero pay-per-view. If he lost, Brian would leave the WWF. If he won, he would get Dustin's wife Marlena, "Or Terri as I know you!", as his personal assistant, 24 hours a day, for 30 days. Goldust turned down the offer, prompting Pillman to declare that Dustin and Terri's daughter Dakota was his love child. As Goldust stormed down the aisle, Marlena spoke up, accepting Brian's proposal to Dustin's surprise.

The angle touched on a very delicate personal situation. Back in 1990, Brian and Terri dated for a brief spell. As things were getting going between the two, Brian got the call from Rochelle that she was pregnant with Brittany. Brian told Terri that they'd put their romance on hold until things became clearer with his incoming child. Months passed and with no sign of a reconciliation, Terri ended up dating Dustin. Brian, feeling like he'd somehow been jilted, left a message on Terri's answering machine asking what happened to their grand plan, saying she'd vowed to wait for him. Dustin hated the idea of doing an angle touching on the real-life relationship with Brian and Terri, but swallowed his pride for the sake of the show.

While Dustin was dealing with the baggage of the past, Brian was struggling to maintain a grip on the present. He'd lived for years for the love of his family and the wrestling business, and he was miserable about his fate in both. He was utterly despondent that after all the years of tape watching, reading and learning about the business, his in-ring output was so limited. His depression about his ability, combined with the increasing pain the more he wrestled, led him further down the rabbit hole. An incident took place in mid-August where Brian was supposed to make a personal appearance, but got so loaded in the airport that he couldn't navigate his way out and missed it.

In addition, things had turned rotten at home with Brian and Melanie going through an acrimonious divorce. A source close to the situation claims that Melanie, who had a reputation for being able to burn through cash, would receive Brian's bi-monthly checks at the house, cash them herself, and spend or store the money elsewhere. Brian even went to Vince McMahon to request he be handed his checks in person to prevent it from happening further. Since he wasn't getting anything and with the rest of his money tied up in the divorce, he had no spending money for the road.

On a flight between shows that many on the crew were on, Pillman called Melanie on the skyphone, and before long a bitter argument started. Brian lost his cool and launched into a furious, profanity-laden tirade at his wife. Pillman, known for his colorful language in tense situations, screamed at Melanie that she was "an AIDS-infested cunt". To show how goofy some members of the dressing room were, one paranoid wrestler took this literally and refused to wrestle Brian in future, thinking there was a chance he could catch the disease.

Things had gotten so bad between the couple that, when back at the house, Brian had taken to staying in the basement. "He told me he walked in the door one time and she jumped off the stairs and attacked him, started beating the crap out of him", says Sheri Benjamin Naud, who had struck up a relationship with Brian in light of the separation and traveled with him frequently. Later, Brian wrote a letter for the children to read, insulting Melanie in the same fashion as the call from the airplane. She responded by putting a restraining order on him to prevent him from entering the Walton home.

"I was worried about him in a sense, because the drug stories were out there and he was really wired", says Dave Meltzer. "I don't remember ever having a conversation with Brian where he was incoherent, but there were times when he was really, really wired. He would even sort of tell me he hadn't slept in 72 hours or whatever. He was just really worried about everything. And I talked to Melanie too so I got her side of it. It was a bad situation, it was a marriage falling apart and there were a bunch of kids involved. Brian was having issues and yeah, he was in a bad way."

The very public airplane outburst opened the eyes of some key people. Talk of drug problems within the company, particularly Brian's, was gaining steam. WWF officials were aware of what was going on and decided to reinstitute testing. Vince McMahon himself met with a few of the more respected members of the locker room to tell them personally and spread the word that the degree of testing would depend on the wrestlers' ability to police from within. At first, they would only test based on apparent patterns of behavior, but the policy would be strictly enforced.

When the news got around the locker room about management's approach, Pillman suddenly found himself in the eye of the storm. Peer pressure from almost all sides began to press on Brian to stop the public lapses, lest it lead to increased testing that would interfere with their own habits. Those who enjoyed partaking undetected were eager for testing to remain a thing of the past.

Alas, it wasn't to be. The first person selected, due to the frequency of his issues, was Brian Pillman. It was a difficult decision, as his supporters found it hard to reconcile the Brian they knew with the Brian they were seeing. "A guy who I was used to knowing as tough, dependable, with it and smart", starts Jim Cornette, "Then a guy whose gimmick became he's fucking nuts, but I know he's working. Then he grows into the gimmick in the wrong way, I guess I thought he was working too much. I mean, I knew things were going on. I knew his home life was not roses." When asked specifically about the drug test and the office perspective leading up to it, Cornette details, "At first, I thought, 'Ah, they're just taking him all too seriously'. By then, I knew we weren't taking him seriously enough."

On a loop of house shows in Canada, Brian's close friend Jim Ross broke the news that he'd be tested, and Pillman was apoplectic. He was enraged, feeling that he was being singled out when there were warning signs everywhere in the company. He protested that he'd never let his use of pain medication affect him in the ring or on interviews and began bringing up recent examples of others who had done just that. He specifically pointed to Shawn Michaels, who was going through his own well-known problems, some of which were televised, and asked why he wasn't being tested first when they all knew what was going on with him.

Ross, who thought the world of Brian, was forced to explain that there was fear for his wellbeing and they just wanted to know what the extent of the problem was. As was Brian's nature, he immediately thought that JR had betrayed him by asking him to take the test and told him so, disgusted at the notion. After being so tight for so long, Brian felt that Ross was selling him down the river by making him a target. Leaving the conversation tremendously offended, Brian told Jim they'd find nothing but painkillers in his system.

It had always been part of Brian's makeup to view people on either end of the spectrum. "Let me tell ya, there aren't many more loyal people out there than Pillman, no question about that", says Mark Madden. "If you were his friend, you were his friend for good. Now, if he thought you were fucking with him, or 'turning' on him as he put it, he got really mad. There was one time he'd heard I had done something or said something and he called my house in an uproar. And I quickly convinced him it had not happened, which it hadn't. But Brian was the kind of guy that you were either with him or against him."

The drug test came back showing high levels of his prescribed pain medicine, as predicted, and trace amounts of decadurabolin (an anabolic steroid). The steroid use was written off due to the small amount found and no further action was taken. "In conversations I've had with JR", says Mike Johnson, "I remember him saying, 'We offered him help, we offered him rehab, and he blew it off'." The damage to the Ross/Pillman relationship was done, and in Brian's ever-troubled mind in that moment, his biggest political ally had abandoned him.

With professional concerns mounting, a situation occurred the same week that augmented his problems. "One of the things that was the beginning of the real downfall was at the end of August, when he came back from Canada", says Sheri Benjamin Naud. Pillman walked right back to his home in Walton, Kentucky, having no regard for the restraining order Melanie had placed on him, to pick up some of his belongings. "First of all, she changed the locks on the house", explains Sheri. "So he broke in, and funnily enough he used one of his horse head canes to get in. She wasn't there, but his stuff was gone.

Come to find out, while he was in Canada she took all his stuff and put it in a storage unit. So he couldn't get to his clothes, he didn't even know where the storage unit was. She wouldn't give it to him, he only had what he had in his bag."

After living a lifestyle for almost his entire adulthood that saw him chasing a dream and living every moment in isolation, he was now utterly trapped. Having moved from fantasy life to fantasy life since college, he suddenly found himself bound with real-world pressures with no sign of escape. At this point, friends say Pillman's habits worsened dramatically. The only distraction from the constant agony and desolation was to numb himself to everything. Brian's personality had undergone significant changes as the burden of despair grew heavier, and his perspective was becoming scarily warped. In a desperate attempt to find resolution to his problems, he blamed the WWF. Telling people that the pressure of the company singling him out had ruined his marriage, he justified it to himself that he could no longer be there.

He called Eric Bischoff in WCW to see if there would be a place to go if he was able to get out of his deal, pitching to rejoin the Four Horsemen. Bischoff would later describe Brian's mood as miserable, and the conversation as dark and deeply unsettling. Pillman then called Jim Ross and asked to be given his release, but was turned down flat. Jim Cornette, at this point still a member of the booking committee, feels that Brian's intentions may have been slightly different. "He didn't want to be released", says Cornette, "He just wanted to show he was suitably offended about the drug test and see if he could keep them from drug testing him. He wasn't anxious to get a release, he was anxious to get them off his back."

In the midst of this personal chaos, Pillman faced Goldust at Ground Zero in a match far superior to their Summerslam shambles. The crowd was hot for the bout and Pillman again upped the ante, taking more risks and gambling with his body. At one point, Goldust threw Brian from the second turnbuckle all the way to the guardrail. In years prior, it would be a spot Pillman would bust out in big matches, but it required a high drop onto his feet. In September 1997, he angled his body to take the brunt of the blow on his chest, arms and face on the barricade. To culminate the contest, Brian snatched Marlena's loaded purse, a reminder of the Summerslam finish, and used it to knock out Goldust and score the pin. As per the stipulations Terri was now forced to become Brian's assistant, and he dragged her into his rental car, speeding away in dramatic fashion as Goldust gave chase.

The next step in the storyline was to revert back to Brian's penchant for the salacious. The less than subtle implication was that Pillman was engaging in an unwilling S&M relationship with Terri, as a series of videos dubbed "Brian Pillman's XXX Files" aired on Raw. The first video was shown the night after the pay-per-view, with Raw emanating from Cincinnati Gardens. Curiously, Brian was never in front of the crowd in his hometown, having taped the footage in a hotel room earlier in the day. The videos showed Brian lying on the bed in his underwear surrounded by lingerie (supposedly Terri's), as well as footage of a steamed-up shower with her inside. As Brian spoke during the piece he'd hit rapid-fire double entendres, ending by saying he was going to have "a hard time…a *real* hard time…getting to sleep tonight." The insinuation was somewhat shocking, even by the standards of an increasingly adult-themed WWF product, and Pillman's personal performance in the role was excellent.

Even with all the recent controversy behind the scenes regarding Brian's condition, he was unable to stay in a lucid state the entire evening. "I was standing there with a couple of the kids that they would use as enhancement talent", recalls Les Thatcher. "They were doing the deal with him and Dustin's wife where he'd taken her. They were out taping that and he came in, he came around the corner and I said something to him. He just stopped and looked at me like he didn't even know me. I said, 'Brian, it's Les.' He paused for a few seconds and said, 'Oh, hi.' He was just out to lunch."

Being back in his home area, Brian had another personal appearance scheduled which saw his longtime mentor Kim Wood stop by. "The last time I saw him", begins Wood, "Our training camp was down in the Lexington area. I stopped at the comic book store that was south of the Ohio River, and he was there signing autographs. I was with my son, and Brian was so fucked up. He knew me, but something was wrong. He was really fucked up on something, and it scared me."

The latest set of divorce papers from Melanie had only driven him to a more fearful and dejected state. "She was asking for everything", says Sheri Benjamin Naud, who read the documents at Pillman's request. A hopeless Brian feared he would lose the house, which he badly wanted in the divorce having worked so hard for it his whole life, and was even more heartbroken that he could possibly lose his children. "He said to me, 'I'll be damned if I'm going to let her take my daughter with Rochelle'", recalls Naud.

The two went to a court proceeding to discuss terms. "Brian told me the night before that they talked on the phone and Melanie said, 'I promise you, when we go in front of the judge tomorrow, I'm not going to bury you'", remembers Sheri. "She did the opposite - she got up there and she tore him apart. She just starts going off about how he's a drug dealer and how he beats her and all kinds of crazy stuff. She really let him have it in front of the judge and she was very specific. It was a public courtroom, there were people in there that knew who he was, and Brian said he was never so mortified. He was in a terrible state when he called me afterwards, very upset." Pillman, for breaking into the house, was ordered to attend anger management sessions starting in October.

On television, the XXX Files videos continued to air on Raw and Shotgun. When Pillman would wrestle, he'd be escorted to the ring by a new look Terri Runnels. Clad in skimpy black dresses and stockings, wearing body piercings and at one point a dog collar, Goldust's wife looked miserable as Brian commanded her around the ring. Making sure that even the dumbest fan understood the connotations of the borderline rape angle, Pillman, when explaining a faux injury to try and get out of a Raw match with Owen Hart, detailed that he'd broken his arm slipping in the bathtub when moving into "that last glorious position" with her.

"I was the producer", recalls Jim Cornette, who was heavily involved in the construction of the Goldust/Pillman angle. "I was loving that, I admit it. I was trying to take that as far as we could without getting kicked off USA. When I would see the risqué stuff, I would say, 'Yes, and do more of it'. But that was them. A lot of him, some her."

Dustin, without his face paint, regularly hit the ring in Brian's matches to build towards the Badd Blood pay-per-view. On that night, it was scheduled to be Pillman versus Dude Love with the stipulation being that if Dude won, Pillman would also have to wrestle Goldust. Additionally, it was announced that on the Raw after the PPV, Goldust and Marlena would renew their wedding vows.

The plan, in standard wrestling fashion, was for Brian to be destroyed in both matches at Badd Blood, but for Terri to reveal during the vows the next night that she'd grown attached to Pillman, ditching a heartbroken Dustin at the altar. As an added provision during the final XXX Files, Pillman insisted that Goldust be handcuffed to the ringpost during the Dude Love match to prevent interference. As he looked across the bed at the sheepish Marlena, Pillman suggested Goldust bring his own handcuffs, as his were being used.

As superb as he was in the role, his real-life behavior still wasn't alleviating concerns. When leaving a show in Philadelphia, Brian stopped off at a bar along the way to pick up some beer. "He came out and was like, 'Do you still want me to drive?' I said 'Yeh, why not?'", says Sheri Naud. "We were going down the Jersey Turnpike and all of a sudden, whatever he must have took when he stopped at the bar, it hit him. And hard. He could not drive, but he was driving. And I'm losing my shit, because I kept telling him to pull over, but he couldn't do it. I kept telling him, 'You have to pull over, you have to turn the wheel!' I don't think I've ever been that scared in my life."

Finally, Brian came to a stop. "We're on the highway", continues Sheri. "I said, 'I'm going to climb over you and you're going to slide under me, it's too dangerous to get out'. But he couldn't do it. He opens the door and gets out of the truck into oncoming traffic. Oh my God, I thought he was going to get killed. So I get out and I'm like, 'Brian, come here! Please come here!' I was terrified, I was in tears and I was just scared. He just wasn't moving."

In September, Pillman totaled three rental cars in the space of two weeks. In an incident near his home, a messed-up Brian fled the scene when he was identified by the driver of a pizza delivery van he crashed into. The driver then called the police, who pulled Pillman over and arrested him, forcing him to spend the night in jail. McMahon was furious with Brian for the incident, with agent Tony Garea scheduling Brian for the 'B' tour of house shows, held in smaller arenas with smaller payoffs, as punishment.

His regular cycle of correspondence was only increasing fears for his wellbeing. "I got the occasional call where I could not understand a word Brian was saying", says Mark Madden. "But what are you going to do? I mean I love the guy, but how do you talk to somebody like that about that? It's impossible. My point is, I'm not sure anybody could have done anything beyond what they did." Brian's circle of friends were becoming increasingly concerned, but given his frame of mind, there was no getting through. Pausing thoughtfully when reflecting on the situation, Madden recapitulates, "The best thing would have been to send Brian home, but that wasn't the way companies did it then."

"I kind of felt like there was danger ahead", echoes Raven. "I think he had a self-destructive streak that he was unaware of. There had to have been because I don't think, if there wasn't, he would have ended up where he did. I really think that. Whether it was conscious or not. Because I really don't think somebody of his intelligence and all his abilities could have driven himself off the cliff, so to speak, if there wasn't something internal driving him that way."

While there were obviously concerns within the company by this point, Pillman's track record didn't make it easy to read the situation. Jim Cornette clarifies his own perspective at the time, declaring, "When you know somebody is working being fucking nuts, but then actually goes nuts, it's hard for you to believe they really are nuts because you've known all along that they were working being nuts. Which is probably the biggest tribute to Brian that I can think of."

Brian was forced to miss the October 3rd house show due to his anger management class. As he went to join the crew in St. Paul, Minnesota, he attempted to get in touch with Bruce Hart, who wasn't home. "My wife told me that Brian phoned her from the airplane phone. I think they cost a fortune", says Bruce. "She told me it was a weird conversation. I asked, 'What did he want?', and she said that was the weird part. He kept her on the phone for about an hour and had really nothing to say, but sounded like he was almost desperate. Like he needed somebody to talk to. He was asking about my kids and the dogs and the weather in Calgary. I told her that it sounds like he's slipping, or reaching out for help. That's what my wife said - he sounded like a drowning man." More worried than ever for the fate of his friend, Bruce immediately arranged to pay him a visit the following week.

Pillman arrived early for the house show in St. Paul on the 4th where he was scheduled to work with Goldust, and seemed clear-headed. After finishing the match, Brian asked Terri if he'd be able to ride with them to St. Louis for the pay-per-view the next day. Pillman had become such a liability that Dustin, on her behalf, said no. Though Brian was liked, he'd scared enough people to the point that even those he was closest too at various points in his life no longer wanted to travel with him. As he got changed out of his gear, he swallowed a handful of pills and stared into space. Ed Sharkey, who worked as a referee that night, later told newspapers that Brian ended up unconscious on the floor of the dressing room after his match.

When the routine night was over, Brian took his suitcase and left the arena, dragging it behind him with a slow stumble. He entered his lonely hotel room at 10:45pm. Brian got in bed, quickly falling asleep for what would prove to be the final time.

An incredible life filled with passion and purpose, magic and miracles, triumph and tragedy, had come to a harrowing end.

22 - 1:09PM

The next morning, a maid at the Budgetel Motel knocked on Brian's door to perform the usual housekeeping duties. There was no response. Police were called and when they entered the room, they found Brian looking sound asleep in bed with the covers pulled over him. Pillman had suffered a massive heart attack in his sleep and passed away, with the official time of death declared as 1:09pm on October 5th, 1997.

"The only thing that ever came easy to him in life was dying", says Linda Pillman with an unequivocal sadness in her voice. "Everything else he had to prove himself and struggle for, all his life. All he had to do to die was go to sleep."

The news moved slowly. WWF officials preparing for the Badd Blood pay-per-view were alarmed when the typically late Bret Hart didn't show up with Brian in tow as expected. After talking to Elliot Pollack, who hadn't heard from Pillman, the WWF's Bruce Pritchard asked Jim Cornette to call the hotel and find out what time Brian had checked out.

"The guy answers, and I said, 'I'm calling to check on a guest who stayed there last night, we're looking for him at his work, he hasn't got here yet. His name's Brian Pillman, when did he check out?", recollects Cornette. "I hear, 'Hold on one second, sir', and I think he's going to check. I can see it now in my head, he went around back rather than say it at the front desk, right? He picks up the phone. 'Sir, Mr. Pillman has passed away.' And the first image in my head is, why the fuck is Brian Pillman standing there? Because now, when the guy left the phone I automatically assumed he's getting instructions from Brian. Why is Brian having this guy tell me that he's fucking dead right now?

Where is this going to lead? And I actually asked the guy, I said, 'Is this a rib?' He said, 'No sir, the police are still here'. And all of a sudden it's like...*okay*. Talk about a fucking mood change."

Jim immediately got the word to Bruce Pritchard and remained alone in the production office trying to find a way to process the news. "I would have expected Brian overslept, Brian was fucked up, Brian was late, Brian was arrested", says Cornette. "I never thought I was going to hear that shit."

Stunned by the news but hoping for the best, the company called Brian's wife Melanie, asking if she'd heard anything with regards to his whereabouts. After confirming that she hadn't either, the WWF softly ended the discussion, asking for her to contact them if she did.

Federation officials alerted Pollack to what they'd been told by the Budgetel and attempted to contact the Minnesota police to see if they would confirm the story. In the meantime, police knocked on the door of the Pillman family home and broke the news of Brian's passing to his wife. Little Brittany, who'd already had her mother kill herself, screamed for fifteen straight minutes in anguish.

The worst-case scenario had come to pass. Through every possible warning sign, every incident and every concerned conversation, things had continued down the same destructive path. And finally, the heart that had carried the weight of the world for so long had given in.

The early information came back as a potential accidental overdose due to the number of pill bottles surrounding his bed, but it wasn't the case. Ever since the 1995 arrest for having a painkiller in his fanny pack, Pillman was vigilant about keeping his prescriptions in bottles and not throwing away any containers. Even if they only had one or two pills left in the bottom, he would keep the tablets where they were supposed to be for fear of being arrested once again on a technicality if he mixed and matched.

A reporter even walked up to the family home and asked if Brian had left a suicide note, due to the pill bottles scattered around. "I said, 'You didn't know my brother'", remembers Linda. "If my brother was going to kill himself, he wouldn't have done it in a hotel in Minneapolis. He would have drove off a bridge in downtown Cincinnati, but first he would have called you all so you'd have been there to film it.' Because he wasn't going to go out quietly, he was going to go out with a bang."

Instead, the coroner's report came back that Brian had died due to arteriosclerotic heart disease with left ventricular hypertrophy. Recent cocaine use was listed as a contributory factor.

Medically speaking, arteriosclerotic heart disease is a condition in which plaque hardens in the arteries and narrows them. The plaque builds up in layers, gradually thinning the arteries and restricting the flow of blood to the heart and major organs. As this builds over time, this alone can cause heart attacks or strokes.

When the heart disease is advanced enough and combined with the use of cocaine, the impact on the heart can be overwhelming. Cocaine use increases heart rate, blood pressure and causes the blood vessels to constrict, effectively reducing the supply of blood to the heart. The drug puts an additional strenuous demand on the heart while at the same time restricting the supply of blood it takes in. In essence, the heart is actually getting the least amount of blood possible when it needs it the most. Adding in the narrowed arteries, it can be fatal.

Left ventricular hypertrophy is a common symptom of steroid abuse, and would appear regularly going forward in a litany of deaths within the profession, the sins of those overinflated physiques of the eighties and nineties coming to pasture. While Brian had done steroids on and off since college, close friends don't have the impression he was a heavy user during his wrestling years. "He looked the same through all his career", says Raven. "Unless he was on steroids the whole time, but if he was, why was he so much bigger when he played football? I always wondered why he didn't go on the gas to get bigger, because he knew his size was the single biggest detriment to him making big money. I asked him before, but he never really answered."

"Brian and I talked steroids all the time", adds Dave Meltzer, "He admitted he used them to me, but it was always in the past as a football player type of a thing. If he was doing them as a wrestler, and I'm sure that there were times he was, he didn't talk about it because he knew I'd be real negative about it."

Brian's use of human growth hormone couldn't have helped. It is accepted wisdom that one of the side effects of HGH is that it enlarges major organs as well as muscles. Growth hormone in the body causes the liver to secrete IGF-1 (Insulin-like Growth Factor 1), which produces the cells that lead to muscle and organ growth. As additional growth hormone is injected, the levels of IGF-1 increase also, having a multiplying effect. The bigger the heart becomes, the more blood it requires to operate, and with his arteries already thinner compounded by the effect of cocaine use, it was a deadly recipe. In his final weeks, Brian had mentioned he was suffering from heartburn.

Local File Number

State File Number

1a Name of Deceased - First	Middle	Last	Suffix
Brian	William	Pillman	

1b Alias		

2 Social Security No.	3 Sex	4 Date of Death found
278-62-4973	Male	October 5, 1997

5 Date of Birth	6a Age (in years)	Under 1 Yr. Days	Under 1 Day Hours / Minutes	7 Place of Birth (city and state/foreign country)
May 22, 1962	35			Cincinnati, Ohio

8a Father's Name (first, middle)	8b Father's Last Name	9 Mother's Name (first, middle, maiden surname)
Howard	Pillman	Mary Perkins

10 Race	11a Hispanic Origin	11b If Yes, Specify Cuban, Mexican, etc.	12 Education (Specify Only Highest Grade Completed)
White	X No ___ Yes →		12a Primary/Secondary (0-12) 12 12b College (1-4, 5+) 4

13a Marital Status	13b Name of Spouse (if wife, specify maiden name)	14 Decedent's Usual Occupation
X Mar. ___ Div. ___ Wid. ___ Never Mar.	Melanie Lawrence	Professional Wrestler

15 Kind of Business or Industry	16 U.S. Veteran	17a State of Residence	17b County of Residence
World Wrestling Federation	X No ___ Yes	Kentucky	Boone

17c City or Township of Residence	17d Address of Decedent (number, street, zip)	
Walton	573 Lassing Way	41094

17e Inside City or Township?	18a City or Township of Death	18c County of Death
does not apply ___ No City Limits ___ No Township Limits	Bloomington	Hennepin

18b Place of Death (specify one)	Specify Budgetel Inn #1098	19b If Hospital (specify one)
___ Hosp. ___ N.H. ___ Res. X Other → 7815 Nicollet, Bloomington		___ Inpatient ___ ER ___ DOA ___ Other

19c Name of Facility Where Death Occurred (if not institution, specify street address)

Budgetel Inn # 1098, 7815 Nicollet

20a Name of Informant	20b Informant is _____ of the deceased (spouse, child, parent, sibling, etc.)
Melanie Pillman	Spouse

21 Method of Disposition (check all that apply)	22 Date of Disposition
___ Burial X Cremation ___ Donation ___ Entombment ___ Other → Specify _____ City _____ State	October 10, 1997

23 Name of Cemetery	25 If Cremation, Specify Name of M.E. / Coroner Authorizing Cremation
Baxter Cremation Company	Cincinnati (Hamilton County) Ohio

24 If Cremation, Specify Name of Crematory	25 If Cremation, Specify Name of M.E. / Coroner Authorizing Cremation
Baxter Cremation Company	Garry F. Peterson, M.D.

26a Name of Funeral Establishment	26b License No.	27a Signature of Funeral Service Licensee	27b License No.	28 Date Signed
Midwest Mortuary and Shipping Service	0685	_(signature)_	2842	10-8-97

29a Name of Person Certifying Cause of Death (please type)	29b Title (check one)	29c License No. of Certifier
Garry F. Peterson, M.D.	___ M.D. XX Coroner / M.E. ___ D.O.	# 19219

29d Address of Certifier (street & number)	29e City	29f State	29g Zip Code
730 South Seventh Street	Minneapolis	Minnesota	55415

30 Signature of M.D. / M.E. / Coroner / D.O.	31 Date Signed	32 Signature of Registrar	33 Date Filed
Kathryn R. Berg, MD _(signature)_	10/16/97	_(signature)_ Deputy	OCT 27 1997

34 PART I IMMEDIATE cause of death (final disease or condition resulting in death). Enter the diseases, injuries, or complications that caused death. Do not enter the mode of dying, such as cardiac or respiratory shock or heart failure. List only one cause per line.

a. *Arteriosclerotic heart disease with left ventricular hypertrophy

Sequentially list conditions, if any, leading to immediate cause. Enter UNDERLYING cause last, (disease or injury that initiated events resulting in death).

b. _____

c. _____

Interval between onset and death

35 I attended the deceased from ____ to ____ and last saw him/her on ____	I viewed the body after death ___ Yes ___ No	36 Time of Death Found 1:09 p.m.

36 PART II Other significant conditions contributing to death but not resulting in the underlying cause given in Part I.

*Recent cocaine use

37 Was Female Pregnant At Death? ___ Yes ___ No ___ Unknown In Last 12 Months? ___ Yes ___ No ___ Unknown	43 Diagnosis Deferred

38 MANNER OF DEATH X Natural	40 M.E./Coroner Notified	41 Autopsy	42 Were autopsy results available when filling in cause of death	
	X Yes ___ No	X Yes ___ No	X Yes ___ No	

MUST BE REFERRED TO M.E. or CORONER {
___ Accident
___ Homicide
___ Suicide
___ Pending Inves.
___ Cannot be Det.
___ Not Classifiable
}

44a Place of Injury (street & number, city / township, state)

44b Describe How Injury Occurred

44c Type of Place Where Injury Occurred	44d Date of Injury	44e Time of Injury	44f Injury at Work? ___ Yes ___ No

It is accurate however, that the arteriosclerotic heart disease wasn't simply brought on by lifestyle choices and personal issues. "I called the coroner", says Brian's sister Linda, "Because all the rumors were on TV about him and the drugs and stuff like that in the room. At the time, we had an 80-year-old mother. We had his kids there and they're hearing it all." Eager to find out the real story about what happened, Linda pressed for more information. "All that stuff was going on and I wanted to hear from the man himself that did the autopsy. He told me that the heart disease had a genetic component. My father died at 50 of a massive heart attack. My older brother Philip died at 55 of a massive stroke. And then Brian died at 35 of a heart attack. My mother's brother in Wales was a professional soccer player and he died fifty years to the day that Brian died, at the same age. He died at 35, on October 5th, back in 1947. Now, Brian did steroids and I'm sure he did recreational drugs too, that just goes with the lifestyle. But that's not what killed him."

The many factors that led to his downfall come back to the same sad reality. After an incredible journey that touched the lives of millions of strangers and a downfall that deeply saddened those closest to him, Brian William Pillman had died. Those in the industry that knew he was in serious trouble were still stunned that it had happened.

"I actually made plans to fly down there after the St. Paul and St. Louis run for the pay-per-view", says Bruce Hart. "I was going to fly down to see Brian in Cincinnati. I was up at my Dad's house, training the guys in the Dungeon. Somebody shouted downstairs that Owen was on the phone from St. Louis, and Owen told me that they'd found Brian dead in his hotel room. It was pretty shocking and troubling because you almost saw it coming, but you were almost sort of powerless to do too much about it."

"It was completely devastating hearing that he died", recounts Colin Bowman. "It just so happened that when I heard the news, 'Freebird' was playing on whatever listening device I had at the time. I just instantly started writing a piece for the WCW Magazine and as soon as it was done, I took off in my car all the way up to St. Augustine and just disappeared for a few days. I just needed to get away, I couldn't fathom it."

"I thought Brian was the kind of guy who might have to go to rehab, or boy we've got to get him straightened out", says Jim Cornette. "Death was not an option, I didn't think. I didn't think it would go that far. It was just so quick. From Brian's new gimmick from start to finish, it was less than two years, and that included time off after the wreck when nobody really saw him."

"It was a very sad day when I heard about the loss", says Mark Coleman, who had kept in touch with Brian. "A very, very sad day. Please make sure you put that in. I loved him, and then he was gone."

"I was angry with him at the beginning", reveals Sheri Benjamin Naud. "I just looked up and said, 'I told you. You said you would never hurt me and look what you did'. I sort of trashed my apartment, but I was totally out of my mind with grief, so I went through all these emotions. He was very good to me and we had great times together."

"You just never thought he'd die", begins Mark Madden, who summarizes the sentiments of many. "You thought after nuclear war that cockroaches and Brian Pillman would still be around. He seemed indestructible, you know? You never dreamed that anything could happen. I remember getting the call and I was just mortified. Obviously, I lost a close friend, but that's just the one guy I never saw it happening to, even though all signs pointed to the possibility." After pausing, Madden repeats, "He just seemed indestructible."

The distressing reality was that some people within wrestling felt differently, and talk had been going around certain circles that the end was near. In the middle of September, Kim Wood had received a phone call that he still remembers clearly today. "My buddy Tom Prophet had talked to Paul Heyman", remembers Kim. "He'd said to him that, 'Pillman's on these Mexican Quaaludes and he'll be dead in two weeks.' And he was dead in two weeks. It was just scary. The wrestling people knew, because they were all covering for him."

"Paul's a real perceptive guy", says Dave Meltzer, who has his own memory of hearing Heyman's foreboding prediction. "This is months ahead of time and they're talking about ECW November to Remember. Brian and Shane Douglas had started something but hadn't gone anywhere with it, and Douglas was doing this thing of, 'Why don't we have me and Brian in November?' And Paul Heyman says, 'Brian's not going to alive in November'. And it was like, 'Oh my God, it must be really bad', because think about somebody saying that in *wrestling*. This is when wrestlers would die all the time, but I never really thought about Brian dying. Until that moment."

"Even knowing the rumors that we had heard, I was dumbfounded and shocked", says Douglas. "Because when I would hear those rumors, I always took it as, 'That's just Brian playing the Loose Cannon'. In my brain, I see him in a hotel room just hopelessly taking these pills to try and maintain his addiction, slumbering off and then passing away. And that to me seems gut-wrenching; that he wouldn't feel that he had the opportunity to open up and talk to anybody or ask anybody for help."

McMahon, in the heat of the moment on October 5th, was expecting the worst in terms of what would come out as the cause of death. As his lieutenants grieved around him, most of them close friends of Brian for years, McMahon snapped at them to regain their composure. After all, they had a pay-per-view to run.

Vince himself announced Brian's death on the "Free For All" pre-game show. Offering up that no real details were known, McMahon had finally seen the walls of plausible deniability come crumbling down. For years, the business had silently encouraged or turned a blind eye to behavior that was not in the best interest of the wrestlers' health. When pressured from the outside, the company would manipulate the truth, vow to do better, or in some cases outright lie to weather the storm. But never had a high-profile performer died on Vince McMahon's watch. With Brian's drug problems well known within the company, McMahon could only fear what ammunition this would give the critics of his organization.

In the years that would follow, WWE would get depressingly practiced in the art of the dead wrestler tribute. In 1997, with no precedent, calling the handling of Pillman's death ham-fisted would be excessively generous.

The Badd Blood pay-per-view card was reworked to add two new matches to replace the time allocated to Pillman's bouts. At the announce table, Vince almost apologetically mentioned that they'd "scrambled a bit" in the wake of Brian's demise, and were offering the best replacement matches they could under duress, due to circumstances "that obviously we couldn't have foreseen". Later in the pay-per-view, McMahon addressed the possibility of a prescription painkiller overdose, and in a remark that could only be interpreted as guarding himself, mentioned that drug problems were an issue in all forms of sports and entertainment. Though vaguely insensitive, in the immediate fallout of such a situation it is certainly forgivable. It would pale in comparison to the following evening.

The next night, while WCW offered their condolences to the Pillman family with a graphic to kick off Nitro, Vince McMahon made the unconscionable call to treat the death with all the tact and grace of the lowest form of tabloid sleaze. Somewhere in the 24 hours between shows, McMahon made the decision to invite Brian's widow, Melanie, to do a live interview. Since the story was potentially big, it was prudent to present and control the narrative to the best of their abilities. Bringing on Melanie to discuss it in their controlled environment, they determined, was the right call. Melanie agreed, and Bruce Pritchard quickly called Les Thatcher and asked him to produce the piece, as they sent a television truck to Walton, Kentucky.

Melanie may well have had the best of intentions, outwardly making comments that were clearly on the money and in no way sugar-coated to protect the WWF or pro wrestling in general. When asked about Brian's use of painkillers, Melanie stated, "I think all athletes to a degree experience a reliance on pain medicine. I knew it was just a matter of time before it happened to someone and unfortunately it was my husband. And I just want everyone to know that...I hope it's a wake-up call to some of you because it could be your husband next, or it could be you."

But from the WWF's perspective, it couldn't have come off worse. The constant plugs for the upcoming interview throughout the show came off as callous and repulsive. While a ten-bell salute to start the show and Jim Ross-narrated video package were nice touches, the goodwill was eliminated as Vince McMahon probed Melanie with shameful questions. "How are the children taking this news and do they understand?", asked McMahon, and worse, "Have you had any opportunity to think about what you, now as a single parent, will do to support your five children?" With the camera moving to close-up shots, the only possible reason for asking such questions would be to generate tears and willingly air the pained sobs of the weeping widow.

"Oh fuck, I *hated* that", laments Jim Cornette to no surprise. "When they told me they were going to do that I just looked at them like they had steaming turds hanging out of their mouths. I couldn't believe I was hearing people say they were going to do that on a wrestling show. It would have been better to say nothing, to me, than to do that."

While the decision to bring Melanie on Raw to try and address the situation may seem logical to some, the combination of the heartless insensitivity and overtones of defensive self-preservation made for chilling viewing. But in what was surely a big deal for McMahon, the interview with Melanie did a 3.4 quarter hour rating, carrying Raw to its best number in over a month.

The move for Melanie to appear on Raw would be as controversial within the family as it was to wrestling fans. It would be fair to say that almost any action or response is understandable in the hours following the death of someone so close, notwithstanding the recent turmoil, due to the shock and emotions involved. Nevertheless, given how badly the relationship with Brian and Melanie had deteriorated in the preceding months, there was certainly doubt as to the sincerity of her words and intentions. Even now, it's a subject of contention. "When you watch that interview where they interview my mother", begins Brian Pillman Jr., "She just looks like she's faking her sadness. She's not sad at all, you can see how cold she is. In her eyes, the way she's talking, the way she's sitting there, the way she makes her voice sound sad. When I watch that video, it's so creepy and so eerie. But I'm almost glad they did it, because it brings me so much enlightenment to her real character."

Brian Jr. adds to his thoughts on the validity of her public heartache, saying, "She had already planned to divorce him before he died. His bags were already packed. She was with my stepdad within the next week and she was ready to go."

The day after Raw, the WWF's General Counsel sent letters to several of the mark doctors with reputations to both the wrestlers and company for being handy with the prescription pad. The correspondence was to emphasize the official company stance that they were prohibited from being backstage at shows. It was a rule that, at the time, was not exactly strictly enforced. The letter also reiterated that any dealings between doctors and wrestlers should occur in their office in a traditional doctor/patient relationship. In what would be an unfortunate pattern for the following decade, the WWF were proving to be reactive rather than proactive, and only until the heat died down. At which point, old habits always tended to return.

In truth, everybody was still in a highly emotional state. At a private wake on October 9th, close friends and family were invited to observe the body. Kim Wood, who was one of the few to go, described the scene to be as bizarre as it was upsetting. "That day they had the biggest car wreck in the history of the interstate there, so there's this huge funeral home down in Kentucky and there's nobody there", says Kim. "Except for me and Dave Meltzer, who came together, Vince McMahon and Jim Ross. And Ross is scared to death that Dave is going to say hello, because Jim Ross and Dave Meltzer were very close friends and probably talked on the phone three or four times a day. But Vince didn't know that. Poor Pillman's mom had had a stroke, and she didn't realize he's dead. Then there's Melanie and she had this creepy guy with her who was the chauffeur for the Ultimate Warrior, named Wendell Weatherby. One of the little girls is jumping up in the casket, she wants to say goodbye to her Dad, and we've got Melanie sitting there crying and looking at the corpse. Ten feet away, lusting after Melanie is this Wendell Weatherby, this guy with bleached blond hair."

Today, Wood laughs as the absurdity of the scene plays back in his mind. "So, we've got JR scared shitless. I talk to Vince for an hour about Hammer Strength, then go over to talk to Dave Meltzer because I came with Dave, but Vince didn't know it. So, all of a sudden Vince wants to fight me, but we're in this huge funeral home. I talk to Mary who is saying, 'Oh Kim, you should come over for lunch with me and Brian again. Brian likes you so much and you're so important to him.' And I'm like, 'Mary, Brian's in the box there'. I'm trying to be nice. Then Vince comes over to talk to her and I just say, 'Good luck, Vince'."

But the strangeness of the scene would be brought back to reality when they went to see Brian. "They did the worst mortician job on him", remembers Kim, who intensely remembers the sight of his fallen friend. "I turn to Meltzer and said, 'Dave, you don't drink, do ya?' And he said no. I said, 'Dave, you know I don't drink'. And he said, 'I know you don't drink Kim'. Then I said to him, 'Dave...let's go get drunk'."

Brian's funeral took place the next day in Walton, Kentucky, before his body was cremated. Though there was no WWF representation at the funeral, the place was filled. "It was the saddest Goddamn funeral I've ever been to", remembers Kim, who explained the prevailing emotion in the ceremony. "Brian was nice to all these people on the way up, and he stayed nice to them. What he'd do when he'd come home to Cincinnati, he'd do the rounds. All the people that were nice to him, he had all these people he'd go visit. All his old coaches and everything. Brian would get friendly with all the headbanger wrestling schools, all these little groups, and he'd go and work out with them. They're all wannabes and little guys, but he was nice to all of them. And at his funeral, I mean there were a lot of people there. He was a very nice person and he had lots of friends. The football guys just loved him."

Family, close friends, football coaches and players paid their respects. From the wrestling business, only Joey Maggs, Bruce Hart, Eric Bischoff, a few ECW wrestlers, Les Thatcher and some of Les' students were in attendance. Steve Austin, Pillman's old tag team partner and close friend, was supposed to give a eulogy. It's been said, though not confirmed, that Steve had also attended the wake early, but upon seeing his friend was beside himself with grief and left. At the last moment, he faxed Melanie to let her know he wouldn't be at the funeral. Instead, Bruce Hart was offered the chance to speak in his place and with little notice, provided a heartfelt and tearful effort that saw him fight to compose himself several times.

The impact of the funeral hit Eric Bischoff hard. The following Monday before Nitro, Bischoff gave a speech to the wrestlers about Brian's death and stated that he wasn't naive enough to truly believe there was no drug use in WCW. Eric offered any wrestler with a problem to come to him and the company would help them. They would treat any necessary rehab as if it were an injury and they wouldn't lose their jobs.

∞

The unique, multifaceted nature of Brian's life spurs the discussion about the role of professional wrestling in his untimely death. 24 hours after his passing, Melanie Pillman had said on Raw that, "He lived for this business, and he died for this business." While there were elements of wrestling he hated, there were others that Brian loved, and many close to him agreed that Melanie's words were a fair assessment.

From one perspective, the business took a promising athlete and with its mind games, politics and prejudices, took Brian on a rollercoaster of peaks and valleys. Having exhausted every logical method to get ahead, he analyzed the surroundings and figured out that in a company that made little sense, that ran on nepotism, cronyism and ego, he'd need to do something equally unorthodox. He concocted a borderline genius method of manipulation and through timing, good luck and intelligence, played the system like a fiddle. In the perfect illustration of how zany wrestling is, it worked. But the obsession led to a critical mistake that cost him everything he'd been building. His unshakeable pride led him to bad choices. In the end, he undoubtedly worked himself, and there seemed to be no answer but to carry on. The business at the time wasn't constructed in such a way to save him from himself and at that point, the ring was the worst place for him.

"The Brian Pillman at the end wasn't the same Brian Pillman people knew", Alex Marvez explains. "I just really think that if you look at it, the wrestling business was the best thing for Brian Pillman and it was the worst thing for Brian Pillman. He was so talented he could have done so many other things outside of wrestling in terms of media, because he was such a charming guy. Great looking guy, larger than life personality and had that aura about him that's a very special thing. And instead, he fell in love with pro wrestling and to his detriment, because I think he became so obsessed with wrestling, his place in it, trying to keep his job, trying to keep his finances going, trying to feed his ego, that it ended up leading to his demise."

"He was very dedicated and committed", says Bruce Hart, "He was extremely conscientious. It almost seemed they were sort of fatal flaws that you see in literature. Character flaws that proved to be the undoing of the individual. To an extent that's what happened with Brian with the drugs."

It can't be ignored that Brian was a wild personality that had a predisposition for some of the darker trappings pro wrestling brings. Many aspects of his personal life were dramatic and brought with them dramatic ends. Bruce Hart asked the same question of his close friend, saying, "You ponder whether the business is a magnet for that, induces that or allows that. Or invites that."

Adding his two cents to Bruce's thoughts, Raven agrees that a certain type of personality was drawn to the business during that period. "People who want to be famous usually have something missing inside", he begins. "They're trying to fill a hole, just like in acting. So it draws a certain kind of individual who's already missing something inside. Not always, and this isn't a perfect metaphor, but it does to a certain extent. Not everybody is one or the other, but the average was."

Further explaining the attraction, he elaborates. "Wrestling is basically a cross between rock and roll and sports", Raven says. "Because you've got the rock and roll lifestyle, you get to cut promos and have an audience in the palm of your hand, but it's also athletic. It's a morality play, it's opera for the masses, and so it used to attract the kind of person that wanted to live that lifestyle. And even if you didn't know that there was so much drinking and drugs going on, just the whole idea of being a wrestler was a pretty cool thing."

Whether or not people had the knowledge going in, the common nature of the bad habits soon became obvious. "It's not a matter of peer pressure", he explains, "But when everybody's having a drink, you're not forced to, but it's also more comfortable to go along to get along. It doesn't seem so toxic when you're around it all the time. You're still trying to fill a void, so it all builds on itself. I swore I would never drink before a match, you know? Then eventually you have one drink, two drinks. Next thing you know it's a six-pack before a show. Finally, next thing you know, I'm drinking when I get out of bed."

Pushed to explain what creates this state of mind, Raven opens up further. "Once people get in, they realize their heroes drank and did drugs, went out, slept with chicks, had a good time, and everybody wants to do that. When every night it's either that or go back to the hotel room, read a book and fall asleep, you go to the bar. You have a couple of drinks, but it's better than sitting in your room by yourself. A couple of drinks leads to a couple more and five years later, it's up to 15 or 20 drinks. The business is really bad if you have addiction because you don't have a support system on the road. Your support system is at home - your wife, your family, your friends, and you're not with them all the time to support you. The boredom leads to drugs. I'm sure for some people the emptiness does too. Like, you walk out of an arena with a billion people cheering for you and now you've got to go back to your hotel room and sit by yourself with your thumb up your ass, it's a letdown. So all these things combined make the business conductive to addiction, whether you have a predilection for it or not."

When asked about the self-awareness of whether the problems existed in himself and Pillman beforehand, Raven answers within a second. "I never thought it was in me. I *never* thought it was", he states definitively. "It's the glamorous lifestyle, but it's really not. Well, it is until it isn't. And once it isn't it's really the opposite, but you don't see that or think of that. I'm lucky I didn't end up dead, I really am."

"I would concur with Raven", says Shane Douglas. "I never ever was around drugs in my life, never smoked pot in my life. I fervently believe in my heart of hearts that the wrestling industry, at that time especially, was creating drug addicts."

This isn't to chase a simplistic answer of who or what is responsible. Brian's case is, however, emblematic of an epidemic that has thankfully slowed in recent years. Perhaps those who succumbed were simply people, due to their status, that had very easy access to dangerous things and believed they were living life to the fullest. Many tended to be naturally eccentric or somewhat emotionally damaged, seeking validation or success in a fantasy world that ambiguously blurs into reality.

There's the bizarre high-school atmosphere of gossip whispers, backstabbing and immature pranks. There's the degradation from promoters who dictate a wrestler's value to the world, and the wrestlers' willingness to accept being told their worth by superiors. Then there's the psychological element of their work or physical appearance not being what it needs to be, leading to them rationalizing the next small yet dangerous leap to advance. Spending so much time on the road, this unusual environment became the real world, as health and family all too often took a backseat to the next town, next payoff and next fleeting moment of glory.

William Gresham's *Nightmare Alley*, the book about carnival life that Pillman read in preparation for the Loose Cannon character, discusses the concept of "the geek" - a circus performer who bites the head off live chickens and drinks the blood before a disgusted, freaked out audience. Being the subject of scorn to carnival attendees, it's the least desirable position to have. Why would somebody ever lower themselves to do such a thing?

In *Nightmare Alley*, it is revealed that "the geek" isn't found, but made. A weak character is recruited, preferably a drunk or someone seeking the high life. They are told the job is only temporary while they find a "real" geek. Until they do, they'll fake it with the new recruit. You won't *really* bite the head off the chicken, and you don't *really* drink the blood. It's all a work. But, they say, you'll get fed, get a bottle of booze and a place to sleep. Just enough to keep them going.

Thinking they now know better, the new recruit accepts the role and find the benefits to be heavenly. When the week is up, they're told it's over. You can't draw a crowd "faking a geek", and they have found a real one to take the role. After having a taste of what could be, the new recruit pleads for another chance. They throw themselves whole-heartedly into being the best geek they can be, grossing out the audience with gusto, biting the head off for real and drinking the blood. They become everything they reviled just weeks before, looked at with contempt by the spectators as the lowest of the low. Of course, there never was a "real geek" coming in.

The parallels to wrestling are worth considering, since the business has always had some questionable practices. There is no union for the participants, and talent are signed as independent contractors despite obviously being regarded as employees judging from what is required, expected, and the power the promotion lauds over them.

It used to be said that Vince McMahon loved to overwork his talent in the eighties, almost turning them into zombies. Eventually, they'd lose sight of who they really were and become immersed in their characters. Vince would tell his performers that their futures were looking so bright they should buy the biggest house they could find and steered them towards Tampa, Florida, where he happened to know the real estate people. The deluded wrestlers would buy the big house, which happened to come with large monthly payments. Needing to keep their jobs in order to make the payment, they became dependent on McMahon and would be far more susceptible to coercion.

Without even considering the days of promoters being tricky with payoffs or blacklisting talent, the physical requirements alone draw comparison. Things like cutting your forehead with a razor blade, taking unprotected chair shots to the head, keeping an impossible schedule and taking dangerous falls high on the head and neck for entertainment are all things that the general public wince at. Particularly for something like pro wrestling that, rightly or wrongly, isn't often regarded fondly in the entertainment or advertising worlds. As recently as Summerslam 2016, Brock Lesnar legitimately elbowed Randy Orton repeatedly in the head until blood was drawn. In an effort to shock and awe the "marks", they chose to forego the fact wrestling is a work. In the process, Randy Orton received a very real concussion. On the premise of a little more money, a little more notoriety and a little more internal approval, wrestlers constantly push past their own boundaries and standards to seek validation from fans and superiors alike.

Looking at the final year of Brian's life, examining what the WWF knew and the moves they could have made, it's easy to suggest negligence or place blame at their feet. Had drug testing not been abandoned in the first place, who knows if it would have made a difference, though it very well could have. The truth is that it took countless tragedies before the company cleaned up, and while the WWF policy of the mid-nineties toned down steroid use, it wasn't particularly successful in preventing addiction to begin with. "The drug testing in the WWF was a fucking joke", states Shane Douglas, who was subject to the policy in 1995. "We would get to the building and there would be a sign on the wall that said, 'Drug test today'. Then guys like me, who at that time didn't take anything, had 25 wrestlers with visine bottles saying, 'Can you piss for me?' Then they would go in and spray my piss into the bottle and that was it. In my experience in the three companies, WWF, WCW and ECW, the drugs were equally bad in all three. I saw rampant drug use in all three companies. It wasn't like this one was a little better or a little worse than the next."

Saying all that, Brian made his own decisions every step of the way, which shouldn't be ignored when putting the business on trial. It's just the way he was. "It was a great tragedy in my own life when Brian died", says Kim Wood. "But my thing to you is - I kinda' got him into wrestling...and I don't feel guilty. I feel bad for what happened, I feel *terrible*. But I don't feel guilty at all, because he didn't have a chance otherwise. He would have been a lost soul, or a drunk, or who knows."

"He, like me, grew up in the seventies, which is an entirely different era than now", says Raven, looking to provide context to Brian's outlook on life. "Sleeping around was looked upon as cool, drinking was something men do, cocaine was cool for rich people, and as long as you didn't do crack or heroin you were just partying. And if you could do that and then go out and have five-star matches, oh my God, you were a superhero! The business is different now, the world is different now. Now that behavior isn't something to aspire to, is possibly frowned upon and it's probably hard to understand why it was then at all, but it was. He was always an alpha male when that was what guys were raised to be. But coming from a home with no dad, that may have inflamed his desire to prove he was the best of the best. And Brian definitely had insecurities."

When WWE did a DVD on Pillman in 2006, they did what they could to paint a picture of a man who overcame the odds to succeed in two fields where the chances of success are slim to none. In looking at Brian's life through the course of this book, the real story is quite different.

Ultimately, the story of Brian Pillman is a man who had all the instincts, talent, drive, acumen and athleticism to succeed in football and wrestling, and while he got somewhere in both fields, he never got what he truly wanted from either.

The size prejudices were too strong in the NFL for him to be given the opportunities his stats and ability warranted, and he soon discovered that the business elements of the game weren't what he expected going in. His vision for the NFL didn't come to be.

In wrestling, he worked harder than most and thought about it on a deeper level to get ahead of the curve and break out of the pack. He surrounded himself with the smartest minds he could to gather intelligence and help him determine his next move. He got over enough on numerous occasions to justify going further with him, but excuses would be given every time to keep him in place. His size would be a convenient out for bookers or critics, even when the evidence dictated that their self-imposed rules were irrelevant. No matter how good the matches, how captivating the promos or how loud the crowd reactions, he was in a company in WCW that, during that era, couldn't make a new star to save their lives.

For isolated moments Brian got what he wanted. But they passed all too quickly and would be followed by circumstances that didn't allow Brian to progress, leaving people wondering what was possible had things been different.

"My Dad used to say that the four saddest words in the English language were, 'What could have been'", says Bruce Hart, "I figure he would have been one of those guys that would have still been around today."

"If he would have got in the business ten years earlier he would have been on top of all the small territories, and if he'd have got in ten years later he would have been on top because the size issue changed", states Raven. "If Brian had got main event money way back when, when he should have started getting it, who knows what would have happened? Would he have still ended up down that road? Or was that strictly because he'd tried to find a way to get there and it led him down a different road than he thought it was going to?"

"If he hadn't of been hurting so bad, with that personality and everything, whichever side he would have been on, he would have been one of their biggest stars", adds Dave Meltzer. "He'd have been real big in the WWF, I think. He was so good at that point. When he would be in a scene with a bunch of people, he always stood out with his eyes and the hair and everything. That's what a main eventer to me is - the guy who stands out in the crowd. So he really had it and the promos were really, really good. They'd really gotten good. He really did have a lot going for him in that regard. God, it's so sad."

Had Brian managed to negotiate with both sides without compromise at the height of the Loose Cannon, he would have gotten the pay rise he was looking for. Would he have been treated like a top star had he stayed in WCW? Maybe somewhat, but he would have remained under the ceiling of higher paid talent such as Hogan, Flair, Sting, Luger, Nash and Hall, unless he'd found another way to navigate to the top. Had he gone to the WWF without the ankle injury and with a big contract, he would have had a very good chance to make it to the top, but there were no guarantees.

Would he have even gone to the WWF without the accident? Possibly not. But then the turmoil and chaos of the next three years of WCW, combined with the reality that he was only going to get so far, may have been enough to send him to McMahon in the end. Especially since so many of his friends and allies were in key positions on and off screen.

"If he had ended up in the WWF, with his ability, in my mind he would have been the Roddy Piper for that generation to Steve Austin's Hulk Hogan", analyzes Mike Johnson. When talking about where the business was before Pillman's impact and his influence on the wrestling boom that followed, Johnson is quick to review. "Brian helped set the table, but he never got to enjoy the meal."

"What the Loose Cannon also did, which was interesting, was it also brought reality into pro wrestling, which has its good and bad", says Alex Marvez. While tying in aspects of real life would be pivotal to the early success of the nWo and Mr. McMahon angles that set both companies on fire, there were many failed efforts to work the wrestlers or refer to backstage incidents on the air stemming from Pillman's success. "Fans don't want to be told the shit's fake", says Marvez. "They want to think there is something that's real, and Brian did a real nice job walking that line as opposed to others that just incorporated it."

Almost everybody, when asked about what was in store when his career was over, felt it wouldn't have been hard for Pillman to thrive. "Brian really, really understood the business", states Mark Madden. "I have no doubt had Brian lived that he would be involved to this day in the creative process somewhere. Even if it was just as a producer. They don't let wrestlers write TV anymore, but I think Brian would have been great at that as well."

"That's the shame of the thing", agrees Jim Cornette, "He'd got to the point where he could have been an announcer or he could have been an agent or he could have been other things if he couldn't physically go."

"It was doubly sad that Brian died", says Kim Wood, "Because he had a future with Vince. He would have listened to Vince, and Vince would have listened to him." When discussing the possibilities, Kim offers his prediction without a moment of pause. "Triple H, when he goes to bed", he starts, "Needs to face the East and pray to Brian Pillman for the fact he was dead by the time Steph came along. Had Brian pulled it off and not died, he would have got there first."

Twenty years after his passing, there are many ways to view Brian Pillman. The wild stories of his toughness and conquests are the stuff of legend. His refusal to let anybody dictate his destiny is revered. A complete wildman that was extremely intelligent, whose actions were decided on a whim yet were highly calculated, as kind, caring and loyal as he could be devious, cunning and crafty. The paradoxical Pillman; an enigma in life, a symbol in death. A man who sparked the curiosity of legions of fans and left a mythological legacy. A performer whose influence had far-reaching consequences, both short and long-term, on the business. A product of the industry he was drawn to, an exception that became a statistic. An icon for the best and worst.

"He was a brilliant, charming fellow who was well versed in the ways of sleaze and smut and scum", laughs Kim Wood. "He was a unique guy because he certainly wasn't high culture, but the stuff he did was the product of thinking and analysis and he was tough enough to pull it off. And that's the kicker."

"I think one of the things about him, he was kind of this combination of different contradictions", says Bruce Hart. "There's a lot of these double-edge things with Brian. It was one of the prevailing themes of his life, was this intermixing of good and bad."

Far more important than wrestling was the fact that children were now going to live without their father, siblings without their brother, a mother without her son. But despite the passage of time, the stories, memories and legacy of Brian Pillman, the person, have lived on. Perfectly in keeping with his spirit it seemingly refuses to quit, as friends and family share stories with a sincere fondness in their voices.

With all the amazing tales, several people were sure to speak of Brian's nature as a father before the wreck. They'd remember him taking his children on drives around Cincinnati to visit people off his list of thirty or forty close friends. They spoke warmly of not only his obvious affection for them, but of the children's reciprocated love and admiration for him. Stories of spending time with them and playing at the house, where the twinkle in his eye would shine brightest and the kids genuinely seemed to love being around him.

"The sad thing was", says Kim Wood, "Brian, even though he had all these kids with all these different mothers, he was a hell of a dad. I mean, he would show up to the Hammer Strength offices with 3 or 4 different little kids on his shoulders, laughing and playing. He had a nice house, and when you looked around, it was all the kids. He was a very caring dad."

When the story of Brian's life is revisited, it's perhaps best illustrated by words spoken by Bruce Hart at his funeral. Paraphrasing Elton John, Bruce compared Brian's way of life to a Roman candle in a hurricane.

"He was like a free ticket at Disneyworld, you know, you were along for the ride", encapsulates sister Linda. "Sometimes the ride got a little bit rough. The good times were good and the bad times were bad. I think we had more good times than bad times."

23 - A SELFLESS DEED

With the blistering pace of the wrestling business at the time, Brian's tragic demise, while mourned, quickly became yesterday's news. Phil Mushnick of the New York Post wrote a piece stating that Pillman's death and the many others like it in the industry, had they taken place in any other sport or entertainment field, would be subject to a federal investigation. But realistically, it only served as that week's story. Bret Hart leaving the WWF and Vince McMahon's famous double-cross, WCW's biggest pay-per-view ever with Starrcade '97, and Mike Tyson appearing in the WWF to contribute to Steve Austin's rise to megastardom all took Pillman's name out of the headlines in the weeks and months following.

But while Brian was gone, he was certainly not forgotten, and in the office of a wrestling school in Cincinnati, one of the more admirable displays of selflessness in the business was in its formative stages.

Les Thatcher, born Dave Malady, had his first wrestling match on July 4th, 1960 at the age of 19. Since then, he'd done just about every job you could in wrestling – from broadcasting to writing and putting together magazines, to production, to booking and promoting. Thatcher founded the Heartland Wrestling Association in 1996 and in the face of his Cincinnati roots, didn't have the deep background with Brian Pillman that many in the area had. In fact, the two didn't cross paths until, while Thatcher was working as a trainer for John Parrillo Performance, Brian came in to see John and met Les in the process. "The only thing I knew about Brian before I met him", says Les, "Was that somebody might say, 'Pillman was in town last week - he beat the shit out of somebody at such and such a nightclub over across the river'."

The two became friends and stayed that way for the remainder of Brian's life. "I have a picture of Brian and all it says is 'To Les,' but I would not sell you that picture for a million dollars", declares Thatcher. Chip Fairway, the wrestler Brian had sent to train at Les' school, also played with Brian and Melanie on the "Loose Cannons", a mixed gender softball team that played in a local league. "I had said to Chip – 'Do me a favor, get Brian to autograph a picture so we can put it up at the gym'", Les elaborates. "So he went to the softball game and Brian got a picture out and a Sharpie and wrote 'To Les,' and the Sharpie dried up. And he's asking, 'Has anybody got a Sharpie?', and nobody did. So Brian handed it back to Chip and said, 'Hang on to this and I'll finish signing it when I get back from Minnesota'."

As fate would have it, Brian died that weekend and never finished signing it. "When Chip came to the gym maybe a week later", says Les, "And brought the picture, he said, 'You probably won't want this', and told me the story. I immediately said, 'Give me the picture'." The photo still hangs in Les' office.

This kind of goodwill and emotion towards Brian quietly permeated the whole industry, with many people having fond memories and holes in their hearts. As Les Thatcher sat in his office at the HWA's gym, an idea crossed his mind. "We said, 'Let's do a little tribute show for Brian'. And the key word was little", he clarifies with a laugh.

The idea was to run a small show on April 29th, 1998, local to the Cincinnati area, to raise some money for Brian's surviving wife and children. With the mindset being to run something true to Pillman's roots, Thatcher booked the Norwood Middle School gym for the event, where Brian had gone as a child. When the nature of the show was explained and with Pillman's death so fresh on the mind, the school didn't bill Les to book the venue, happy to honor one of their own free of charge. "We had a lot of great cooperation from the school and the coaches", recalls Thatcher. "The football coach Brian played for was still there. The lady that was head of the recreational department in the city of Norwood had gone to school with Brian and was a personal friend of the family, so they were cooperative too." The outpouring of charitable sentiment was contagious, and it didn't take long for word to spread of a show in memory of Brian, with the goal of financially assisting his family.

"We started putting it together and had a couple of people volunteer to come", remembered Les, "And then, Jericho and Benoit chimed in." Chris Jericho and Chris Benoit both had history with Brian, and although they were under WCW contract at the time, they offered to work on their day off, also free of charge, to help the show out and raise money. The phone calls kept coming, this time from the other side of the fence. The WWF's Steve Austin, who at this point was rapidly becoming the biggest star in the entire business, dialed Thatcher's number and vowed to participate. "Of course, Austin was going to come because they were close, but the WWF didn't want him to wrestle", says Les. "Which was fine, just the fact he was going to show up was tremendous."

Indeed, having WWF and WCW talent on the same show, with both promotions red-hot, fiercely at war and in the middle of a wrestling boom, was a rare novelty. Excited, Thatcher called Dave Meltzer and told him what was lined up for the show. "Well you know", said Meltzer, "Now all you need is ECW and you'll have all three."

With so much positive momentum behind the project, Les was keen to oblige. "At the time I hadn't met Paul Heyman", says Les. "But of course, Chris Candido and I were friends from Smoky Mountain Wrestling, and Al Snow, who at the time was working ECW, he lives a few miles up I-75 from Cincinnati." Thatcher called Candido and encouraged him to talk to Paul Heyman and see what could be put together. After talking to Paul, Chris called back with the news that he was given the green light to book Candido Vs. Snow.

"I left a message on Meltzer's phone and said, 'We've hit the trifecta!'", chuckles Les. "And that was how it all started. Once WCW was involved, WWF had to or look bad, ECW had to or look bad, and they all paid for the airfare, hotels and local transportation, so there was no out of pocket."

With the incredible scenario in place for every major American promotion to send representation, it was up to Les to present a class show, and a tremendous effort was put forward to ensure that was the case. "We picked them all up in limos or shuttle vans at the airport to take them to the hotel. They were treated like they should be, like VIPs, because they were there giving up their day off to work for nothing", says Thatcher of his approach. "We had a hot table with chicken breasts, rice, baked potatoes and vegetables and all that; it was in the building from the time the wrestlers arrived until the show was over. It was kept so that there was always food there for everybody."

Show time finally came, and the public response far outperformed even the loftiest of expectations. "The day of the show it was drizzling rain here, and I thought, 'Wow, that's kinda gonna hurt our crowd'", explains Les. "We were doing photos with the VIPs, which were Snow, Jericho, Benoit, Sunny, Austin and Candido. I'm running all over the place trying to make sure everything is where it should be and everything is set up, and somebody came in and said, 'You're not gonna believe this – we'll never get all the photographs shot'. I said 'Why?', and he said, 'They're lined up all the way around the building'. Those fans were standing outside in the drizzling rain."

A stickler for starting shows on time, Les had a dilemma on his hands. But with the wrestlers willing to do whatever was needed for Brian's memory, it ended up being easy. "We had to shut down some of the people who had bought photographs with the stars, but the wrestlers stayed afterwards so the fans that had purchased the photos could get their pictures taken", says Thatcher.

Having had his name in local papers and magazines since 1979, the turnout for the first Brian Pillman Memorial Show was more than the Norwood Middle School gym could handle. "We had the place filled. We actually turned away between three and four hundred people that we could not fit in the building", states Les.

With the show ready to start in front of a packed house, the promoter was approached by his two main eventers, who offered up an unusual question. "Jericho and Benoit came to me and said, 'What do you want?'", reminisces Les. "I said, 'Whaddya mean, what do I want?' 'Well, what kind of match?' I said, 'I want the match that you want to give me, I want you guys to feel it'." As a general rule for the show, the babyfaces went over to send the crowd home happy, but with the exception of the HWA-trained talent that might have a finish laid out for them, the major stars were given free reign. "I said, 'You guys go out there and play it by ear, do whatever the hell you want', and they went out and tore the house down that first year."

Benoit and Jericho went hell for leather, going all out in a pay-per-view quality match that saw Jericho split open, the blood running down his face turning his long blond hair a shade of crimson red. Terry Taylor, who was booking WCW along with Kevin Sullivan at the time, sat up in the bleachers with Thatcher to watch the match unfold. Halfway through, seeing the effort poured out in the name of their fallen comrade, Taylor turned to Les, saying, "My God, these guys are working harder for you for nothing than they do for me for pay."

"It was one of those things that people say, 'You have to have been there', but to have been there and felt the energy that all the boys put off, it was just an amazing thing", responds Thatcher, when asked how special the show felt in the moment. "The first year when it was over I came back to the house, but I had to be back to take guys to the airport at 6am. It was almost 4am by the time I got back, so I was almost dead on my feet by the time we got everybody there. I remember going into my office at the gym, I was just drained in terms of energy, because I'd been going since probably 6am the morning before with a couple of hours sleep. But I just thought, 'Wow, we did this, and it was such a success...let's do it again!' None of it was pre-planned, and each year it was never definite that there would be another show."

But there would be, and with the roaring success of the first, it was only appropriate to set the bar higher and do even more to commemorate the life of Brian Pillman. After having to turn people away in 1998, Thatcher booked the Cincinnati Gardens for 1999, as the scope of the organizing required increased massively. "I had a committee of ten people which handled catering, transportation, hotels, a little bit of everything. For seven months before the event, we met at HWA at the gym on Monday evenings to plan and put the whole thing together. So yeah, we worked at it for seven months before the actual show", says Les.

With no financial gain for himself, Thatcher worked diligently to put together the next event to raise more money for the Pillman family, and the reputation of the first show was such that people from all over the country wanted to be involved. Independent wrestlers from coast to coast were offering to pay their own way to travel to the show and wrestle for free. A number of them were used alongside HWA talent on the 1999 event in a Brian Pillman Memorial Cruiserweight Tournament, and every year after, the HWA office was flooded with requests to appear.

More stars from WWF, WCW and ECW appeared on the second event, with Rey Mysterio Jr., Konnan, Dean Malenko, Mick Foley, Road Dogg and D-Lo Brown wrestling on the show, and Ric Flair appearing as a special guest. The show also ran an auction (which became a tradition at the events), as items such as D-Lo Brown's chest protector, ring-worn wrestling boots from Chris Benoit and one of Ric Flair's robes were sold to the highest bidder. Most importantly of all, the magic from the first event bled over. "It was never like the boys from WWF or WCW or ECW were competing with each other, but it was almost like, 'Well those guys just lit the place up, so we've got to go out there and do the same thing'", articulates Les. "But it was an unspoken thing, I never heard anybody say, 'We're gonna' go out there and kick your ass!' It was never that way."

That intangible, heartfelt, organic element that made the Pillman Memorial Shows unique led to a lot of memorable moments being produced. "It seemed like every year there was something special", Les begins. "Not that it was scripted, not that it was planned, there was just something special. The first year, it was the Benoit and Jericho match. Nobody expected Jericho to need stitches, but they worked that hard. The second year it was a situation that took place with Mark Curtis."

Brian Hildebrand, who worked as a referee in WCW under the alias of Mark Curtis, was suffering from stomach cancer at the time. A highly regarded individual and an absolute student of pro wrestling, it pained Brian's close friends to hear about his battle with the disease. At this point, Brian had a feeding tube in his stomach to help him as his body was no longer able to accept him eating normally. The main event of the show was scheduled to be Konnan and Rey Mysterio Jr. against Chris Benoit and Dean Malenko, and Hildebrand wanted to be part of it. "We had the Brian Hildebrand/Mark Curtis faction - Jericho, Benoit, Malenko, Guerrero, myself, a bunch of us were really tight, in a way because of Mark. So he'd wanted to referee that match", says Les. Unfortunately, with his health being such an issue, it was looking like it just wasn't meant to be.

A few weeks before the show with HWA training in session, Brian Hildebrand's wife Pam called the office and asked to speak to Les. "I'm thinking 'Oh my God, something's happened'", Les remembers. "I go in, and she said, 'Brian's weight is just dropping too fast, we're taking him to the hospital so they can feed him better and we can get his weight up. But we wanted you to know in case you called - we don't want you to worry.'" In the background of the call, however, Thatcher was able to make out Brian's voice – "Tell him I'll be at the show! Tell him I'm making the show! I'm not missing the show!" Thatcher responded to Pam, "Just tell that little asshole to go to the hospital and get well."

Hildebrand's struggle with weight continued, and Les had a tough decision to make. Les utters, "I said, 'You can ref the old timers' match.' And really, they weren't that, it was Terry Taylor versus Tom Pritchard. But I said, 'They'll go at a slower pace than that main event', and so that was how we'd figured it."

As it came time for the final match of the evening, Thatcher, who also doubled as the ring announcer for the first two events, entered the squared circle to introduce the participants. Before he began, his eye was drawn to the curtain as Mark Curtis walked out the dressing room and climbed in the ring, bound and determined to officiate the match involving his close friends. Les approached him in the ring.

"I thought you weren't gonna do this?", quizzed Les

"Well I'm out here, I'm gonna do it", responded Curtis.

"Are you gonna be okay?"

"Well, are you gonna stay out here?"

"Yeah, why?"

"Well, if I can't make it, you can carry me to the back, can't you?"

Les paused to take in the gravity of the statement, before warmly answering. "Yeah, I can do that."

"That little son of a bitch", begins Les, "And I say that with all the affection in the world, pound for pound was one of the toughest people I've ever known in my life. He fought that and he was gonna be part of this damn show whether he was on his deathbed or what. He was going to be there. And that was so special." Only four months later, on September 8th, Brian Hildebrand passed away.

After the show in Cincinnati Gardens, a group of Pillman's friends celebrated his life with a visit to Sorrento's sports bar, just as they did after Brian's first match in the building all the way back in 1990. Sadness at that realization blended with pride and a sense of achievement, as the event had been a hit once again.

The event continued to grow, and people were clamoring for the third annual Memorial Show. Les booked Xavier University's Schmidt Field House for Pillman 2000, and the barrage of volunteers wanting to appear exploded further. As the three major companies continued to pick up the tab for their guys' attendance as a gesture of generosity, Les began the show earlier with what came to be known as the "Independent Showcase". It was essentially a pre-show, spotlighting those that wanted to come from all across America to either be seen at a major event or pay tribute to Brian Pillman in their own way. Additionally, some of the baseball players from MLB's Cincinnati Reds appeared as guests to raise money on the night. When discussing the special moments that defined the shows, there was one very obvious standout on Pillman 2000, and easily the most famous match of any of the events.

Steven Regal had been a pushed midcard performer in WCW for several years through the mid-nineties, but major drug issues had threatened to ruin his career and destroy his life for good. After being fired by WCW he'd been hired by the WWF in 1998, only to be fired from there as well. WCW picked him back up, but he wasn't used with any prominence and he was once again let go. By 2000, after a stint in rehab that took, the WWF had given him another chance and sent him to Memphis Championship Wrestling to work with the developmental talent. Regal, once earmarked as a potential opponent for Steve Austin in 1998, had seen his stock drop drastically, but was being groomed for a return to the big time and relished the opportunity to redeem himself. That opportunity came on May 25th, 2000, when he was booked to wrestle Chris Benoit at the third annual Brian Pillman Memorial Show.

"The funny thing", says Les, when asked about his expectations going in, "When I said I wanted Benoit and Regal, a lot of people said, 'Why are you having that match?' And I said to them, 'Well, bring a pencil and paper, because you're going to school'. I mean, I knew what it was going to be, and that's why I wanted it."

As the match began, the crowd was somewhat lukewarm as the two exchanged holds, not knowing what to expect. "If you turn the volume up, you can hear a couple of hecklers saying 'Boring' or something", Thatcher remembers. "But I use that particular match as a teaching tool, because I tell the kids - some idiot on the internet yells boring and you jump up and start running highspots, you've just made him the booker."

Indeed, Regal and Benoit were telling their story and the crowd slowly but surely started to come along. The match was very diverse compared to what was typically expected in mainstream American wrestling at the time, particularly with Regal's forehead busted open hardway after exchanging full contact headbutts with Benoit. "I was kneeling in front of the sound guys' table, which was probably 25 yards from the ring", says Les. "And as that match started to unfold, you could just feel it building, feel the people coming. Being an old wrestler, I wanted to be as close to it as I could get, so I'm edging my way down to ringside and finally I'm leaning on the apron."

He wasn't the only one drawn in. With the layout of the Schmidt Field House, the dressing rooms were downstairs. The other wrestlers weren't typically inclined to come upstairs to watch the matches, given the sheer number of name stars on the show. But as the crowd started to rise, the other guys could hear it and began coming upstairs to see what was going on. By the end, they were elbowing each other out of the way to get a better spot to see the contest climax.

"To begin with it was lukewarm, and by the end they had two thousand people on their feet chanting. It was so amazing", proclaims Thatcher. "I tell people to watch that match over and over and over, because you can learn so much."

Finally, Benoit put Regal in the Crippler Crossface and forced the submission. The emotion was such that Les himself jumped on the apron to hug Benoit at the conclusion of the match. While it was Benoit's hand raised, it was a true victory for Steven Regal, who achieved a manner of personal redemption most human beings never truly experience. With the nature of the final year of Brian Pillman's life, Regal's comeback from drug problems and career resurgence taking place on a show in memory of Brian was all the more poignant.

"People were crying in the crowd at that match", recalls Kim Wood, who watched it live. "It reminded them of what wrestling used to be and what they thought it might never be again."

After such an incredible match, and since the show in general was once again a success, Les immediately knew what he wanted for the following year. "I knew the main event of the show, and I knew what the title was going to be. Pillman '01: Regal Vs. Benoit - The Return." As it turned out, it didn't come to pass. Benoit suffered a broken neck three months before the show and required fusion surgery that would keep him out of action for over a year. This posed an issue with Regal, who called Les to tell him that the match he had with Benoit in 2000 was one that he could only have with a couple of other people, and none of them were in the same hemisphere. Feeling it would be an insult to Chris and a disservice to the show to put out a lesser effort, he requested not to work with anyone else. Regal offered to come and help out in any way he could, attending instead as a guest for photos and presentations.

By the time the 2001 edition came around, it was a monster. Rattling off the schedule, Les proudly details the course of events. "Photos started at noon. The Independent Showcase started at 5pm and ran until about 6:45pm. Then we took a break and came back between 7pm and 7:15pm to start the main show. But then of course there were intermissions, presentations and the auction. The guy that made our HWA belts, each year he made a special Brian Pillman belt, with the design we had on the t-shirts that year on the main plate of the belt. We had artists do paintings they donated to raffle off, we did whatever we could to help Brian's wife and kids."

Emanating from the Oak Hills High School, the fourth Memorial Show had a different vibe, in that the wrestling landscape had changed in the interim. Part of the distinct charm of the shows was that it was the only place to see WWF, WCW and ECW performers on the same card. By August 2001, both WCW and ECW had gone out of business and there was now only one major promotion to draw from. The show was still loaded to the gills with seventeen matches. "The fourth year was very, very good", says Les. "The big surprise we had there was Dean Malenko announcing his retirement. Each year, something unplanned came up that made that particular year special."

As it turned out, the 2001 Brian Pillman Memorial Show ended up being the final one. When asked about what brought the series of shows to an end and the multiple published reports that it had ended badly, Les indulged. "There were several reasons", Thatcher prefaces. "A few of the people in the committee that were so relevant to the event had moved. I had a young man who was on the public relations department of the Cincinnati Reds baseball team. So, of course he had access to getting advertisement out that I could never duplicate, and he handled a lot of that. He had taken a position with the athletic department at the Naval academy in Indianapolis. A couple of other people who were handling sound and lighting for me, who were professionals, were relocating to the West Coast. They were things and people we couldn't just replace." In addition, Thatcher's HWA had become an official developmental territory for the WWF, and the time that was dedicated to that job made it difficult to prepare the Pillman shows simultaneously.

There was also a gut feeling nagging away at Les when it came to the quality of the show and the nature of everybody's selfless spirit. "To me, you can play 'can you top this' for so long and then at some point, you can't. I mean, you've hit the ceiling and there's no way you can duplicate it or get better than that."

Another thing that became an issue was Melanie Pillman's new husband. Less than a year after Brian had died, Melanie had gotten married to a man named Mike King. The general sense was that Mike and Mel had started their relationship prior to Brian's death, and Brian's daughter Brittany has since publicly stated (which was also the consensus opinion back then) that the child Melanie was pregnant with at the time of Brian's passing, Skylar, was actually Mike's biological daughter.

Mike hadn't attended the first three Pillman Memorial Shows but made an appearance in 2001. "He was jealous of Brian, and jealous of the attention he was getting", says Les. "When he came to the show, to this day I do not know what was said, but a couple of the guys were turned off. He went to the back and introduced himself, and this was when the boys themselves kind of thought, 'Enough's enough, she's got a husband, we've tried to support her and the family. Maybe it's time for us to stay at home with our families for a little bit'."

More than anything else, the Pillman Memorial shows were about benefiting his widow, Melanie, and their children. Without a doubt, one of the major contributing factors to the conclusion of the events was Melanie herself. "She was invited to the committee meetings to help plan the stuff. She never, ever showed up. But she always showed up to get the check", explains Les. "The problem was that she wanted to stay in the big house they were in when Brian was alive and making money."

From a financial perspective, the setup was fairly simple. A Brian Pillman Memorial account was opened in a bank in Northern Kentucky. In addition to the check Melanie would get from Thatcher, people were able to make donations directly to the bank. When Steve Austin was unable to appear one year, he sent $10,000 to the fund. "Other than the box office and the concessions, we handled no money at all", Thatcher elaborates.

By the time the 2001 show rolled around, Melanie wasn't endearing herself to many. "She became a major pain in the ass the last year", says Les bluntly. "The guy that handled security and lighting and sound for me, he came to me and he said, 'Les, my security guys are having a problem with Mrs. Pillman.' I said, 'What the hell kind of problem is she giving you?' And of course, unless you had an all access pass, you weren't to be popping in the back. So anyway, she started to haul a bunch of her children's neighborhood friends into the back. The security guy said, 'Well they don't have passes', and she said, 'This is my show and I'll take them wherever I want!'"

Les dealt with the situation as best he could, allowing Melanie to take the children backstage, but before long there were more problems cropping up. "I was walking to the back and Raven called me off to the side", remembers Les. "He said, 'I don't mean to be a pain in the ass, and I don't know how this is going to sound, but I know every year you'd always be sure the hot table was here with food for the boys and everything.' I said, 'Yeah Scotty, what's the problem?' He goes, 'Well, Melanie is feeding the neighborhood children at the hot table, and everybody's running out of food'. And there was no talking to her in that respect", says Les. "Again, it was the attitude of 'I'm

Brian Pillman's widow and the business owes me'."

Melanie had already got on the wrong side of Debra Marshall, who at that time was the wife of Steve Austin, by calling the house and curtly asking to speak to Steve without identifying herself. Her subsequent rudeness to Debra on the phone put Austin between a rock and a hard place. "She ended up pissing off a lot of people. It was a sad state of affairs", said Thatcher.

With all of the above, it was still with a heavy heart that the decision was made to not run a Pillman Memorial show in 2002. Les sat alone in his office after everybody at the HWA school had gone home for the day. Chris Benoit, who was rehabbing his neck in Les' gym at the time, had stepped out with the intention of returning later. Thatcher's voice softens as he recounts having to pick up the phone and break the news. "I was really down about having to call Melanie and having to tell her that in 2002 we couldn't run a show. And I was ready to explain to her about the committee and about the boys", he says. "I called, and I got as far as saying we can't do another show, and she went off on me."

Melanie told Les that she had expected him to run the Memorial shows for a decade. "I thought to myself, 'Ten years?'", says Les. "You didn't expect me to run one! And of course, then she told me that she had made me famous by running these shows and that's how I got the job with WWE as a trainer. And now that I had that job, I didn't need her anymore. And I thought, 'You don't appreciate a friggin' thing, do you?'"

As Melanie continued her onslaught with the suggestion Les was selfish in his decision, Thatcher thought back to the lengths he went to put together such an undertaking. For the 2001 show, in order to cover the overhead for deposits, programs and other essentials, Les had taken out a short-term loan of $15,000 to use as front money.

"I said, 'Mel, do you realize I don't take a dime? Everything that doesn't go to the overhead goes to you. Do you realize that if the show hadn't drawn, who would have had to pay the bank?' And she just goes, 'Well, why didn't you take the money from the fund?' All I could say was, 'Because I thought you and the kids needed it'."

In the midst of the conversation, Chris Benoit returned to the room and sat down in the office. Only privy to Les' half of the discussion, Benoit looked on quizzically. "So finally", says Les, "She basically says fuck you, in so many words, and we hang up. And as I put the phone down, Benoit said, 'What the hell was that about'. So I told him. And he sat there, looked at me and said,

'If she doesn't call you by tomorrow and apologize, then the next time you talk to her, you tell her to go fuck herself'."

In the fallout, Melanie took to the internet to criticize the decision, and Les to boot. It was Harley Race's wife, B.J., who came to Thatcher's defense, saying, "He was a nice guy when he was giving you $25,000 a year wasn't he? What the hell has changed?"

It was an unfortunate end to something that started with the best of intentions and was a true credit to the profession. But regardless of how it concluded, that's not how the Brian Pillman Memorial Shows are remembered by Les, or anybody that attended, participated, or donated. What's enduring about the shows is exactly what should be – the altruism displayed by an industry that, all too often, callously forgets its own in the quest for greed and glory. A sincere collaboration by people who wanted to honor Brian Pillman in death for the great memories he'd given them in life.

"Over the four years, we raised a little over $120,000", says Les. "I'm so, so proud of what we did. It was a labor of love for everybody. That first year we were selling all the tickets out of our little office for HWA, and that was a madhouse. And of course, we realized when we went to Cincinnati Gardens, from that point on we worked with Ticketmaster and people like that because it was just insane. The crazy thing is we had people coming in from all over the country. We had fans from Oklahoma, from all over. The energy and the involvement of the boys, the committee and volunteers that worked with everything, I couldn't tell you how proud I am of all of them. I know people say, 'You were the promoter', and yes, I was the promoter and I was the booker. But it couldn't have happened without all these people."

When asked to explain the rush and the magic of the shows as best he could, Les obliged. "The high of this show, it was almost like a drug. Year two, three and four I stayed at the hotel with the boys, because I wasn't going to come home to get two or three hours sleep then head back out and start loading people up to take them to the airport. I'd be physically and mentally tired, but it was euphoric, it was an amazing thing. Brian's mother and sister wrote me just the greatest letter. We set out to do one little show and it turned into four. It just had a life of its own, and it grew."

24 - THE STORY EVER SINCE

Irrespective of the overwhelming positivity aimed towards the Pillman family, things went down a dark and unfortunate path in the years following. Melanie's marriage to Mike was prompt and while they soon welcomed the sixth child onto the scene, the makeup of the house quickly changed. Danielle was raised by her mother Jan, who was a very protective and religious lady. Jesse moved back down to Atlanta to live with his father. Their relationships with the rest of the children were sporadic, with occasional visits set up to allow them to spend time together. Eventually, the family moved from the house Brian had bought to a more middle-class area in Florence, Kentucky.

Mike, who came from a wealthy, upstanding family, worked for his father's trucking company. As a stepdad, he was especially strict on Brian Jr. and Brittany, most likely due to the looming shadow of their famous father. Melanie played the good cop parent, often telling the grounded children not to be concerned with Mike's orders and generally took a very laissez-faire approach. As time went on, things got progressively worse. Before long, Mike would allegedly be physically disciplining Brian Jr, even though he wasn't his own child.

"When I was real young, I literally got my ass beat for like, nothing", remembers Brian. "He beat the shit out of me and was a dick to me, called me names." Brian remembers an unsettling situation where the family dog, mirroring Mike's hostile attitude towards him, would lunge at and bite him on occasion. He'd be constantly ordered to remain on his bed for no real reason.

Brittany, unfortunately, had to deal with similar neglect. "Brian and I pretty much got treated the same", she begins. "The only difference was he was more physically abused. I was more like Cinderella growing up, I had to do all the chores. I wasn't allowed to leave the house unless the dishes were done and the house was cleaned." As the daughter with no biological ties to either parent, there seemed to be little responsibility to care for Brittany properly. The emotional toll this would take was understandably severe.

As time went by it seemed as if Melanie's approach to parenting became more and more distant. "She did nothing", says Brian bluntly. "She literally would sleep 80% of the day. I don't even think I ever saw her awake in the daytime ever, because she would just be passed out from drugs all day."

With her habits worsening the burden would fall to Mike, making him more antagonistic as a result. The home atmosphere continued to deteriorate. The trucking company eventually collapsed, leading Mike to turn to the same vices as his wife. Little by little, the money that Brian Pillman had worked for, that the wrestling business generated in his honor and that WWE would send in royalties vanished as the parents spiraled out of control. "It makes me sick that all the money was wasted on her and my step dad on their drugs", says Brittany. "He (Mike) went to jail many different times. For stealing, writing bad checks and using drugs."

The family ended up moving again, this time to a much worse neighborhood. The lack of parental leadership started to show in Brian. After being treated like a bad kid for so long, he began to believe it. "When I got into my teenage rebellious years, I was trying to rebel so hard against my strict-ass abusive stepfather that I did start becoming a little thug to the neighborhood", jokes Brian. "And that's when he didn't even try. For my early teens, he didn't even try to discipline me, he would just pass out. He and my Mom would do drugs and pass out. That's when I had free reign to get it out of my system. We'd be throwing parties with cases of beer and I was a freshman in high school."

As money got tighter, the children say things got even less hands-on from Mike and Melanie. Often times there'd be no food in the fridge, or unpaid bills would lead to services being shut off. Linda Pillman remembers giving Brian and Brittany cell phones in order to keep in touch with her, as the phone line was constantly being cut. Even that effort ended up backfiring.

"I found out Melanie's husband was taking Brian's phone", begins Linda. "And the only way I knew - every time I called Brian there would be no answer. I called Brittany and she said, 'I think Mike's got it'. So, then I would just have the phone turned off, and when I did he'd just give it back to Brian. Then we'd get it turned back on. Back then, I only bought so many minutes for the phones for the kids since they were just to get in touch with me. When Mike would take the phone, he'd run up all these minutes and I'd get $700 phone bills because he was going over the minutes all the time. And they didn't have the money to be paying the bill."

Over time, it was becoming clear that something wasn't right, and Linda offered for Brian and Brittany to move in with her and her mother Mary (who she was caring for at the time). However, the distance between the two locations and pivotal time in school and social lives made it difficult, though the invite was there.

Brian was coming to a crossroads in his own life. With his parents preoccupied on other things, he had free reign to act however he wanted. "I grew up faster than a lot of kids needed to", he says. "To say that I was burned out on partying at 16 is nuts. It was a wild upbringing, a lot of ups and downs. I had access to as much alcohol as I wanted at 14 years old. I'd drink vodka on the way to school in the car, or I would put it in a water bottle and drink on the school bus." Thankfully, he started to realize he was capable of far more and just needed the right outlet to express it. That outlet came in the form of football at Dixie Heights high school. The camaraderie, the dedication to fitness and the love of the game gave Brian focus.

"When I was 13 or 14 was when the fork in the road came", elaborates Brian. "Because I was bad, I was getting in trouble with the law. I was doing stupid shit, but I hadn't gotten into all the drugs. That's where the fork came. It was like, do I keep hanging out with these bad kids that are terrorizing the neighborhood, vandalizing and doing drugs? Or do I veer to the right and hang out with the people playing football? When the stuff they do in school is to get good grades so they can keep playing, getting in the weight room and improving themselves?"

He made the right decision and played at linebacker, just like his father. He was originally stuck on a junior varsity team that went 9-1 while the varsity team struggled. "They realized, oh, we have all these good kids in JV that should be playing varsity, but where do we put them?", says Brian. "I walked up to the coach, and said, 'I'm tired of your bullshit and your politics, your defensive line sucks. Put me on nose guard.' I was 185 pounds."

They did, and Brian threw himself into the sport with the same vigor as his dad. His stance as nose guard at the line of scrimmage was remarkably similar to his father's. When thinking about why he chose the path pointing away from drugs, his answer was simple. "I saw how much destruction that was", he says. "I saw that it had already fucked up my dad and my mom. I learned that lesson young."

Unfortunately, there was more tragedy to come for the family. Alexis, Melanie's daughter, had gotten into the wrestling business locally in 2008 as a manager under the guise of "Sexy" Lexi Pillman. She also worked as a stripper at a local establishment. "She was taking on the roles of both parents, she was really living it up", jokes Brian. Both industries can attract shady characters, however, and before long she got caught up with the wrong crowd.

On November 26th, 2009, Alexis was leaving the club she worked at after a shift. She'd been partying, and an eyewitness stated she was tipsy leaving the bar. As she drove home on a foggy night, Alexis had to pull the car over after getting a flat tire. The roads had sound barriers, making it harder to maneuver. With no way out, she stepped out of the car and tried to cross the wide, barely-visible road. On her walk across the tarmac, she was brutally hit head-on by a semi-truck and killed instantly at the age of 28.

"She was a wild thing, a wild spirit", remembers Brian. "But she worked hard. She took pride in her dancing and she took pride in her wrestling. But in a sense, she was surrounded by the wrong people. She didn't respect that dark side the way I do now."

Eventually, the fractured family began to go their separate ways. Skylar, the youngest daughter, was eventually taken by Mike's mother, who has since raised her as her own.

Jesse got into the army after dropping out of college and had a close call in an explosion during his time in Afghanistan. He also lost a close friend on duty, both incidents mentally scarring him. After being discharged, he moved back in with Melanie. "I don't really talk to him anymore because he shares many of the same traits as her", says Brian, matter-of-factly.

Brian's first daughter, Danielle, still looks a lot like her dad. After being raised in a very sheltered environment, she developed into her own person with a little bit of a rebellious streak. She dated an MMA fighter and had a child with him, a baby boy named Jackson. Eventually they split, and she now lives in Cincinnati working as a waitress. She's flirted with the idea of getting into wrestling and has recently reached out to some of her dad's old friends to learn more about him. Sadly, Danielle, Brittany and Brian have no real memories of their father at all.

Melanie finally broke up with Mike, but by that point the children's view of her had been cast. Since May 2005, she's been arrested over a dozen times on various charges. To this day, she receives thousands of dollars from WWE every quarter in residuals for her late husband's body of work, but has little contact with the rest of the family.

Reason being that, contrasting the amount of heartbreak and misfortune that seemingly plagued the situation, there was a happy ending in sight. Linda Pillman was increasingly concerned for Brian and Brittany and did everything she could to help. "I couldn't let them go by the wayside", states Linda. "A lot of stuff I didn't know was going on, because Melanie was threatening that if they told me they'd get in trouble." Linda did everything from buying groceries to paying the bills on the house to try and provide some normalcy and guidance to the kids. Sacrificing herself, Linda went broke trying to keep two houses running.

"She is our angel", begins Brittany. "The mother we never had. We would be lost without her. I just pray one day we're able to give back for all she has done for us. I know we will never be able to repay for everything, but to get her out of debt would be a dream come true. I don't care to have anything as long as she is taken care of."

Linda purchased a house in Edgewood, Kentucky to allow Brian and Brittany to move away from Melanie and live with her. With the loving help of their aunt, they've turned their lives into gratifying, positive stories.

After losing both of her parents so young and experiencing more tragedy firsthand than any youngster ever should, Brittany dealt with issues for many years. "I have suffered with depression and major anxiety disorder", she explains. "It's been a long struggle for me, but I'm finally overcoming some of my struggles. Mental illness is the worst."

With a healthy home environment and a strong support system, Brittany found further salvation in religion, which she says saved her life. In 2016, she graduated college with a criminal justice degree. After coming so far, her instinct is now to help others. "I would love to work with kids that live in troubled homes", says Brittany. "Give them hope and inspire them through my overcomings."

As for Brian, he obtained his college degree in computer science and quickly got an office job. "My whole goal in life was just to be normal", he explains. "Just to get a damn job and be just like the middle-class people that my friends were raised by. My friends were so good, and I always thought they were rich. 'Oh my God, they're rich, I want to hang out at their house where their parents feed them and shit!'"

Following graduation, Brian moved out of Linda's house in Edgewood and lived with a couple of his friends. Soon, the normal life he'd strived for wasn't enough. After getting back in shape by taking hot yoga classes, his gears began turning and his heart started telling him he had a destiny to fulfill. After talking it over with family, he emailed Lance Storm and applied for a spot at the Storm Wrestling Academy in Calgary, Alberta, Canada. He enrolled in the September 2017 class.

The poetry in Brian Pillman Jr. training to wrestle in Calgary isn't lost on him. Like his father, Brian wasn't a devout follower of pro wrestling in his youth with so much negativity towards the business boiling within his family.

"I wasn't really thrilled about the wrestling when he said it", offers Linda Pillman, "Because I know what Brian went through. But Brian Jr. has a foot in the door already I think, because of my brother. I don't think it'll be as hard for him. Brian's got a good head on his shoulders and he knows a little bit of what he's getting into, what could happen."

Readily aware of the bad side of the wrestling business, Brian had more than enough reason to second guess his decision. Contrary to that, however, he's seemingly relentless in his pursuit. "If he doesn't try, he's always going to wonder", says Linda. "This way, if he tries and he's successful, great. If not, at least he tried, and he won't have that 'What if?' If it doesn't work out, he's got his degree to fall back on."

Not doing anything by half measures, Brian went from hot yoga to advanced classes, moving to CrossFit training to prepare for Lance's school. With both Brian and Brittany facing $40,000 of debt from school loans, the funding for Brian's excursion could have been challenging, but ultimately came from an unlikely source.

John Harbaugh of the Baltimore Ravens has remained in touch with Linda, Brian and Brittany, and been an active part in their lives. "He reached out to me a few years ago when I was still in school", utters Brian. "He really started helping out with me and Linda financially because he knew about the whole situation we were in. He's such a nice dude, really clean cut." Whenever the Ravens swing by Cincinnati to play the Bengals, they'll meet up, and John will arrange for them to attend the game. When the Ravens went to the Super Bowl in 2013 against the San Francisco 49ers, Harbaugh got Super Bowl seats for the family. "John is a very, very nice man", says Linda. "He truly is a nice man. His whole family is like that. He's been very good to the kids."

When Brian told John about his desire to follow in his father's footsteps, Harbaugh immediately offered to bankroll the trip so he could learn the ropes properly. John's involvement with the family to this day is a testament to the bond formed in the dorms of Miami of Ohio some thirty-five-plus years ago. A framed picture of Brian and John jokingly walking hand-in-hand, clad in their Redskins uniforms, still rests on the wall of the family home.

Harbaugh isn't the only old friend of Brian's to reach out to his son as he starts the next chapter of life. Steve Austin contacted the younger Pillman to talk about his decision and his father. As a show of support, Steve sent Brian his dad's weightlifting belt, with "FLYIN" stitched in the back, that Austin had kept over the years for sentimental reasons.

Eager to begin, Brian moved back in with Linda and started training the fundamentals at the OVW wrestling school under Rip Rogers. He continued to work at getting himself in the best possible condition for Calgary, getting his weight up to 225 and squatting 400 pounds. "He's eating good, I can attest to that", says Linda with a laugh. "It has come full circle. Instead of me, my mother and Brian, it's me, Brittany and Brian doing the same thing." Bringing it even closer to home, Brian's Sunday dinners in preparation for wrestling training were eaten off the exact same meat platter his dad used when looking to bulk up in college.

"Obviously they're huge shoes to fill", says Brian. "But to think that I have the opportunity to try and put myself in those shoes and live up to that is going to be a fun adventure."

When asked about similarities between father and son, Brittany jests, "He is my Dad's mini-me!" Unlike others, she has no reservations about her half-brother's decision. "Brian is going to finish what my father started and I can't wait to watch it all unfold. He has a very unique character, just like my father did. I think he's perfect for the wrestling industry."

The next volume of the story begins anew, not shackled by the demons of the past, but guided by hope for the future. Through the incredible, selfless, commendable actions of their aunt Linda, Brian and Brittany have the rest of their lives back in the palm of their hands through good choices, hard work and determination. The outlook is nothing but optimistic, their resilience inspiring.

Without a doubt, their father would be proud.

Printed in Germany
by Amazon Distribution
GmbH, Leipzig